# The British Growth Crisis

*Building a Sustainable Political Recovery: SPERI Research & Policy*

*Series Editors*: **Colin Hay** and **Anthony Payne**, Co-Directors of the Sheffield Political Economy Research Institute (SPERI) at the University of Sheffield, UK.

SPERI is an innovation in higher education research and outreach. It brings together leading international researchers in the social sciences, policy makers, journalists and opinion formers to reassess and develop proposals in response to the political and economic issues posed by the current combination of financial crisis, shifting economic power and environmental threat. *Building a Sustainable Political Economy: SPERI Research & Policy* will serve as a key outlet for SPERI's published work. Each title will summarise and disseminate to an audience of academics, postgraduate students and directly to policy makers and journalists, key policy-oriented research findings designed to further the development of a more sustainable future for the national, regional and world economy following the global financial crisis. It takes a holistic and interdisciplinary view of political economy in which the local, regional, national and global interact at all times and in complex ways. The SPERI research agenda, and hence the focus of the series, seeks to explore the core economic and political questions that require us to develop a new sustainable model of political economy.

# The British Growth Crisis
## The Search for a New Model

Edited by

Jeremy Green
*Research Fellow, University of Sheffield, UK*

Colin Hay
*Professor of Political Science, University of Sheffield, UK*

and

Peter Taylor-Gooby
*Professor of Social Policy, University of Kent at Canterbury, UK*

First published 2015 by
PALGRAVE MACMILLAN

Palgrave Macmillan in the UK is an imprint of Macmillan Publishers Limited, registered in England, company number 785998, of Houndsmills, Basingstoke, Hampshire, RG21 6XS.

Palgrave Macmillan in the US is a division of St Martin's Press LLC, 175 Fifth Avenue, New York, NY 10010.

Palgrave Macmillan is the global academic imprint of the above companies and has companies and representatives throughout the world.

Palgrave® and Macmillan® are registered trademarks in the United States, the United Kingdom, Europe and other countries

ISBN: 978–1–137–44151–5

This book is printed on paper suitable for recycling and made from fully managed and sustained forest sources. Logging, pulping and manufacturing processes are expected to conform to the environmental regulations of the country of origin.

A catalogue record for this book is available from the British Library.

A catalog record for this book is available from the Library of Congress.

# Contents

# List of Figures

# List of Tables

# Notes on Contributors

**Craig Berry** is Research Fellow at SPERI and was previously Pensions Policy Officer at the Trade Union Congress as well as Policy Adviser at HM Treasury. Craig's research focuses on the development of an alternative model for economic growth in Britain, following the apparent failure of the Anglo-liberal growth strategy which emerged during the 1980s.

**Ben Clift** is Professor of Political Economy at the University of Warwick. His research engages with international political economy, comparative political economy, the French model of capitalism and the evolving policy discourse of the IMF.

**Dan Corry** is Visiting Fellow at Southampton University and was formerly a Downing Street and Treasury Advisor to the Labour government. He is also the Chief Executive of New Philanthropy Capital.

**Ken Coutts** is Assistant Director in the Faculty of Economics at the University of Cambridge. His research interests include open-economy models of debt dynamics, visible and invisible earnings in the balance of payments and macroeconomic policy.

**Andrew Cumbers** is Professor in Management at the University of Glasgow. His research employs a geographical political economy perspective in order to problematise uneven development within capitalist societies.

**David Featherstone** is Senior Lecturer in the University of Glasgow's School of Geographical and Earth Sciences. David's research focuses upon the political geographies of globalisation, examining issues related to the relations between resistance, space and politics.

**Jeremy Green** is Lecturer in Politics at the University of Bristol and Honorary Research Fellow, SPERI. His research focuses upon British development, global finance and Anglo-American political economy.

**Graham Gudgin** is Research Associate at the Centre for Business Research at the University of Cambridge and a part-time Senior Economic Advisor with Oxford Economics. He is currently researching a new Keynesian model of the UK economy with colleagues in Cambridge and elsewhere.

**Colin Hay** is Professor of Political Analysis at the University of Sheffield and a co-director of the Sheffield Political Economy Research Institute (SPERI). His research primarily engages with issues relevant to political analysis, British politics and the political economy of globalisation.

**Jason Heyes** is Professor of Employment Relations in the School of Management at the University of Sheffield. Jason's work explores the connections between employment relations, labour markets and public policy.

**Paul Lewis** is Lecturer in Political Economy in the Birmingham Business School. His research utilises comparative statistical and institutional approaches to understanding national economic development.

**Danny MacKinnon** is Professor of Regional Development and Governance at Newcastle University. His research focuses upon the institutions and politics of local and regional development.

**Jonathan Perraton** is Senior Lecturer in Economics at the University of Sheffield. Jonathan's research focuses upon processes of globalisation and their impact upon different national economies.

**Frank Pyke** is a researcher, advisor and lecturer, and his work focuses upon local and regional employment strategies.

**Paulina Ramirez** is Lecturer in International Business and Innovation at the Birmingham Business School. Her work focuses upon the impact of globalisation on new organisational forms and international knowledge flows, as well as comparative studies of national institutions.

**Gerry Stoker** is Professor of Governance and Director of the Centre for Citizenship, Globalization and Governance at the University of Southampton. His research examines issues of governance, democratic politics, urban politics, public participation and public service reform.

**Peter Taylor-Gooby** is Research Professor of Social Policy at the University of Kent's School of Social Policy, Sociology and Social Research. His major research interests lie in the areas of welfare state developments, austerity and welfare state restructuring, social divisions associated with inequality and struggles over multiculturalism.

**Daniela Tepe-Belfrage** is Research Fellow at the University of Sheffield. Her research interests cover gender, international political economy and critical theory.

**Andrew Tylecote** is Professor of the Economics and Management of Technological Change at the University of Sheffield. Andrew's research encompasses concern with the institutions of the economy and the role of technology within economic development.

# Introduction: The British Growth Crisis

*Jeremy Green, Colin Hay and Peter Taylor-Gooby*

Since 2007 the question of growth has plagued the British economy. Though, at the time of writing in the early summer of 2014, growth has returned, a pervasive anxiety about the solidity, stability and sustainability of that growth persists, even in the most hallowed of elite political circles. Thus, even the recently appointed Governor of the Bank of England, Mark Carney, is concerned that the short-term boost in economic output that has occurred since 2013 is a product of the re-stoking of an inherently unstable and, indeed, further de-stabilising housing bubble, much like that which burst to precipitate the crisis in the first place. Britain, even in his terms, would appear to be dancing on the edge of the precipice once again. For the much-vaunted 'rebalancing', presented as a necessary pre-condition of any return to a stable growth dynamic by the principal parties and the cornerstone of the Coalition's economic policy rationale, has yet to materialise. By almost all available economic indicators the British economy is more unbalanced today than it was in 2007 (for a more detailed assessment of which see Berry & Hay 2014), and that gives a rather different complexion to the return to growth since 2013. Re-contextualised in this way it looks all too like the product of a rather desperate, short-term, and carefully targeted pump-priming of the housing market (using tools like the Coalition's Help to Buy scheme). This, as Carney himself is close to admitting, can only end badly.

That this is so, we argue, is the product of Britain's failure to find a new growth model to replace the one that took us over the precipice once before and threatens, in its new incarnation, to do so a second time. As that suggests, Britain's growth crisis continues. It is that crisis that forms the subject of this volume.

Thus, despite superficial impressions to the contrary, Britain remains in the midst of the most severe and prolonged economic crisis that it has faced since the 1930s. The financial crash of 2007 brought British growth to a sharp halt and the subsequent double-dip recession and unbalanced and potentially illusory recovery has eaten away at living standards and dampened longer-term growth prospects while making the transition to a more sustainable growth dynamic less rather than more likely. The deepening inequalities that marked the pre-crisis growth model have also continued unabated. The Bank of England's Quantitative Easing programme has differentially benefitted the wealthiest percentiles of asset-holders (BofE 2012), while the labour market has witnessed the most prolonged period of real wage decline since the late nineteenth century (Groom 2013). On top of these worrying distributional trends, household debt levels are once more approaching their pre-crisis peak level (Smith 2013). These are hardly the foundations of a more sustainable and equitable growth model for Britain.

Within the context of prolonged recessionary conditions, themselves exacerbated by a commitment to public austerity set to endure for two decades or more, the question of growth has acquired a renewed urgency, taking centre stage within British politics. Britain's old growth model, based on asset price inflation in the housing market and cheap consumer credit, is now defunct. But as yet no credible alternative has been proposed in its wake. The old growth model is dying but a new one has yet to be born.

With the Coalition government's austerity project now in place and with all three principal political parties signed up to it in some form (now, and beyond the 2015 General Election), a critical exploration of Britain's crisis response strategy, and the potential alternatives that have been overlooked, is long overdue. Our aim, as editors of this volume, has been to bring the full range of analytical insights of contemporary political economy to bear upon the British growth crisis, exploring its roots, ramifications and potential remedies. For, strangely perhaps, and despite a wide array of literature dealing with the global financial crisis itself (notably Krugman 2008; Gamble 2009a; Schwartz 2009), there is as yet no single volume dedicated to exploring the impact of the crisis upon Britain's political economy. This book corrects that deficiency by linking the financial crisis to a broader crisis within Britain's growth model.

The crisis has raised many questions about the future of British growth: is the attempt to reduce deficits and lower debt the right strategy to foster long-term recovery? Can a new growth model deliver growth that is socially and environmentally sustainable? And will the benefits of growth be shared more evenly in the future? To date these questions have been met with few convincing answers.

What is certain is that the question of growth has supplanted decline as the principal contemporary narrative for understanding British political economy. But this shift has not yet been adequately reflected within the literature, with scholarly commentary on the British growth crisis so far confined to journal articles (Gamble 2009b; Hay 2011). There is, we suggest, a real and pressing need for a more detailed multi-perspective and multi-author treatment of these issues, focused for the first time explicitly on the problem of the British growth crisis. This book aspires to meet this need. It does so by drawing on a range of contributions, developed over the past two years, but first discussed in outline form at the inaugural annual conference of the Sheffield Political Economy Research Institute (SPERI). This provided the rare opportunity to bring together a range of key analysts and commentators on Britain's economic plight to begin the dialogue that culminates in this volume.

If the volume builds from a central core premise, it is that crises are, to a considerable extent, what we make of them. For what we do in response to a crisis depends on how we perceive the problem; we respond not to the condition itself but to our diagnosis of it. What is clear is that the dominant political discourse in Britain has come to conceive of our affliction as *a crisis of debt*. Our shared conviction is that this is not the only way in which the crisis could be understood, and it is not how the crisis *should* be understood. For us, this is a crisis of growth not of debt (see also Hay 2013).

The point is that it is only by conceiving of the crisis as one of debt rather than growth that austerity and deficit reduction become the logical solution. Change our sense of the crisis and we change the range of responses considered appropriate. Thus, were the crisis conceived of differently, as a *crisis of growth* not a *crisis of debt*, then austerity and deficit reduction would be no solution at all. Indeed, they would almost certainly be seen as likely to compound the problem.

Consequently, if we are to put right what went wrong, it is first imperative that we get our diagnosis of the affliction correct. From the perspective of this collection, to see the British crisis or, indeed, the Eurozone crisis as one of debt, is to mistake a symptom for the condition itself; and the risk is that, in mistaking the symptom for the condition, we choose a course of medicine only destined to reduce further the life expectancy of the patient.

Yet wrong though it may be, it is not at all difficult to see why a crisis of debt discourse might have taken hold in Britain. It is not very threatening; it does not entail a change in economic paradigm; and it leads readily to a simple diagnosis – deficit reduction and austerity – which is arguably quite in accordance with the liberal market disposition of recent British governments. The alternative crisis of growth discourse is, in a sense, a far more challenging one. For it would entail a rejection of the prevailing economic paradigm informing policy since at least the 1980s. More significantly still, it would almost certainly require a rejection of the old growth model and the search for a new one.

As this suggests, while the crisis of debt discourse is paradigm-reinforcing, the crisis of growth discourse is paradigm-challenging. And, if there is one thing that we have learned from previous crises, it is that prevailing economic paradigms are not readily abandoned. They tend, if anything, to be tested to destruction. Arguably, this is what happened in the 1930s; and it may well be what is happening today.

## Structure of the volume

The distinguished array of contributors we have assembled raise key questions about Britain's growth model and attempt to provide convincing answers that will be of use to academics, commentators and policy-makers alike. The different sections respond to the multifaceted nature of the British growth crisis.

In section one, *Diagnosing the Crisis*, the authors tackle the roots of the present crisis. But, rather than focusing upon the immediate causes of the crisis, these chapters reach deeper to provide an analysis of the longer-term direction of British economic development and its bearing upon the current crisis.

In their extremely important contribution, Graham Gudgin and Ken Coutts assess the extent to which the liberal economic policies consistently pursued in Britain since the 1980s are culpable for the crisis we have witnessed – and now prevent us from finding an alternative growth dynamic. They chart, in sometimes painfully graphic detail, the depth of the crisis and the unparalleled long-term damage this has done to the British economy. And they are very clear about its cause. Following Wynne Godley, they suggest that the period since 1979 saw a remarkable increase in the ratio of household debt to income, that this was always likely to prove unsustainable and that the product of the growth to limits of this ratio was always likely to be recession and the subsequent long-term suppression of growth going forward. They also show that growth during the three decades culminating in the 'great moderation' was not superior to the previous three decades – the trend rate of growth did not rise, the rate of growth of productivity fell and the volatility of real GDP was greater, at a time of steeply rising inequality and with a step-level increase in the rate of unemployment. As they show, there was a substantial social and economic cost of the control of inflation. They conclude that liberal economic policies have suppressed rather than stimulated growth and that the crisis provides us with the opportunity to begin to put this right in a way that starts to address the profound imbalance in the economy that has developed over the last thirty years and the pronounced polarisation in social inequality with which is has been associated.

The second contribution to this section comes from a very different source, Dan Corry, and presents a very different case. Corry was a special advisor in the New Labour years in a number of ministerial departments, chairing the Council of Economic Advisors in the UK Treasury between 2006 and 2007 and serving as Senior Economic Advisor to the Prime Minister between 2007 and 2010 and head of the Number 10 Policy Unit from 2007 to 2008. His equally rich chapter presents a detailed empirical assessment of the New Labour years which seeks to draw out the lessons for progressive economic thinking in the wake of the crisis. He suggests that, in terms of productivity and the labour market, performance was good – while the 'bubble' sectors of the economy certainly performed well, productivity growth was in fact higher in other sectors. Moreover, if growth is decomposed in terms of factor inputs, what emerges is a picture of the successful transformation of the economy to make better use of human capital and new technologies. This Corry sees as crucial to any strategy to rebalance the economy away from the 'bubble' sectors in the years ahead. His carefully balanced account suggests that although there were many clear failings in economic governance and, in particular, financial regulation in the New Labour years in office, there are also clear positive lessons to be learned as we strive to build a more sustainable model of growth for a more inclusive society and a more balanced economy in the next decade.

Finally in this section, we have Jeremy Green's important and timely intervention on the origins of Anglo-American capitalism, its liberal disposition and the implications of this new historical perspective for our understanding of crisis. Green argues that while the characteristic pathologies of the Anglo-liberal growth model are now well understood and well described in the literature, what we invariably fail to appreciate is their much longer pre-history. This history he seeks to chart in some detail. He shows that Britain and America share a longstanding commitment to the promotion of international trade and investment.

This shared interest has been central to the prominent role that both economies have played in the evolution of the global economy since 1945. In particular, he charts in some detail the way in which the Anglo-American endorsement of open international trade and investment has impacted upon the British economy. The chapter traces the re-emergence of the City of London as an international financial centre and its intimate inter-connections to the development of American finance. It then discusses the processes of financial liberalisation and deregulation driven in large part by Britain and America, highlighting their relationship with foreign direct investment flows and the growth of income inequality in Britain. Green suggests that the Anglo-American developmental model has been a major factor in Britain's overdependence upon financial services, and in rising income inequality, using statistical evidence to support these claims. This tendency, he shows, became increasingly pronounced during the mergers and acquisitions booms of the 1990s and 2000s, which boosted City incomes and further increased levels of income inequality. The chapter concludes by identifying rising income inequality as a key failure of Britain's pre-crisis economic development, suggesting that raising levels of equality should be a central goal for Britain's future economic strategy.

In the second part of the book, *Evaluating Responses*, contributors critically review the trajectory of crisis politics and propose alternative directions and progressive remedies to the British growth crisis. They trace the transformations that have occurred since the crisis, examine the rise to prominence of debt and deficit discourse, and look towards the future resolution of the challenges that Britain faces.

Gerry Stoker's thought-provoking and original contribution on the prospects of a 'governance for the long-term' gets this section underway. Emphasising the need to develop a long-term political strategy to cope with the many challenges faced by the British economy in the wake of its failed growth model, Stoker reviews the ingredients required to foster coalitions of long-term policy support for alternative economic strategies. Stoker argues that the rise of neoliberal, short-termist and consumerist politics in the pre-crisis era has undermined faith in the capacity of politics to deliver collectively beneficial outcomes. After reviewing rational choice interpretations of democratic political models, he then offers a critical appraisal that counteracts the rather gloomy prognoses for democratic vitality offered up by these approaches. Instead, Stoker moves beyond simplified rational choice models of democracy and examines a range of alternative factors that might contribute to the development of a politics for the long-term. Stressing the contingency and non-determinacy of the prospects for long-term politics, he identifies a number of conditions for the success of such a project, including the effective management of political conflict, building trust in the competence and capacity of government, and devolving power wherever possible. Ultimately, Stoker concludes that long-termist politics is an eminently achievable goal, particularly if a more genuine dialogue between citizens and government can be created alongside a more robust sense of localism and a geographical rebalancing of economic power within the UK.

In the second contribution to this section, Peter Taylor-Gooby provides an illuminating analysis of the current predicament of progressive politics. In a rather more sobering account than Stoker's, Taylor-Gooby examines the crisis from the vantage point of progressive politics and makes clear the magnitude of the challenge at hand. That challenge is captured by what he terms the 'Left Trilemma' in public policy. The Left's response to the crisis must balance between three goals: achieving the perception of competence and credibility in handling the crisis; addressing established themes within public policy to be electable; and developing generous and inclusive policies in order to be progressive. Through a review of a range of public policy programmes advocated by the Left, Taylor-Gooby demonstrates that tensions exist both within and between all three components of the 'trilemma'. Thus, responding to Britain's mounting fiscal challenges in the wake of the crisis squeezes the space to enact progressive measures. Added to this, greater inequality has corroded the public sense of solidarity required to underpin social provisioning. Hardening public opinion and a pervasive mood of 'anti-politics' present further obstacles for Left revitalisation by undermining the foundations of progressive redistribution and positive state intervention. He concludes his review of Left policy programmes with the recognition that no single proposed policy package holds all of the answers. Any progressive future in Britain will have to rely upon a flexible combination of different policy approaches, one that embeds micro-level policies within an overall outlook that seeks to foster growth through greater investment in infrastructure, production and social provision, as well as a higher tax take from the better-off. The popular political basis for these measures can only be achieved if the Left displays the required ambition to shift public discourse in a more progressive direction.

We then move towards a more exclusively macroeconomic analysis of Britain's response to the growth crisis with Ben Clift's fascinating examination of the changing character of the economic ideas that have informed fiscal policy post-crisis. Clift's contribution focuses upon the context and content of debates over Keynesianism, with particular emphasis upon the interaction between the IMF's interventions in the debate and the Coalition government's evolving position. Stressing the importance of ideas and inter-subjective beliefs in shaping the debate over 'fiscal rectitude', he traces the linkage between that debate and the attendant policy outcomes. What emerges from the analysis is a very clear picture of the tension between the government's construction of a 'crisis of debt', on the one hand, and the IMF's contending view that the UK government had a considerably greater degree of room for fiscal manoeuver, on the other. Despite criticism from the IMF, the government continued to cling to an outlying and widely discredited notion of 'expansionary austerity', which stressed the growth dividends of public sector retrenchment. Clift shows that, despite its public endorsement of expansionary austerity, the government did in fact switch to an unstated 'Plan B' from summer 2012 by slowing the pace of fiscal retrenchment. For Clift, these debates and their impact upon policy demonstrate the 'contingency and malleability' of the politics of fiscal rectitude. There was, in fact, much more space for the government to enact a very different fiscal policy response to the crisis, but an underlying ideological opposition to counter-cyclical policy and a desire to change the size of the British state, from within the Coalition, put paid to any possibility of a more expansionary fiscal stance.

The final contribution to this section isolates the fortunes of a single, but hugely important, sector of the economy within Britain's failed growth model and the politics of the crisis. Craig Berry revisits the question of the malaise of British manufacturing with a timely and insightful analysis that stresses the need to break down Britain's growth model into its component sectors. Beginning with a review of the traditional 'declinist' interpretation of the ills of British manufacturing, Berry updates the literature by critically examining the Coalition government's 'rebalancing agenda', suggesting that it is based on a serious over-simplification of the relationship between sectors. The key argument is that the continuing deterioration of British manufacturing is principally a consequence of the failure of the political elite to address the impact of Britain's bloated financial sector upon other sectors. British financial institutions have continued to fail the manufacturing sector, by providing an inadequate flow of credit. This predicament has continued in the aftermath of the crisis, with only a very limited recovery of manufacturing despite a huge depreciation in the value of sterling. Crucially, Berry convincingly demonstrates the socially destructive consequences of a failing manufacturing sector, suggesting that the dearth of high-quality and high-wage jobs in Britain is a direct consequence of the diminishment of high-productivity manufacturing sector employment. Britain's lop-sided growth model has privileged finance while neglecting manufacturing, resulting in an earnings squeeze among workers as the manufacturing sector has shrunk. Arresting the further decline of manufacturing will require, Berry concludes, a major reorientation of the relationship between the financial sector and the wider economy.

The British growth crisis is multifaceted, reaching into many different sectors and articulated within local, national and global frameworks. This is reflected in the third part of this volume, *Global, Local and Sectoral Dimensions*, in which the authors address the dynamics of the crisis in relation to different dimensions of the British growth model. Contributors explore the refocusing of political emphasis around the local scale, while critically reviewing the redefinition of the 'local' in the post-crisis era. The different contributions explore the impact of the crisis upon the labour market, address the question of growth from the perspective of institutional shareholders and examine the ways in which Britain's relationship with the wider global economy has fed into the crisis.

The first chapter in this section, by Danny MacKinnon, Andrew Cumbers and David Featherstone, discusses policies for local and regional economic development. In the context of a shift towards a 'new regionalism' or 'new localism' in many developed countries, the UK stands out as having a strong centralised government. The recent devolution of powers to Scotland, Wales and Northern Ireland may be seen as fostering the growth of centralised forms within those areas. In addition, the UK has an exceptionally high level of spatial inequality between regions and a highly centralised system of local finance. The authors argue that the limited decentralisation and the reproduction of centralised rule are critical weaknesses in the British growth model.

The chapter first reviews the development of local and regional policy since the late 1990s. It examines how the 2010 Coalition has pursued a form of 'austerity localism', imposing heavy cuts in finance on local government and seeking to dismantle some of the inherited structures of regional policymaking and central scrutiny. The new patchwork of business-led Local Enterprise Partnerships introduces substantial regional variation. This is compounded by the introduction of City Deals, which allow the centre to offer very different levels of support and funding in different cities. The chapter concludes with a discussion of how a new 'progressive localism' might be constructed around four general principles. These are: genuine autonomy, with a constitutionally guaranteed status for local government; greater local financial autonomy; new approaches to policy innovation; learning between authorities as key elements in a 'cooperative localism'; and, finally, an important role for the centre in setting service standards, re-distributing revenues and co-ordinating local policy development.

The second contribution, by Jason Heyes and Paul Lewis, provides a rigorous and critical examination of a claim that lies at the heart of Coalition government labour market policy: that employment protection legislation damages competitiveness and leads to higher unemployment. This assumption underpins a series of reforms that make dismissal easier and weaken workers' rights to claim compensation. Heyes and Lewis examine the background to the current UK policy debate and place recent labour market policy in the European context. They demonstrate that the reforms will not stimulate growth in good quality employment. The Coalition's approach fails to address Britain's skill shortage and is unlikely to create more high-valued added employment or enhance productivity.

Jonathon Perraton returns to the theme of globalisation in his contribution to this section. In recent years UK governments have increasingly emphasised the challenge of globalisation in relation to labour market policy, education and training, research and development and macroeconomic and industrial policy. The chapter points out that the British economy has long had a high level of international involvement, with relatively high trade integration, major engagement in global financial markets and established multinationals going back to eighteenth and nineteenth century trading companies. Official analyses of globalisation have argued that the appropriate response is to promote deregulation, a competitive tax regime and flexible labour, product and capital markets with a limited role for state intervention. These arguments lead to the view that Britain, with its relatively flexible liberal economy, is well placed to reap the benefits of a more globalised world.

Perraton points out that successive UK governments have in fact failed to address the deteriorating trade balance in manufactured goods and that it is not obvious that service sector trade will make up the shortfall. Advantage in areas such as finance, insurance and education is balanced by weakness in the rapidly expanding field of tourism. He shows that the UK's position remains weak in emerging markets. His chapter reinforces the argument made elsewhere in this volume that Britain suffers from its failure under recent governments to develop a coherent industrial strategy and that reliance on globalisation as a possible basis for the rebalancing of the economy is likely to be misplaced.

In the final chapter of this section, Andrew Tylecote and Paulina Ramirez address the influential argument developed by Hall and Soskice (2001) that liberal market economies, such as the UK and the US, tend to have a comparative advantage in radical innovation, and thus in high-tech industry (for example aerospace, pharmaceuticals and IT), whereas co-ordinated market economies, such as Germany and Japan, tend to have an advantage in incremental innovation and in medium-tech industries (motor vehicles, machinery and chemicals). Hall and Soskice and others argue that the high degree of engagement by shareholders and financiers in business in the latter group of stakeholder economies facilitates development within the framework of current thinking. The more disruptive innovations, which enable business to progress in the high-tech areas, are more readily achieved when other actors are less immediately involved in firms.

Tylecote and Ramirez show that, while it is true that co-ordinated economies appear to lead in medium-tech business, it is not obvious that the shareholder capitalism of the more liberal economies is uniquely fitted for the high-tech sector. Both the Nordic countries and Japan are generally agreed to have highly co-ordinated economies, yet appear successful in the high-tech area. The authors then turn to the UK experience and point out a sharp and continuing decline in research and development investment, which has now fallen to a level below any of its rivals apart from Italy. They conclude that, while it is unlikely that any UK government would be able to make a substantial impression on the finance sector bias of the economy, there are worthwhile reforms that can be pursued. Government could invest more in training and seek to engage business in it, for example by reviving the old Industrial Training Boards. It could also develop state-supported banks to finance innovation and introduce public sector co-funding for research and development.

These four chapters review recent policy developments in a range of areas: local government, trade balance, training and industrial policy. All argue that the flexible liberal stance of the Coalition is failing to provide a satisfactory solution to Britain's entrenched problems of growth and productivity and that it is likely to lead to further long-term economic difficulties in the context of growing social and economic inequality.

In the final section of this volume, *Alternatives: Beyond Growth?*, contributors interrogate the framework of growth itself, exploring the practical limits of the existing growth strategy and stepping back to critically examine the status of growth as the guiding aspiration, and dominant metric, of economic development. In different ways, they question whether this is a crisis *of* growth or indeed a crisis *for* growth?

In addressing this question as part of a critique of existing growth strategies, the authors address the labour and gendered dimensions of the British growth crisis.

Daniela Tepe-Belfrage's highly innovative chapter presents the first detailed feminist critique of the Coalition government's community cohesion policies which have developed since the onset of the crisis and which are so intimately associated with the popular mantra of David Cameron in particular that 'we are all in it together'. Drawing analytical inspiration from recent trends in critical criminology, notably the work of Löic Wacquant, Tepe-Belfrage shows that we are not. In so doing, she examines in rich detail the way in which the theme of Britain's 'broken society' has been constructed as a hindrance and impediment to growth and prosperity and how this, in turn, has shaped the politics of the 'big society'. The chapter examines the production and reproduction of masculinities and femininities through poverty targeting programmes and the resulting consequences for the organisation of production and social reproduction drawing out, in particular, the implications for community cohesion projects. Tepe-Belfrage shows, passionately and persuasively, how the lives of women, particularly single mothers, have been impacted by the inegalitarian, disciplining and criminalising politics to which the Coalitions' austerity agenda and its aggressive politics of community have given rise.

The final contribution to the volume comes from Frank Pyke, who provides a compelling overview of the prospects for a new growth strategy based upon the ILO's notion of 'decent work'. Pyke uses 'decent work' as a synonym for an enlarged social dimension within economic development, suggesting that there are serious growth benefits to be accrued through promoting better working conditions. Pointing to an alarming increase in precarious work, a wider deterioration of employment conditions and mounting inequality in Britain, Pyke argues that these factors will likely undermine the sustainability of Britain's growth model. Identifying the dominant 'business first' approach to growth, Pyke then counterposes an alternative 'decent work first' perspective that sees decent work as a key input into growth and competitiveness, rather than an outcome. By mobilising a wide range of supporting evidence, Pyke makes a strong case for the beneficial impacts of decent work upon productivity and competitiveness. If we do not enact such a strategy, Pyke warns us, then Britain's long-term economic sustainability will be gravely imperilled by the continued casualisation, precarity and inequality that erode the sources of domestic demand.

As a whole, the conclusions to be drawn from the volume are sobering indeed. The Coalition government has failed to break from the damaging course upon which the British economy was steered in the pre-crisis period. Instead, the Government's unprecedented austerity agenda and avowed market-liberal commitments have deepened and exacerbated many of the most debilitating idiosyncrasies associated with the British growth model. Headline figures of GDP growth may paper over these weaknesses in the short-term, but the sustainability and stability of growth remain gravely imperilled in the longer-term. The threat of a new crisis, perhaps of even greater magnitude and duration, looms large. Only with a new growth strategy that convincingly departs from the hallmark failings of the old model, will we move closer to an enduring solution to the problem of British growth.

Yet, despite the rather depressing failure to change course since 2008, the contributions to this volume provide a note of optimism and the sense of possibility, as well as practical prescriptions for policy, that will be required for the achievement of a more progressive and enduring growth model for Britain. As Coutts and Gudgin show in their chapter, it is time to break from the rigid commitment to liberal economic policies, which have suppressed growth rather than stimulating it. We need a growth model that addresses and resolves inequalities and imbalances, rather than one which aggravates and entrenches them further. That task will not be easy, as Peter Taylor-Gooby's review of the 'Left Trilemma' makes all too clear, but there are concrete steps that can be taken towards this goal.

As the contributions from Frank Pyke, as well as Heyes and Lewis demonstrate with great clarity, strengthening employment protections and promoting decent work should be central here. The entrenchment of precarity, casualisation and insecurity offer only the flimsiest of foundations for a growth model. We must surely aspire to much more than this. Building the foundations of a new growth model will also require a long-term outlook, as Gerry Stoker counsels to compelling effect. It will require a re-engagement between government and citizens and a reinvigorated notion of localism that empowers communities and builds capacity. But, as Mackinnon et al. show so convincingly, it will require the right kind of localism; not one that devolves austerity while further centralising the real levers of power and control. Instead, we need a progressive localism that can present a genuine challenge to the debilitating pathologies of a model forged in Westminster. And finally, any new growth model, if it is to stand the test of time and meet the requirement of sustainability, must genuinely be seen to work for all of us, as Daniela Tepe-Belfrage makes clear. A strategy that seeks to deliver growth through the marginalisation and exploitation of the disempowered cannot provide a defensible basis for economic development and it certainly will not offer a firm foundation for community cohesion or civic sentiment. The challenges at hand for Britain are considerable. But what this volume confirms is that the resources, remedies, and ideas are available if the right choices are made.

## References

Bank of England (BofE) (2012) 'The distributional effects of asset purchases', *Quarterly Bulletin*, Q3, pp. 254–266. Available from http://www.bankofengland. co.uk/publications/Documents/quarterlybulletin/qb120306.pdf [accessed 12 February 2014].

Berry, C. and Hay, C. (2014) 'The Great British 'rebalancing' act: communicative dissonance in the construction and implementation of an economic imperative for exceptional times', SPERI, unpublished manuscript.

Gamble, A. (2009a) 'British Politics and the Financial Crisis', *British Politics*, 4: 450–462.

Gamble, A. (2009b) *The Spectre at the Feast: Capitalist Crisis and the Politics of Recession*. London: Palgrave.

Groom, B. (2013) 'When will the big squeeze on wages end?' *The Financial Times.* Available from http://www.ft.com/cms/s/0/1abaeafe-161e-11e3-856f00144fe-abdc0.html?siteedition=uk#axzz33ZytjUU3 [accessed 20 May 2014].

Hall, P. and Soskice, D. (2001, eds) *Varieties of Capitalism. The Institutional Foundations of Comparative Advantage*. Oxford: Oxford University Press.

Hay, C. (2011) 'Pathology without crisis? The strange demise of the Anglo-liberal growth model', *Government and Opposition*, 46(1): 1–31.

Hay, C. (2013) *The Failure of Anglo-Liberal Capitalism*. Basingstoke: Palgrave Macmillan.

Krugman, P. (2008) *The Return of Depression Economics and the Crisis of 2008*. New York: WW Norton & Company.

Schwartz, H. (2009) *Subprime Nation: American Power, Global Capital, and the Housing Bubble*. Cornell: Cornell University Press.

Smith, N. (2013) 'The British economy: a crisis of Anglo-liberal capitalism?' *Renewal*. Available from http://renewal.org.uk/articles/the-british-economy-a-crisis-of-anglo-liberal-capitalism/ [accessed 10 February 2014].

# Part I
# Diagnosing the Crisis

# 1
# Should the UK Continue to Follow Liberal Economic Policies?

*Graham Gudgin and Ken Coutts*

## Introduction

The current economic crisis in the UK, which began in 2008, has been the deepest and most prolonged for over a century. The level of output, or gross domestic product (GDP), is now 20 per cent below the pre-2008 trend,[1] and the cumulative loss of income since 2007 is equivalent to a whole year's GDP. Even with the recent upturn in growth, no economic forecaster currently expects full convergence back towards the pre-2008 trend.[2] That trend had been well established, at least since 1948 when modern records began. Since there was also continuous growth from the early 1930s to 1948, this means that the UK economy is in new territory not previously experienced in most people's lifetime.

This is the time to question whether the UK is following the most appropriate form of capitalism. Conventional wisdom, notwithstanding the recent recession, is that the liberal market policies followed since Mrs Thatcher's election victory in 1979 (and, to some extent, a few years earlier) remain the best model for the UK economy, albeit with additional safeguards to prevent future banking collapses. This belief is based on a view that liberal market policies reinvigorated a failing economy and underpinned a resurgence of UK prosperity from 1980 onwards. For several decades this view appeared to be supported by the facts on the ground and by a rejection of Keynesian economic theory in many university economics departments.

Most people, including most economists, still view the period 1979–2007 as one of faster economic growth and greater prosperity, as well as one of lower inflation, greater industrial peace and higher efficiency in the privatised, formerly state-owned, companies.[3] In this chapter we ask whether this benign view of the post-1979 world is a true reflection of

17

the economic facts. The aim is not to conduct an exercise in economic history for its own sake, but to investigate the extent to which the switch to a liberal market model is an essential underpinning for our prosperity. Those who believe in the free market economic model must be able to show that economic performance after 1979 was better than it would have been under the 'corporatist' economic policies of earlier decades. The easiest way to do this is to show that performance was better than during the decades prior to 1979. We show that the most important economic indicators, including GDP per head, were not better in the post-1979 decades. This makes it incumbent upon supporters of liberal market policies to explain why what they believe to be a superior economic system did not produce the goods.

This chapter thus compares the three decades of 'corporatist' economic policy prior to 1979 with the three 'liberal' market decades from 1979–2012 to assess which, on balance, were the more favourable. The end of the latter period saw the largest recession for a century, and this in itself is an indictment of a liberal market regime. While it is not the purpose of this chapter to describe the causes of the recent economic crisis in detail, we can say that the crisis was clearly caused by the build-up of household debt over three decades of financial liberalisation, leading eventually to a vastly over-extended banking system dependent on loans backed by over-valued housing assets. The value of housing had been unrealistically increased by easily available credit in a liberalised banking system, and individuals were willing to gear themselves to realise huge capital gains. As Minsky (1995)[4] clearly predicted, years before the crash, credit-based bubbles always end in economic crashes as the demand for credit disappears once asset prices begin to fall, and the supply of credit from troubled banks dries up.

The economic crash of 2008/2009 caused many to question the validity of the liberal market model. The main international policy response to these questions has been to strengthen rules on bank reserves to avoid future financial stresses causing the collapse of major banks. Otherwise the liberal market model remains intact. This chapter asks the much more general question, extending well beyond banking, of whether liberalising the economy led to faster economic growth and greater stability as modern economic theory suggests it should.

## Definitions

While we do not propose to conduct a lengthy review of the nature of liberal market policies the broad characteristics are easily summarised. Several of them could be included within a definition of 'globalisation'.

They are:

- Free markets, including:
  - Free trade, low tariffs and absence of non-tariff barriers
  - Free movement of capital and labour
  - Light regulation of business and labour markets
  - Light-touch regulation of banking and removal of restrictions on the Building Society movement
  - Private ownership of most production and services
  - Low income taxes
  - Weak trades unions
  - Strong competition law.

The contrasting policy regime that dominated the three decades prior to 1979 is often described as 'corporatist'.[5] During the 1950s, 1960s and 1970s the economy was highly regulated with relatively high tariffs on trade,[6] controls on capital movements, large-scale industrial subsidies and regional investment controls, cartels and weak competition rules, substantial public ownership of production,[7] and close involvement of powerful trade unions in determining economic policy.[8] Wage and price controls were also intermittently in force during periods of high inflation, and average and marginal income tax rates were high by post-1980 standards.

After 1979 all of this was to change. Fixed exchange rates had already been abandoned internationally in 1971 and a start was made on UK financial deregulation in the same year. Capital controls were quickly removed in 1979 followed by wage, price and investment controls. Over the 1980s a whole series of deregulatory measures were introduced in the financial and commercial sectors. Although the level of taxation was not permanently reduced there was a major switch away from high marginal income taxes and towards indirect taxes. Competition law was strengthened[9] and trades union laws introduced. Finally, a major programme of privatisation transferred the ownership of many public corporations to the private sector. In some cases this was a reversal of earlier nationalisations, but in the utilities this was a sell-off of organisations that were originally developed by local or central government.

The key question is whether these liberal market reforms led to faster economic growth and higher productivity across the UK economy as a whole. There is a widespread consensus that market liberalisation reforms since the 1970s have strengthened the competitiveness of the UK economy, ended a long period of relative economic decline and introduced a sustained period of rapid and stable growth. For instance, Professor John Van Reenan, Director of the Centre For Economic Performance at the LSE, wrote in April 2012, 'Mrs Thatcher's reforms helped to end a century of relative UK economic decline'.[10] The widely quoted economic historian Professor Nick Crafts takes a similar view.[11] Crafts (2011) concludes that 'applied economists in the UK are now generally agreed that strengthening competition in product markets is good for productivity performance'. Crafts reviews a range of studies showing that price-fixing and cartels, market concentration, separation of ownership and control, and strong trades unions all tend to reduce growth in productivity, as do barriers to trade and to new entrants in a sector. By 1979 it was relative decline which dominated interpretations of the post-war period. At the same time economic turbulence, and especially the high inflation of the 1970s, led to a reaction to the 'corporatist' model that had prevailed under both Labour and Conservative governments until 1979. High inflation, frequent and damaging strikes, and dissatisfaction with the performance of a range of nationalised industries all contributed to the Thatcher victory in 1979 and the subsequent free market revolution.[12]

## Evaluating the impact of free market reforms since 1979

The economic changes undertaken since the 1970s are so numerous and interwoven that an evaluation is necessarily complex. In this chapter we focus primarily on growth and productivity in the macroeconomy and on inflation, although we will have something to say about the impact of individual changes, such as the privatisation programme and deregulation. The starting point in making a judgement on the impact of the liberal reforms is to conduct comparisons. Our main comparison is of UK economic performance in the three decades since 1979 with the three preceding decades. In doing so, we also compare UK performance with other advanced economies over the two periods to address the issue of *relative* growth and decline. A number of studies have investigated the impact of deregulation and increased competition by comparing individual sectors and firms.[13] These studies are valuable and informative, but also partial. A necessary starting point in our view is to look at the performance of the UK economy as a whole, and to use sectoral and other studies as an aid to interpretation. The 30 years since the election victory that brought the Thatcher government to power is a long enough period to attempt an assessment of the impact of this revolution on the UK economy.[14]

## The salient facts

### Per capita GDP

Looking back over the past sixty years, the evidence now clearly shows that there was no sustained improvement in the trend growth of per capita GDP in the UK after 1979.[15] Indeed, per capita GDP has only once returned to the pre-1979 trend, at the pinnacle of the 1980s boom in 1989 (Figure 1.1). The current level of per capita GDP in 2014 was 20 per cent below what it would have been if the 1950–1979 trend had continued. This suggests two things. Firstly, any claim that market liberalisation in the UK raised the growth rate in per capita GDP depends entirely on the view that in the absence of liberal reforms the trend would have deteriorated after 1979. Any assessment of the impact of market liberalisation in the UK thus needs to examine the plausibility of the proposition that, in the absence of the liberal reforms, deterioration in the growth trend would have set in after 1979.

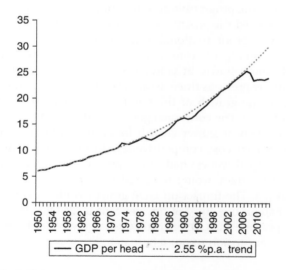

*Figure 1.1*   Real GDP per capita in the UK (£000, 2003 price reference year)

*Source:* GDP in constant prices (chain-linked 2010 reference year) from ONS UK National Accounts December 2013. Population is from the same source. The trend is fitted by least squares regression to real GDP per head over the period 1950–1979. The trend in 1950 was one per cent below the actual GDP per head. This accords with Dow's estimate of the position of the economic cycle in that year (J.C.R Dow The Management of the British Economy 1945–1960 NIESR CUP 1965).

Secondly, the superior trend over the three decades before 1979 was achieved despite the presence of all of the corporatist apparatus listed above, which is now generally, but in our view unnecessarily, regarded as damaging to economic growth and productivity. As well as high marginal income tax rates and higher inflation (the latter being mainly confined to the period from the late sixties to the early eighties), much of the period was characterised by wage, price and investment controls,[16] fixed exchange rates, greater public ownership, subsidisation and regulation of industry, alleged poor management and restrictive labour practices,[17] together with a less favourable record of strikes and industrial relations.

Any claim that the economic record has been better under a more liberal economic regime must explain why faster growth was possible under the more corporatist and interventionist regime that characterised the period up to 1979. Such a claim also needs to establish why a continuation of the corporatist regime after 1979 would have led to a poorer economic record than it did prior to 1979. In the latter case two possible reasons for a worsening economic growth performance in the UK are available. First, world trade grew more slowly in the second period. Second, the progressive adoption of free trade under GATT rules could have reduced the growth of UK exports by exposing uncompetitive firms to greater international competition.

On the first point, it is true that world trade in manufactures grew considerably more slowly in volume terms in the three decades after 1979 than in the previous three decades (Table 1.1). There was, however, no slowing in the growth of the volume of UK exports of goods and services after 1979. The continued good growth rate of UK exports after 1979, in a context of slower growth for world trade in manufactures, reflected improved cost competitiveness through much of next two decades. If competitiveness had not improved we estimate that slower growth in world trade would have reduced growth in UK exports by 0.7 per cent p.a. The impact on GDP growth is likely to have been of the order of about one third of one per cent p.a.[18] Our view is that this downward pressure on GDP growth was largely offset by the positive impact of the expansion in household debt.[19]

*Table 1.1*   Annual percentage growth in export volumes

|  | 1950–1979 | 1979–2007 |
|---|---|---|
| World Exports Volume (mfrs) | 8.9 | 6.4 |
| UK Exports Volume (goods and services) | 4.3 | 4.5 |

On the second point, trends in cost competitiveness are examined below together with the UK share of world trade. The conclusion is that there was a prolonged improvement in UK export competitiveness after 1979 but this was reversed from the mid-1990s as the sterling effective exchange rate soared. If increasingly free trade affected UK exports between 1979 and 1995 the impact was more than offset up to the mid-1990s by increased cost competitiveness. After the mid-1990s the UK share of world trade fell strongly and consistently but most of this is likely to be due to the lack of cost competitiveness under a strong sterling exchange rate. Similarly, import penetration remained stable up to the mid-1990s but has risen strongly since then.

## Increased volatility of growth

Economic growth also became more volatile after 1979 in the sense that departures from the long-term trend became deeper and more prolonged, even if they were less frequent. Between 1950 and 1979, in what were then called 'stop-go cycles', the 'stop' years were slow-downs in the rate of growth rather than recessions with actual declines in GDP. The only years in which real GDP was lower than the previous year were 1974 and 1975, following the first global oil price hike.[20] Since 1979, there have been three major recessions, with the latest one being the deepest for a century. Departures from the 2.25 per cent p.a. growth trend have been much more serious and prolonged in the post-1979 period. Many economists have focused on the lengthy period of concerted growth between recessions. The period 1992–2007 was often referred to as the Great Moderation because of its combination of growth with quiescent inflation. The recession of 2008–2009 destroyed the idea that boom and bust had been abolished and it strains credibility to interpret the entire post-1979 period as one of stability.

## Productivity

It seems that after 1979 GDP per head remained below the pre-1979 trend. This poor performance can be examined further by disaggregating per capita GDP into components. Per capita GDP is the arithmetic product of productivity (GDP per hour), hours worked per employed person, employment rate (numbers employed divided by population of working age) and a dependency ratio (inverse of working age population divided by total population). The evidence on productivity shows that the pre-1979 trend in productivity (GDP per hour) was maintained for a few years into the early 1980s but deteriorated after that, coming to a halt after 2007 (Figure 1.2).[21] The employment rate was generally lower after 1979 despite the expansion of the female workforce, the growth of part-time employment and, most recently, the increase in employment of people aged over 64 (Figure 1.3). The lower employment rate

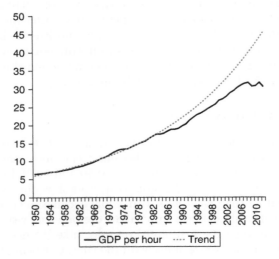

*Figure 1.2*   Productivity (GDP per hour, £ 2010 prices)

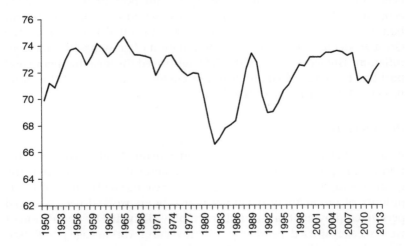

*Figure 1.3*   Employment rate (percentage of working age population)

*Source:* ONS Employment Rate is the number of employed people as percentage of population aged 16–64.

contributed to a lower level of GDP per head, but its negative impact was more than offset by a lower dependency ratio and a cessation of the previous falling trend in hours worked per employee (see Figure 1.10).

## Unemployment

The clearest and largest failure of the liberal market policy era has been unemployment. The average unemployment rate since 1979 has been 7.8 per cent , a rate two and a half times higher than the average for 1950–1979 (Figure 1.4). Unemployment rates have been higher in every year since 1979 than any previous year with the exception of the short period 2000–2004. This is not what supporters of free market policies would expect. Reduced regulation in business and labour markets should, in theory, have led closer to full employment. The fact that it has not done so has led to the development of the currently dominant 'New Keynesian' school of macroeconomic theory. This tries to explain away remaining high unemployment through various unconvincing 'frictions' in the job search process. Our Keynesian view is that the level of effective demand has not been sufficiently high to maintain full employment. This view is strengthened by the fact that measured unemployment is only part of the problem of joblessness. Fothergill, Beatty and Gore (2012) argue that 900,000 people on Employment and Support Allowance (formerly Incapacity Benefit) should be considered a form of concealed long-term unemployment.

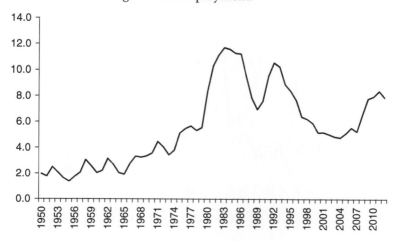

*Figure 1.4*  Unemployment rate (percentage of labour force)

*Source:* LFS (ONS) persons actively seeking work as a percentage of employed persons plus unemployed persons.

## Inflation

More than anything else it was the huge rise in inflation during the 1970s that stimulated the change in economic policies from 1979 onwards.[22] UK inflation was generally higher than in the US through the 1950s and 1960s, although the gap narrowed as Vietnam War expenditure stimulated demand in the US in the later 1960s. Inflation in the US, and most other advanced economies, peaked after the 1974 and 1980 oil price hikes, but UK inflation rose by much more (Figure 1.5). UK inflation rose after the 1968 devaluation of sterling and again from 1971 in the so-called 'Barber Boom' following the first round of financial deregulation in 1971. The impact of the first oil price hike in 1974 was greatly magnified by inept wage indexation polices under the Heath government in which 'threshold' wage increases were built upon price rises.[23] Further devaluation of sterling under the post-1973 floating rate regime kept inflation high through much of the 1970s, although the Callaghan-Healey wages squeeze of 1976–1979 helped to bring down wage inflation at the same time as global inflation was moderating. The squeeze proved too rigorous and led to the breakdown of the policy after the Winter of Discontent and another bout of high inflation exacerbated by the second oil price hike in 1980.

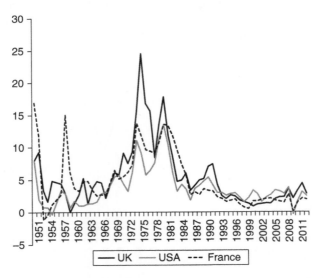

*Figure 1.5*   Inflation rate: annual percentage changes in consumer price index

*Source*: US Bureau of Labour Statistics. www.bls.gov/fls/intl_consumer_prices.xls

It was this record of high inflation that caused the incoming Conservative government to adopt its Medium-term Financial Strategy (MTFS). This used government expenditure cuts and high interest rates to reduce inflation in place of wages policies. Inflation did fall rapidly in the early 1980s, but this was a global phenomenon and it was not obvious that the UK inflation record over the period 1980–1992 was much better vis-à-vis the US than it had been in the 1950s or 1960s, even though unemployment was very much higher in the 1980s. UK inflation peaked once more at the beginning of the 1990s following an extended period of rapid economic growth despite the fact that unemployment remained high. After 1992 the impact of globalised trade and low import prices kept inflation low in all advanced countries, including the UK, until the sharp depreciation of sterling in 2008 which set off another rise in prices.

The impact of liberal market policies in this complex history of inflation is important but not straightforward. UK inflation tended to follow world price changes after 1979 mediated by changes in the sterling exchange rate. The impact of global trade liberalisation was strong, particularly after 1992, in bringing China, India and other emerging economies into trade in manufactures and, to some extent, services.

## Industrial disputes

Poor industrial relations were a particular feature of corporatist Britain prior to the 1980s. They improved under the liberal market regime, and the reduction in the annual number of days lost in strikes was dramatic. The number of days lost ranged between one and two million in the 1970s and early 1980s, with a peak of four and a half million during the winter of discontent of 1978/1979. By the 1990s the average number of days lost had fallen to around 250,000 p.a. High unemployment in the 1980s, the reform of trade union legislation and practice, and government determination as displayed during the 1984 miners' strike, all played a role. The reduction in strikes, and related industrial disruption, was welcomed by business, and must have helped management to raise productivity. Clearly, the impact on GDP growth is not a large one. The growth in productivity in the UK has not risen as the number of days lost in strikes has fallen. Other factors are clearly involved and it seems that the reduction in industrial disruption has not been a large enough factor to overcome other influences leading to lower productivity growth.

## Other changes

Consumers' expenditure returned to the pre-1979 trend by the end of the 1980s and remained close to this trend until 2007. This was a rather better performance than for GDP per head because consumers' expenditure reversed its previously falling trend in its share of GDP after 1979 mainly due to increased household borrowing. Lower income taxes in the post-1979 period helped to maintain growth of household incomes but were offset by higher indirect tax rates. Overall, taxation was higher through most of the 1980s than in the 1970s but fell after 1992 to levels a little lower than the 1970s.

Crucially for economic growth, business investment grew more slowly after 1979 and from 1990 ceased to grow at all. In both periods the UK had the lowest level of business investment of any advanced economy. This was accompanied by a much less favourable performance of manufacturing output in the later period. Manufacturing output grew rapidly until 1973 but has expanded little since then. The UK now has proportionately the smallest manufacturing sector of any OECD country. Regional inequalities in per capita GDP have also widened since 1979, reflecting a collapse in manufacturing employment in much of the North and the Midlands. As a result there are now large tax revenue flows out of the Greater South East to support public expenditure in other regions (the current outflow of revenues is estimated to be 7 per cent of GDP of the Greater South East).[24]

The reduction in international trade barriers, a key plank of liberalisation, has played an important role in the declining importance of manufacturing through easing the path of firms to relocate production in lower cost countries. This has also increased markets for UK-based service exports but these are heavily concentrated in London and the South East. Globalisation in this sense has also underpinned the growing inequality of incomes since 1979. The weakness of trade unions has played a role but the ease with which firms can relocate production and bring in foreign labour strengthens the power of managers relative to the workforce.

We can conclude that the evidence for an absolute improvement in UK economic performance after 1979 is mixed. Inflation was lower and industrial disputes were reduced in number and impact. However, the level of GDP per head was lower than would have been the case had the pre-1979 trend continued. In addition, the growth rate of productivity clearly deteriorated after the early 1980s. Crafts (2011) argues that competitive conditions in British product markets were strengthened but fails to explain why reforms from the 1970s, which abolished or weakened constraints to competitiveness, failed to raise the trend growth rate for UK productivity (GDP per hour) or for per capita GDP.[25] Much of the support for liberal market reforms comes from a belief that the UK's economic performance improved relative to Western European competitors (although not relative to the US) and it is to this issue that we now turn.

## The UK's relative performance

Other than the support of what we regard as not always appropriate theories currently dominant in much of university economics, it has been the UK's improved performance *relative* to major European competitors that has underpinned the consensus around the economic benefits of market liberalisation. In the immediate post-war years, levels of productivity and per capita GDP in the UK were well above those of most of Western Europe. The advantage had disappeared by 1979 as productivity in other EU countries improved faster than in the UK, but after 1979 the UK matched or bettered growth in per capita GDP in the original EEC members (Figure 1.6). However, there is little evidence, as we have seen, that this improvement in relativities was caused by any improvement in the actual growth of UK GDP. Rather, it was caused by

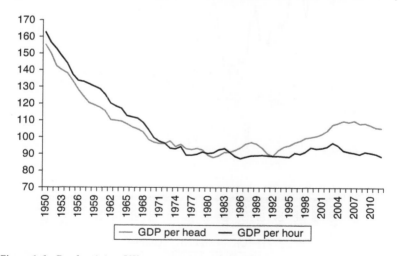

*Figure 1.6*   Productivity: UK as percentage of the EU6

*Source:* Conference Board Total economy database data in US$ at 1990ppp. The EU6 consists of Belgium, France, Germany, Italy, Luxembourg and the Netherlands.

a dramatic slowing in the growth of continental EU economies from the early 1970s onwards. GDP at constant prices in these economies grew rapidly at an annual rate of 4.5 per cent p.a. from 1950–1973, slowing to 2.5 per cent p.a. in 1973–1979, but it was only 1.6 per cent p.a. from 1979–2007.

The war-affected economies of Western Europe experienced rapid post-war recovery with rapid catch-up to the international technology frontier aided by political stability and expanding free trade within the EU and under GATT trade rules.[26] Madison's historical data on economic productivity levels (GDP per head) suggest that the recovery of France and Germany from the low war-ravished levels of 1945 continued rapidly until around 1960, and more sedately until the early 1970s when they regained the levels relative to the US previously experienced in the interwar and pre-WW1 periods (Figure 1.7). The UK gained less from post-war reconstruction, having suffered much less wartime damage and was initially much less far behind the technology frontier.[27] Growth in per capita GDP in the UK was more typical of an economy closer to the technology frontier both before and after the 1970s, even though

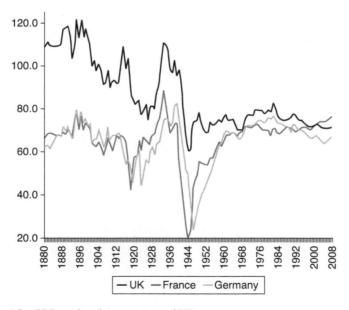

*Figure 1.7*   GDP per head (percentage of US)

*Source:* Madison. Historical Statistics of the World Economy.

the UK has never managed to close the whole of the wide productivity gap with the US that opened up during and after WW2. After 1970 there was little further European convergence towards US levels of per capita GDP.[28] This interpretation suggests that the panic around economic decline that swept 1970s Britain was unwarranted and that already by the late 1970s the UK was matching productivity growth in the EU. To the extent that the decision to join the European Economic Community in 1973 was taken to gain access to fast-growing markets, this decision was based on a false premise.

As we noted above, GDP per head is not a direct measure of productivity. It is not only influenced by labour productivity (GDP per hour worked), but also determined by other factors, including the proportion of the population working and the number of hours worked per employee. The general rule for productivity in a globalised world economy is that countries tend to catch up with the technologically most advanced economy through inward investment, competition and the transfer of knowledge.

Differences in the rates of European convergence to the technology frontier, as represented by the US, are shown in Figure 1.8. In France and Germany labour productivity (GDP per hour worked) converged more rapidly towards the US level over the post-war decades than was the case in the UK. There was clearly something deficient in the UK's performance, since the UK convergence trend was under half the rates achieved by France or Germany. The important point in relation to economic liberalisation, however, is that the UK convergence trend did not accelerate after 1979. Indeed, the same slow convergence trend continued until the mid-1990s when it stalled at 80 per cent of the US level.

French and West German productivity converged close to the US level by the early 1990s and from this date slowed down to below the long-term US rate of just less than two per cent p.a. Because the slower UK convergence continued for a few more years the gap between the UK and France/Germany narrowed a little after 1990. UK productivity levels remain well below those of France and the US (and West Germany). They were also below the level that would have prevailed if the pre-1979 convergence trend had continued right up to the present. There is thus little in this record to suggest that free market reforms improved UK performance. Productivity in the UK remains well below that of major competitors and is not converging.

Productivity has grown a little more slowly in all of the major European economies since the mid-1990s. The US productivity spurt of the late 1990s, due largely to Walmart and other large US retailers (and

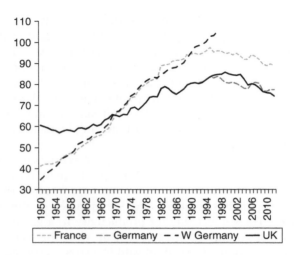

*Figure 1.8*   Productivity comparisons: GDP per hour worked (US=100)
*Source:* Conference Board (2013).

to financial dealers), was not reflected in Europe where higher population densities mean that planning regulations constrain the development of very large-scale retail operations. In the current recession US
productivity growth has again outpaced that in Europe, as US employment fell more rapidly than in Europe.

In the US itself there has also been little evidence that deregulation
and other liberal market policies since 1980 have boosted productivity.
In the period up to 1970, with fixed exchange rates, US productivity
grew at two and a half per cent p.a., Since the Reagan era the trend
rate has dropped below two per cent , with only minor and temporary
changes, including the productivity spurt of the late 1990s.[29]

While productivity in the UK remains below US, French and German
levels, other components of per capita GDP bring the UK closer to France
and Germany but not the US. The UK employment rate has always been
relatively high, while that in France and Germany has always been lower
(Figure 1.9). There is evidence that low productivity workers are disproportionately excluded from employment by institutional arrangements
in countries with low employment rates.[30]

The number of hours worked by employees tends to fall as countries
become richer. This has happened in all western economies, but occurred
much more slowly in the US than in Western Europe (Figure 1.10). Until

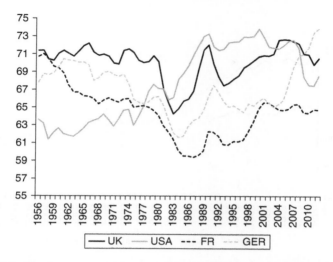

*Figure 1.9*   Employment rates: persons employed as percentage of population aged 15–64

*Source:* OECD dataset ALFS Summary tables. Germany is West Germany up to 1990.

1979 the UK behaved like a European economy with falling working hours per employee, but after 1979 the decline in hours worked was much closer to the US. In the US the decline in the number of hours worked went at an even slower pace after 1980 and the US now works longer hours than any western economy. Since US employees used to have shorter hours than Europeans until the 1980s, the current long hours are unlikely to represent a cultural preference for income over leisure. An important reason is the low number of days of annual holiday in the US, and one reason for this is likely to be job insecurity. Whatever the reason, the longer hours worked in the US and the UK serve to raise the level of per capita GDP relative to those in the rest of the EU. In the UK this goes some way towards compensating for low levels of labour productivity.

## The UK share of world trade

Another set of facts used to suggest an economic revival from the 1970s onwards concerns the UK's share of world trade. At the end of WW2 the UK share of world goods exports was almost 14 per cent, or six times its share of world population. This share fell rapidly over the 1950s

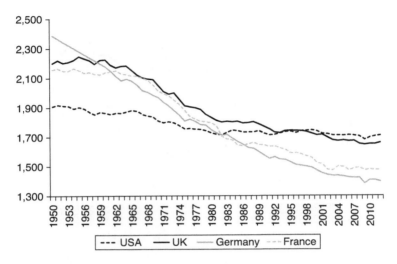

*Figure 1.10*   Annual hours worked per employee
*Source:* Conference Board.

and 1960s, but stabilised at around five per cent from 1973 until the mid-1990s, after which it declined once more, reaching three per cent by 2010 (Figure 1.11). The sharp improvement in the falling trend of the UK share of world trade suggests a marked improvement in competitiveness. The UK share of world trade had fallen by close to 2.7 per cent p.a. up to 1979 and by 2012 was only nine per cent above this pre-1979 trend. Over the 15 years from 1984–1999 the UK share of world trade improved relative to the previously falling trend, indicating an improvement in competitiveness. From the late 1990s this improvement went sharply into reverse and by 2012 the share was close to what it would have been had the pre-1979 trend continued.

The accelerated downturn from 1999 suggests a reaction to the 25 per cent increase in UK relative unit labour costs between 1996 and 1998 caused by a sharp appreciation of sterling (Figure 1.12). Similarly, the improved performance from 1984–1999 reflected generally low unit labour costs over this period.

One further point to note is that the UK balance of trade was closer to that prior to 1979 than it has been subsequently (as it had to be, in an era of fixed exchange rates) (Figure 1.13). The 2.25 per cent p.a. trend in per capita GDP was thus maintained with a more favourable trade balance before the 1970s than subsequently. The deteriorating trade

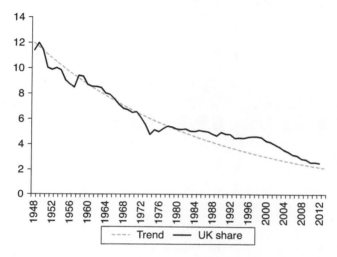

*Figure 1.11*   UK Exports of non-oil goods as a percentage of world exports (and −2.7% p.a. trend)

*Source:* IMF Direction of Trade Statistics.

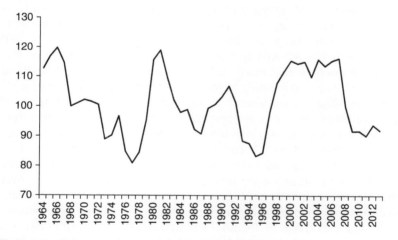

*Figure 1.12*   UK relative unit labour costs (2008=100)

*Source:* OECD relative Unit Labour costs (IMF NRULC for 1964–1969, linked).

balance after 1979 was largely due to a strongly worsening balance of goods trade, despite the build-up of North Sea oil production. The services balance was little changed through most of the period since 1979, but has improved considerably since 2002.

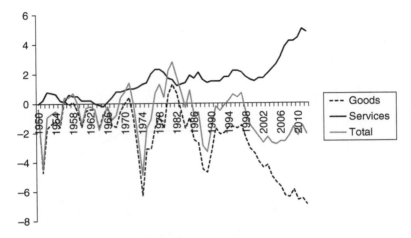

*Figure 1.13*   UK trade balance (percentage of GDP)
*Source:* ONS.

The unfavourable goods and services balance over recent decades is the counterpart of an excess of domestic expenditure over domestic income. In part this excess has occurred because of rising household debt, which has allowed spending to grow faster than income. The level of household debt has risen from around 60 per cent of household income to over 160 per cent in the most recent years. Our econometric estimates suggest that around 15 per cent of increases in household debt contribute to private sector spending (through new housebuilding, spending associated with moving home, and other spending financed through equity release). If so, then the rise in household debt since the early 1980s, equivalent to 100 per cent of private sector disposable income, may have raised private expenditure by around 15 per cent over the 30 years from 1980 to 2010. It is of course also the rise in debt (and mainly mortgage debt) that was responsible for the house price bubbles of the late 1980s, late 1990s and the noughties. The apparent increase in wealth in these bubbles may also have led to a higher level of consumer expenditure.

## Discussion

To recap, it seems clear that the growth of the UK economy in the three decades since 1979 during which market liberalisation occurred has not been demonstrably superior to the previous three decades. The trend rate of growth in per capita GDP did not rise, the growth rate of productivity fell and the volatility of real GDP was greater. Unemployment has been much higher since 1979 than over previous decades and inequalities of income and regional prosperity have increased. The main economic indicators that clearly improved since 1979 were price inflation and the level of disruption through industrial disputes. Neither of these improvements has however been able to raise growth rates in output or productivity to the levels experienced prior to 1979. Nor do we expect future growth to even match that of the 1979–2007 period. Household debt levels are now too high to generate sustained growth, and governments across the developed world are holding down growth in attempts to reduce public debt.

Without an actual improvement in the growth rates of UK output and productivity the argument that UK prosperity over recent decades was the result of liberal market reforms requires the assumption that, without the reforms, economic growth would have deteriorated after the 1970s. Slower growth in world trade is one factor that is likely to have reduced the growth rate of GDP. We estimate that the reduction would have been relatively small and the only periods in which actual GDP exceeded the trend adjusted for world trade was when household borrowing was rising rapidly, which was in the 1980s and after the mid-1990s. Fast growth in household borrowing was largely due to financial liberalisation, but as the crash of 2008/2009 showed, this could not provide a sustainable stimulus to the economy. Other than the unsustainable stimulus from greater lending there is little evidence that liberal market policies boosted growth. Our conclusion is that liberal market policies are not a necessary requirement for satisfactory growth of the UK economy. Just as the 'Rogernomics' liberal reforms did not accelerate growth in New Zealand, the evidence is that UK growth was slower and more volatile after 1979 compared with the previous 'corporatist' era.

This does not mean that all such reforms should be reversed, but it does suggest that there is a greater potential choice of mixed economy than is usually admitted by many economists. This choice, in our view, should attempt to avoid some of the socially damaging aspects of a liberal regime, such as increased cyclical volatility and greater inequalities in income and wealth. Financial deregulation, the main cause of increased cyclical volatility, is being unwound but the re-introduction of regulations that worked well for decades could be taken much further than is currently proposed. Higher government spending (perhaps with lower taxation) is likely to be necessary to maintain effective demand, and the

Nordic economies show that this can work well. Stronger trades unions are likely to be necessary for a more equal distribution of incomes and, although this is a fraught area of policy, agreements between government and unions work reasonably well in some countries. Free trade and capital movements have worked well to bring greater prosperity to over a billion people in emerging economies, and the UK should strive to succeed within the existing trade rules but more could be done to ensure that UK-owned firms serve the UK national interest through such things as protecting national ownership and control.[31] Without reforms, slow growth rates are likely to continue. In our view the liberal market regime – business as usual – will do no more in the future than it has in the past. The Coalition government has temporarily revived the economy through stimulating mortgage borrowing once again, but household debt levels remain much too high for such a stimulus to last long.

## Notes

1. The trend used here for GDP per head is 2.25 per cent p.a. see Figure 1.1.
2. The UK economy would have to grow at an unprecedented 5 per cent p.a. every year to regain the trend within ten years. The Office For Budget Responsibility (OBR) in its March 2014 forecasts (Economic and Fiscal Outlook) expected growth in GDP to settle down at 2.5 per cent p.a.. This growth rate would be the same as the trend but would not be fast enough to allow any convergence back to the level of the pre-2008 trend.
3. It is the growing inequality of incomes, and most recently the long recession since 2007, that have begun to cast doubt on the liberal market approach, or at least on the financial deregulation aspects of the liberal market model.
4. Minsky H (1986) Stabilising An Unstable Economy. Republished 2008. McGraw-Hill Professional.
5. We recognise that the move towards free markets pre-dated Mrs Thatcher's government and included, *inter alia*, the end of the Bretton Woods system of fixed exchange rates in 1971 and the end of direct restrictions on bank lending under Competition and Credit Control, also in 1971.
6. The average effective rate of protection fell from 9.3 per cent in 1968 to 4.7 per cent in 1979, and 1.2 per cent in 1986 (Ennew C, Greenaway, D and Reed G, Further evidence on effective tariffs and effective protection in the UK. *Oxford Bulletin of Economics and Statistics*, 52, 69–78). Membership of the EEC in 1973 and European single market legislation contributed to the fall in protection but tariff rates were falling more widely under the various GATT rounds.
7. Employment in public corporations was close to two million from 1961–1981 (8 per cent of all employment) and fell steadily to 370,000 (1.3 per cent) on the eve of the Labour general election victory in 1997. Since then public corporation employment has remained in the range of 1–1.3 per cent of total employment (excluding NHS Trusts and publicly-owned banks).

8. Crafts (2011) *op. cit.* p.11 describes UK industrial relations in the post-war decades as 'idiosyncratic and unreformed', 'characterised by craft control, multi-unionism, legal immunities for trades unions and strong but decentralised collective bargaining' with 'increasing trades union density and the proliferation of shop-stewards'.

9. Anti-trust law was strengthened by the Competition Act of 1998 and the Enterprise Act of 2003. Crafts states that these Acts increased the independence of the competition authorities, removed the old 'public interest' defence, and introduced criminal penalties for running cartels. Crafts *op cit* p.13. By international standards UK competition rules were still weak in 1995 but were much stronger by 2005.

10. The Times 16 April 2012.

11. N Crafts (2011). British Economic Decline Revisited. University of Warwick, May 2011. For instance p.19, 'when competition was strengthened in later decades (i.e. after the 1950s and 1960s) there was a strong productivity response.'

12. Nigel Lawson, Conservative Financial Secretary and later Chancellor from 1983–1989 outlined the need for liberal market reforms in his autobiography ('The View From No.11'. Bantam Press. 1992). His worry was 'the long-term decline of the British economy' and the fact that growth 'lagged well behind the rest of Europe and Japan' (p.29). Most immediately, 'over the six years from the cyclical peak of 1973 to that of 1979...the British economy all but stopped growing altogether. Excluding North Sea Oil...the average annual rate of growth over that period was a half of one per cent' (p.29). Other concerns were the 'inexorable ... rise of inflation', trade union power, and sinking profits (p.30). Margaret Thatcher made similar points in her autobiography *The Downing Street Years*, Harper Collins, 1993. She described the 'democratic socialism' of the decades prior to 1979 as 'a miserable failure in every respect' (p.7). Like Lawson she draws attention to the slower growth in the UK relative to Western Europe, but adds 'as the 1970s wore grimly on, we began to fail absolutely as well as relatively' (p.7). As far as GDP was concerned this was not true. Lawson's points on economic growth also appear to be selective and exaggerated. The period 1973–1979 includes the first major post-war recession caused by the quadrupling of world oil prices in 1974. In the recovery from 1975–1979 annual growth in GDP averaged 2.8 per cent p.a. Even excluding the contribution of North Sea Oil to GDP, growth over the 1975–1979 period averaged 2 per cent p.a.

13. These studies are summarised in Crafts (2011) *op cit.*

14. It is also 40 years since the antecedents of the Thatcher revolution in the form of the liberalisation of banking under the Competition and Credit Control reforms and the introduction of market determined exchange rates. See Goodhart C A E (1984) *Monetary Theory and Practice: The UK Experience*, Macmillan, London.

15. Some economists argue that 1973 is a better candidate than 1979 as the key turning point in post-war economic history. There is some merit in this idea and it does seem true for the US. However, the later 1970s were reasonably close to the 1950–1979 trend for GDP per head. The final year, 1979, was only 1 per cent below this trend and closer to the trend than virtually any later year. See also, footnote 12 for details on economic growth in the later 1970s.

16. Through much of the 1950s consumer rationing and significant tariffs were also in force.

17. See N Crafts (2011) *British Relative Economic Decline Revisited.* CEPR Discussion Paper DP8384 May 2011.

18. We take a Keynesian view that the main exogenous variables driving growth in UK demand are exports and government spending (with consumer spending and private investment endogenous). Since exports are around half of the combined exogenous expenditure, demand for GDP will decline by about half of the reduction in growth of exports. UK export volumes grew by 4.3 per cent p.a. in the pre-1979 period while world trade in manufactures was expanding at 8.9 per cent p.a. If world trade had continued to grow at this rate in the three decades after 1979, then UK exports might have also continued to grow at 4.3 per cent p.a. The slower rate of growth in world trade in this post-1979 period would have reduced the growth rate of UK exports to 3.8 per cent p.a. This is calculated as the observed growth rate of UK exports 1979–2007 at 4.5 per cent p.a. adjusted for the fact that by 2007 actual export volumes in the UK were 22.2 per cent above the expected volume based on the growth of world trade and the UK's falling share of that trade (i.e. 1.045 divided by 1.0072 which is the annual growth rate required to achieve a cumulative growth of 22 per cent over 28 years). The reduction in export growth between the two periods is thus 0.7 per cent p.a. If the impact on GDP is half of this, then this impact would be around 0.35 per cent p.a.

19. Household debt rose by 7 per cent p.a. in real terms over the period 1979–2007 compared with 4.4 per cent p.a. over the previous three decades. Our econometric equation for real consumer spending suggests that a 7 per cent increase in real household debt will raise real household consumption by 0.7 per cent. This in turn would raise real GDP by 0.5 per cent p.a. The same calculation for the earlier 1950–1979 period suggests that rising debt boosted GDP by around 0.25 per cent p.a. The increase in the boost in the post-1979 period was thus of the order of 0.25 per cent p.a.

20. The quadrupling of OPEC oil prices in 1973 was itself a reaction to the depreciation of the real value of oil revenues as inflation accelerated in the late 1960s and early 1970s following US government decisions to expand defence spending and social benefits without concomitant increases in tax. The most plausible explanation for the subsequent recession (which was quite mild by post-1979 standards) was the difficulty of recycling the huge increase in OPEC revenues through a relatively under-developed international financial system. These were eventually recycled to less developed countries at the cost of a round of sovereign defaults in the early 1980s.

21. There is evidence of slow productivity growth during the 1950s when price-fixing and cartels dominated Broadberry S N and Crafts N R (2001) Competition and innovation in 1950s Britain. *Business History*, 43; and Crafts N (2011) *op cit* p.11. However productivity accelerated over the 1960s to regain the long-term trend in GDP per hour of 2.68 per cent p.a.

22. The disruptive nature of the large number of strikes during the 'Winter of Discontent' 1978/1979 was a more immediate and pressing factor underlying the Conservative Party victory in the 1979 election.

23. For a summary of incomes policies during this period, see Henry and Ormerod (1978).

24. Oxford Economics (2010) Regional Winners and Losers in UK Public Finances. *Economic Outlook*. Oxford Economics Ltd.
25. Crafts also presents no real explanation for the marked slowdown in EU productivity growth from the 1970s, despite the growing international movement towards liberalisation in the form of reduced tariffs and freer capital flows.
26. Abramovitz M and David P A (1996) Convergence and delayed catch-up: productivity leadership and the waning of American exceptionalism. In Landau R, Taylor T and Wright G (eds) *The Mosaic of Economic Growth*. Stanford UP. The authors suggested that the post-war catch-up proceeded better than in the interwar period because incentive structures were better and because US technology became more cost effective in European circumstances.
27. Like the US the UK also gained from war-related R&D and production in industries including aircraft, telecommunications, radar and chemicals. See Barnett C (1986) *The Audit of War*, e.g. p. 146 showing a tenfold increase in aircraft production between 1938 and 1943.
28. In his Milliman lecture (19 May 2011), 'The US Recession of 2007–201?' R E Lucas argues that the failure of EU economies to fully converge on US levels of GDP per head depends on the greater regulation of markets in the EU. This appears to confuse productivity (GDP per hour worked) with per capita GDP. The main reason for higher US levels of per capita GDP lies in the longer hours worked. The US is unusual among advanced economies in not reducing its working time as it becomes richer.
29. After a long period from 1975–1998, in which GDP per hour grew at only 1.4 per cent p.a. there was a productivity spurt between 1998 and 2004 with a productivity growth of 2.4 per cent p.a. Much of this occurred in the large distribution sector dominated by Walmart.
30. Crafts *op cit*, p.12. W Lewis makes the same point for France in the McKinsey report on Productivity (W W Lewis, 2005 *The Power of Productivity. Wealth, Poverty and the Threat to Global Stability*, Chicago: University of Chicago Press).
31. As one example of the potential disadvantages of foreign control, the sale of the iconic British-owned company Cadbury's to the American Kraft corporation (now Mondalez International) in 2010 lacked much in the way of economic logic but, although unpopular, it was not opposed by government since no vital national interest appeared to be at stake. However, control was transferred to Zurich (where the corporation tax rate was a third of that in the UK) following the takeover, and the firm is now believed to pay little in corporation tax in the UK. This is a loss to the UK even though a Financial Times report (20/6/2013) reported that Cadbury's had adopted aggressive tax avoidance schemes before the takeover, paying only around six per cent of profits in tax in the decade prior to 2010. Kraft quickly closed the Cadbury factory near Bristol, although it promised not to, having relocated the Terry's factory in York to Poland in an earlier takeover in 2005.

# References

Abramovitz, M. and David, P. A. (1996) 'Convergence and Delayed Catch-up: Productivity Leadership and the Waning of American Exceptionalism', in

R. Landau, T. Taylor and G. Wright (eds), *The Mosaic of Economic Growth*. Stanford: Stanford University Press.

Barnett, C. (1986) *The Audit of War; The Illusion and Reality of Britain as a Great Power*. Macmillan.

Broadberry, S. N. and Crafts, N. R. (2001) 'Competition and Innovation in 1950s Britain', *Business History*, 43.

Crafts, N. R. (2011) *British Relative Economic Decline Revisited*. University of Warwick, May.

Dow, J. C. R. (1965) *The Management of the British Economy 1945–60*. NIESR CUP.

Ennew C., Greenaway D. and Reed G. (1990) 'Further evidence on effective tariffs and effective protection in the UK', *Oxford Bulletin of Economics and Statistics*, 52, 1, 69–78.

Fothergill, S., Beatty, C. and Gore, T. (2012) 'The Real Level of Unemployment 2012', *Centre For Regional Economic and Social Research*. Sheffield Hallam University.

Goodhart, C. A. E. (1984) *Monetary Theory and Practice: The UK Experience*. London: Macmillan.

Henry, S. G. B. and Ormerod, P. A. (1978) 'Incomes Policy and Wage Inflation: Empirical Evidence for the UK 1961–1977', *National Institute Economic Review*. August, 85, 1, 31–39.

Jin, W., Joyce, R., Phillips, D. and Sobieta, L. (2011) 'Poverty and Inequality in the UK 2011', *Institute of Fiscal Studies*.

Lawson, N. (1992) *The View from No. 11*. Bantam Press.

Lewis, W. W. (2005) *The Power of Productivity: Wealth, Poverty and the Threat to Global Stability*. McKinsey.

Lucas, R. E. (2011) *The US Recession of 2007–201?* Milliman Lecture, University of Washington, May.

Oxford Economics (2010) 'Regional Winners and Losers in UK public Finances', *Economic Outlook*. Oxford Economics Ltd.

Thatcher, M. (1993) *The Downing Street Years*. Harper Collins.

Waterson, J. (2012) 'World Economics', *Commonwealth Growth Monitor,* June.

# 2
# UK Economic Performance Under New Labour 1997–2010: Facts, Lessons and Pointers

*Dan Corry*

## Introduction

The way that people think about policies for the future is greatly influenced by their take on what has happened in the past. This pattern is even more pronounced on the left with its tendency to be hypercritical. It is important therefore to look carefully at the experience of the UK Labour government 1997–2010 in order to understand what progressive policy making can and cannot achieve in the modern era. This chapter seeks to do that.

This period saw a particular version of progressive economic policy. Things went wrong, but many things went right. However, much of the understanding of the period has been coloured and overshadowed by the fact that there was a banking crash in 2007–2008 followed by a period of deep recession. Some wish to dismiss the whole period as a great mistake. From the right, some argue that New Labour's programme was too left wing, too interventionist and engaged in too much public spending (Cooke et al., 2011). From the left, some argue that the project was too neo-liberal and light touch (Coates, 2011). Rather than indulge in rhetoric and posturing it is useful to look at the facts; to look at what actually happened and to try to assess these issues from that foundation.

To do this, this chapter focuses on the economic performance of the UK in the Labour years, leaving aside issues like distribution and equity covered elsewhere in this volume (Taylor-Gooby, Tepe-Belfrage and Pyke). It begins by laying out some of the overall facts of economic performance since 1997 and puts them in an international and historical context. The focus, however, is on productivity both at the aggregate national economy level and in terms of the contribution of different sectors, such as finance, and different factor inputs, such as capital and skills.

Overall, we find that British performance between 1997 and 2010 was good compared to other major countries, both in terms of productivity and the labour market. The productivity performance was not primarily driven by the 'bubble' sectors of finance, property or government services. Rather, human capital, ICT and efficiency improvements were the dominant forces, especially in the business services and distribution sectors. A number of important mistakes were also made. The focus however, is on what lessons can be learnt for successful, progressive growth policies to create a better form of market based economy in the future.[1]

## Analysis of aggregate trends in national income and productivity

We begin by comparing the macro-level economic performance of the UK with its major international comparator states. There is an argument for focusing our analysis of the Labour period only up to 2008 (i.e. before the Great Recession) since the financial crash of this period was in essence a global shock, albeit one that hit the UK and its dominant banking sector harder than in many other nations. However, a tougher test is to look across the whole period in which Labour was in government through to 2010.

UK GDP growth from 1997–2010 was second only to the US (around 2 per cent p.a. vs. 2.22 per cent p.a.).[2] In terms of GDP per capita, a better measure of economic welfare, the UK averaged around 1.4 per cent. As Figure 2.1 shows, this was better than all the G6 countries we compare with, perhaps a surprise given the current rhetoric about the New Labour years.

If we look at GDP per adult, in order to take out any demographic effects across countries, then the UK performance is similar to that of Germany above all the other comparator states. Table 2.1 below shows some of the same data, including how the data looks if we stop in 2007. Clearly the UK performance looks extremely good in that case.

In order to try to appraise Labour's impact on the economy, we also compare the UK's performance over 1997–2010 to the period 1979–1997 which corresponds to the Thatcher–Major-led Conservative governments. Was it any different from the previous trend?

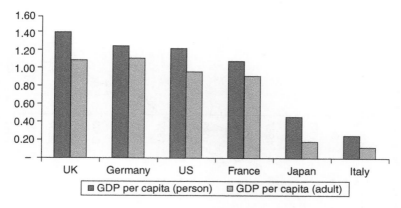

*Figure 2.1*   UK growth in GDP per capita faster than every other G6 country. Annual average growth GDP per capita & GDP per adult, 1997–2010

*Notes*: Conference Board data GDP is US$, constant prices, constant PPPs (CB based year: 2011). Adults are civilian population over 16. US Bureau of Labour Force Statistics. Data for Unified Germany from 1991.

*Table 2.1*   Growth of GDP, GDP per person and GDP per adult, 1997–2010

|  | 1997–2010 (whole period of Labour) | | | 1997–2007 (up until Great Recession) | | |
|---|---|---|---|---|---|---|
|  | GDP | GDP per capita (person) | GDP per capita (adult) | GDP | GDP per capita (person) | GDP per capita (adult) |
| UK | 1.93 | 1.42 | 1.22 | 2.89 | 2.43 | 2.20 |
| US | 2.22 | 1.22 | 0.99 | 3.00 | 1.96 | 1.64 |
| Germany | 1.24 | 1.26 | 1.01 | 1.67 | 1.64 | 1.35 |
| France | 1.66 | 1.04 | 0.92 | 2.31 | 1.66 | 1.51 |
| Japan | 0.59 | 0.52 | 0.31 | 1.15 | 1.02 | 0.79 |
| Italy | 0.69 | 0.22 | 0.19 | 1.45 | 1.01 | 0.99 |

*Notes*: Cumulative annual growth rates (in %). Analysis based on OECD data (extracted on 28 Oct 2011 from OECD.Stat). GDP is US$, constant prices, constant PPPs, OECD base year (2005) from GDP database. Adult refers to "working age adults", obtained from US Bureau of Labour Force Statistics, and includes the civilian population aged over 16. Data for Unified Germany from 1991.

Figure 2.2 can help us to answer this question. We base each series in 1997 to show the cumulative performance of the UK and other countries before and after the 1997 election, so the slope of the line can be interpreted as growth rates.

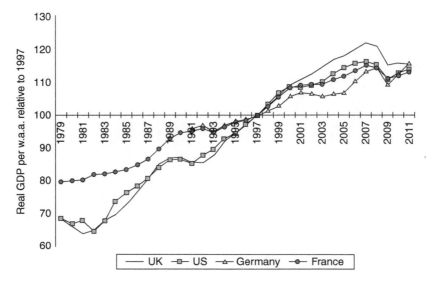

*Figure 2.2*   GDP per adult growth (1997=100) in UK, US, France and Germany

*Notes:* CB data GDP is US$, constant prices, constant PPPs, (CB based year: 2011). Adults are civilian population over 16. US Bureau of Labour Force Statistics. Data for Unified Germany from 1991.

In terms of comparison with the Conservative years, the trends seem similar, at least after around 1981. But with respect to our peers the results are a little more complex. Relative to the US the UK appears to do better post-1997 than before, despite this being the period of the US's 'productivity miracle'. On the other hand the catch-up with France seems to have been faster pre-1997 although we were still pulling away from France for most of the New Labour period. The situation is similar with respect to Germany.

It is useful to go one level down to examine what is contributing to this performance on GDP per capita. GDP per capita can be decomposed into productivity growth and labour market performance since as an accounting identity, GDP per capita = GDP per employee (productivity) x employees per capita (the employment rate). This type of decomposition allows us to determine how much of a country's growth performance is due to working smarter (i.e. productivity gains) versus working harder (higher employment rates or hours per average adult). Ideally, we want both to be high and increasing (although on average hours it may depend on how many are doing fewer hours than they want to start with). Panel A of Figure 2.3 uses GDP per worker as a measure of labour productivity. It shows that the UK did well, with the UK's GDP per worker growth as fast as that in the US between 1997 and 2008. This is impressive as these were the years of the US 'productivity miracle' (Jorgenson, 2001). US productivity has outstripped that of the UK in the Great Recession, which reflects the far more aggressive job shedding in the US in response to the downturn. UK productivity growth was better than that of Continental Europe, however. Again, UK productivity performance was also strong in the pre-1997 period. In fact, between 1979–1997 (under the Conservatives) UK GDP per worker grew faster than both the US and France.

Panel B of Figure 2.3 sets out employment rates and shows a good UK performance, especially post-1997. Its performance is strikingly steady relative to the US and Germany (at least until recently, since in Germany unemployment has hardly risen at all during the Great Recession). Over the period 1997–2007, the growth of the employment rate in the UK was similar to that of France and Germany. The US by contrast had a very poor jobs performance with the employment rate falling by nearly 5 per cent by 2008 before plummeting in the Great Recession. This is reflected in the fact that US unemployment rates rose from 5 per cent to almost 10 per cent, whereas in the UK the increase in unemployment was more modest. This was in spite of a larger fall in GDP. The UK's employment rate was similar at the beginning and at the end of the Conservative period, not rising like in the US, but not falling like in France. What is more striking is how volatile the jobs market was in the pre-1997 period in the UK, with a huge boom in the late 1980s and busts in the early 1980s and early 1990s.

This analysis gives a fairly clear story of Britain's performance under Labour. GDP per capita outstripped the other major economies because the UK did well in terms of both productivity (only a little worse than the US and better than the EU) and of its labour market performance (better than the US and only a little worse than the EU). This was a solid performance, contrary to what political discussion about the period might suggest (Landale, 2013). However, it is also true that the UK did well in terms of productivity in the Conservative years of 1979–1997, so UK performance is more likely to be a continuation of a post-1979 trend rather than a sharp break with the past.

In addition we must keep in mind the fact that although the UK's overall productivity growth has been strong, the UK still lags behind other countries despite the gap narrowing since the early 1990s (Figure 2.4)

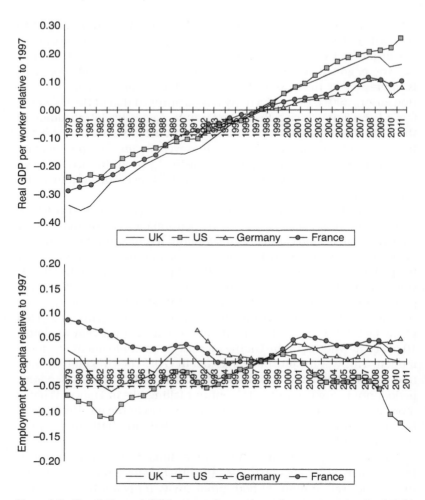

*Figure 2.3* Trends in real GDP per worker and employment per capita (adult) relative to 1997. Panel A GDP per employee; Panel B Employment per capita

*Notes*: Analysis based on OECD data (extracted on 28 October 2011 from OECD.Stat). GDP is US$, constant prices, constant PPPs, OECD base year (2005) from GDP database. Employment data from OECD productivity database. Adult refers to "working age adults", obtained from US Bureau of Labour Force Statistics, and includes the civilian population aged over 16. Data for Unified Germany from 1991.Workers are all persons engaged. For each country the logged series is set to zero in 1997, so the level of the line in any year indicates the cumulative growth rate (e.g. a value of 0.1 in 2001 indicates that the series has grown by exp(0.10)–1=11% between 1997 and 2001). The steeper the slope of the line, the faster growth has been over that period.

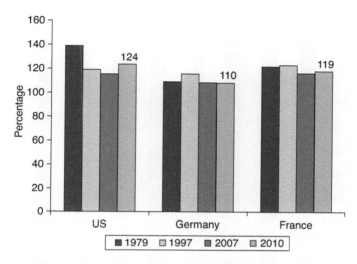

*Figure 2.4*   UK still lags behind in total economy productivity levels. GDP per hour levels (UK=100)

*Notes*: Analysis based on Conference Board data (2012). GDP is US$, constant prices, constant PPPs, CB base year (2011).

## Where did the growth in UK productivity come from?

To understand a bit better what lies beneath these relatively positive aggregate trends in UK productivity it helps to decompose the 'boom' years (up to 2007) in two ways. First, we examine the contributions of various industries to the aggregate productivity performance of the UK against its key comparators. Second, we look at the contributions of the factor inputs to growth (i.e. the quantity and quality of capital and labour).[3]

### Which sectors grew overall?

Before looking at productivity Figure 2.5 shows how aggregate value added has split between different sectors since 1979 in different countries. In all countries, there has been a strong trend away from manufacturing and other goods producing sectors towards services. But this trend is particularly strong in the UK with a shift towards business services (its share of aggregate value added rises from 7 per cent to 13 per cent).

Significantly, Figure 2.5 shows that the growth in the public sector, finance and real estate sectors between the Conservative and the Labour

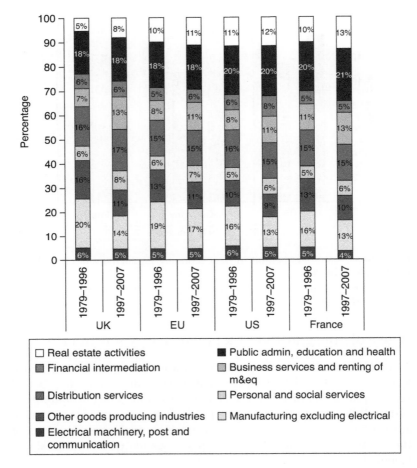

*Figure 2.5*    Sector shares of total economy GVA

*Notes*: Data: EU KLEMS. EU represents all EU-15 countries for which growth accounting could be performed, i.e. AUT, BEL, DNK, ESP, FIN, FRA, GER, ITA, NLD & UK. Data for France and the EU are available from 1981 onwards. Market economy only.

periods has been less than often imagined. Financial intermediation is about 6 per cent of aggregate value added in both periods and a broadly defined public sector (public administration, health and education) also remains constant at 18 per cent of value added. Real estate activities have grown, but only from 5 per cent to 8 per cent. According to

Figure 2.5 the share of the market economy was only three percentage points smaller under Labour than in the previous period. This fall was less than in France (which saw a 4 percentage point fall) but more than in the US and EU as a whole (which had a 1 percentage point fall).

For the rest of the analysis we now focus on the better measured market economy, both because productivity in the public services is so hard to measure – especially across countries – and in order to exclude real estate.

Overall, average annual growth in value added in the market economy in the UK was 3.2 per cent over 1997–2007, only slightly behind the US (3.4 per cent), and much faster than the EU average (2.5 per cent) and France (2.6 per cent). In addition, this was faster than the pre-1997 period, when the average annual growth rate was 2.3 per cent. However, this performance was largely due to the contribution of total hours worked (driven by rising employment). If we strip out the contribution of hours to UK growth of 0.4 per cent, we are left with labour productivity growth of 2.8 per cent, very similar to the pre-1997 period of 2.7 per cent.

### Which sectors are responsible for productivity growth? And how much was growth due to the financial bubble?

Figure 2.6 breaks down average annual productivity growth in the market economy between 1979–1997 and 1997–2007.[4] Overall productivity growth here was pretty similar but there were big changes in composition, with an especially big increase in business services and a decline in 'other goods producing industries'.

Most interestingly, financial intermediation was responsible for only 0.4 percentage points of the 2.8 percentage points annual growth in productivity under Labour. Accounting for 14 per cent (= 100*0.4/2.8) of productivity growth with only 9 per cent of the market economy value added is no small achievement, but this sector *already* accounted for 0.2 percentage points of the growth under the Conservatives (when it constituted 8 per cent of market economy value added). This leaves 86 per cent of aggregate market economy growth due to other sectors. Further, the contribution of finance also increased in other economies, as Figure 2.7 shows, its contribution more than doubled in the US over the same periods (from 0.2 to 0.5), and doubled in France and in the EU as a whole (0.1–0.2). So, while there are issues with the increasing share of GDP contributed by the financial sector in this period, any suggestion that productivity growth in the UK relative to others was mainly due to a 'bubble' in finance does not seem

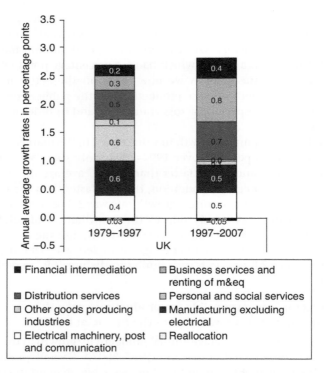

*Figure 2.6*   Sector contributions to market economy productivity growth, UK, 1979–2007

*Notes*: Analysis based on EU KLEMS data. Average sectoral growth rates for the periods 1979–1997 and 1997–2007 are weighted by each sector's average share in market economy nominal GVA (GDP less taxes, plus subsidies) over the relevant period. Reallocation effect refers to the labour productivity effects of reallocations of labour between sectors that have different productivity.

to square with the evidence. Furthermore, if we exclude the effect of finance altogether, productivity growth in the UK would have been broadly constant at around 2.5 per cent per annum in the pre- and post-1997 periods.

Although the productivity growth performance does not seem directly attributable to the 'bubble' sectors of finance, property and the public sector, there could be some other indirect mechanism. Could productivity in business services, for example, be driven by the demands from financial services? This seems unlikely, since many parts of business services (e.g. consultancy and legal) are serving primarily non-financial

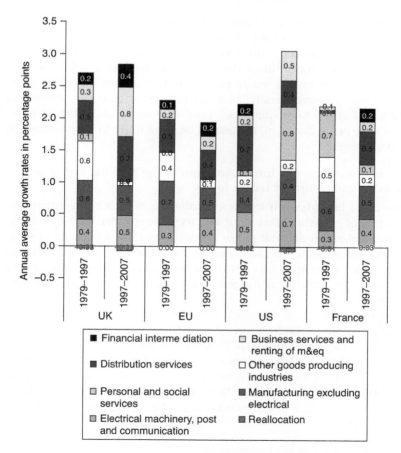

*Figure 2.7* Sector contributions to market economy productivity growth, 1979–2007

*Notes*: Analysis based on EU KLEMS data. Average sectoral growth rates for the periods 1979–1997 and 1997–2007 are weighted by each sector's average share in market economy nominal GVA (GDP less taxes, plus subsidies) over the relevant period. Reallocation effect refers to the labour productivity effects of reallocations of labour between sectors that have different productivity. EU represents all EU-15 countries for which growth accounting could be performed, i.e. AUT, BEL, DNK, ESP, FIN, FRA, GER, ITA, NLD & UK. Data for France and EU are available from 1981 onwards.

firms. A more subtle argument is that the financial bubble created a kind of unsustainable excess consumption demand that was propping up fundamentally inefficient companies. However, Giles (2011) shows that the data do not support the assertion that there was a great consumer boom before the financial crisis. In fact, there was a drop in household consumption as a share of national income, from 63.3 per cent in 2002 to 61.3 per cent in 2007. Furthermore, even if this consumption bubble story were true, it is unlikely that this would artificially inflate productivity. A general bubble would increase output and employment hours (temporarily) above sustainable levels. But it is unclear why this would flatter the productivity numbers. In fact, if generally unproductive activities were being drawn in, this would be more likely to lower measured productivity.

### Decomposing growth into factor inputs: The growing importance of skills and computer technologies

The other breakdown is by the contribution of each factor input, the product of growth in that input and its share in value added, and also the contribution of Total Factor Productivity (TFP, a measure of technical change) which is calculated as a residual. The labour composition index takes into account differences in the composition of the workforce in terms of skills, gender and age (O'Mahony and Timmer, 2009).

As Figure 2.8 shows, although TFP growth was similar, at about 1 per cent per annum in both the pre- and post-1997 periods, the contribution of labour composition and ICT capital increased in importance post-1997 and the contribution of non-ICT capital has fallen. Overall, contribution from the knowledge economy (labour composition, ICT capital and TFP) has increased in the UK from 2 to 2.3 per cent, compared to a fall in the EU and a larger increase in the US, driven mainly by higher TFP growth.

*Other measures of business performance*

We have focused on productivity because, for economists, this is the key measure of long-run economic performance. But we can look at other indicators of business performance to see what story they tell and if it is consistent with our overall argument. These include investment (domestic and foreign direct), innovation, management, education and skills, entrepreneurship, exports, profits and regional differences, all of which are examined in detail in Corry et al. (2011). This is more of a mixed bag, but overall these alternative indicators support the conclusion that there was a continuation of the positive trends in business performance since 1997, but with many problems relative to other countries' performances on the same indicators.

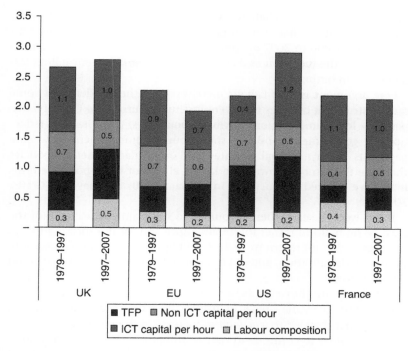

*Figure 2.8* Sources of labour productivity growth, market economy

*Notes*: Data: EU KLEMS. EU represents all EU-15 countries for which growth accounting could be performed, i.e. AUT, BEL, DNK, ESP, FIN, FRA, GER, ITA, NLD & UK. Data for France and EU are available from 1981 onwards. ICT = Information and Communication Technology and TFP = Total Factor Productivity.

## Was the UK's strong post-1997 performance anything to do with Labour's policies?

The assessment so far suggests that the performance of the UK economy between 1997 and 2010 was good by international standards. UK per capita GDP grew faster than all other major advanced countries and only the US had a better productivity growth record. A natural question to ask, however, is whether any of this was due to Labour policies?

Indeed, as noted earlier, the UK's growth of GDP per adult was about 1.4 per cent p.a. during 1997–2010 compared to 2 per cent p.a. under the Conservatives between 1979 and 1997. So although Labour did better relative to other countries on this measure it did not do better in comparison to the Thatcher–Major years. The picture looks better for Labour (with similar growth rates of around 2 per cent p.a. in both periods) if we end in 2007 of course, as productivity has fallen dramatically during the recession as a consequence of employment falling less quickly than output.

One argument is that Labour merely reaped the dividends of some radical structural changes that were instituted during the Conservative period – for example, more flexible labour laws, privatisation, reductions in government subsidies, some tougher enforcement of welfare payments, lower marginal tax rates, and other market-friendly policies that take time to bed down. The lagged effects of these policy reforms may have boosted productivity in the late 1990s and beyond (Crafts, 2011).

If this were the case, then Labour could still claim some credit for the glass being half-full rather than half-empty and for not messing things up. Labour did not return to 1970s style high rates of marginal taxation, or to re-nationalisation, and did not reinstate pro-union laws that could damage growth.

A deeper point, however, is that although many of the reforms under the Conservatives may have increased the level of productivity, it is unlikely that they led to a *permanent* increase in the rate of productivity *growth*. In order to continue to narrow the productivity gap with other countries, continuous reform is likely to be necessary; especially as many other countries have also been reforming their labour and product markets. It seems unlikely, for instance, that anti-union laws would have a permanent effect on productivity growth. Unions would have to have a seriously negative effect on innovation and there is no compelling evidence of this (Menezes-Filho and Van Reenen, 2003).

It is therefore likely that Labour policies did contribute to the good productivity performance during the period in question. In the next section we look briefly at what those policies were and which lessons might be learned, with the proviso that there is a lack of proper evaluation of most UK policies, so much is informed and intelligent conjecture.

## Did the Great Recession change everything?

The analysis shows a very good economic performance from Labour, at least until 2007/2008, a period we should therefore surely try to learn lessons from. However, some resist this for a number of reasons.

First, because of the economic problems of recent years there is an argument that productivity improvements up to 2007 were an illusion.

Second, perhaps the Great Recession itself was, in fact, due to Labour policies – so, whatever the benefit of these policies for a short period, in the end they led to the crash and should not be a model for future progressive policy makers. Third, some argue that Labour policies left the UK more vulnerable to the effects of the downturn than other countries. Finally, it could be argued that Labour did the wrong things when the crash took place because they were following the logic of their own policies in 1997–2007, which was the wrong approach to take in a crisis.

### Were the 1997–2007 productivity improvements a statistical illusion?

In pride of place is the argument that the productivity improvements from 1997 to 2007 were mainly froth, driven by a finance and real estate bubble. Thus, when the crash happened the mask was removed and the UK was revealed to have a much lower trend rate of growth and productivity than had been previously maintained. Potential output was lower than we had thought and so, despite a massive fall-off in output compared to what it would have been if the trend had been maintained, the UK (still) has virtually no gap between potential and actual output. This argument does not really stack up. As we have seen, the financial sector only contributed about 0.4 per cent of the 2.8 per cent annual growth in the UK market economy, which excludes the public sector and real estate, both of which held back aggregate productivity. We also saw that productivity increases were mainly based in business services and distribution and generated through the increased importance of human capital and ICT (compared to low-tech capital). It is therefore difficult to see why such activities could be solely generated by an artificial financial or property bubble.

### Was the Great Recession due to Labour's policies?

The second argument is that the crash itself was the result of Labour policies. One reason for this was Labour's weak regulation of the financial sector, which clearly had a role to play in causing the financial crisis. However, this light touch regulation was supported by the previous government, and the financial crisis was a global phenomenon with the catalyst being in the US and not the UK – even if the crisis revealed some major underlying weaknesses in the UK economy, particularly in the housing market (Hay, 2013). Many countries with different types of financial regulations also suffered as the banks got into trouble, so it is hard to blame the global crash on UK policies, even if stronger regulations should have been in place in retrospect.

## Did Labour's policies leave the UK more vulnerable to the effects of the downturn than other countries?

The strongest challenge is that the UK economy was particularly vulnerable to a downturn because of policy mistakes made by Labour, as well as by the Thatcher and Major administrations before them. The primary mistakes are to do with financial regulation and public debt.

### Financial market regulation

Financial market regulation clearly failed. The UK had pioneered a light touch approach to guiding financial markets well before Labour came to power and the Financial Services Authority (FSA) had been created. The direction of travel was similar to many other countries, such as the US, but the UK was clearly a supporter, or even a leader in some of these areas. Other nations – such as Canada – were more prudent, and this is one reason why they weathered the financial storm more successfully.

Light touch regulation helped the development of the financial services industry and there have been benefits of this in terms of access to credit. But it was clear that this process went too far (although nowhere nearly as bad as in the US sub-prime fiasco). The wholesale end of the finance sector concentrated in the City of London is the strongest cluster in the UK and created huge amounts of tax revenue and high paying jobs. It also drew a lot of talented people in the UK towards this sector and out of other industries that would be more favourable to long-term growth. Because the UK has a larger financial sector than other countries it took a harder hit in the downturn. On the positive side, however, if there is now a reallocation of British talent away from finance towards sectors that are creating more real and durable output, this could boost national income in the long-term.

In retrospect, a major problem was that certain banks based in the City had become 'too big to fail'. Equity and bond holders of financial institutions were given too many implicit and explicit guarantees of protection if they got into trouble. This encouraged banks to take excessive risks and disguise these risks by creating exotic and opaque financial instruments. By being protected on the downside for the risks, but being handsomely rewarded on the upside, this created a form of structural moral hazard so that all agents, from shareholders to CEOs to traders, were incentivised to take excessive risks. When the crisis hit the state had little choice but to bail out the failing institutions. In hindsight, it is clear that regulatory policy should have been more vigilant in all countries in: (a) creating a mechanism for the orderly break-up of failing banks (such as, so-called, living wills); (b) demanding higher capital requirements to prevent the excessive leveraging of debt (à la Basel 3); (c) maintaining a greater separation between the casino (investment) and utility (retail) arms of banking; (d) controlling the exposure of utility banking to raising finance in the wholesale market (Northern Rock's problem); and (e) paying more attention to asset bubbles (such as in housing).

Labour's policies towards the financial sector were remiss and a better approach to the financial sector would have reduced some of the costs in lost output. On the other hand, it is likely that Conservative policies would have been broadly similar. The failure of financial market regulation was really a global problem, whose consequences we will live with for a long time to come.

### Public debt

In retrospect, it is clear that public debt levels were too high for the stage of the cycle in 2008 in the UK (alongside many other countries like the US, Ireland and Spain). This reflected the large increase in public spending after 2000 with what we now can see were insufficient increases in tax to pay fully for it, which meant that the budget deficits were running up debt. The debt position has exacerbated the pain of recession. However, the structural element of the deficit, excluding investment spending, that was not related to the cycle was only about 1 per cent of GDP in 2008 (Portes, 2011). Over the next two years this jumped to 5 per cent because of the crisis. This demonstrates that the poor state of the public finances was a consequence of the recession, not a cause of it (Wren-Lewis, 2013a).

Having said this, the UK's debt and deficit position is not catastrophic in an historical context. In 2010 national debt stood at 52 per cent of GDP, high in comparison to the 1980s and 1990s (see OECD, Economic Outlook Database, 2010), but lower than during much of the twentieth century (between 1750 and 1850 debt exceeded 100 per cent of GDP). Compared to other countries the maturity of UK sovereign debt is very long, which means that the Chancellor does not have to raise finance frequently (like in the case of Italy). In other words, the UK is not Greece.

Labour left office with a plan to eliminate the structural deficit in eight years. In July 2010, the Coalition replaced this with a plan to eliminate the structural deficit in four years. Thus, there was and is a cross-party consensus over the medium-term to reduce the deficit; the point of contention has been more to do with its pace and timing. This is perhaps a second order issue but it is a crucial one nevertheless.

## Did Labour do the wrong things after the crash occurred?

The last argument is that the wrong things were done once the crash occurred. Labour's long-standing, light touch approach to economic management up to 2007 meant that, when the crisis broke, the party did not shift to a more interventionist Keynesian stance quickly enough.

This argument does not stand up to close examination. As the work presented above shows, the record was not that bad, even through to 2010. In fact, vigorous counter-cyclical and interventionist actions were taken which had real and 'confidence' effects from 2008. This meant that output and employment did not fall nearly as much as they could have. Productivity fell, but primarily because employment stayed much higher than would be expected compared to previous recessions (Gregg and Wadsworth, 2011). Real wages have fallen substantially since the Great Recession, and this has been an important factor in keeping unemployment much lower than we would expect – in addition to the growth of 'non voluntary' part-time and self-employment. Additionally, the effectiveness of the Employment Service, heavily reformed since the early 1990s, is greater than in previous recessions.

## Summary

The Great Recession does not overturn our assessment of real productivity improvements pre-2007 and certainly does not show that Labour was to blame for the recession. The failure to properly regulate finance and perhaps to bring the deficit down by a bit more during the good times did, in retrospect, leave the country more vulnerable to the downturn. But this does not mean that we should not learn lessons from the period for future progressive economic policies. The biggest mistakes have been made post-2010!

We do well to recall that arguably the biggest mistakes on macro (as opposed to financial regulation) policy came after 2010 as the new government tried to get to grips with the situation.

Growth in 2010 (the last year that can be attributed mainly to Labour) was in fact pretty healthy at a rate of 1.7 per cent. Unemployment had not risen nearly as much one might expect in a recession while home repossessions, business failures and so on remained remarkably low.

After 2010 the situation markedly deteriorated. Growth fell back sharply to 1.1 per cent in 2011 and to just 0.2 per cent in 2012 (a recovery of sorts seemed to be finally emerging in 2013). Despite low growth, inflation was high at 4.5 per cent in 2011 and 2.8 per cent in 2012 and the unemployment rate rose to 8.4 per cent, although again not as much as the negative GDP growth might have suggested.

Of course, some of this is due to external factors, not least the Eurozone crisis, but at least a large proportion must be put down to the consequences of policy decisions by the new government. While whoever had won the election of 2010 would have had to have kept a tight rein on spending, the relish with which the Coalition government went about its austerity programme undoubtedly deepened and prolonged the recession (see Jorda and Taylor, 2013) for more recent analysis of this.

Looking ahead there is huge uncertainty over whether a more pessimistic or optimistic view of the economy is closer to the truth. Has the great recession led to a permanently reduced amount of potential output (and productivity) or not? Pessimists see the current level of output as at near full capacity, whereas optimists believe there has been for many years, and still remains, a substantial output gap. As a result of this, there is room for expanding demand without sparking more inflation. While a lack of demand is depressing productivity, the precise size of the output gap is uncertain. Based upon the analysis above it does not appear that the recession is simply a bursting of the financial bubble with no hope of returning to pre-recession growth trends. Consequently, the more optimistic view of the UK economy seems correct, and the recent uptick in growth and growth projections (from very low levels) may be a sign of this, even if the degree to which is it based on a deliberate kick-starting of the housing market spells trouble ahead.[5]

## Creating a better form of capitalism for the future

### Introduction

Given the view that the Labour years 1997–2010 were a successful period in terms of GDP per capita and productivity growth, what lessons for progressive policy making should be drawn from this?

In the UK we focus on promoting long-term growth and on expanding the potential of the economy, rather than focusing on how to recover from recession. While many of the factors that will determine UK growth and productivity are outside the direct influence of economic policy – for example the Eurozone crisis, US policy and the sustainability of growth in India and China – UK policy still matters a great deal.

### New Labour's attempt to create a new capitalist model

The micro and growth orientated policies during the New Labour period in office were based on knowledge derived from academic research and thinking, be that around the importance of agglomeration and of incentives and governance at sub-national levels, the fundamental significance of innovation and human capital, or the importance of product market competition and so on.[6]

But in my view it went further than that. It was an attempt – within the constraints that were faced at the time – to create something closer to a social democratic version of a market economy. This model is best described as a mixture of stakeholderism – trying to increase long-termism, boost investment – and Clintonomics – skills, education, competition, innovation (see Corry, 2002, 2011a).

New Labour was not setting out to try to create a totally different type of economy nor to offer a full-on challenge to what is often categorised as the 'Washington consensus'–privatisation, deregulation, free trade, fiscal discipline, shareholder value, financialisation, and so on (see e.g. Gamble, 2009). But explicitly or implicitly the aim was undoubtedly to change the context in which capitalism – its firms and economic agents – operated.

It may sound obvious, but it is worth re-stating, that building institutions for a reformed model of capitalism is difficult. It is not one or two big changes that matter, but a whole nexus of them that, in aggregate, alter the incentives for markets and other players.

Broadly speaking three types of change were pursued: alterations to the external environment faced by firms and their set of incentives (e.g. competition policy); altering how firms utilised and accessed labour and capital (e.g. skills); and attempts to alter how firms operated (e.g. corporate governance).

In some places the policies worked well, as with the minimum wage; but some did not work, as is the way with policy. And the machinery of economic decision making and implementation in the UK did not always help (Corry, 2011b). In some cases, Labour was not ambitious enough or pulled back, partly due to a perceived need to keep business on board. In other cases, policies did not work or were badly implemented (e.g. Individual Learning Accounts, ILAs). Equally important, some policies are simply difficult to implement successfully in a world of open, globalised markets and free movement of capital (and labour) with a tax-resistant voting population.

In the remainder of the chapter we look briefly at a number of areas of policy: what was done, whether it worked and what might be done in the future.

## Some policy lessons from the New Labour period

### Competition

A robust finding from a host of studies suggests that increases in product market competition boost productivity (for example, Nickell, 1996;

Blundell et al., 1999 on UK productivity; Bloom and Van Reenen, 2007, 2010 on management and Holmes and Schmitz, 2010, for a survey). Crafts (2011) argues that the reduction in competitive intensity in the inter-war period was a major cause of the relative decline of UK productivity, which only turned around after pro-competition reforms were implemented post-1979.

Labour acted strongly in this area. Several pieces of legislation significantly strengthened competition policy. The 1998 Competition Act and the 2002 Enterprise Act both strengthened the hand of the competition authorities. There was also a de-politicisation of merger reviews, tougher punishments for cartels and more support for whistle-blowers. Perhaps some of this went a little too far in terms of allowing short-term decision making to trump long-term investment. Ideas in the 2010 Labour manifesto to put a bit more 'grit in the wheels' of the takeover merry-go-round make lots of sense. Similarly, governments must not be blinded by their commitment to competition policy to the strategic needs of major firms nor to the dangers of asset strippers – both from home and abroad.

Utility regulation was also reformed. A criticism of the privatisations of the previous Tory period was that, in many cases, public sector monopolies were allowed to remain private sector monopolies who could exploit their market power. Labour was more aggressive in moving from regulation to effective competition, fostering greater entry of newcomers into the business markets of the incumbents, but then allowing these incumbents more freedom to set prices and compete.

While the record was mixed across the utilities, most commentators see the strengthening of competition in telecoms as a success story with lower prices, improved quality, high innovation and greater customer choice. Particularly important in this regard were the moves which were made in the 2003 Communications Act that created a unified regulator for the communications sector (Ofcom). More generally, utility regulation suffered because the government wasn't clear enough on its strategy on energy, water and other areas. One lesson from these years is that regulation is no substitute for clarity (Corry, 2003; Helm, 2004).

In addition, Labour continued to argue for open markets in trade relations. It needs to resist the dangers of trade protectionism and distancing itself from the EU as we move forward.

### Corporate governance

The governance of firms helps determine the way that they act. Labour made some important changes – including empowering shareholders more in terms of executive pay – although this made less difference than had been hoped and this agenda needs revisiting.

However, a major review of company law brought in important changes but was never really seen through into powerful legislation. A key element of this, a requirement on firms to report on their more general activities in an operating and financial review, was dropped late in the day in 2005. This agenda – often termed the stewardship approach – is a key one and the degree to which voluntarism will advance us is unclear. Certainly, areas where there are incentives to short-termism must be tackled more in future, like in the case of quarterly reporting (PIRC, 2011).

## Education and skills

Education and skills have direct effects on productivity through raising the quality of labour inputs. But education is likely to have an effect on productivity that is even stronger than would be suggested by conventional growth accounting, particularly if there are spill overs which increase innovation.

Labour worked hard on education both in terms of investment and in terms of some important reforms in the sector.

Public investment in education increased in the UK between 1995 and 2007, from 5 per cent to 5.4 per cent of GDP. In 2007, public expenditure on education in the UK exceeded that in the US (5.3 per cent) and Germany (4.5 per cent) and was just below that of France (5.6 per cent).

It appears that over the period things did improve as Table 2.3 shows. From 1997 to 2008, the proportion of tertiary (or post-secondary school) educated adults rose from 23 per cent to 33 per cent in the UK, representing an average annual growth rate of 3.2 per cent, which is higher than in the case of comparator states. The UK did better than Germany

*Table 2.2*  Public expenditure on education as a percentage of total GDP (% total public expenditure)

|         | 1995       | 2000       | 2007       |
|---------|------------|------------|------------|
| UK      | 5.0 (11.4) | 4.3 (11.0) | 5.4 (11.7) |
| US      | 4.7 (12.6) | 4.9 (14.4) | 5.3 (14.1) |
| Germany | 4.6 (8.5)  | 4.4 (9.8)  | 4.5 (10.3) |
| France  | 6.3 (11)   | 6.0 (12.5) | 5.6 (12.5) |

*Notes:* Expenditure on educational institutions as a percentage of GDP, reproduced from IPPR (Lent and Nash, 2011) based on OECD Education at a glance data. Note that Public expenditure presented here includes subsidies to households for living costs (scholarships and grants to students/households and students loans).

*Table 2.3* Percentage of 25- to 64-year old population by educational level

| | | 1997 | 1998 | 1999 | 2000 | 2001 | 2002 | 2003 | 2004 | 2005 | 2006 | 2007 | 2008 | ave growth |
|---|---|---|---|---|---|---|---|---|---|---|---|---|---|---|
| UK | Below upper secondary | 41 | 40 | 38 | 37 | 37 | 36 | 35 | 34 | 33 | 32 | 32 | 30 | -2.7 |
| | Upper Secondary and post-secondary non-tertiary | 37 | 36 | 37 | 37 | 37 | 37 | 37 | 37 | 37 | 38 | 37 | 37 | 0.2 |
| | Tertiary education | 23 | 24 | 25 | 26 | 26 | 27 | 28 | 29 | 30 | 31 | 32 | 33 | 3.2 |
| US | Below upper secondary | 14 | 14 | 13 | 13 | 12 | 13 | 12 | 12 | 12 | 12 | 12 | 11 | -1.8 |
| | Upper Secondary and post-secondary non-tertiary | 52 | 52 | 51 | 51 | 50 | 49 | 49 | 49 | 49 | 48 | 48 | 48 | -0.8 |
| | Tertiary education | 34 | 35 | 36 | 36 | 37 | 38 | 38 | 39 | 39 | 39 | 40 | 41 | 1.7 |
| Germany | Below upper secondary | 17 | 16 | 19 | 18 | 17 | 17 | 17 | 16 | 17 | 17 | 16 | 15 | -1.0 |
| | Upper Secondary and post-secondary non-tertiary | 61 | 61 | 58 | 58 | 59 | 60 | 59 | 59 | 59 | 59 | 60 | 60 | -0.1 |
| | Tertiary education | 23 | 23 | 23 | 23 | 23 | 23 | 24 | 25 | 25 | 24 | 24 | 25 | 1.0 |
| France | Below upper secondary | 41 | 39 | 38 | 37 | 36 | 35 | 35 | 34 | 33 | 33 | 31 | 30 | -2.6 |
| | Upper Secondary and post-secondary non-tertiary | 39 | 40 | 40 | 41 | 41 | 41 | 41 | 41 | 41 | 41 | 42 | 43 | 0.6 |
| | Tertiary education | 20 | 21 | 21 | 22 | 23 | 24 | 24 | 24 | 25 | 26 | 27 | 27 | 2.9 |

*Notes:* OECD Education at a glance, www.oecd.org/edu/eag2010, See Annex 3 for notes (www.oecd.org/edu/eag2010).

and France with 25 per cent and 27 per cent respectively in 2008; however it still lagged behind the US where 41 per cent of 25–64 year olds have a tertiary education.

The UK does more poorly with upper secondary and non-tertiary education (which tends to represent vocational courses). Only 37 per cent of 25–64 year olds in the UK have education at this level, compared with 43 per cent, 48 per cent and 60 per cent in France, the US and Germany respectively. However, this proportion rose between 1997 and 2008, with an average annual growth rate of 0.2 per cent (compared with a decline in US and Germany but a greater rise in France).

Finally, the percentage of 25–64 year olds with below upper secondary education is 30 per cent in the UK in 2008. This fell sharply from 41 per cent in 1997, at an average annual rate of 2.7 per cent, representing a faster decline than in its comparators. In 2008, the unskilled proportion of the workforce in the UK was of a similar level to France, even if it was higher than in the cases of Germany (15 per cent) and the US (11 per cent). Therefore, it appears that since 1997 progress was made at faster rates than in comparator countries, even if the UK continues to lag behind its comparators in key areas.

Some elements of educational reform, such as the literacy and numeracy hours, do appear to demonstrate positive improvements (McNally, 2010), while the number of schools in deprived areas where few got five good GCSEs fell sharply, especially in London. The City Academies movement, for example, which focused on the most troubled schools in the most challenging areas, appears to have improved outcomes for pupils in deprived areas (Machin and Venoit, 2011). If quantity increased, quality is a little harder to ascertain as there remain some concerns that, despite some progress, other countries were moving faster and that there may have been some grade inflation over the period. The lesson seems to be that schools need a combination of accountability, support and freedom/responsibility to maximise outcomes and the search for the right balance must go on.

Increasing the staying-on rates past the compulsory schooling age of 16 is another key policy for progressives. This was aided by Labour policies, such as the Education Maintenance Allowance (EMA), which subsidised young people from low income families to stay on in education. High quality evaluations of this program suggest that the EMA significantly increased participation rates (Dearden et al., 2009), and passed a cost-benefit test which made its scrapping by the Coalition disappointing. Towards the end of its term Labour also brought in plans (continued by the Coalition) to raise the education leaving age to 18 by

2015. Using this golden opportunity to change the pathways of many young people needs to be grasped in the future.

Higher Education is a sector where the UK has some comparative advantage, with its globally recognised universities attracting the second largest proportion of overseas students in the world. Recent Coalition policies that threaten our share of the overseas student market are likely to be economically damaging. Arguably, the government should be doing the exact opposite and making it much easier for the very talented to come to the UK to work and study. This will boost a major sector, increase innovation and productivity, and may even help to curtail inequality by providing more competition for the highly educated.

Despite overall progress in the tertiary, post-secondary school areas, and on skills uplift for those already in the labour market, Labour's policies made less progress than was hoped for. The Leitch review (Leitch, 2006) that led to the Train to Gain scheme, tried to get many more people in work doing Level 2 qualifications. But it did not really work and it may be that the ambitious ILA approach should be tried again (Corry, 2011a). Apprenticeships need to be pursued especially for the under-19s. This is something that the current Coalition government has also had problems in recruiting for. However, the quality of these programmes must be raised.

### Infrastructure

One reason for the UK's historical productivity gap has been a low level of public investment, which Labour did increase and that was a catalyst for improvement. At the current juncture of very low global interest rates, investment in infrastructure seems a very attractive proposition and is unlikely to scare the markets in the same way that government consumption would.

Approaches to financing and organising such investment have to be done carefully to maximise effectiveness and value for money. While some elements of guarantees to get the private sector investing will definitely continue to be required – including some off balance sheet funding – lessons need to be learned from the way PFI was used and abused and from the fact that schemes like Building Schools for the Future went too slow and probably inflated costs. More attention in the future needs to be paid to the details as well as to the broad concepts.

As the Eddington and other reviews suggested (Eddington, 2006), small often works better in terms of infrastructure investment. Rather than relying on grand projects, such as the planned high speed rail links, the government should consider the myriad smaller schemes of road and rail investments that could have larger and less risky returns.

Finally, Labour put massive amounts of investment into science spending. While there may be doubts as to its exact allocation, this does seem a sensible way forward.

### Finance for industry

There is clearly much to be done in terms of the regulation of financial markets. This was an area Labour got badly wrong but, very quickly after the crash, began to put in the building blocks to make the future more secure through higher capital requirements (Basel 3), living wills, greater transparency and more vigilant regulation. It will be necessary to keep under review the degree of separation of the 'utility' part of banking (for example in retail, which has taxpayer insurance) from the 'casino' part of banking (investment, which does not) which has come out of the current government's response to the Vickers Report (Vickers, 2011). We also need to remain vigilant as to whether these reforms are pursued quickly and aggressively enough (in the face of bank opposition).

More generally, there is still an issue of the banks remaining short-termist in their behaviour and very London based, something that was somewhat disguised during the boom years up until 2007, not least because Labour policies had made venture capital and similar sources of finance easier to access. To secure the right portfolio of support to encourage finance for start-ups and post-entry growth, there is now a growing case for state-backed guarantees to smaller and growth firms, via a bank like the KfW in Germany. The Green Investment Bank could play this role to a degree but there are perhaps other sectors that could do with such a body. A properly constituted National Investment Bank therefore remains very much a live issue.

### Regional policy

Labour tried hard to address the regional economic inequality that has bedevilled the UK. Regional Development Agencies (RDAs) were developed and empowered to some degree while Public Service Agreements (PSAs) and other targets were used to try to make departments care more about this. Assessing how well they worked is difficult, especially given the counterfactual of what would have happened without the RDAs. Some assessments say they were adding at least something (Department for Business, Enterprise & Regulatory Reform, 2009). Perhaps fuller government support from across Whitehall might have helped, especially if the referendum in the North East had been successful.

One conclusion – added to by the Heseltine report under the Coalition government – is that a sub-national tier higher than the city or council is needed to bring strategy and spend together on a relevant scale and spatial area if we are to counter regional inequalities. Much analysis suggests that city regions are the place for this and Labour needs to continue to develop ideas for their appropriate governance and the best ways to devolve powers to them.

### Labour market and regulation

A major lesson from the Labour years is that labour market regulation, if done carefully and intelligently, is good all round. Labour market regulation increased after 1997, there were: more rights for trade unions (employers have to grant recognition if a majority of workers vote for it); more opportunities for flexible work and maternity/paternity leave; the first national minimum wage; and a shorter time period before employees qualified for unfair dismissal. Productivity growth did not seem to falter in the face of these regulations, and the (small) empirical literature examining these details does not seem to have uncovered any large negative productivity effects (Draca et al., 2011). However, it would be wrong to believe that the economy can cope with ceaseless labour market regulation. The UK retains a relatively flexible labour market since Labour did not return to the heavily regulated labour market of the 1970s with militant trade unions.

These lessons go beyond labour markets. While overregulation – especially tempting to progressives – is a danger, there is very limited hard evidence of real negative impacts on productivity, despite lots of rhetoric from lobbying groups. Indeed, intelligent regulation can help new sectors emerge and thrive, as in the environmental area. Equally, poor and inadequate regulation can let the consumer suffer while excessive profits survive.

### Public sector productivity

Achieving productivity growth in public services is crucial for many reasons. So it is perplexing that public sector productivity in the UK was more or less flat from 1997 to 2010. Only part of this can conceivably be due to measurement problems or the amount of output not being able to keep up with the substantial increase in public expenditure after 1999.

So how can public sector productivity improve? Competition, information and choice do appear to help in at least some areas, as some innovations from the new Labour period show. In healthcare, for instance, there is a growing body of research that the combination of greater autonomy (e.g. Foundation Trusts), money following the patient (e.g. Payment by Results), and greater patient choice with information (e.g. Choose and Book) gave sharper incentives to hospitals to attract patients through improving quality. Econometric studies have found that this competition significantly raised clinical quality and efficiency (Cooper et al., 2011).

Of course, one needs to be very careful that in markets where there is so much asymmetric information and other issues of market failure, such moves do not have the opposite effect and simply push up costs, especially where the private sector is involved. Much depends on the particular circumstance and the way that quasi-markets are implemented and regulated. For example, price competition in health can reduce clinical quality, as it did in the internal market period (Propper et al., 2008).

More radical approaches will also be needed over time, like a switch to early intervention spending that reduces costs over time, including more integration of health and social care.

It would also be unwise to completely dump New Labour's other mechanisms for driving change. Top-down targets, league tables and inspectorates can go too far, but they do have a role.

## Industrial policy

Economists have been rightly wary of a more interventionist growth stance that goes beyond simply focusing on the broad, economic environment and considers more specific and pro-active interventions. In its first phase, New Labour embraced this 'orthodoxy' almost too much, frightened of being accused of embracing discredited industrial policy or, worse yet, of picking winners.

In the later period from 2008, when Peter Mandelson was back at the business department, a more hands-on approach was taken, not least as the crisis hit (for e.g. see BERR, 2009). This was sensible and got the balance right, although the temptation to then go over the top is a tightrope that must be walked.

Most governments do have a *de facto* industrial policy and recent work suggests that there can be some role in principle for industrial policies (Aghion et al., 2011). An implicit industrial policy can be seen not only in government attitudes towards exports and FDI, but also in every time they make decisions on procurement and regulation, for example in health, education and the environment. The key issue is how to make these decisions in a way that allows for, but is not dominated by, their business and industrial strategy implications.

An effective long-run growth policy requires governments and civil society to consider two key factors. First, where are the likely areas of growth? Second, where does the UK have some comparative advantage? The intersection between the areas of global growth and comparative advantage is where policy makers should focus. Are there barriers stifling the potential growth of these industries in the form of laws, regulations and policies that could be removed? Are there some pro-active policies that could foster the development of such sectors, including on tax? The government is inevitably involved in one way or another as procurer, regulator and investor across many fields and in many sectors. As a result, sensible, considered use of its leverage can be used to help key sectors (without creating competitive distortions).

Guessing future growth sectors may seem like a fool's errand, but areas like healthcare, education, bio-pharmaceuticals, financial and business services, creative industries and some areas of ICT must be in the mix.

## Innovation

Growth theory puts innovation at the centre of productivity growth over the long-term, a key ingredient of which is R&D. The theory of spill-overs suggests that normally there will be underinvestment in R&D. There is good international evidence that R&D is a major source of productivity growth and that such fiscal incentives are an effective way to increase research (e.g. Hall and Van Reenen, 2000; Bloom et al., 2002a). Science also seems to have a major multiplier effect (Haskel and Wallis, 2010).

Labour acted strongly in this area. The UK introduced its first R&D tax credits in 2001 (for small firms) and 2003 (for large firms). There were substantial increases in the science budget. One consequence of this activity was that the R&D/GDP ratio, which had been in decline in the UK since the late 1970s in contrast to the increases in other nations (Van Reenen, 1997), rose, albeit slightly, as a proportion of GDP between 1997 and 2008 as Figure 2.9 shows. The fact that at 1.8 per cent the ratio is lower than in other major developed countries. and that the UK lags behind the US and Germany with respect to patents granted (though it has been tracking France since the 1990s), also shows there is a need for further action.

Innovation in the era of Google and design is increasingly about intangibles. These are difficult to measure and to compare across countries. On one set of recent data the inclusion of intangibles indicates that the UK had a higher share of value added in intangibles than all other G7 nations (BIS, 2010c). Other sources of intangible data however show

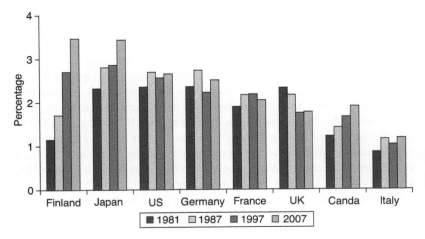

*Figure 2.9*   Gross domestic expenditure on R&D (GERD) (% GDP)

*Notes*: Analysis based on OECD MSTI June 2010. Data not available on a consistent basic prior to 1981.

the UK in a less favourable light compared to other countries (e.g. some OECD data).

Clearly, active policy in areas to encourage innovation like R&D, high-tech clusters, spin-outs from HE and support for venture capital, can work. But to make Britain a more innovative economy requires prolonged support and a myriad actions.

## Conclusion

The years from 1997 to 2010 are not just a period to be put aside, a big mistake, an embarrassing uncle. That temptation is natural, especially since the period ended with a crash, a major election loss and a public who tended to (simplistically) see the whole period through that lens.

In fact, a lot that was tried, worked and should be pursued again. Some policies did not work and should be scrapped. But lessons can be drawn from many policies that were in essence sound but which were not pursued strongly enough or did not have enough time to develop.

Finally, the lesson that change is difficult and can be slow to take effect needs to be appreciated. A progressive government can make an enormous difference to the way society and an economy evolves. Every little decision matters. Moving the economy decisively away from the trajectory that the Coalition has put it on and towards a more responsible version of capitalism is a tough task. This project will require learning and patience, rather than more cries of betrayal and accusations that the Labour party suffers from a lack of political will.

## Acknowledgements

Much of the detailed productivity work summarised in the first half of this paper comes from Corry et al. (2011). Van Reenen has done further work on productivity, for which see, for instance, Van Reenen (2013).

## Notes

Visiting fellow at Southampton University, chief executive of charity think tank and consultancy NPC. Was special adviser in various departments in many of the New Labour years including chairing the Council of Economic Advisers in HMT 2006–2007 and Senior Economic Adviser to the PM 2007–2010 and Head of No 10 Policy Unit 2007–2008.

1. I should note that I was a special adviser to the Labour government during much of this period – not a totally disinterested party!
2. This data was mainly extracted in late 2011 with some revised in 2012 when this paper was given at the SPERI conference. Some data has been revised further since, making the drop in GDP from peak to trough in the UK even larger. But other revisions have 'improved' the Labour record, for instance: average GDP growth per working age adult to 2010 is estimated at nearly 1.4 per cent; while the figures from 1997–2007 in Table 2.1 all look stronger now, see Van Reenen (2013) and Pessoa and Van Reenen's forthcoming look at more recent data. But the story does not essentially change.
3. For these purposes we use the KLEMS database , available at http://www. euklems.net/ (Timmer, 2007), which was the best available source of harmonised productivity data at the time most of the data in this paper were compiled in October 2011) for the major countries that we want to look at. See also O'Mahony and Timmer (2009).
4. Note that a sector's contribution to overall market economy productivity growth depends on both its productivity growth and its size (share of total market economy GVA). Nationwide aggregate productivity growth can increase either because a sector increases productivity (within effect) or a high productivity sector grows in size at the expense of a low productivity sector (between effect).
5. As it appeared when this was written in September 2013.
6. Wren-Lewis (2013b) points out that Labour, more than most governments, followed the best practice that mainstream economists were suggesting in this period, for good or ill.

# References

Aghion, P., Dewatripont, M., Du, L., Harrison, A. and Legros, P. (2011) Industrial Policy and Competition, National Bureau of Economic Research Paper No. 18084.

Berr (2009) New Indsutry New Jobs, http://www.berr.gov.uk/files/file51023.pdf

BIS (2010a) Economic Growth. *BIS Economics Paper No.9.*

BIS, N. (2010c) Annual Innovation Report.

Bloom, N., Draca, M. and Van Reenen, J. (2011) 'Trade Induced Technical Change? The Impact of Chinese Imports on Innovation, IT and Productivity', *NBER Working Paper, 16717.*

Bloom, N., Griffith, R. and Van Reenen, J. (2002a) 'Do R&D Tax Credits Work? Evidence from a Panel of Countries 1979–1997', *Journal of Public Economics*, 85, 1–31.

Bloom, N., Sadun, R. and Van Reenen, J. (2011b) 'Americans Do I.T. Better: U.S. Multinationals and the Productivity Miracle', *American Economic Review.*

Bloom, N. and Van Reenen, J. (2007) 'Measuring and Explaining Management Practices across Firms and Countries', *Quarterly Journal of Economics*, 122, 1351–1408.

Bloom, N. and Van Reenen, J. (2010) 'Why Do Management Practices Differ across Firms and Countries?' *Journal of Economic Perspectives*, 24, 203–224.

Blundell, R., Griffith, R. and Van Reenen, J. (1999) 'Market Share, Market Value and Innovation in a Panel of British Manufacturing Firms', *Review of Economic Studies*, 66, 529–554.

Coates, D. (2009) 'Chickens Coming Home to Roost? New Labour at the Eleventh Hour', *British Politics*, 4, 4, December, 421–433.

Cooke, G., Lent, A., Painter, A., and Sen, H. (2001) 'In the Black Labour', *Policy Network.*

Cooper, Z., Gibbons, S., Jones, S. and Mcguire, A. (2010) 'Does Hospital Competition Improve Efficiency? An Analysis of the Recent Market-based Reforms to the English NHS', *Centre for Economic Performance.*

Cooper, Z., Gibbons, S., Jones, S. and Mcguire, A. (2011) 'Does Hospital Competition Save Lives? Evidence from the English Nhs Patient Choice Reforms', *Economic Journal*, 121, F228–F260.

Corry, D. (2001) 'Labour's Industrial Policy: A Break with the Past?' *New Economy*, 8, 3, September, 127–133.

Corry, D. (2003) 'The Regulatory State : Labour and the Utilities 1997–2002', ippr.

Corry, D. (2011a) 'Labour and the Economy, 1997–2010: More than a Faustian Pact', In P. Diamond and M. Kenny (eds), *Reassessing New Labour: Market, State and Society under Blair and Brown.*

Corry, D. (2011b) 'Power at the Centre: Is the National Economic Council a Model for a New Way of Organising Things?' *The Political Quarterly*, 82, 459–468.

Corry, D., Valero, A., and Van Reenen, J. (2011) 'UK Economic Performance since 1997, Growth productivity and Jobs', CEP, LSE, November. http://cep.lse.ac.uk/conference_papers/15b_11_2011/CEP_Report_UK_Business_15112011.pdf

Crafts, N. (2011) 'British Relative Economic Decline Revisited: The Role of Competition', *CEPR Discussion Paper Series.*

Dal Borgo, M., Goodridge, P., Haskel, J. E. and Pesole, A. (2011) 'Productivity and Growth in UK Industries: An Intangible Investment Approach', *Imperial College.*

Dearden, L., Emmerson, C., Frayne, C. and Meghir, C. (2009) 'Conditional Cash Transfers and School Dropout Rates', *Journal of Human Resources,* 44, 827–857.

Department for Business, Enterprise & Regulatory Reform (2009) 'Impact of RDA Spending – National Report', http://www.berr.gov.uk/files/file50735.pdf

Draca, M., Machin, S. and Van Reenen, J. (2011) 'Minimum Wages and Firm Profitability', *American Economic Journal-Applied Economics,* 3, 129–151.

Eddington, R. (2006) 'Study on Transport', Department for Transport/HMT.

Giles, C. (2011) 'Busting the Myths on the Economy', *Financial times.*

Gamble, A. (2009) *The Spectre at the Feast: Capitalist Crisis and the Politics of Recession.* Basingstoke: Palgrave MacMillian.

Gregg, P. and Wadsworth, J. (2011) 'Jobs in the Recession', *CentrePiece Summer 2011.*

Hall, B. and Van Reenen, J. (2000) 'How Effective are Fiscal Incentives for R&D? A Review of the Evidence', *Research Policy,* 29, 449–469.

Haskel, J. E., Pereira, S. C. and Slaughter, M. J. (2007) 'Does Inward Foreign Direct Investment Boost the Productivity of Domestic Firms?' *Review of Economics and Statistics,* 89, 482–496.

Haskel, J. E. and Wallis, G. (2010) 'Public Support for Innovation, Intangible Investment and Productivity Growth in the UK Market Sector', *IZA Discussion Papers 4772.*

Hay, C. (2013) *The Failure of Anglo-Liberal Capitalism.* Palgrave Macmillan.

Helm, D. (2004) *Energy, the State, and the Market: British Energy Policy Since 1979,* Oxford: Oxford University Press.

HMT (2010) Budget 2010: Securing the Recovery.

Holmes, T. J. and Schmitz, J. A. (2010) ,Competition and Productivity: A Review of Evidence', *Federal Reserve Bank of Minneapolis, Research Department Staff Report.*

Jordà, O. and Taylor, A. M. (2013) 'The Time for Austerity: Estimating the Average Treatment Effect of Fiscal Policy', *NBER Working Paper No. 19414.*

Jorgenson, D. W. (2001) 'Information Technology and the US Economy', *American Economic Review,* 91, 1–32.

Landale, J. (2013) 'Labour's the Point', http://www.bbc.co.uk/news/uk-politics-24371521

Leitch, S. (2006) 'Review of Skills: Final Report, Prosperity for All in the Global Economy – World Class Skills', HMSO.

Lent, A. and Nash, D. (2011) 'Surviving the Asian Century', *IPPR, New Era Economics Report.*

Machin, S. and Venoit, J. (2011) 'Academies and Their Impact on Educational Achievement CEP', UCL.

Mcnally, S. (2010) 'Evaluating Education Policies: The Evidence from Economic Research', *CEP Election Analysis.*

Menezes-Filho, N. and Van Reenen, J. (2003) 'Unions and Innovation: A Survey of the Theory and Empirical Evidence', in J. Addison and C. Schnabel (eds), *International Handbook of Trade Unions.* Cheltenham: Edward Elgar.

Nickell, S. (1996) 'Competition and Corporate Performance', *Journal of Political Economy,* 104, 4, 726–746.

O'Mahony, M. and Timmer, M. P. (2009) 'Output, Input and Productivity Measures at the Industry Level: The EU KLEMS Database', *Economic Journal*, 119, F374–F403.

PIRC (2011) 'A Long-Term Focus for Corporate Britain: Response to A Call for Evidence from BIS January', http://www.pirc.co.uk/sites/default/files/PIRC%20response%20to%20short-termism%20review.pdf

Portes, J. (2011) 'The Coalition's Confidence Trick', *The New Statesman*.

Propper, C., Burgess, S. and Gossage, D. (2008) 'Competition and Quality: Evidence from the NHS Internal Market 1991–9', *Economic Journal*, 118, 138–170.

Timmer, M. P. (2007) 'EU KLEMS Growth and Productivity Accounts: An Overview', *National Institute Economic Review*, 200, 64.

Timmer, M. P., Inklaar, R., O'Mahony, M. and Van Ark, B. (2010) *Economic Growth in Europe: A Comparative Industry Perspective*. United Kingdom: Cambridge University Press.

Valero, A. and Van Reenen, J. (2011) *Slow Growth Does Not Have to be Our 'New Normal'. Government Needs to Change the Way it Looks at the Growth Problem in the Long Term* [Online], available at http://blogs.lse.ac.uk/politicsandpolicy/2011/08/02/slow-growth-not-new-normal/.

Van Reenen, J. (1997) 'Why has Britain had Slower R&D Growth?' *Research Policy*, 26, 493–507.

Van Reenen J. (2013) 'Productivity under the 1997–2010 Labour Government', *Oxf Rev Econ Policy*, 29, 1, 113–141.

Vickers, J. (2011) 'Final Report: Recommendations', *Independent Commission on Banking*.

Wren-Lewis, S. (2013a) 'Aggregate Fiscal Policy under the Labour Government, 1997–2010', *Oxf Rev Econ Policy*, 29, 1, 25–46.

Wren-Lewis, S. (2013b) 'The last Labour Government: Has the Influence of Economists Ever Been Greater?' http://mainlymacro.blogspot.co.uk/2013/06/the-last-labour-government-has.html

# 3
# Anglo-American Financial Interdependence and the Rise of Income Inequality

*Jeremy Green*

Understanding the roots of Britain's failing economic model requires a deeper historicisation of British economic development than is commonly ventured. This leads us towards the Anglo-American dimension of British development and, in particular, the role that foreign direct investment (FDI) has played within a shared Anglo-American commitment to the promotion of an open, liberal, international political economy. As hosts to the world's two major international financial centres, London and New York, state officials and bankers in Britain and the US, through their interactions and interdependence, were central to driving the politics of financial globalisation and capital market liberalisation in the post-war period.

Contemporary analyses of Britain's faltering economic performance, which have identified a defective Anglo-liberal growth model at the heart of the UK economy, correctly acknowledge the centrality of these Anglo-American developmental dynamics (Gamble, 2009: 454, Hay, 2011: 6, 2013: 2).[1] What these accounts do not do, however, is to move beyond a simple recognition of Anglo-American (or Anglo-liberal) dynamics towards an attempt to trace the historical processes of Anglo-American development that have fed into the constitution of the contemporary British growth model. Furthermore, while these accounts have identified the role of deregulation in Britain and the US in contributing to the permissive regulatory climate and broader financialisation that prepared the ground for the financial crisis of 2008, they have not drawn sufficient attention to the significance of FDI as a component of the British growth model derived from Anglo-American development in the post-war period.

This is a major shortcoming because FDI has been key to two interconnected and important issues within the political economy of the British crisis: concerns over rising income inequality, that were expressed both nationally and globally within the Occupy movement and have become increasingly important within popular commentary (Deprez and Dodge, 2011; Hutton, 2014), on the one hand, and public anger at the size of bankers' bonuses (Asthana, 2010), on the other.

As a corrective to these deficiencies, this chapter traces the impact upon British economic development of Anglo-American endorsements of open international trade, foreign investment and capital market liberalisation. High and growing levels of income inequality have been a hallmark of Britain's prevailing economic strategy. In order to problematise this, the chapter focuses upon the relationship between rising income inequality and its relationship to FDI.

This relationship is contextualised within the historical re-emergence of the City of London as an international financial centre closely connected to the expansion of American finance. The chapter then discuss processes of financial liberalisation and deregulation driven in large part by the developmental interdependence of Britain and America, highlighting the relationship between these processes, FDI flows and the growth of income inequality in Britain. The chapter suggest that Anglo-American developmental dynamics have been a major factor in driving rising income inequality. This tendency, the chapter argues, became increasingly pronounced during the mergers and acquisitions booms of the 1990s and 2000s, which boosted City incomes and aggravated inequality. The chapter concludes by identifying rising income inequality as a key failure of Britain's pre-crisis economic development, suggesting that raising levels of equality should be a central goal for any progressive economic strategy.

## Foreign investment and Anglo-American development

As a component of Anglo-American development foreign investment has rarely been problematised. Robert Gilpin's work is a rare exception in this regard and provides a useful entry point for an assessment of the role of foreign investment within Anglo-American development. Gilpin's analysis was essentially an attempt to critique what he saw as an overreliance upon outward FDI within American international economic policy during the 1970s. In this vein, Gilpin (1975: 5) suggested that the stuttering US hegemon was following the path of former hegemonic powers, Britain and the Netherlands, down the road of long-term economic decline by 'overinvesting abroad to the detriment of the home economy'. In order to make his case, Gilpin drew attention to the parallels between British and American development.

This comparison provides useful clues as to the role of foreign investment within Anglo-American development. While Britain had tended to rely more upon foreign portfolio investment during its economic development, the US tended to rely much more heavily upon FDI. What united both countries, however, was that after a first phase of rising hegemonic power during which foreign investment was a sign of strength, it subsequently came to reflect economic weakness during a subsequent phase of economic decline (Gilpin, 1975: 46).

By focusing on foreign investment as an explanans for the rise and decline of hegemonic powers, Gilpin obscures the potential to trace the role of foreign investment within Anglo-American development in the post-war period. His concern is with Britain and the US as parallel historical cases of hegemonic rise and decline, rather than interdependent components of an Anglo-American sphere of post-war economic development. Despite this, Gilpin does provide some interesting clues, arguing that the Anglo-American reliance upon heavy foreign investment has been underpinned by a strong commitment to the maintenance of a liberal economic order, both at home and abroad. According to Gilpin (1975: 60), the political and economic leadership of Britain and the US have, 'shared this liberal perspective and have projected this vision to the international sphere'. Within both countries, public policy and liberal ideology combined to stimulate very large exports of capital and the ownership of foreign assets on a massive scale.

Gilpin's assessment of the role of foreign investment in the development of Britain and the US signals something very significant: the crucial importance of the broader international political economic framework within which foreign investment has occurred and the centrality of Britain and the US within it. Britain and America have shared much more than a common liberal outlook. In fact, their development has been framed within a context of *uneven interdependence* based upon the symbiotic relationship between banking in London and New York and the intertwined politics of the pound and the dollar. America's post-war ascendancy was articulated *through* the post-war deterioration of British power. Although British power was gravely weakened there was a *mutual need* for cooperation. Britain was financially dependent upon the US, but American State officials and the New York banking community recognised that British support for multilateralism and the restoration of sterling convertibility were key to the successful re-launching of global capitalism (Block, 1977: 52; Helleiner, 1994: 41; Eichengreen, 2008: 123).

The close developmental interdependence of Britain and the US continues to be absolutely central to understanding Britain's economic model. Contemporary literature on the British growth model recognises the centrality of an 'excessively liberalised Anglo-American form of capitalism' (Hay, 2013: 1), but does not move beyond this recognition towards an excavation of the developmental processes and institutional interdependencies that account for the situation of British capitalism within this broader Anglo-American context. Consequently, ideological complementarities that are said to have intensified with the inauguration of neoliberalism brought about under Margaret Thatcher and Ronald Reagan during the 1980s, or later incremental shifts within Anglo-American credit markets and regulatory orders, tend to carry most of the analytical burden (Montgomerie, 2007: 14; Baker, 2010: 648; Hay, 2013: 1).

This overlooks a series of institutionally structured connections established during the early decades of the post-war era, which provided much of the foundation for the neoliberal transformations of the 1970s and 1980s: the interdependence of sterling and the dollar as key currencies under the Bretton Woods order; the increasingly connected role of the City and New York within global finance, beginning with the Euromarkets; and the need for coordination of monetary policy between the Bank and the Fed dating back to the 1960s (Green, 2014). The synchronised rise of monetarism and neoliberalism within Britain and the US had much to do with these underlying forms of financial interdependence established during the Bretton Woods era.

Reorienting the British growth model will, then, likely require more than simple regulatory recalibration. It will also bring into question the institutional interdependencies that have been established within Anglo-America during the post-war era. Most significantly, a fundamental shift in the City of London's role within both the British growth model *and* the wider global political economy (the two are likely tightly connected), that might involve privileging the interests of domestic credit supply and industrial financing at the expense of more internationally oriented investment banking business, would inevitably have serious consequences for Britain's status within the Anglo-American sphere. This throws up the key question of whether Britain must fundamentally reconsider the Anglo-American interdependencies within which it has long been embedded, in order to arrive at a more sustainable and egalitarian trajectory of growth and development?

Understanding these forms of interdependence requires us to move beyond the analysis of parallel processes of rise and decline and towards a synthetic conception of Anglo-American development that helps account for the trajectory of modern British economic development and the contours of the contemporary British malaise. As we shall see below, the empirical evidence supports Gilpin's contention that foreign investment has played a key role in the development of both Britain and the US and has been central to a shared vision for the international economy.

FDI refers to the process by which firms operating across national boundaries are created or expanded (Graham and Krugman, 1993: 21).[2] It is, therefore, intimately connected to the formation of multinational corporations and is a key indicator of the progression of globalisation. Historically, Britain has been at the forefront of FDI flows. This was in part owing to Britain's status as the first industrialised country and in part due to the overseas expansion of British capital under the aegis of the British Empire. Early FDI flows, during the nineteenth century, developed in accordance with colonial relationships of dependency, with capital from the imperial centres flowing out to their colonial dependencies (Clegg, 1996: 42). At its peak, Britain's share of total global foreign investment (both FDI and portfolio) stood at around 80 per cent, with one third of total British savings devoted to overseas investment between 1870–1914 and British foreign investment increasing by 250 per cent during the same period (Obstfeld and Taylor, 2002: 55, 238; Gilpin, 1975: 86). Britain's nineteenth century dominance did not last however, with the financial exhaustion caused by Britain's involvement in two World Wars severely undermining its ownership of foreign assets (Burnham, 1990: 18). Britain's financial exhaustion presented the opportunity for the most striking transformation in global foreign investment patterns during the twentieth century; the massive increase in the American ownership of foreign assets (Gilpin, 1975: 15).

In 1938, Britain accounted for 43 per cent of total global capital stocks, while the US accounted for 22 per cent. But by 1945, Britain's share had fallen to 40 per cent, while the US's share had risen to 43 per cent and eventually peaked at a staggering 50 per cent in 1960 (Obstfeld and Taylor, 2005: 52–53). The transition between British and American dominance in terms of ownership of foreign assets occurred in a highly interdependent manner, with US FDI into Britain increasing enormously during the 1950s. In fact, it occurred through processes of Anglo-American development that integrated the political economies

of Britain and the US around the interdependency of London and
New York.

## The Euromarkets and the birth of financial globalisation

By the late 1950s American FDI was pouring into Europe. In Britain,
American private capital had begun to flow in earlier, with an increase
of American direct private investment in the UK from $519 million
to $847 million between 1943 and 1950. Between 1950 and 1958,
American investment in the British manufacturing industry increased
by 151 per cent (Overbeek, 1990: 105) and by 1955 the value of the US
FDI stake in British manufacturing industry reached a record figure of
$6,322 million or 32.9 per cent of America's foreign capital holdings
(Dunning, 1998: 30).

But this was only part of a larger expansion of American capital into the
continent that gathered momentum during the 1950s. Manufacturing
FDI in Europe tripled between 1955 and 1965, while by 1966 there were
9,000 US subsidiaries in Europe. The period also saw a related rise in
European inward investment in the US, as European and American
capitalism became increasingly integrated (Panitch and Gindin, 2012:
114–115).

This rapid increase in international investment, and of US inward FDI
into Europe in particular, was fuelled by developments in international
capital markets that massively increased the availability of private capital.
The major innovation in this regard was the birth of the Eurodollar and
Eurobond markets, known collectively as the Euromarkets.[3] Although
offshore, both markets were hosted in the City of London and, crucially,
both were products of Anglo-American developmental interdependency. This Anglo-American interdependency would play a crucial role
in undermining the Bretton Woods system of fixed exchange rates and
capital controls, giving rise ultimately to an increasingly open and liberalised global financial system with deeply integrated capital markets in
London and New York at their heart. These two cities, London and New
York, became the twin-engine rooms of financial globalisation. There
was, then, a clearly identifiable Anglo-American axis underpinning
financial globalisation.

Facing restrictions on the use of sterling as an international trade and
financing currency due to Britain's chronic balance of payments deficits,
merchant bankers in the City turned to a growing pool of expatriate
dollars known as Eurodollars (Martenson, 1964: 14; Bell, 1973: 8; Schenk,
1998: 223). These had originally been deposited in European banks by

Soviet and Chinese officials that feared the requisition of their dollar holdings for political reasons if they were maintained with American banks (Higgonet, 1985:27; Burn, 1999: 229). As an offshore currency the Eurodollar was effectively outside any national regulatory remit and thus unencumbered by what were, in the view of Britain's merchant bankers, onerous restrictions upon the use of sterling.

Tapping into the supply of offshore Eurodollars, which grew rapidly during the 1960s as US balance of payments deficits continued, British banks were able to maintain their high international standing and insulate themselves from the travails of sterling. In the process, they augmented the status of the dollar as the world's international currency. The flourishing business also drew American banks into the City. Dollar deposits had been attracted to the Euromarkets in London because of the interest rate differential between the City and New York. Through regulatory arbitrage, the different regulatory contexts on either side of the Atlantic drove vast dollar movements between New York and London, as banks and investors sought the highest possible returns. London banks, outside the interest rate ceilings on short-term loans that were in place in the US as part of Regulation Q and the New Deal regulatory architecture, were able to offer higher rates and pull dollars away from US banks. In response, American banks sidestepped Regulation Q by setting up branches in London and then funnelling dollars back to their home branches during times of dollar shortage.

This dynamic between the British and American money markets intensified from the mid-1960s as the US attempted various different measures in order to arrest the deterioration in the balance of payments associated with the 'Triffin Dilemma' (Eichengreen, 2008: 126; Gowa, 1983: 55).[4] Under both the Johnson and Kennedy administrations, attempts were made to rein in capital outflows. But these measures were rendered increasingly ineffective by the offshore supply of dollars that could be funnelled back into the US (Kane, 1981: 13). Through the interdependency of sterling and the dollar, and via bankers in London and New York, the Euromarkets created a vast and liberalised international capital market that was central to the unfolding of financial globalisation. The Euromarkets complemented the New York capital markets, by providing an offshore space for American bank branches, which could now continue to supply capital to globalising American corporations despite domestic efforts to tighten the money supply and assuage balance of payments difficulties.

Anglo-American financial synthesis restored the City's predominance as an international financial centre, securing its power within the British economy and cementing the international dominance of the dollar. By creating the conditions for vast international capital markets, dominated by the dollar, the Euromarkets laid the foundations for financial globalisation and provided a major impetus towards further capital market liberalisation globally. Anglo-American developmental dynamics were, therefore, absolutely integral to the liberal reconstitution of the global economy during the early decades of the post-war era. The vast levels of FDI flows in the post-war world economy would have been practically unthinkable without the role played by the Euromarkets.

The provision of capital on a huge scale through private financial markets undermined the political allocation of capital through the World Bank and the IMF, which had been inaugurated at Bretton Woods. Those institutions and multilateral financial avenues, more broadly, were dwarfed by the massive growth of private capital flows, with the Euromarkets at the centre. Eurodollar bond issues, a central means of securing corporate financing for domestic and overseas expansion, rose from $148 million in 1963 to $2.7 billion by 1970 (Panitch and Gindin, 2012: 118). By 1999, the figure for annual Eurobond issues had risen to over 3,500, with a face value of $857.3 billion (Claes et al., 2002: 374).

The Euromarkets had a major impact upon trans-Atlantic regulatory orders. The lax regulatory climate in the City challenged New York's competitiveness and led American bankers to lament the restrictive stipulations of the New Deal regulatory framework (Burn, 2006: 142–143). The influx of American competitors during the 1960s exposed Britain's banks to a competitive challenge and destabilised the prevailing regulatory order in the City. With the Bank of England now having to deal with a larger number of banks and a growing presence of foreign banks, the traditional relationship that it had maintained with a concentrated and cartelised banking sector began to break down (Moran, 1986: 2; Michie, 2004: 44). As credit markets became increasingly responsive to global demand fluctuations, rather than to the requirements of the British government, economic planning and government management of financial markets became increasingly difficult.

To compete with their well-capitalised American counterparts, British banks moved towards universal banking and away from traditional divisions between merchant and commercial banking (Battilossi, 2002: 114–116). These transformations required a corresponding regulatory recalibration and the Conservative government's Competition and Credit Control policy offered exactly that. It broke from the moves towards credit rationing by administrative decree, which had proliferated during the tight money policy of the 1960s, freeing up credit markets by substituting price levels for government controls as the decisive determinant of credit levels (Moran, 1986: 30).

In fact then, the origins of the deregulatory dynamics of the 1970s and 1980s, commonly associated with the rise of neoliberalism, can be located within the transformation of financial markets during the 1960s. It is only with a deeper historicisation of Anglo-American development that we are able to reveal the extent to which these deregulatory dynamics were driven by the competitive interaction and integration of financial markets in London and New York. Mirroring the imperatives of Competition and Credit Control and increasingly conscious of the competitive challenge that the City posed to New York, deregulation began to gather pace in the US. Nixon called for the gradual phasing out of interest rate ceilings in 1973 while the Securities and Exchange Commission (SEC) brought about New York's 'Big Bang' in 1975, breaking from its longstanding support for the cartel-like organisations that had dominated American capital markets since the 1930s (Panitch and Gindin, 2012: 149).

Regulatory transformations in the US then fed back into Britain, with further liberalisation during the 1980s and Thatcher's own Big Bang carried out after British officials had visited the US in order to learn from the American regulatory apparatus (Moran, 1994: 168). Much of the permissive financial deregulation associated with the Anglo-liberal growth model can, therefore, be identified as having a much deeper lineage within the development of transatlantic financial markets during the 1960s. It was under the smouldering tensions of the post-war Keynesian era, rather than the white heat of neoliberalism, that many of these deregulatory dynamics were originally ignited.

How do these seemingly distant developments bear upon Britain's contemporary political economy? The key factor here is the role of the Euromarkets in maintaining the dominance of the City within British capitalism. By drawing in the dollar and accepting the arrival of American banks, the City was able to maintain its dominance despite the rapid demise of sterling's international status. It now became an Americanised enclave, with sections of the City tapping in to global flows of dollar-denominated trade and investment, quite independent from the fortunes of Britain's wider political economy and the plight of sterling (Coakley and Harris, 1983: 23). Importantly, therefore, the City's traditional commitments to open international trade and investment have remained paramount within the policy goals of Britain's political class. The City's success in promoting financial liberalisation, through the birth of the Euromarkets, the abolition of exchange controls in 1979 and the enactment of the Big Bang in 1986 (to name just a few key signposts on that journey), has guaranteed Britain's continued commitment to the prevailing policy paradigm. But, as the chapter demonstrate below, the impacts of that orientation have been hugely harmful to British society and have fuelled rapidly rising income inequality.

## The problem of income inequality

Rising levels of income inequality are a defining feature of the neoliberal era and of British economic development since the election of Margaret Thatcher in 1979. As Figure 3.1 demonstrates, income inequality in Britain has risen incredibly sharply since the late 1970s. The dataset below uses the category of the top 1 per cent of income earners, which has been popularised by the Occupy Wall Street movement. This is an

*Figure 3.1*   UK top 1 per cent income share, 1949–2009

*Source*: Atkinson, Anthony B. (2007). 'The Distribution of Top Incomes in the United Kingdom 1908–2000', in Atkinson, A. B. and Piketty, T. (ed.) *Top Incomes over the Twentieth Century. A Contrast Between Continental European and English-Speaking Countries*, Oxford University Press, chapter 4. Series updated by Atkinson. Accessed through World Top Incomes Database, http://g-mond.parisschoolofeconomics.eu/topincomes/.

important category for understanding rising income inequality given the massive increase in income accruing to this top decile of income earners. Between 1980 and 2007, the top 1 per cent share of national income rose by around 135 per cent in the US and Britain (Alvaredo et al., 2013: 3–5).

Income inequality began to rise from the late 1970s, reversing the long-standing trend of a declining share of income for the top 1 per cent of income earners underway since WW2. But income inequality really accelerated sharply during Margaret Thatcher's premiership. Thatcher introduced a range of policy changes that radically altered the landscape of British capitalism, inaugurating an enduring trajectory of rapidly rising income inequality. In distributional terms, her policies essentially relied upon an upward, regressive, redistribution of wealth towards the wealthiest individuals within society (Stark, 1989: 181).

One component of Thatcherite redistribution was the transformation of taxation policies in a process that was mirrored by Ronald Reagan in the US. The de-legitimation of the existing taxation system went further in the US than it did in Britain, but nevertheless Britain's progressive taxation system, which had been firmly in place since the 1950s, came under attack. Thatcher's government held ideological objections to progressive redistributive taxation policies but they were also able to tap into growing popular resentment of the tax system. The inflationary context of the 1960s and 1970s pushed more and more workers into liability for income tax and forced many into higher tax bands. Thus inflation eroded public support for progressive taxation by altering the distributional consequences of, 'relatively invariant tax rates' (Cronin and Radtke, 1987: 286–287). This broader context enabled Thatcher's government to slash income tax, with a particularly sharp drop in the top rate of taxation, from 83 per cent down to 60 per cent, under its first budget. These tax cuts were funded by an increase in regressive, indirect taxes such as VAT (Stark, 1989: 177). The effects of these changes to the tax system were principally distributive; there was no major decrease in the level of absolute taxation, but the burden was shifted more towards the working class and poorer members of society. This direction in taxation politics was strengthened by a series of measures introduced after 1980, including reductions in capital gains tax, the investment income surcharge, and inheritance and gift taxes. The Thatcher government also granted a series of special concessions to the City in order to boost its international competitiveness (Cronin and Radtke, 1987: 289).

A further strut of Thatcher's redistributive politics was the clampdown on union power. The rapidity with which labour market institutions have declined in Britain since the late 1970s has been unparalleled within advanced capitalist states. Whereas in 1980 54 per cent of the labour force had been a member of trade unions, that figure had fallen to 32 per cent fifteen years later. Thatcher's government introduced a series of anti-union laws and won landmark battles against the union movement, most notably with the defeat of the bitter miner's strike in 1984. From the later 1970s, the gap between the highest and lowest paid workers in Britain rose markedly, while wage dispersion grew much more rapidly in the non-union sector under Thatcher (Machin, 1997: 647–653). Although advanced industrialised countries as a whole have witnessed a decline in the power of organised labour since the 1980s, that trend has been much more pronounced in Britain and the US (Weeks, 2007: 169; Lansley, 2011: 40).

That pattern of rising inequality, which was activated during the Thatcher government, continued under John Major's Conservative government and did not abate during the years of New Labour.[5] Indeed, Peter Mandelson, a key figure within New Labour, famously declared that his party was 'intensely relaxed about people getting filthy rich' (Malik, 2012). Thatcher's policies, then, represented an epochal shift in the terrain of British capitalism that set in place many of the failings that have continued to inform the dominant policy paradigm of both the Tories and Labour. A less well understood component of this shift has been the rise in the volume of FDI flows and the impact of these flows upon income inequality. It is to this dimension that we now turn our analysis.

## FDI flows and income inequality

In general terms, the relationship between FDI and income inequality is difficult to pin down. As the above analysis has suggested, the causes of deepening inequality in Britain are varied. But despite this varia-tion, certain patterns involving the relationship between FDI flows and income inequality are discernible. Indeed, the rise in income inequality in Britain over the last three decades has been highly episodic (Blundell and Ethridge, 2010: 76). There was an 'inequality boom' in the early 1980s and then a period of stabilised income distribution, but at a higher level of inequality. There was then a further sharp rise in income inequality during the late 1990s.

Importantly, the rise in inequality in the UK largely occurred due to the rising employment income of workers in the financial services sector (Blundell and Ethridge, 2010: 85). In the more recent past, and particularly since the late 1990s, the increase in income inequality in Britain (and also the US) has been focused principally at the very top end of wage distribution. In particular, bonus payments to financial services workers have been key. In Britain a staggering 60 per cent of increased income has gone to financial service sector workers. This is despite the fact that they only constitute 5 per cent of the workforce (Bell and Van Reenen, 2010: 3). Within this wage increase bonus payments have played a key role, with 82 per cent of top percentile workers receiving a bonus in 2008. Indeed, Bell and Van Reenen (2010: 11) conclude their study into the impact of bankers' pay upon wage inequality in the UK by suggesting that, 'the rise in bonus payments to bankers more than explains the rise in overall extreme wage inequality'.

Clearly, then, bonus payments to financial services workers have had a serious impact upon wage inequality in the UK. But Bell and Van Reenen do not attempt to identify what processes lie behind the booming bonus culture in the City. What these studies have not revealed is the role that massive FDI flows, linked to waves of mergers and acquisitions from the late 1990s, have played in driving episodic increases in income inequality in the UK. Figure 3.2 demonstrates this relationship.

We can see from Figure 3.2 that the rising income share of the top 1 per cent has corresponded with a rising volume of FDI flows. For the period as a whole the correlation coefficient is 0.75, suggesting a strong correlation between the two variables which is further revealed by the qualitative analysis and evidence provided below. The cyclical peaks of these FDI flows, during the mid to late 1980s, the late 1990s and the mid to late 2000s, correspond with cyclical increases in the income share of the top 1 per cent during the same periods. This is particularly the case with the two phases of intensified FDI flows during the late 1990s and the mid to late 2000s. Figure 3.3 shows the same data sets, but with the data smoothed out through the use of five-year moving averages to produce a clearer picture of the long-term relationship. The graph shows that both the top 1 per cent income share and real gross FDI flows have trended upwards together. Regarding FDI flows, the important thing to notice here is that both the cyclical peak volumes and the general levels of FDI flows in and out of the UK economy have increased markedly as the transnationalisation of ownership has accelerated since the 1970s.

The data raise an important question about the cyclical relationship between FDI flows and the income share of the top 1 per cent. How do we explain the cyclical peaks in FDI flows? The answer lies in the increasing significance of mergers and acquisitions (M&As), and the

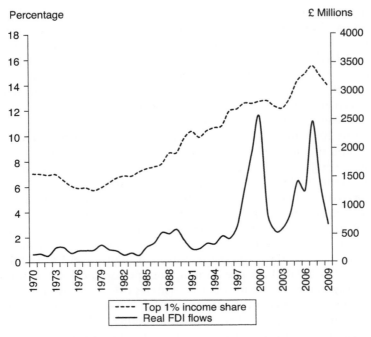

*Figure 3.2*  UK top 1 per cent income share and UK real FDI flows, 1970–2009

Sources: UNCTADstat inward and outward foreign direct investment flows, annual, 1970–2012 through UNCTAD database. Real flows calculated by dividing gross flows by Consumer Price Index data from IMF international statistics through Global Insight database. Top 1 per cent income share data from Atkinson, Anthony B. (2007). *The Distribution of Top Incomes in the United Kingdom 1908–2000.*

reduced role of greenfield expansion, in accounting for the vast volumes of FDI flows. Since the 1980s there has been a shift in the purpose of FDI flows, moving away from greenfield expansion and towards FDI flows involved in M&As (Foot, 1993: 3; Nitzan and Bichler, 2009: 359). Indeed, in 2000 cross-border M&As accounted for over 75 per cent of all global FDI (Nitzan and Bichler, 2009: 359). Crucially, the predominance of M&A activity as a constituent of FDI flows has had a serious impact both upon the structure of British capitalism and the acceleration of income inequality.

From the late 1990s, the top income earners in Britain and the US began to generate revenue by employing new business practices, manipulating the financial structures of existing firms in order to generate short-term returns.[6] As Stewart Lansley has noted, 'Business activity today

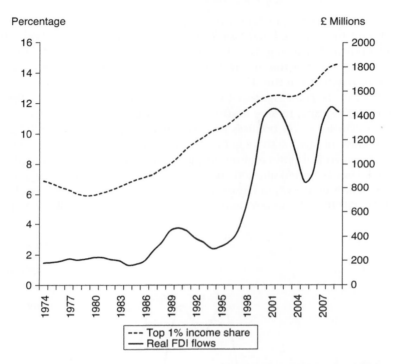

*Figure 3.3*   UK top 1 per cent income share and UK real gross FDI flows, five-year moving averages, 1974–2009

*Sources*: UNCTADstat inward and outward foreign direct investment flows, annual, 1970–2012 through UNCTAD database. Real flows calculated by dividing gross flows by Consumer Price Index data from IMF international statistics through Global Insight database. Top 1 per cent income share data from Atkinson, Anthony B. (2007). *The Distribution of Top Incomes in the United Kingdom 1908–2000.*

means mergers, hostile takeovers and rearranging balance sheets', as boardrooms have become increasingly focused upon, 'buying, merging, breaking up, repackaging and selling on existing companies' (Lansley, 2011: 8). This new phase of capitalism, focusing more upon transforming the existing ownership structures of firms rather than greenfield investment and growth, has been marked by a major increase in the volume and size of M&As and leveraged buyouts (LBOs). This development in capitalism has fed into increasing income inequality. Indeed, in the decade up to 2008, 'three quarters of the increase in the income concentration among the top 1 per cent went to finance workers, virtually all of it in bonuses' (Lansley, 2011: 24). Bonus payments in the top income decile are highly significant, with 82 per cent of those workers receiving a bonus in 2008 (Bell and Van Reenen, 2010: 10). Figure 3.4 shows the relationship between gross FDI flows, largely accountable for in terms of the M&A wave of the mid to late 2000s, and finance/insurance sector bonus payments in the UK.[7]

We can see from Figure 3.4 that as the M&A wave of the late 1990s/early 2000s came to an end, financial sector bonuses also dropped, but both FDI flows and bonuses increased markedly from 2003–2007 as a new wave of M&A activity got underway.[8] In both cases there is a slight lag between FDI flows and bonus payments that may be accounted for on the basis of when quarterly results are published and bonus payments are made after the capital flows occur. Importantly, for the politics of the financial crisis, bonus payments rebounded between 2009–2011, despite

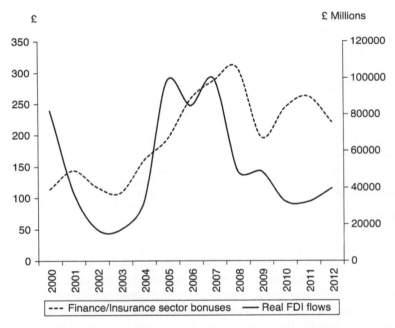

*Figure 3.4*   UK finance/insurance sector yearly bonuses and UK real gross FDI flows, 2000–2012

*Source*: UNCTADstat inward and outward foreign direct investment flows, annual, 1970–2012 through UNCTAD database. Real flows calculated by dividing gross flows by Consumer Price Index data from IMF international statistics through Global Insight database. Finance and insurance sector bonuses data from Office for National Statistics Dataset 'EARN03June2013', Average Weekly Earnings by Industry.

the fact that capital flows did not recover to their pre-crisis levels. This, coupled with the analysis below, suggests that the relationship between bonuses and FDI flows that existed before the crisis became uncoupled in the years after the crisis began.

In the aftermath of the crisis there has been a marked shift in the bonus hierarchy within finance. Whereas in the pre-crisis heyday M&A bankers sat at the top of hierarchy, the dominant earners are now those responsible for the flotation of Initial Public Offerings (IPOs) within a buoyant stock market stimulated by quantitative easing and loose monetary policy. In this context it has become increasingly clear that, 'the old-school advisers to Fortune 500 clients on strategic mergers and acquisitions – made famous by the likes of Felix Rohatyn and the late Bruce Wasserstein – are unlikely to be the big rainmakers anymore'. M&A bankers have now been overtaken by, 'hedge funds, asset managers and anyone who has anything to do with initial public offerings', players who are benefiting from rapidly rising stock markets, 'with the stock market up and more money pouring in every day, bonuses will be showered generously on employees connected to that world' (Sorkin, 2013).

M&A bankers had continued to experience rising bonuses after the crisis, 'even though they weren't bringing in the same kind of revenue that they once did, given the drought in mega-mergers and private equity buyouts'. But the fees involved outside M&A activity are considerably smaller leading to a situation whereby a declining M&A business has led to relatively smaller bonuses for M&A investment bankers while the banks themselves are, 'trying to figure out what to do with a staff that often looks bigger than it should be relative to the revenue they bring in' (Sorkin, 2013). UK investment banking fees for IPOs rose by an enormous 111 per cent during 2013, 'reflecting the revival of company flotations on the London Stock Exchange'. During the same period, M&A fees in the UK fell from $1.57 billion to $1.35 billion (Armstrong, 2014).

Banks have adjusted their business strategies in order to adapt to changing circumstances post-2007, with a booming stock market, fuelled by unorthodox monetary policy, shifting the bonus hierarchy within the City and Wall Street. The larger bonuses paid out in 2009 may also have arisen due to the large state guarantees that had been given to banks such as Barclays in Britain, while major Wall Street investment banks, employing tens of thousands in the City, made use of the security generated by TARP funding to continue doling out huge bonuses despite faltering performances (Harris, 2009; Treanor, 2010; Grocer, 2010).

The aggregate value of M&A deals in the early 2000s was a remarkable twenty times the level of the early 1980s. Some of the major deals here were the £112 billion Vodafone takeover of Mannesman in 2000, the GlaxoWellcome buyout of Smithkline also in 2000 and the 1999 BP takeover of Amoco. There were further huge deals towards the end of the 2000s, notably the $100 billion takeover of ABM Amro, the Dutch bank, by RBS in 2007. The 2000s were a decade in which there was much greater emphasis on M&As, with investment bankers cold-calling firms in order to encourage them to undertake mergers on the promise of vastly increased share prices post-consolidation (Lansley, 2011: 124–125). Investment banks profited massively from these deals given their key role in the M&A process (Rosenbaum and Pearl, 2009: 162–164). The enormous fees that investment banks accrued through these deals were fed into the escalating bonuses among top bankers in the City. Indeed, M&A bankers were widely known to have received some of the largest bonus payments during the boom years, while M&A activity has generally been at the heart of investment bankers' bonus earnings, accounting for the bumper pay-outs at the tail-end of the M&A wave in 2007 (White et al., 2012; Armstrong, 2014).

Lansley describes these major deals (2011: 129), achieved through leveraged finance, as a 'huge personal gravy-train for the top participants'. For the Vodafone takeover of Mannesman alone, participating investment banks trousered advisory fees over £400 million, while the 2004 Glaxo and Smithkline merger generated £122 million in fees and the RBS takeover of Natwest (a British acquisition but funded through foreign finance) brought in around £300 million in fees. That deal was underwritten by Goldman Sachs and Merrill Lynch, two blue chip American investment banks working from the City, and involved the Australian insurance firm CGU taking a major stake in RBS.[9]

The presence of these dominant investment banks within London has much to do with the way in which the City has repositioned itself by drawing in American financial power. After the Big Bang, in 1986, larger American investment banks bought out many of the traditional British merchant banks, banks who had been at the top of the City tree in 1983 when a deal was struck with the stock exchange that fed into the 1986 Big Bang reforms. But by the mid 1990s many of these traditional British merchant banks had been bought up by their larger and more aggressive American counterparts as the American investment banks looked to use the City as a launch pad for increasing their share of European business, bringing in new tactics and a more intensive work ethic that had been honed on Wall Street (Augar, 2000: 76). The 1980s boom on

Wall Street gave these banks, 'the confidence and financial resources to attack London'. By the mid 1990s, Morgan Stanley and Goldman Sachs had become, 'established parts of the corporate finance scene in the UK and Europe' (Augar, 2000: 214). The American expansion into London has been part of a more general deepening of the power of American investment banking since the 1980s (Hager, 2012: 5).

By the 1990s and 2000s, then, decades of interdependent Anglo-American development, centred upon the interaction between banking in London and New York, had repositioned the City as a major hub for capital flows and investment banking. Thus, income inequality in Britain needs to be understood not simply in terms of neoliberal ideology or contemporary policy programmes, but as a consequence of deeper processes by which Britain, and the City in particular, has positioned itself within the global political economy since WW2. We are now seeing the damaging social consequences of decades of Anglo-American development and the restoration of the City's international pre-eminence.

Playing host to a major financial centre drives up income inequality in Britain and deepens social divisions between rich and poor, the social implications of this dynamic are grave. Stagnant wages for the majority of the population also continue to present a problem of aggregate demand within the British economy, reducing the purchasing power of workers and forcing them to rely upon credit in order to sustain living standards, further deepening the credit dependency of the British economy and paving the way for future financial instability (Lansley, 2011: 31; Hutton, 2014).

## Conclusion: the cost of inequality

In their influential study, 'The Spirit Level', Wilkinson and Pickett chart the corrosive impacts of inequality at length. Their central conclusion is that the social problems in contemporary Western societies, with Britain exemplary in this regard, arise not from a lack of aggregate wealth but rather as a consequence of, 'the scale of material differences between people within each society being too big. What matters is where we stand in relation to others in our own society' (Wilkinson and Pickett, 2009: 25). Income inequality signifies the hierarchical nature of a society and the distance between different groups within that society. On this metric, Britain's performance is appalling. What's more, higher levels of inequality are linked to a wide array of negative social and health phenomena as part of a marked deterioration in social wellbeing and social relations (Wilkinson and Pickett, 2009: 174; Schuerkens, 2010: 7).

Restoring higher levels of equality should be a key component of any project that aims towards a progressive transformation of British capitalism. Achieving this goal will, however, require more than a recalibration of tax policy along more progressive lines or an increase in wages for those lower down in the income hierarchy. It must also entail a broader reconsideration of the entwinement of British capitalism with American financial power and the role of the City as a major international financial centre. Problems of British economic transformation are thus inherently intertwined with the broader contours of the global political economy and, in particular, the support for, and integration of, Britain within an international economic system shaped by American power.

To conclude, this chapter has argued that rising levels of income inequality in Britain, a hallmark of Britain's contemporary political economy, have arisen as a consequence of post-war Anglo-American development. Tracing the way in which the Anglo-American endorsement of foreign investment and capital market liberalisation has impacted British economic development, the chapter have suggested that the increasing levels of income inequality in Britain are linked to the manner in which the City of London was restored as a global social space for financial flows through integration with American financial power. That process began with the emergence of the Euromarkets, but it continued to unfold during subsequent decades and produced further financial liberalisation on both sides of the Atlantic. By drawing in the dollar and accepting the arrival of American banks, the City was able to maintain its longstanding dominance within Britain's political economy, despite the rapid demise of sterling's status as an international currency. This meant that the City's traditional commitments to open international trade and investment have remained at the centre of British economic policy. Finally, the chapter have argued that it is this Anglo-American developmental interactivity that provided the wider context within which the City's investment banking elite were able to prosper from the increased FDI lows linked to several waves of mergers and acquisitions activity between the late 1990s and the late 2000s. The social consequences of rising levels of income inequality, fuelled by rocketing incomes in the City, are stark.

Achieving a more equitable form of economic development within Britain, therefore, is more than just a question of subtle domestic policy recalibrations. It will necessarily and inescapably also be a question of how Britain, and the City of London in particular, is integrated within the broader global political economy. Deepening inequality will continue to erode the civic foundations of British society and create a further polarisation of interests. If Britain is to continue endorsing a globalised economy with a liberal system of international capital flows, those flows must be made to work for the benefit of the wider economy and not just for the enrichment of a privileged few.

## Notes

1. Hay's acknowledgement (2011: 6, 2013: 4) of Anglo-American dynamics in the gestation of the crisis centres upon the importation of American mortgage market reforms into the UK through processes of Anglo-American deregulatory arbitrage centred upon the competitive interaction between London and New York. The broader continuum of Anglo-American financial development remains absent from this account however. Andrew Gamble's assessment of the crisis explicitly identifies (2009: 454) the centrality of finance within a new type of dominant 'Anglo-American capitalism' but offers no substantive explanation of the central actors and processes that comprise Anglo-American capitalism.
2. FDI is distinguished from portfolio investment by the size of asset transfer; 10 per cent or over of the target company's equity has to be purchased in order to qualify as FDI (Nitzan and Bichler, 2009: 356).
3. The term Euromarkets applies to transactions in two distinct but related markets: Eurocurrency/Eurodollar and Eurobond. But the Euro prefix is misleading as the term is, in fact, used as an umbrella to describe transactions of offshore currency traded outside of nationally prescribed banking authority (Burn, 1999: 226). Essentially, it describes an offshore market in foreign currency. The market is wholesale, predominantly comprising of large-scale operators such as commercial banks, governments and large companies (Higgonet, 1985: 30).
4. The Triffin Dilemma referred to a key problem in the international economy that had been identified by the American economist, Robert Triffin. Triffin realised that the US deficit had become the key source of international liquidity and that maintaining this deficit would be crucial to the supplying the flow of dollars required for financing international trade, exchange and the build-up of reserves (Gowa, 1983: 42). Unfortunately, there was a major problem; continued deficit spending would weaken confidence in the dollar's fixed convertibility to gold and, over time, could lead to a run on the gold stocks, dollar devaluation and the end of Bretton Woods. This was, in fact, the actual outcome when Nixon unilaterally delinked the dollar from gold in 1971.
5. Although inequality continued to rise under New Labour, there were attempts to redirect resources to the poor through specific policy measures (Godman, 2001: 92). Prior to the financial crisis, the top rate of income tax remained unaltered under New Labour as part of a 'hands off' approach to top income earners that emerged from the way that 'Third Way' philosophy reconceived of inequality in terms of opportunities rather than outcomes (Sefton and Sutherland, 2005: 232–233).
6. Sponsors of LBOs typically seek a 20 per cent or more annualised return and an exit from the investment within five years (Rosenbaum and Pearl, 2009: 161).

7.  There is, unfortunately, no further disaggregation of sectoral bonus payments available, meaning that finance bonuses have to be examined in conjunction with insurance sector bonus payments.
8.  This is not to say, of course, that bonus payments are entirely determined by FDI flows. Financial sector firms' business strategies are much broader than a mere dependence upon these cross-border flows.
9.  CGU agreed to purchase a large volume of shares within RBS, with a subscription price of £1 per share, while Merrill Lynch, Goldman Sachs and Warburg Dillon Read provided a combined liquidity facility of £3.5 billion (RBS, 2000: 13–14).

## References

Alvaredo, F., Atkinson, A., Piketty, T. and Saez, E. (2013) 'The Top 1 Percent in International and Historical Perspective', *Journal of Economic Perspectives*, 27, 3, 3–20.

Armstrong, A. (2014) 'Is This the Last Happy New Year for Bankers' Bonuses?' *The Telegraph* online, 4 January, Available at <http://www.telegraph.co.uk/finance/newsbysector/banksandfinance/10551079/Is-this-the-last-happy-new-year-for-bankers-bonuses.html> (accessed 14 January 2014).

Asthana, A. (2010) 'New Poll Reveals Depth of Outrage at Bankers' Bonuses', *The Guardian*, online, 21 February, Available at <http://www.theguardian.com/business/2010/feb/21/bank-bonuses-outrage-opinion-poll> (accessed 15 September 2013).

Augar, P. (2000) *The Death of Gentlemanly Capitalism: The Rise and Fall of London's Investment Bank.* London: Penguin.

Baker, A. (2010) 'Restraining Regulatory Capture? Anglo-America, Crisis Politics and Trajectories of Change in Global Financial Governance', *International Affairs*, 86, 3, 647–663.

Battilossi, S. (2002) 'Banking with Multinationals: British Clearing Banks and the Euromarkets' Challenge, 1958–1976', in S. Battilossi and Y. Cassis (eds), *European Banks and the American Challenge: Competition and Cooperation in International Banking Under Bretton Woods*, Oxford: Oxford University Press, pp. 103–135.

Bell, G. (1973) *The Euro-dollar Market and the International Financial System.* London: Macmillan.

Bell, B. and Van Reenen, J. (2010) 'Bankers' Pay and Extreme Wage Inequality in the UK', LSE Centre for Economic Performance.

Block, F. (1977) *The Origins of International Economic Disorder: A Study of United States International Monetary Policy from World War II to the Present.* Berkeley: University of California Press.

Blundell, R. and Ethridge, B. (2010) 'Consumption Income and Earnings Inequality in Britain', *Review of Economic Dynamics*, 13, 76–102.

Burn, G. (1999) 'The State, the City and the Euromarkets', *Review of International Political Economy*, 6, 2, 225–261.

Burn, G. (2006) *The Re-Emergence of Global Finance.* Basingstoke: Palgrave Macmillan.

Claes, A., De Ceuster, M. and Polfiet, R. (2002) 'Anatomy of the Eurobond Market 1980–2000', *European Financial Management*, 8, 3, 373–386.

Clegg, J. (1996) 'The United Kingdom: A Par Excellence Two-way Direct Investor', in J. Dunning and R. Narula (eds), *Foreign Direct Investment and Governments: Catalysts for Economic Restructuring*. Routledge: London, pp. 42–78.

Coakley, J. and Harris, L. (1983) *The City of Capital: London's Role As a Financial Centre*. Oxford: Basil Blackwell.

Cronin, J. and Radtke, T. (1987) 'The Old and the New Politics of Taxation: Thatcher and Reagan in Historical Perspective', *The Socialist Register*, 263–296.

Deprez, E. and Dodge, C. (2011) 'Occupy Wall Street Protests Inject Income Inequality into Political Debate', *Bloomberg News* online, 9 November, available at <http://www.bloomberg.com/news/2011-11-09/occupy-wall-street-protests-inject-income-inequality-into-political-debate.html> (accessed 20 November 2013).

Dunning, J. (1998) *American Investment in British Manufacturing Industry*. London: Routledge.

Eichengreen, B. (2008) *Globalizing Capital: A History of the International Monetary System*. Princeton: Princeton University Press.

Foot, K. (1993) 'Introduction', in K. Foot (ed.), *Foreign Direct Investment*. Chicago: University of Chicago Press, pp. 1–13.

Gamble, A. (2009) 'British Politics and the Financial Crisis', *British Politics*, 4, 4, 450–462.

Gilpin, R. (1975) *US Power and the Multinational Corporation: The Political Economy of Foreign Direct Investment*. New York: Basic Books.

Godman, A. (2001) Income Inequality: What has Happened under New Labour?' *New Economy*, 8, 2, 92–97.

Gowa, J. (1983) *Closing the Gold Window: Domestic Politics and the End of Bretton Woods*. Ithaca: Cornell University Press.

Graham, E. and Krugman, P. (1993) 'The Surge in Foreign Direct Investment in the 1980s', in K. Foot (ed.), *Foreign Direct Investment*. Chicago: University of Chicago Press, pp. 13–37.

Grocer, S. (2010) 'Banks Set for Record Pay', *Wall Street Journal* online, 14 January, available at <http://online.wsj.com/news/articles/SB10001424052748704281204575003351773983136> (accessed 22 November 2013).

Harris, J. (2009) 'George Osborne Attacks 'Unacceptable' City Bonuses', *The Guardian* online, 14 August, available at <http://www.theguardian.com/business/2009/aug/14/george-osborne-barclays-bankers-bonuses> (accessed 5 November 2013).

Hay, C. (2011) 'Pathology Without Crisis? The Strange Demise of the Anglo-Liberal Growth Model', *Government and Opposition*, 46, 1, 1–31.

Hay, C. (2013) 'The British Growth Crisis: A Crisis *of* and *for* Growth', *SPERI Paper* No. 1, 1–27.

Helleiner, E. (1994) *States and the Reemergence of Global Finance: From Bretton Woods to the 1990s*. London: Cornell University Press.

Higonnet, R. (1985) 'Eurobanks, Eurodollars and International Debt', in P. Savona and G. Sutja (eds) *Eurodollars and International Banking*. Basingstoke: Macmillan, 15–52.

Hutton, W. (2014) 'Britain is Scared to Face the Real Issue – It's All About Inequality', *The Guardian* online, 19 January, available at <http://www.theguardian.com/commentisfree/2014/jan/19/inequality-threat-recovery-poverty-pay> (accessed 20 January 2014).

Kristal, T. (2010) 'Good Times, Bad Times: Postwar Labor's Share of National Income in Capitalist Democracies', *American Sociological Review*, 75, 729–763.

Lansley, S. (2011) *The Cost of Inequality: Three Decades of the Super-Rich and the Economy*. London: Gibson Square.

Machin, S. (1997) 'The Decline of Labour Market Institutions and the Rise in Wage Inequality in Britain', *European Economic Review*, 41, 3–5, 647–657.

Malik, S. (2012) 'Peter Mandelson Gets Nervous about People Getting 'filthy rich', *The Guardian* online, 26 January, available at <http://www.theguardian.com/politics/2012/jan/26/mandelson-people-getting-filthy-rich> (accessed 22 November 2013).

Martenson, G. (1964) *The Euro-dollar Market*. Boston: The Banker's Publishing Company.

Michie, R. (2004) 'The City of London and the British Government: The Changing Relationship', in R. Michie and P. Williamson (eds), *The British Government and the City of London in the Twentieth Century*. Cambridge: Cambridge University Press.

Montgomerie, J. (2006) 'Giving Credit where it's Due: Public Policy and Household Debt in the United States, the United Kingdom and Canada', *Policy and Society*, 25, 3, 109–141.

Montgomerie, J. (2007) 'Financialization and Consumption: An Alternative Account of Rising Consumer Debt Levels in Anglo-America', *CRESC Working Paper* No. 43, 1–29.

Moran, M. (1986) *The Politics of Banking*. London: Macmillan Press.

Moran, M. (1994) 'The State and the Financial Services Revolution: A Comparative Analysis', *West European Politics*, 17, 3, 158–177.

Nitzan, J. and Bichler, S. (2009) *Capital as Power: A Study of Order and Creorder*. New York: Routledge.

Obstfeld, M. and Taylor, A. (2002) 'Globalization and Capital Markets', *National Bureau of Economic Research*, 1–67.

Obstfeld, M. and Taylor, A. (2005) *Global Capital Markets: Integration, Crisis and Growth*. Cambridge: Cambridge University Press.

Overbeek, H. (1990) *Global Capitalism and National Decline: The Thatcher Decade in Perspective*. London: Unwin Hyman.

Panitch, L. and Gindin, S. (2012) *The Making of Global Capitalism: The Political Economy of American Empire*. London: Verso.

Rosenbaum, J. and Pearl, J. (2009) *Investment Banking: Valuation, Leveraged Buyouts and Mergers and Acquisitions*. New Jersey: Wiley.

Royal Bank of Scotland (2000) 'Supplementary Listing Particulars: Increased Offer for National Westminster Bank PLC (pdf) Royal Bank of Scotland', available at <http://www.investors.rbs.com/acquisition_natwest> (accessed 20 November 2013).

Schuerkens, U. (2010) 'Globalization and Transformations of Social Inequality', in U. Schuerkens (ed.), *Globalization and Transformations of Social Inequality*. New York: Routledge.

Schenk, C. (1998) 'The Origins of the Eurodollar Market in London: 1955–63', *Explorations in Economic History*, 35, 221–238.

Sefton, T. and Sutherland, H. (2005) 'Inequality and poverty under New Labour', in J. Hills and K. Stewart (eds), *A More Equal Society? New Labour, Poverty, Inequality and Exclusion*. Bristol: The Policy Press, 231–251.

Sorkin, A. (2013) 'Big Bonuses, but a Shift in Who Gets the Biggest', *CNBC* online, 17 December, available at <http://www.cnbc.com/id/101278207> (accessed 14 January 2014).

Stark, T. (1989) 'The Changing Distribution of Income under Mrs Thatcher', in F. Green (ed.), *The Restructuring of the UK Economy*. London: Harvester Wheatsheaf, 177–196.

Strange, S. (1972) 'The Dollar Crisis 1971', *International Affairs*, 48, 2, 191–216.

Treanor, J. (2010) 'Bonus Time as Banks Pay Out £40 bn', *The Guardian* online, 8 January, available at <http://www.theguardian.com/business/2010/jan/08/bonus-time-city-banks> (accessed 18 November 2013).

Weeks, J. (2007) 'Inequality Trends in Some Developed OECD Countries', in K. Jomo and J. Baudot (eds), *Flat World, Big Gaps: Economic Liberalization, Globalization, Poverty and Inequality*. London: Zed Books.

White, S., White, L. and Horowitz, J. (2012) 'Bullish Bankers Struggle to Adjust to Bonus Cutbacks', *Reuters News* online, 22 November, available at <http://uk.reuters.com/article/2012/11/22/us-banks-bonuses-idUKBRE8-AL0KK20121122> (accessed 14 January 2014).

Wilkinson, R. and Pickett, K. (2009) *The Spirit Level: Why Greater Equality Makes Societies Stronger*. London: Bloomsbury Press.

# Part II
# Evaluating Responses

# 4
# Economic Recovery and Governance for the Long-Term

*Gerry Stoker*

## Introduction

A challenge for any government is to be able to operate effectively in the short-term and to think and act for the long-term. Any economic recovery strategy is likely to involve a capacity to govern in a way that enables the imposition of social costs long before economic benefits in terms of recovery arrive. Can governance for the long-term be assembled?

A capacity for long-term politics is not easy to achieve in any circumstances in democratic politics and has arguably become harder to muster. The boom years (1990–2007) in which the old growth model dominated has left many established democracies with legacies that will be difficult to overcome, not only in terms of economic or financial problems but also with a certain model of politics that is short-term in focus, consumerist in style and neo-liberal in ideology, which seems ill-fitted to the task of taking a new economic path.

There are some that go further and argue that short-termism is inherent in democratic politics. Their prescription appears to be that the only hope for long-term policy processes to emerge is to take issues away from democratic politics. This chapter challenges the view that democratic politics cannot deliver long-termism by offering a broader framework for analysis that identifies some of the ingredients necessary to deliver a politics that is capable of managing loss and building coalitions of long-term policy support for alternative economic strategies. A further section considers the settings and conditions under which a politics of long-termism are most likely to emerge.

## The old growth model and consumerist politics: an adverse legacy

Andrew Gamble (2011) characterises the growth model adopted in the UK and other countries from the 1980s – built on financial services, retail, property and construction in the private sector, matched by growth in education, health and universities – as 'remarkably successful' but facing critical questions given the problems that surfaced from 2007 onwards. Can the model be relaunched after some minor adjustment and a period of recovery? Do more radical repairs to the model need to be undertaken? Does a different growth model need to be developed and put in place?

Any response to these questions is, in part, an issue of economic policy but it is also constrained by the forms of politics that might be available. A different growth model is likely to require a different politics that can provide positive answers to some tough questions. Can politics confront tough choices? Can it legitimate short-term sacrifices for long-term gain? Can it take on and defeat powerful and vested interests? If you had to characterise the nature of much of the politics practised in democracies, especially the established democracies, for the last three decades you might have grounds for some considerable doubts about its capacity to meet these challenges and in particular its capacity for long-termism. A politics for the collective good, requiring short-term sacrifice, seems a long way away from politics as practised in the twenty-first century, which has become consumerist rather than collectivist in style (Stoker, 2006).

The role of political parties as bastions of collective loyalty and identity has shifted more to a practice of catch-all institutions looking to market themselves to a wide range of free-floating voters. The major institutions of engagement, including trade unions, churches and formal membership associations, have seen their role decline and instead interest politics is more dominated by single-issue campaigns and organisations that demand not loyalty and engagement from their membership, but funding and fees to support professional and sleek campaign organisers.

Citizens at the start of the twenty-first century in many established democracies relate to politics through a complex mix of broadcast, print and internet media but rarely directly through face-to-face contact with politicians or campaigners. Many public service delivery mechanisms operate in a world beyond the formal levers of government and representative democracy and instead through the murkier world of governance.

Citizens may be surveyed, consulted and provided for but forms of public accountability often appear either opaque or non-existent, save for the sense that you can, as a citizen, look for another provider to meet your needs, give an unsatisfactory rating to your current provider, or protest to the market regulator about your public service provider. Whether it's the relationship between voter and politician, campaigner and interest group or client and service provider, the citizen is cast as a consumer first and a citizen hardly at all.

This emergence of consumerist political practice has been matched by the rise of a neo-liberal understanding of the public realm. Neo-liberalism constitutes the most successful ideology of the last three decades, which has shown a resilience and capacity to survive even in the context of an economic downturn. Neo-liberal thinking offers a powerful critique of the idea of the civic and the public realm. As Raymond Plant (2004) explains, the starting point for neo-liberal thought is that liberty is the key goal, and that the only form of liberty that can and should be promoted is freedom from coercion. So when the collective is constructed it needs to keep what the government can do to a minimum. A framework of non-coercion and civil rights to protect citizens from interference is all that is needed. The goal of neo-liberals is a minimal state to frame and support free markets and to allow individuals to pursue their own good.

After this period of neo-liberal hegemony we are left with two factors that work against the search for a political solution towards promoting new economic strategies. First, for many citizens politics appears to be a rather unedifying process that they would rather not have much to do with. Attempts by most citizens to engage in politics are ad hoc and sporadic. Most substantial politics is done by a mixed, but small, cadre of elected politicians, unaccountable officials, specialist lobbyists, narrowly focused experts and professionalised protesters. That world, in turn, is reported to us by a media that focuses on personality conflicts, controversy and a mix of reporting and commentary that can enlighten, but more often confuses. The average citizen is alienated from politics and far from convinced of its value. As an ideology, neo-liberalism has helped to undermine the case for politics and any faith that politics might deliver something of collective value.

The second issue is that even when politics does engage citizens it does so only on the basis of short-term promises and delivery, which is at odds with the long-term delivery and intervening sacrifices required by new economic strategies and models. This short-termism is seen as a flaw of modern policy making by observers from both right and left.

The Adam Smith Institute, a think tank that strongly promotes a broad neo-liberal ideology, comments:

> How do you deal with the fact that politicians typically only think as far as the next election, and as such do not as a rule pay much attention to the long term effects of their decisions? Short-termism in politics is a chronic affliction, manifesting itself both in inaction (let's not bother reforming social security – its eventual collapse is going to be someone else's problem) and in action (let's have a fiscal giveaway now and worry about the deficit once we've bought ourselves the next election). (Cloughterly, 2011)

For the right, short-termism enables sloppy and inappropriate government intervention and the rolling back of the state. From a more left or progressive perspective, short-termism in politics is seen as something that disables effective government intervention, undermining the prospects for reform. According to Victor Andersen (2011) writing in *The Guardian:*

> The problems of the market are often reflected in problems in political systems. The short-termism of the way markets often function, creating instability for business and for whole national economies ... can unfortunately be amplified by the short-termism of democratic political systems. Where we should be able to look to politics and government to correct, regulate, or compensate for, the failings of the market, we often instead get 'political failure' alongside 'market failure'. For the 'good transition' to a green economy, the problem of short-termism in government and politics is a key problem.

The last three decades of consumerist politics has left us with a politics no longer fit for purpose, at least, not fit to drive the search for long-term alternative economic strategies or to deliver on the practice and implementation of those strategies. A politics bent towards short-termism that does not engage most citizens and where politicians and the democratic processes are widely distrusted hardly seems to be in a robust condition to deliver policy goals, such as reducing public debt or restructuring the economy, 'that require governments to arrange losses and gains in a particular temporal order: to impose social costs long before most benefits will arrive'(Jacobs, 2008). It would appear many current political practices in established democracies are very ill-suited to the task of delivering long-term policy goals, such as those required for an economic renewal which appears to involve some mix of austerity and economic redirection.

## Water and oil: democratic politics and long-termism

A complex, unhelpful legacy of short-term politics presents problems to policy makers but what if the challenge is even greater? There are some who argue that democracies are just not compatible with long-term policy making and subsequently argue that the only way forward is to take decisions out of normal politics. There are several current policy variations of this argument. One solution mooted for the crisis in the eurozone is for national budgets and banking systems to be subject to oversight from Brussels-based officialdom within the EU. Another option, often touted, is to enforce spending control by creating transparent legislative and regulative mechanisms to limit the discretion available to politicians. The justifications for these various options to by-pass normal politics tend to rest not only on a sense of pressing crisis but also implicitly, and sometimes, explicitly on a particular understanding of politics offered within a rational choice framework of thinking in which all actors are viewed as self-interested in their motivations and instrumental in that selection of courses of action.

The logic provided by a rational choice framing of issues offers a powerful narrative. The collective choices of societies led by democratic governments are inherently short-term because of the dynamics of electoral competition. Politicians have no incentive to focus on the long-term and as a result, in the words of William Nordhaus (1975: 188), the author of a key original substantial theoretical statement on the issue, is that 'democratic myopia' creates a problem in a whole range of policy issues that require long-term commitment. His work, based on a stylised model of a representative democracy, views politicians and voters as driven by self-interested calculation. Voters will judge parties on their performance in delivery for them in the short run and incumbent politicians are therefore under irresistible pressure to deliver short-term gains or risk being voted out of office. As a result democracies 'will make decisions biased against future generations' (Nordhaus, 1975: 187). In the economic field, in particular, the result is a 'predictable pattern of policy, starting with relative austerity in early years and ending with the potlatch right before the elections' (Nordhaus, 1975: 188).[1] With respect to public spending then the pattern is prudence followed by a big giveaway. More generally, the model predicts that 'politicians should *never* be willing to impose short-term costs for future gain' (Jacobs, 2008: 201).

When reflecting on long-term policy choice much of our thinking in both academic and wider public debate is framed by variations of this rational choice paradigm. The Nordhaus model has received serious attention and multiple developments and there is some evidence to suggest that economic and spending policy does tend to follow the cycle that the model suggests (Alt and Dreyer, 2006). The rational strategies inevitably favoured by citizens and politicians mean a virtually iron-grip for short-termism. Politicians may start off with a commitment to austerity and sacrifice but as election time draws near the pressure to please voters in the here and now becomes too great.

How can sacrifice be delivered in the context of an electoral cycle that demands a focus on short-term delivery by politicians to citizens? Staying within the confines of the rational choice framing developed by Nordhaus and many others it is possible to think of some ameliorative measures. Familiar ones are discussed by Nordhaus but dismissed as likely to be ineffectual. The idea that additional information or independent audit would transform voters from inattentive judges to more long-term reflectors is viewed as implausible. Extending election terms to a sufficient degree to meet the challenges of overcoming short-termism would lead to a loss of democratic legitimacy that would undermine any gains made. If Nordhaus had been presented the option of hiving off decisions to unelected EU bureaucrats he might have doubted whether the solution would work on similar grounds.

Most of the options considered more viable by those with a rational choice perspective involve somehow or other removing decision-making from the normal run of politics. Politicians set broad guidelines so legitimacy is preserved but detailed decisions are left to unelected regulators. For example, decisions could be passed to an independent group of actors not bound by electoral constraints. The practice that is seen as an exemplar of this is passing on the control of monetary policy to an independent central bank. Equally, legislation could be passed that bound both politicians' and citizens' hands on balancing the budget or climate change targets. Indeed, given the problem of short time horizons it is rational to try to bind the hands of both yourself and your successors. Through different mechanisms for delivering 'credible commitments' it would appear that short-term time horizons do not count automatically against the potential for far-sighted policy making. The key is not to allow the inherent short-termism of politics to railroad the process by putting decisions at one remove and limiting the discretion available to future decision-makers.

There is no sense among advocates of these kinds of mechanisms that they are confident that any measures will guarantee a longer-term focus to decision-making. They appear to recognise that short-term political pressures could lead to pressures on 'independent' decision-makers to change tack and that binding commitments can be unbound or honoured in some way that takes away their bite. What we are offered at best is a number of interventions that, in benign circumstances, could deliver long-term policy making.

For the remainder of this chapter it will be argued that this rational choice inspired form of thinking runs the risk of creating a rationality trap where, given assumptions that actors have full information and act in a self-interested manner, there appears to be no way out of the social dilemma identified. But there is an argument to suggest that these prescriptions are based on too limited an understanding of what politics can and cannot be expected to deliver. Indeed, far from limiting political discretion it could be suggested that it would be good to encourage it if long-term policy making is the goal. But to make sense of that proposition it is necessary to go beyond the simplified model of the operation of representative democracy knowingly offered by Nordhaus and it would appear, naively adopted, by others.

## The ingredients for long-term politics: an analytical framework

The sense that we are constrained by a rationality trap that preordains short-termism in democratic politics is mistaken. Democratic politics is not inherently myopic. To understand how political space can be constructed for long-term policy making three factors need to be considered, each one, if present, could support long-term policy making. First, the potential importance of attentive organised interests as opposed to an inattentive public in the policy process means that backing for long-term solutions can emerge without direct citizen initiation, especially if institutions supporting power sharing among interests are present. Second, strategies for promoting long-term policy making, including insulating and mitigating devices, are available to politicians in structuring their relationship to citizens. It is also possible to identify more radical and less manipulative options for greater engagement with citizens that could support a politics of the long-term. This section of the paper looks at each of these factors in turn.

### Organised interests where power is dispersed

The elected politician–citizen relationship is not like that of the buyer and supplier at the time of a purchase, most of the time citizens are not paying attention to politicians and a lot of the time politicians are not paying attention to citizens. Nearly all citizens fail to follow politics in detail, indeed the dominant feature of most liberal democracies is the inattentiveness of most voters. Politicians, in turn, are not so much driven in their decision-making by a focus on citizens but by their relationships with international partners, party or coalition colleagues, powerful organised interests and the media, which provide a set of significant and more proximate influences. In short, politicians are more insulated from electors than the Nordhaus inspired models of representative democracy recognise. Moreover, they can use that insulation to present policies in ways that allow space for long-term decision-making.

Politics is about groups and interests as much as it is about citizens and the state. Policy can be made and unmade in the world of organised interests, which usually have professional staff and act to represent the interests of particular functional groups, causes, projects or programmes. They matter to elected politicians because: they can mobilise public opinion and voters; through funding they can support particular political parties or candidates; their leaders can be networked and even have social ties that give them access to political representatives and unelected officials. As well as these options for positive influence, interested organisations are often in positions where they need to be taken into account in decision-making because they are central to effective implementation or because their welfare is central to that of so many citizens (as in the privileged position of business in market economies, given their importance to job and wealth creation) (Lindblom, 1977).

The presence of organised interests changes the calculus more in favour of long-term policy (Jacobs, 2008). The leaders of interest organisations are attentive and able to track policies and be concerned about their implications way beyond the time framework of an election cycle. The institutional character of interest organisations provides a capacity for investing in the future. That is not to deny that interest organisations are concerned with short-term issues but they are attuned to routinely seek policy consequences that are advantageous in the long-term.

The commitment from organised interests to make an investment in long-term policy may be enhanced in settings where power is dispersed. As Jacobs (2008: 206) puts it: 'all else being equal, the broader the coalition required for policy change in a given context, the harder it will be for one social group to shift its own long-term problem onto another'. A political system that disperses power creates more veto points and at the same time makes cross-sectional redistribution harder, opening up the door for inter-temporal policy choices that meet the challenge of long-termism, usually by giving up something now for something later.

If an organised interest can shift burdens on to others it will not accept short-term pain for long-term gain. But if that avenue for cross-sectional redistribution is blocked an organised coalition of interests, willing to partner in some shared pain for long-term gain, becomes a possibility.

Organised interests matter in politics and the dynamic of their interventions is affected by the institutional frame in which they are operating. If political leaders have special relationships with particular interests then those interests will exploit that relationship to extract favours for themselves and put costs on to others. Westminster-style systems may be particularly prone to such problems; while those with more dispersed power may be more open to long-term policy development. There are, of course, many countervailing factors that must be considered in any full assessment of what is the right institutional framework to encourage long-term policy making and the empirical evidence is a far from conclusive, but dispersing power, perhaps counter-intuitively for some, might be the key to triggering a long-term orientation, at least among organised interests.

Long-termism makes a lot more sense in the context of local and regional decision-making as they can build the regime of partners needed to deliver success (Stoker, 1995). Manchester, Leeds and several other major cities and regions have already shown how long-term ambitions for moving to successful post-industrial economic success can be delivered (Hildreth and Bailey, 2013). Around Europe it is localities that are driving the economic turnaround. Long-term strategies are more viable at the local and regional level for several reasons. First, politics is less partisan at the local level in that all parties and interests can share in the ambitions for the success of their locality. Second, local politics is less wrapped up in the 24-hour media world and so faces less pressure to be short-term. Third, there is a cadre of officials with the technical and local knowledge to deliver effective long-term strategies. Finally, citizens themselves have a loyalty to their locality that can help political leaders buy the time they need to follow long-term strategies.

### Citizens are inattentive and mitigating strategies can employed

The response of citizens remains central to any politics of the long-term but the relative inattentiveness of most citizens to politics, a feature of democracies exasperated by the consumerist politics of the last three decades as noted earlier, means that there are opportunities for politicians to manage citizens' expectations in ways that a rational choice model of myopic politics does not take into account. The general inattentiveness of citizens to politics reflects a number of factors. Some explanations can be taken from the stealth model of politics (Hibbing and Elizabeth Theiss-Morse, 2002) developed to explain how in many democracies politics takes place undetected by citizens' political radar; just as stealth technology delivers fighter planes invisible to radar. How does this occur?

Citizens have no strong views on most issues and are therefore willing to concede decision-making authority to others, as long as decisions appear to be being made in the public interest or, more particularly, are not being usurped by self-interested politicians or organised interests. Under these circumstances citizens will not spend large amounts of effort in reasoning about the short- or long-term consequences of policy and instead will rely on cues or heuristics to judge their support, or otherwise, for what is going on. Some citizens may be particularly likely to mobilise against changes in policy that are likely to impose losses on them in the short-run, but mobilisation is only a reluctant choice. Under these conditions it is easy to imagine that there are a myriad opportunities for political leaders to manipulate citizens to gain their acquiescence, at least, to long-term policies that demand short-term sacrifices.

Studies suggest that there are many strategies for managing pain and making the case for long-term delivery rather than short-term satisfaction (Pal and Weaver, 2003). Adapting work on how governments go about avoiding blame and inflicting loss suggests that three broad categories of manipulation might work. First, *procedures can be changed to lower the visibility* of the policy, which plays on the inattentiveness of citizens. Classic examples of this kind of strategy involve delegating decisions to regulatory or other governmental bodies so they, rather than the elected leaders who made the decision, have to impose the losses and shoulder the blame. Cuts or unpopular decisions can be passed to local or regional governments to make. Military chiefs can be asked to shrink their budget but are given discretion over where the axe should fall, diverting attention to those decisions. In a similar manner, long-term policies could be passed to a low profile agency for implementation in the hope that they remain below the radar or, if they do become contentious, politicians are left with a plausible deniability strategy.

The next option is *manipulating perceptions*. Obfuscation of the damaging implications of long-term policy changes is an option and, for example, is quite common in taxation policy. Another option is to clearly identify a scapegoat for long-term decisions that have short-term unpopular consequences. Useful targets here include previous governments and their failings (look at the deficit, lack of infrastructure, divided society, etc. they left us). International forces or organisations or markets that can be presented as offering no choice but to make painful long-term decisions are another option. Or perhaps one section of society can be the scapegoat, such as migrants, the unemployed or bankers. Another option for getting to 'there is no alternative' is to get cross-interest or cross-party support for what you are doing. The rhetoric of the UK's coalition government in its first year 2010/2011 made heavy use of that line (Taylor-Gooby and Stoker, 2011). The Labour government from the mid-2000s onwards developed a policy for a long-term shift to using a greater proportion of nuclear power as part of the energy mix in the UK – a policy that carried considerable political dangers given the financial and safety fears created by nuclear power – but deliberately sought to buy the, then, main opposition party into the process by involving its shadow minister in decisions, meetings and conferences in developing the policy (Baker and Stoker, 2011, 2012).

The final option open to political leaders seeking to justify short-term losses for long-term gains involves *manipulating pay-offs*. One option is to try to share the pain as widely as possible. Another is to concentrate it on particular citizens who, for some reason, will not fight back. Another option is to give compensation to those who might be particularly prone to protest or exempt them from some of the worst effects of the long-term policy. When shifting the basis of a pension's policy over the long-term those coming up to pension age may lose fewer benefits; while those a long way from retirement may face the full force of the change but feel less immediate angst and therefore be less likely to mobilise against the policy.

It is important to recognise that, just as proponents of long-term policies can use some of the strategies identified, so too can opponents; using variations of the tactics to undermine long-term policy options (Pal and Weaver, 2003): they can work hard to increase the visibility of the policy; they can take on proponents for change in the battle of perceptions; they can extend the scope and range of citizens who notice that they are adversely affected by the policy; above all, they can expose the manipulations by supporters of long-term policy for what they are. The point is that the long-term policy can take its chances in the play of power and politics. It is not a mission impossible.

The stealth depiction of the way democracy works is both an empirical depiction of what is commonplace political practice and is normatively underwritten by claims that it is reasonable for citizens not to pay attention to politics and that as long as elites compete then citizens still have a choice as to whether to go along with long-term policies or move against them. The stealth understanding draws on a long tradition of how democracy does and should work through competing elites, but gives it a particularly strong realpolitik or amoral twist (Stoker, 2012). Manipulation does not guarantee success for long-term policy but it does open up exploitable opportunities and indicates that while myopia is a feature of democratic politics it is a feature that can be addressed by political practices familiar to humankind from before the days of Machiavelli.

The underlying claim of this section is that democratic politics is not an arena in which information and understanding flow freely but is one where claims are subject to manipulation and conflict and during that process long-term policy making is a potential outcome, which undermines claims that myopia is an automatic output from democracy. There are some that argue that this political jousting not only provides a pragmatic way to long-termism but is also a legitimate route. Others may express more doubt. They argue that the inattentiveness of citizens most of the time makes long-termism possible but there is a fragility to approaches that rest on manipulative exploitation of that situation. This morally loaded critique does, however, offer its own formula for raising the prospect of long-term thinking from citizens.

## Citizens are engaged through mechanisms of democratic innovation

Contrary to the idea that smart leaders can get to long-term policy making by manipulating public opinion there is a strong school of thought that suggests that including citizens in decision-making and trusting their judgement is a better way to get the same outcome. The sunshine perspective on democracy (Neblo et al., 2010) is one which favours greater engagement of citizens through mechanisms of democratic innovation and points to another path to long-termism. Democracy needs the sunshine of more public debate, shared information, mechanisms of accountability and openness to citizen engagement. Again, this is a perspective that has a normative position and reflects a long tradition of participative commitment in democratic thinking (Stoker, 2012) but its advocates also argue that there is an empirical base to its claims. From the evidence of this perspective citizens are inattentive because they judge they are powerless, given the dominance of special interests in politics, and if they felt that politics was more open to influence, and if the right mechanisms could be found, then they would engage (Stoker and Hay, 2012). Moreover, implicit in a lot of the arguments for democratic innovations, involving deliberation and decision-making by citizens, is that, given access to information and institutional mechanisms that encourage thinking about issues in an other-regarding manner, a long-term perspective can emerge. Deliberation-inspired democratic innovations could inspire respect for, and focus on, the needs of future generations and not just the concerns of those who can be engaged in a decision in the present (Ekeli, 2009).

Involving citizens to a greater degree, through more deliberative and reflective mechanisms, might be valued as an intrinsic expression of full citizenship[2]. But it might be seen as a route to long-termism because of its impact on the way citizens decide and its legitimating quality. Deliberation claims to have a transformative effect on the way that citizens approach an issue. A combination of information and awareness of the perspective of others encourages more reasoned decision-making and public-spiritedness. Having to publicly defend a position encourages reasonableness and participation over time will foster civic virtues, making citizens more reflective and more willing to think long-term. Deliberation and engagement can also enhance the legitimacy of decisions by involving all those affected by the decision, which matches a widely held sense of fairness and could enhance the 'stickability' of a policy, in the sense that it might be more difficult to overturn if it had been through a process of widespread endorsement.

There are a myriad democratic innovations that have been put into practice which could be bent to the purposes of long-termism (Smith, 2009). For example, referenda on major constitutional issues are often presented as once in a generation decisions that then have to last a generation and the same principle could be applied to some long-term policy making issues. Deliberative fora about climate change and its implications, with detailed evidence about the long-term changes likely to affect individual communities, have been shown to sweep aside positions taken in the inattentive phase of citizens' political practice and although consensus may not emerge a more reasoned debate can occur (Hobson and Niemeyer, 2011). Might such mechanisms be capable of generating a long-term policy perspective and support for short-term sacrifices? It might even be possible to build a future oriented system of checks and balances into political systems, building on the idea put into practice in the Israeli Knesset for a commissioner for future generations (Ekeli, 2009). Perhaps a second chamber elected, as proposed by the UK Coalition government in 2012, with long, non-renewal tenure, would encourage a greater willingness to think in terms of the long-term in decision-making?

None of these democratic innovations can take away from a fundamental feature of politics that there may be significant differences about what constitutes the interests of posterity or, more generally, what the right long-term choice is. The point is that democratic innovations could plausibly get long-termism onto the agenda of policy making. We know from survey evidence that both stealth and sunshine understandings of democracy are widely present among citizens in several established democracies (Stoker and Hay, 2012). What emerges from the discussion of the stealth and sunshine responses is that short-termism present in democratic politics could be addressed whichever understanding is to the fore.

## The conditions for success of long-term policy making: issues, institutional forms and cultural factors

Any strategy for long-term policy making is likely to involve some mix of the ingredients identified above. A long-term policy programme would need the buy-in of a range of organised interests and some mix of presentational and engagement strategies aimed at citizens. This section explores the conditions under which a successful long-term policy is likely to emerge and investigates how that might reflect the nature of the issue in contention, cultural factors, including trust in government, and the institutional environment for decision-making.

### Issues: sources of conflict

The construction of long-term policy making does not require the taking away of the very rationale of politics. It does not require the removal of conflict. Consensus is not essential. Rather, what is essential is the political capacity to manage conflict. Conflict between interests is not an inherently undermining factor as far as long-term policy making is concerned. A never-ending series of conflicts is characteristic of established democracies and market societies, and these conflicts can be managed as long as they are divisible, that is conflicts over actors getting more or less. Such conflicts lend themselves to compromise and the art of politics. Although they are never resolved 'once and for all' the goal of long-term policy making is to extend the time horizons of the policy area as much as possible and keep future negotiation to matters of detailed implementation rather than first principles.

What can be disabling to long-termism and a cause of failure is conflict where the issue is not divisible. Conflicts which are driven by matters of religion, race, language or ideology, which have an 'either–or' character, present considerable difficulties (Hirschman, 1995: chapter 20). They are not inherently irresolvable but, insofar as they figure strongly, they are likely to make the politics of long-termism more problematic. The issues at stake in the field of economics tend to be more divisible and, as a result, make it more possible to manage short-term sacrifice for long-term gain in this arena. Value or identity based conflicts may create decisions that are unbridgeable, but material issues may be more open to give and take or can, perhaps, be more effectively constructed as positive sum rather than zero sum games, in which everyone gains something in the end.

Pal and Weaver (2003) identify different categories of loss imposition. Some may be framed as conflicts between groups where a deal can be cut or where participants are not strong enough to block the loss. Losses imposed on one group are driven by a combination of deal making and the power dynamic in operation. Another category is geographically concentrated loss, such as closing a particular factory or military base, where the key is to contain the conflict to the local arena. Value-based conflicts and issues, which involve threats to ways of life, are undoubtedly the most problematic to manage because government will find it difficult to compensate losers, for example by 'splitting the difference' or compensating losses in some way. If your position is that something should be a social norm you are unlikely to be persuaded that it is OK for you to follow the norm and for others to ignore it. Long-term policy making is therefore easier over some issues than others.

## Culture: trust and complexity

Political strategies, whether of the manipulative or deliberative variety, associated with long-termism also require that if the government asks for some sacrifices in the short-term that future benefits are viewed as credible. Given that acceptance of the policy and its delivery inevitably take place non-simultaneously there has to be some belief that what the government says it will do, it will do. There are two tests involved. A test of good faith, can the government be trusted? And a test of capacity, can the government do what it says? Beyond that there may be an element of a leap of faith, where lack of sufficient evidence means that there is no reason to take a chance but a commitment still emerges.

Let us assume that citizens, like other decision-makers, are inclined to be short-term in their policy orientations, such an assumption would be consistent with the presence of bounded rationality in decision-making. All things being equal citizens prefer short-term to long-term pay offs. A rare study (Jacobs and Matthews, 2012) has explored what it is that drives short-termism. Using an experimental design to test responses among citizens to a range of long-term policy options Jacobs and Matthews found that it was not so much impatience or a desire to smooth out consumption that drove interest in short-termism, rather it was that citizens do not trust government or doubt its ability to actually deliver, even if its commitment was genuine. In the absence of these factors citizens would be left to reason with a leap of faith and say, for example, that for reasons of solidarity or because we are all in this together we will make a commitment to long-termism despite any real sense that success will occur. The spirit of 'I would rather die in a ditch with you than live without you' is a motto that might be embraced in families and communities and could provide a base for long-termism, but how can it be conjured up?

Long-termism demands, then, what the political culture in many established democracies conspicuously appears to lack: trust in the good faith of government to keep its promises and its word and trust in the competence of government to deal with the complexities of delivery in the context of long-term policy. Beyond that a capacity to trigger a leap of faith that would enable citizens and organisations to commit to a long-term approach is, in much of modern governance, a scarce commodity. While the tractable nature of the issues embedded in economic policy, perhaps, lend themselves to long-termism it would appear that the political culture to provide a context for trust and credibility is likely to be harder to deliver. Again, the argument here is that the prospects for long-term policy making are contingent and not predeterminately doomed. Creating a political culture supportive of long-termism requires a sense that governments in future can and will deliver. It is a major obstacle to overcome but a challenge that could be met with a successful political strategy.

### Institutions: devolved decision-making

To consider the range of institutional factors that might support a politics of the long-term would require far more space and detailed empirical understanding than is available to this author. Instead, in this section I concentrate on one general issue which emerges as an important dividing line in the literature (Jacobs, 2008; Pal and Weaver, 2003): whether centralised or decentralised governance systems are better at long-termism?

The case for central control would appear to be that decision-makers can: be insulated to some degree from a range of competing forces;

develop a shared vision of what needs to be done; and have the capacity to provide the resources, legal instruments and administration necessary for the delivery of long-term policy. A centralised system is less easily blown off course. The case for a devolved system is that when power is shared citizens and organisations are more inclined to accept the demands of others and accommodate themselves to some losses in the hope of future gains.

As Jacobs (2008: 219) argues 'the likelihood of policy investment should rise as it becomes more difficult for social groups to redistribute their long-run burdens'. He explores the case of developing long-term reforms to pension plans, where a centralised decision-making environment with a strong leader and strong executive government under Mrs Thatcher made less progress than the checks and balances, multi-veto system of the United States. In the UK close ties between organised interests and the government led to the lay-off of costs on to other interests with less access and influence. In the United States the greater dispersal of power meant that a more radical long-term policy became possible. Other evidence (Pal and Weaver, 2003) suggests that the relative advantages of centralised systems in redirecting pain is mixed, so the argument for a dispersed form of institutional power as a better context for long-termism is not conclusive but it should be enough to challenge the assumption that long-termism requires a form of benign dictatorship and that it may, on the contrary, demand a form of considered devolution of power.

In building the arguments for dispersing previously developed power I would argue that local and regional government may have a particular role in promoting long-termism for the reason that it is an expression of dispersed but often relatively stable representative politics (because electoral competition is often more limited given the concentration of preferences and interests in different populations). Long-term policies and long-term coalitions of support, especially around the issue of economic development, have been a feature of local politics for some time. Local government is free to use both manipulative and deliberative strategies for reaching out to citizens and can appeal to local identity and community as a basis for 'leap of faith' partnerships with both citizens and organised interests. Add to these considerations that local government tends to be seen as more trustworthy than central government (Stoker, 2011), at least in the UK, and might also be seen as a more competent long-term deliverer, and the case for local and/or a regional institutional lead on long-termism becomes stronger.

## Conclusions: the politics of long-term growth strategies in the UK

The politics that came to prominence in the consumer boom era is ill-equipped to deliver the political strategies that might be associated with economic recovery. Progressive economic growth strategies based on a search for a more effective and sustainable alternative growth model demand long-term politics. This chapter argues that long-termism is not some kind of mission impossible for modern democratic government. But it will require a different politics and the challenge of renewing and reshaping politics will need to be grappled with, just as much as the development of new economic policies and practices.

Politics does have a remarkable capacity to deliver in extremely difficult circumstances. The play of power and the effective manipulation of information, the tools of persuasion and the forging of alliances gives politics a creative dynamic that some analysts overlook. For those who favour a more radical economic redirection the challenge of designing a matching politics is considerable and remains to be met. The challenges presented by institutional inertia and path dependency and the power of vested interests[3] would have to be met if the old economic model was going to be replaced by a substantially new one, but a clear political strategy for delivery would aid in that process. This chapter has identified at least some of the paths that might need to be followed. Key mechanisms for reinstating a politics for the long-term could be: one, a greater emphasis on deliberative dialogue with citizens; two, a capacity to link with organised interests focused on delivering economic growth; and three, an institutionalised power sharing giving a much wider role to local and regional government in developing long-term economic policies for growth. Some or all of these mechanisms have been present in Britain in the past and are present in other countries. In short, the politics of the long-term is not about a utopian ambition but about delivering an effective political strategy.

So, what would help in the delivery of the conditions for a long-term strategy for growth? First, what is required is a rebalancing of the nature of the dialogue between political elites and citizens; too often all the latter get are sound bites, headline grabbing initiatives that lack substance, and various forms of grandstanding. A more deliberative dialogue with citizens does not necessarily involve abandoning the cut and thrust of modern politics, but it does mean using all the means available to the political system to create space for more reflective debate. Just as over the issue of climate change some progress on these issues has been made so an effective political strategy for growth needs to find its platforms. These could include: multiple parliamentary committee investigations into long-term concerns; it may mean bringing more attention to the fore-sight activities already undertaken by governments; and active funding of third sector organisations to launch local versions of these debates to get citizens online and offline thinking long-term. This chapter begins the process of identifying the structure and form of such a strategy in the context of a democratic polity that is flawed but not without hope.

Second, long-termism means embracing localism. There are signs that across the political spectrum more lip service is being paid to the potential role of city regions (Hildreth and Bailey, 2013), but more ambitions for localism would be more radical still. I think that long-term policy making requires a dramatic break from the centralised decision-making that pervades the British system. We need powerful and democratically acceptable city region government that has the finance raising powers for the job of developing the different niche economies of their area to their full potential. What is good enough for London government should be the basic starting point of what is required elsewhere. Beyond that we need a much less London-centric vision of our economic future and we need to free and support the city regions of the North to rebalance our economy. So, long-termism is not about special deals for cities set up by a controlling central government, it is about recognising that a full scale institutional devolution in England is essential for long-term economic growth policies. Matched, of course, by substantial devolved capacity in Wales, Northern Ireland and Scotland.

By shifting the political culture and institutional framework for policy making, long-termism becomes less of a pipe dream and more of an achievable reality. At that point the play of politics can kick in and will determine the success or failure of the ambition for a long-term focus on economic growth. The analysis presented here is not that long-termism can be guaranteed, but that it has more potential for delivery than the naysayers suggest if the right context is created. Politicians will need to do their politics and organised interests will have to choose long-term benefit over short-term gain and if that dynamic is created then a long-term and sustainable economic growth is not a forlorn hope but an achievable target.

## Notes

The chapter draws on research funded by the UK's ESRC (RES-000–22-4441) undertaken by teams from Sheffield and Southampton Universities and the Hansard Society.

1. Potlach is a festival of giving.
2. The discussion below draws on Ekeli (2009).
3. All these challenges are identified in Gamble (2011).

# References

Alt, James E. and David Dreyer Transparency (2006) 'Political Polarization, and Political Budget Cycles in OECD Countries', *American Journal of Political Science*, 50, 3, 530–550.

Anderson, V. (2011) 'Addressing Short-termism in Government and Politics', *The Guardian*, 2 May 2011, available at http://www.guardian.co.uk/sustainable-business/government-politics-short-termism-unsustainability Downloaded 16 June 2012.

Baker, K. and Gerry S. (2011) '*Metagovernance* and the UK Nuclear Industry: A Limiting Case' in J. Torfing and P. Triankafillou (eds), *Interactive Policy Making, Metagovernance and Democracy*. Colchester: ECPR Press.

Baker, K. and Stoker, G. (2012) 'Governance and Nuclear Power: Why Governing is Easier Said than Done', *Political Studies*, 61, 3, 580–598.

Cloughterty, Tom (2011) *Tackling Short-termism*, The Adam Smith Institute, Wednesday 3 August 2011. Available at http://www.adamsmith.org/blog/tax-and-economy/tackling-short-termism Downloaded 16 June 2012.

Ekeli, Kristian (2009) 'Constitutional Experiments: Representing Future Generations Through Submajority Rules', *The Journal of Political Philosophy*, 17, 4, 440–461.

Gamble, Andrew (2011) *Economic Futures*, New Paradigms in Public Policy, The British Academy, 20 September 2011.

Hibbing, John R. and Elizabeth Theiss-Morse (2002) *Stealth Democracy: Americans' Beliefs about How Government Should Work*. Cambridge: Cambridge University Press.

Hildreth, P. and Bailey, D. (2013) 'The Economics Behind the Move to Localism', *Cambridge Journal of Regions, Economy and Society*, advanced access.

Hirschman, A. (1995) *A Propensity to Self-Subversion*. Cambridge, Massachusetts: Harvard University Press.

Hobson, K. and Niemeyer, S. (2011) 'Public Responses to Climate Change: The Role of Deliberation in Building Capacity for Adaptive Action', *Global Environmental Change*, 21, 3, 957–971.

Jacobs, A. (2008) 'The Politics of When: Redistribution, Investment and Policy Making for the Long Term', *British Journal of Political Science*, 38, 193–220.

Jacobs, A. and S. J. Matthews (2012) 'Why Do Citizens Discount the Future? Public Opinion and the Timing of Policy Consequences', *British Journal of Political Science*, 42, 4, 903–935.

Lindblom, Charles (1977) *Politics and Markets: The World's Political-Economic Systems*. New York: Basic.

Neblo, M., K. Esterling, R. Kennedy, D. Lazer and A. Sokhey (2010) 'Who Wants to Deliberate – And Why?' *American Political Science Review*, 104, 3, 566–583.

Nordhaus, W. D. (1975) 'The Political Business Cycle', *Review of Economic Studies*, 42, 2, 169–190.

Pal, L. A. and K. R. Weaver (2003) *The Government Taketh Away. The Politics of Pain in the United States and Canada.* Washington: Georgetown University Press.

Plant, R. (2004) 'Neo-liberalism and the Theory of the State: from *Wohlfahrtsstaat* to *Rechtsstaat*', *The Political Quarterly*, 75, s1, 24–37.

Smith, G. (2009) *Democratic Innovations.* Cambridge: Cambridge University Press.

Stoker, G. (1995) 'Regime Theory and Urban Politics', in D. Judge, G. Stoker and H. Wolman (eds), *Theories of Urban Politics.* London: Sage Publications.

Stoker, G. (2006) *Why Politics Matters.* Basingstoke: Palgrave Macmillan.

Stoker, G. (2011) 'Anti-Politics in Britain', in R. Heffernan, P. Cowley and C. Hay (eds), *Developments in British Politics: Nine.* Basingstoke: Palgrave Macmillan.

Stoker, Gerry (2012) *Building a New Politics?* London: British Academy. Available at http://www.britac.ac.uk/policy/Building_a_new_politics.cfm

Stoker, G. and Hay, C. (2012) 'Comparing Folk Theories of Democratic Politics: Stealth and Sunshine', PSA (UK) Annual Conference, Belfast, 3–5April 2012. Available at http://www.psa.ac.uk/journals/pdf/5/2012/10_144.pdf

Taylor-Gooby, P. and Stoker, G. (2011) The Coalition Programme: A New Vision for Britain or Politics as Usual? *The Political Quarterly*, 82, 1, 4–15.

# 5
# Public Policy Futures: A Left Trilemma?

*Peter Taylor-Gooby*

Why is it so hard for the Left to produce a coherent and progressive response to the crisis, when markets and private enterprise have so obviously failed? One answer is that the Left faces a trilemma in public policy: it must respond adequately to the economic crisis to be seen as competent; it must address the established themes in public opinion to be electable; and it must develop generous and inclusive policies to be progressive. This chapter identifies conflicts in all three areas where low public sector productivity growth and demographic shifts tighten already harsh spending constraints. Entrenched public suspicions of higher taxes for any but the distant rich and a public discourse which makes rigid distinctions between those deserving and undeserving of state welfare conflict with egalitarian or redistributive policies. Most Left strategies include higher public spending and more equal social provisions, but public opinion rejects both tax rises and greater generosity to the poor of working age. The Coalition strategy, by contrast, rests on private enterprise-led recovery, work ethic values and policies that exclude less deserving groups. It does not face the same problems. This chapter analyses a range of policy programmes suggested by commentators on the Left in the light of these points. It concludes that a progressive strategy must draw on multiple themes, and must seek to shift public discourse in a more supportive direction.

The first section reviews the economic pressures, the current Coalition government's strategy and the constraints on future policy directions. The second section considers the difficulties in reconciling more progressive policies with some of the themes in public opinion and with patterns of political support for the Left. The third section reviews various proposals for developing a feasible, progressive and electable social policy programme. In the fourth we conclude that there is no simple overarching strategy and that any programme will need to build solidarity gradually by representing more and more groups among those seen as members of society who make a real contribution and are not responsible for their own vulnerability.

## Economic pressures: current challenges and future-proofing

The Coalition government's cuts from the 2010 Emergency Budget onwards can be looked at in two ways. On the one hand, the 2010 programme, and its extension in the 2011Autumn Statement to 2016–2017 in view of a weak economic performance, represents the largest and most precipitate cuts in public and social spending at least since the Geddes Axe in 1921–1922 (HM Treasury, 2011: 1–2). Various commentators argue that it will increase poverty (Brewer et al., 2011) and homelessness (Fitzpatrick et al., 2011), unfairly damage opportunities for women (WBG, 2011; Cooper, 2011), exert further pressures on the 'squeezed middle' (Whittaker, 2012), severely undermine the NHS (BMA, 2012), erode public health provision and weaken child and elder care services (Yeates et al., 2011).

On the other hand, it is also true that the cutbacks simply return spending close to the overall post-war trend level of slightly below 40 per cent of GDP (Gamble, 2011; Gough, 2011). Indeed, the sharpest departure from the post-war trend was the 2001–2010 increase to 47 per cent under Labour. Another way of looking at it is to point out that Labour plans in their May 2010 budget accepted cutbacks to stabilise public spending but limited their extent, applied them more gradually and recouped more of the deficit through taxation (HM Treasury May, 2010). The Coalition's 2010 plan simply takes spending levels (though not the distribution of spending) to where they would have been under Labour's 2007–2008 plans by 2010–2011, but does so four years later (Hills, 2012).

Both these viewpoints are compelling. The recession and sluggish growth cost the UK at least 6 per cent of GDP between 2007 and 2011, compared with what might have been achieved if the previous trajectory had continued. On the Office of Budgetary Responsibility November 2011 projections, growth will not return to 2007 levels until 2016–2017 (OBR, 2011: chart 1.1). By then, output will be some 13 per cent below what had been predicted in 2006 (IFS, 2012: 74). The response to the recession cost real money in spending on unemployed people, bailouts and 'quantitative easing' (Gough, 2011a: 53–56). Any plans must accommodate the dual pressures of fewer resources and extra spending. This implies measures to stimulate growth, cuts in public spending and increases in taxation. The problem of adequacy under these circumstances can speedily be made more onerous by including three further considerations: demographic pressures; low state sector productivity growth; and rising inequalities. A fourth concern, the cost of managing climate change (Sterne, 2006; Gough, 2011a), is omitted from this discussion.

### The long-term

The OBR Fiscal Sustainability Report (OBR, 2011b) attempts to project future government spending and revenues over a fifty-year period. Such projections are subject to considerable uncertainty, since it is impossible to predict growth, interest rates, economic and productivity growth, migration and other factors with any certainty. A number of different scenarios under differing assumptions are developed. The basic finding is that 'public finances are likely to come under pressure over the longer-term, principally as a result of an ageing population ... Government would have to spend more ... on ... pensions and healthcare. But the same demographic trends would leave government revenue roughly stable.' (2011b: 3) The central (and optimistic) assumption (Figure 5.1) shows that the 8 per cent gap between spending and revenue in 2010–2011 is

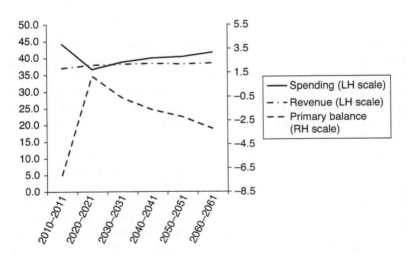

*Figure 5.1*   OBR central long-term projection: spending, revenue and balance (as per cent of GDP)

removed by 2020–2021 as a result of stringent cuts that bring spending as a proportion of GDP to 1998 levels, assuming a return to pre-crisis growth. Spending then returns to long-term trend levels and the balance deteriorates, with a gap of 0.6 per cent of GDP in 2030–2031 widening to 3.2 per cent by 2060–2061. This implies net borrowing of 7.7 per cent of GDP and a debt of 107 per cent of GDP (calculated from OBR, 2011b: table 3.6).

Three points should be noted. First, the report generally assumes current Coalition plans will be realised, except that short-term benefits will be uprated by earnings rather than CPI, the latter being the current policy. Maintaining CPI uprating would cut spending by about 1.6 per cent by 2030–2031, with further cumulative savings (OBR, 2011b: Annex C, 32). This would resolve the problems of the spending gap, at severe cost to very poor people, by reducing benefits for those of working age by about 14 per cent compared with general inflation and nearly three times that compared with projected earnings (OBR, 2011b: Annex C, 34).

## Productivity

Second, the projections assume real improvements in productivity across the public sector in line with those in the rest of the economy. If such improvements are not achieved and public sector workers do not have their pay cut compared to others (perhaps through privatisations), the real cost of maintaining standards in the public sector, and the proportion of GDP it absorbs, rises (OBR, 2011b: Annex D, 39–40). Productivity is hard to measure in the public sector, mainly because outputs include qualitative as well as quantitative aspects (for example the dignity with which patients are treated as well as the mortality rate). Improvements have proved very hard to achieve (Judd, 2011). NHS productivity has fluctuated between 1996 and 2009, with a very slight net fall, mainly due to increases in the drugs bill and staff pay (Hardie et al., 2011). For education, productivity also fluctuated, mainly due to changes in the school population, but it has shown no overall improvement (Ayoubkhani et al., 2010). More recently, efforts to improve productivity have redoubled. A drive to generate 4.4 per cent annual savings between 2010 and 2015 for reinvestment and to meet spending pressures has so far achieved cost-efficiencies at about half that rate, half of which are not permanent (HoC Public Accounts Committee, 2011; HoC Health Committee, 2012).

The NHS is probably a particularly difficult area in which to achieve cost-efficiencies because standards are so politically salient, high-skilled staff are needed and other costs, such as drugs and medical technology, may also rise. An alternative possibility analysed by OBR considers NHS productivity rising at 1 per cent below the whole economy. This would require a further 1.7 per cent of GDP to be directed to health care spending by 2030–2031 and an extra 5 per cent by 2060–2061 to maintain standards.

These points make clear that there is considerable uncertainty in the public spending predictions, but that real pressures are likely to continue beyond the current period of austerity. Adjustments to spending in such areas as pensions, bus passes, fuel allowances and military procurement, and to revenue in energy taxes, vehicle duties, inheritance and capital taxes are possible (see for example Glennerster, 2011, PST, 2020). The problems, which are likely to emerge over a half-century when it is hoped real growth will have returned, are not insuperable. However, a progressive programme, which does not envisage the kind of cuts in living standards for working age claimers and state sector workers with which the current government implicitly plans to balance the books, and which expects to achieve real improvements in health care and else-where, must respond to these pressures.

One further point, current policies involve a profound restructuring of public provision which requires extra upfront spending and addi-tional longer-term commitments (Taylor-Gooby, 2012). Would it be possible to square the triangle of rising demand, diminished resources and weakened capacity to meet needs by directing cutbacks differently? The Government provides estimates in relation to NHS reform of £1.7bn (rejected by the HoC Health Committee, 2011: para 92, who suggested a figure closer to £3bn, see also Walshe, 2010). The universal credit reforms are estimated at £3bn by OBR (2011b: 65) and the student loan system at 30 per cent of loans written off, or about £3bn at current prices (OBR, 2011b: 70). Plans simply assume that restructuring will deliver NHS efficiency savings faster than ever before and that benefit reforms will increase employment. For student loans, spending will not be recouped within the 30-year time-horizon examined, and possibly never. However, these sums amount to less than 0.3 per cent of public spending annually over the period, but abandoning the plans, however unhelpful they are, would not resolve the problem. In any case, the Coalition is pursuing these restructurings in order to embed and make permanent the current cuts. Axing them might be seen to risk an increase in spending.

### Inequality

Society has grown more unequal during the last three decades (NEP, 2010: S3; Atkinson et al., 2011). The distribution of income and wealth seems likely to fan out further. The modest post-war trend towards greater equality of opportunity may well be in reverse (Blanden and Machin, 2007). These points matter, because greater inequality appears to reduce willingness to support social provision, because of the impact on the interests of advantaged groups and on social values: those who hold the majority of resources are better able to meet their own needs privately and have less interest in provision for the poor (Horton and Gregory, 2009); inequality undermines collective solidarity and public trust in state institutions (Uslaner, 2008). Progressive social policies will have more to do, with less public support.

A helpful analysis distinguishes the trend to greater fanning-out of income for the mass of the population (as better-off groups improve their position relative to the median, while that of lower-income groups deteriorates) from the trend of small very rich minorities to gain large relative improvements (Bailey, 2011). The first trend seems to apply to most developed countries during the past three decades, the latter is more a feature of the Anglo-Saxon world, most notably of the US and the UK (Atkinson, 2007). Public policy in the UK appears to have arrested the deterioration of the relative position of those at the bottom during the early and mid-2000s (Hills et al., 2009: 28). How easy it will be to pursue similar strategies in the future is unclear.

Overall, the general tenor of debate is that there are likely to be real but not insuperable additional costs to maintaining welfare standards, even when stable growth returns. Current estimates of those costs are, if anything, on the low side. This raises the bar for any attempts to develop a more progressive policy approach than that pursued by the government. Policies which are both realistic and progressive must avoid the damage of the current cuts, which bear very heavily on those least able to cope. They must take into account the real resource losses outlined in the first paragraph. They must set a course that will meet needs in the longer-term at least as well as they are met at present, and do so in a way that resists the shift to greater inequality. They cannot rely on assumptions about sharp improvements in the cost-efficiency of the restructured services.

## Further constraints: political feasibility and social progressivity

There are at least three further criteria for progressive policies.[1] First, any reform programme must mobilise support from voters. The recent debate between those who believed Labour in 2010 may have alienated traditional working class voters (Glasman et al., 2011; Clarke and Gardner, 2011; Scholes et al,, 2011) and those who stress the importance of retaining middle class support (Radice and Diamond, 2010; Philpott, 2011) strengthens this concern. Second, an electable programme needs to reflect at least some of the main directions in public opinion and must fit within the parameters of discourse established by the UK media and by opinion leaders. Third, it must be capable of development in a way that leads public opinion in a progressive direction, understood as inclusive and generous. Principles of social justice and equality provide a normative yardstick for left policy-making, but are prone to controversy. The focus on inclusivity and generosity covers areas which are likely to be part of any left idea of social justice and should be seen as realistic.

## Traditional vs. aspirational Labour voters

Middle class Labour voters are often seen as more aspirational and concerned with greater opportunities, while the core working class values basic public services and policies to address inequalities, but at the same time strongly endorses work ethic distinctions between deserving and undeserving groups. New Labour succeeded in attracting votes from both middle and working class people from 1997. In 2010 support declined among most social groups. One interpretation of election polls supports the view that the loss of support was most marked among semi and unskilled working class voters (Miliband, 2010: 56–57, see Radice and Diamond, 2010 for a detailed statement of this view). Prominent commentators (Gann, 2011: 143–144; Whitty, 2011: 25–26) refer to statistics from Ipsos MORI which show a striking collapse of support among the groups most likely to vote Labour in 2005: an 11 per cent fall among C2s (skilled manual workers) and 8 per cent among the semi and unskilled DE core working class group. However, these statistics are generated by amalgamating all Ipsos MORI polls taken during the six-week campaign period to produce a combined sample of 10,000 (Table 5.1). They may reflect events at different stages in the campaign, the changing contexts in which questions were asked and the problems of mixing and reweighting poll data. It is noteworthy than a second Ipsos MORI poll taken after the election and given in alternate columns of Table 5.1 in italics, shows a different picture: the collapse in Labour support was about half that estimated in the widely-quoted combined polls among the DE group and more evenly spread across middle class AB and C1 higher, intermediate and junior managerial and professional groups. Labour voters in the C2 group are often the focus of concerns about how well Labour appeals to 'aspiring' people on lower to middle

*Table 5.1* Ipsos MORI combined pre-election and post-election poll statistics

| | Con | | Lab | | Lib Dem | |
|---|---|---|---|---|---|---|
| | Pre-election combined | *Post-election* | Pre-election combined | *Post-election* | Pre-election combined | *Post-election* |
| AB | 39 (+2) | *40 (+3)* | 26 (−2) | *23 (−5)* | 29 (0) | *31 (+2)* |
| C1 | 39 (+2) | *40 (+3)* | 28 (−4) | *28 (−4)* | 24 (+1) | *28 (+5)* |
| C2 | 37 (+4) | *25 (−8)* | 29 (−11) | *39 (−1)* | 22 (+3) | *28 (+9)* |
| DE | 31 (+6) | *29 (+4)* | 40 (−8) | *42 (−6)* | 17 (−1) | *22 (+4)* |

*Notes:*
1. Change since 2005 in brackets
2. Pre-election combined amalgamates all Ipsos MORI polls between 19.3.10 and 5.5.10 (10, 211 adults). http://www.ipsos-mori.com/researchpublications/researcharchive/poll.aspx?oItemId=2613
3. Post-election: 12–13 May national survey (1023 adults) http://www.ipsos-mori.com/Assets/Docs/Polls/NoTW%20Post%20Election_website.pdf

incomes. Support among this group fell by only 1 per cent as against the 11 per cent shown in the earlier combined surveys.

The poll figures are not conclusive, but indicate that concerns about alienating either middle or working class Labour supporters may be exaggerated. This is confirmed in the available analyses of the academic 2010 British Election Survey: 'those in the "working class" (supervisors and manual occupations) were slightly more likely to vote Labour... the decline [between 2005 and 2010] was no larger among manual than among routine non-manual and professional workers' (Johnston and Pattie, 2011: 287–288).

### Compatibility with public discourse

Quantitative and qualitative attitude studies and analyses of media discourse point to five general patterns in public opinion:

- First, some groups and some service areas are more highly valued than others (Van Oorschott, 2000). There appear to be two main dimensions to this division, between mass and minority provision (the NHS, pensions and education vs. working age benefits and social housing) and, of particular importance, between provision for deserving as against undeserving groups, favouring those who are not responsible for their dependence on benefits (children, disabled people) or those with demonstrable commitment to a work or family ethic (Curtice, 2010: 26; van Oorschott, 2006). As Tepe-Belfrage points out (this volume), recent cuts to benefits and services for women and children raise important questions of desert.

- Second, reciprocity emerges as a theme in much analysis, favouring as deserving those who are seen to make a contribution in return for entitlement (Mau, 2004; Mau and Veghte, 2007).
- Third, there is support for redistribution from rich to worse off, but it diminishes as the threshold of wealth is brought closer to average incomes (Sefton, 2005; Hills, 2004: 32–35; Bamfield and Horton, 2009; Orton and Rowlingson, 2007).
- Fourth, most people fail to make any link between the capacity of government to finance public spending and the tax that they and others pay. When pressed they tend to suggest that efficiency savings can reconcile better services with lower taxes (Taylor-Gooby and Hastie, 2002).
- Fifth, poverty is consistently understood in absolute and minimal rather than relative terms (Hills, 2001).

In addition to these five directions identified in attitude surveys, a sixth current idea is also relevant. This is to do with a growing sense of disillusionment with, or distrust of, the state and the public sector (Taylor-Gooby, 2009: chapters 6 & 7). It emerges in the growing political disengagement termed 'anti-politics' (Stoker, 2006; Hay, 2007). These points indicate difficulties in promoting an inclusive and generous programme. They also imply real opportunities. The fourth point makes it hard to address inequalities as opposed to basic need, and the first is particularly powerful in limiting the scope of progressive policy. The second and third constrain the capacity to raise revenues and to redistribute, leading to a policy bias towards cutbacks that is strengthened by concerns about the deficit. The fifth creates further difficulties in marshalling support for progressive change.

The opportunities lie in the possibility that, because the boundaries of deservingness are vague, the notion may be expanded to cover a broad range of needs (point one), that the possible linkage of entitlement to contribution legitimates contribution-based policies (point two) and that growing inequalities may strengthen the appeal of redistribution (point three). The task of developing policies to cope with continuing pressures will be easier if basic trust in government returns (point six). The uncertainty over election polls adds to these concerns. The more commentators emphasise a distinctive collapse of core working class support, the more they are inclined to place weight on the issues of desert (point one) and of tax resistance (point three).

## Leading in a progressive direction

As well as gaining public acceptance, progressive policies must help lead the way people understand welfare towards more inclusive and generous provision. Inclusiveness relates to the identification of net recipients and net givers and to reciprocity between them. A strong tradition in social psychology (Tajfel, 1978) and sociology (for example, Parkin's exclusionary theory, 1979) stresses the power of in-group and out-group cleavages. To overcome these barriers, services should endeavour to include as many as possible and should seek to ensure greater recognition of the needs and capacities of others. Complementary work in social anthropology (Mauss, 1922, republished 1990), political science (Ostrom and Walker, 1997), decision theory (Gintis et al., 2005: chapter 1) and social policy (Titmuss, 1970) demonstrates the importance of reciprocity in social relationships. This may strengthen links between those able to help each other, but confirm divisions between those engaged and those defined as non-contributors.

Generosity concerns recognition of need and willingness to address it. Analysis of opinion surveys and media discourse indicates a shift in the established pattern of greater generosity in hard times occurring about 2007–2008. Figure 5.2 shows that for most of the 1990s and early 2000s agreement with the statement that 'benefits for unemployed people are too low and cause hardship' from British Social Attitudes surveys, and media references to 'scroungers' tended to mirror unemployment rates. Higher unemployment was associated with greater concern about benefit levels and fewer references to scroungers. However, the tendency to greater punitiveness across the period of declining unemployment appears to continue as unemployment starts to rise after 2007. Whether this is simply an attitudinal lag or indicates a secular shift in attitudes is currently unclear. If it is the former, public opinion may move slowly to accept greater redistribution as need increases. If the latter, the current campaign to label claimers as undeserving will have produced a real shift in attitudes, creating further problems for progressives.

Figure 5.3 shows a similar pattern in relation to poverty. A substantial majority believe that inequality is too great, although this view has declined slightly during the past decade just as inequalities increased. The view that government should spend more on the poor, however, shows a continuing downward trend (with a brief fluctuation in the early 2000s) despite the fact that poverty levels increased sharply after 2006 and are set to increase further in the future. This reinforces the evidence that those most harshly affected by labour market and social changes

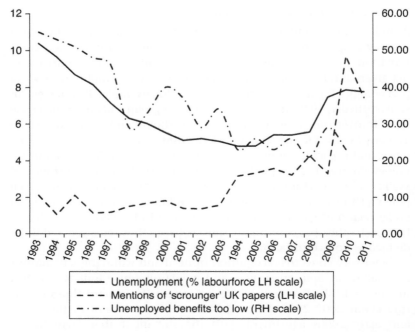

*Figure 5.2* Unemployment as percentage of labour force (WEO harmonised rates), media discourse (Nexis) and benefit generosity (BSA)

**BSA Question:** 'Which of these two statements comes closest to your own view...benefits for unemployed people are too low and cause hardship, OR benefits for unemployed people are too high and discourage them from finding jobs?' Data is percentage choosing the first option. **Media Discourse** is measured as the number of mentions each year in UK National Newspapers of the word 'scroungers' divided by 100.

and now by the austerity programme receive little public sympathy. This makes the task of establishing generous and inclusive welfare harder.

## Current proposals

Current proposals for progressive reform may conveniently be divided between those who operate at a macro-level, directed at reform of the economic system or the social structure as a whole, and micro-level reforms, concerned with improving the lives of individual citizens.

### Macro-level

At the macro-level the main themes are to do with slowing or deferring cutbacks to maintain the level of demand and to expand infrastructure

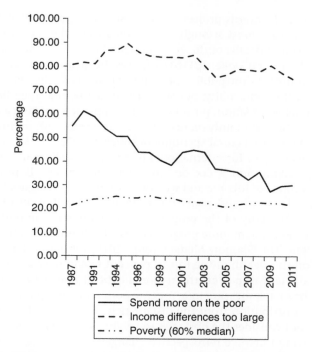

*Figure 5.3* Views on incomes differences and spending on the poor and the level of poverty (BSA)

spending, especially on environmentally friendly projects and tax reform. All the programmes that include a macroeconomic element mention these themes with different degrees of emphasis (see Dolphin, 2011). The underlying concern is to create the conditions for real growth. The Coalition argues that private enterprise will generate growth provided intervention is limited. Progressives follow Keynes in pointing to a major role for the state during the downswing of the economic cycle, although they differ on the extent of intervention during an upswing.

Compass Plan B (2011: 5, 19–24) probably puts the strongest emphasis on the importance of maintaining demand, followed by IPPR (for example Cooke, 2011b), but the theme also emerges in *Red Labour* (Clarke and Gardner, 2011), *Purple Labour* (Philpott, 2011) and *What Next for Labour* (Scholes, 2011). All these programmes include a state investment bank with a bias towards environmentally friendly projects in such areas as energy generation, public transport and home insulation, and towards projects that boost employment. Plan B again develops the case most strongly with estimates of the return on such investments and details of the environmental case. The brief pamphlet *In the Black Labour* (Cooke, 2011b) expresses the greatest concerns about how commitments on public spending will damage electoral perceptions of fiscal responsibility, but supports infrastructural spending. The Social Market Foundation, pursues a similar approach, making a case for further specific cuts mainly on tax reliefs for the better-off, to finance an extra £15bn infrastructural spending (Mulheirn, 2012, 7).

Plan B also argues for international financial regulation and management of banking and a tax on financial transactions. It provides a detailed account of income and wealth inequalities and argues for more progressive taxation and plans for a gradual redistribution of wealth (2011: 22–23). Many of the programmes also stress the importance of making the tax system more progressive but this is not generally worked out in detail. The Glasgow Media Group (2010) estimates that a 20 per cent tax on the wealth of the top 10 per cent would raise some £800bn and be sufficient to pay off the national debt. It points to 80 per cent support for such a measure in a YouGov poll, reflecting public endorsement of redistribution from the distant rich. The plan is briefly stated and does not consider the obstacles to levying such a tax, the extent to which it would involve retrospective changes to legislation in relation to pensions, trusts and other areas and might influence the behaviour of potential payers.

### Micro-level

At the micro-level the range of initiatives is greater. Five major themes may be identified in the debate: social spending as social investment; building social solidarity; responding to the deserving/undeserving distinction; the importance of engaging users directly in service provision; and the logic of pre-distribution as against redistribution. The proposals are set out below and then analysed in more detail.

### Social investment

The clearest and most developed argument for social investment is contained in IPPR work on returns from child-care (Ben-Galim, 2011). This shows a possible return of £20,000 over four years for each woman returning to work after one year's maternity leave, reducing to £5,000 when income figures are based on the pay-rates of women returners rather than workforce averages. In either case the return is impressive. Plan B refers generally to social investment, giving the uncosted examples of obesity reduction and other behavioural changes to reduce pressures on the NHS (Compass, 2011: 32). The returns on investment, for example in improvements to the quality of social housing or in public health, are often diffuse, long-term and dependent on factors outside the state sector. Previous research shows that the most impressive returns on social investments are found in education (Dickson and Smith, 2011), but that it is more difficult to establish a clear picture in other areas.

### Building solidarity

A substantial stream of work on the factors that have contributed to successful redistributive and integrative welfare in the UK, drawing on historical analysis, cross-national comparison and attitude surveys, concludes that welfare policies must be inclusive if they are to succeed in meeting the needs of the poor (Horton and Gregory, 2009: xix). Highly-targeted provision typically fails to enlist the support of the mass of the population and leads to a downward spiral of increasing restriction and exclusion. These authors seek to reconcile commitment to universalism with the realities of deserving/undeserving distinctions through a welfare system that incorporates as many groups as practicably possible. They propose a range of measures, including: a combined housing benefit that incorporates subsidies to all tenure groups and reduces the divisions between them; a merged tax allowance and benefit system which effectively uses tax allowance credits to support lower paid groups; a self-conscious basing of benefit entitlement for working age claimers on social participation (xiii); and real sanctions for claimers who refuse to engage in activities that make a social contribution (xxiv–xxv).

The objective is to ensure that the welfare state includes citizens and does so by reinforcing relationships of reciprocity rather than moralistic divisions or individual interest. One problem lies in ensuring that all groups can engage in activities that most people will understand as making a realistic social contribution. The research carried out by Horton and colleagues indicates that full-time caring for children or frail elderly or sick and disabled relatives, full-time studying for useful qualifications and some kinds of full-time voluntary activity are recognised in this way. These activities would form the basis of an inclusive welfare state.

### Responding to social divisions

An alternative response to public opinion is to seek to devise policies that work with existing divisions. This is attractive to those who believe that the Labour party became detached from traditional working class roots during the early 2000s (for example, Glasman et al., 2011; Byrne in Philpott, 2011: 140–141). The resulting logic of 'something-for-something' welfare (Miliband, 2011) is designed to link the notions of reciprocity and inclusiveness to the theme of desert. Social contribution justifies the receipt of benefit. Many proposals centre on the idea of social insurance, a theme which has had some success in protecting welfare systems in corporatist European countries (Field, 2001).

This approach is attractive in many ways. One problem is illustrated by the National Salary Insurance scheme of Purnell (Cooke, 2011a), which is often seen as a key example. This scheme would allow those whose employment is interrupted by illness or redundancy to claim a relatively high benefit which will then be recouped through a supplement to tax when they return to work. This is essentially a loan system underwritten by the state rather than a benefit or insurance. As Baumberg (2012) points out, the approach is of limited application. It cannot address the needs of those who have a weak employment record, who face extended periods of unemployment, or who are low-paid and unable to finance their own benefits. In short, it entrenches a deserving/undeserving distinction among claimants, the issue that recognition of a wider range of socially desirable activities seeks to address in the Horton and Gregory model.

### User engagement

User engagement emerges in a range of ideas from co-production, where services users are actively involved in providing, managing and sometimes financing the services they use, through to the expansion of mutual and co-operatives. Plan B draws heavily on the work of the New Economics Foundation (for example, 2008) in its discussion of co-production. Current work in this area has applied the idea with some success in health and social care (Glasby et al., 2010). How it would be extended to other areas, especially those involving substantial professional inputs or cash transfers, is not worked out in detail. Co-operatives are discussed in a number of the essays in *Purple Labour* (Richards, 2011: 50–51). Provider co-operatives would operate to stabilise firms and to moderate pay inequalities, a theme that has recently been taken up by mainstream politicians (Clegg, 2012). Co-operatives that included users in the areas of social care, for example, might lead to more responsive services and a stronger trust in social provision. If co-operatives succeed in engaging the public, they may help to rebuild a trust in the state that will facilitate further progressive reform.

The co-operative approach offers a management model for such areas, but can only address issues of inclusion if specifically designed to facilitate entry by outsiders. Mutuals which provided services or support for members might be subject to all the in-group biases identified by social psychologists, anthropologists and sociologists and be unwilling to extend the service to new members who did not have demonstrable resources to contribute. This requires careful attention to how co-operatives recruit members and interact with outsiders.

## Pre-distribution

The grand tradition of state welfare has rested on redistribution through taxation of the better-off or of individuals at life-cycle stages when income exceeds resources, to provide welfare when they are in need. Pre-distribution addresses inequalities at source, through state interventions into the operation of market systems to reduce income inequalities and shift power towards the lower-paid. The most powerful arguments for this approach rest on the claim that state welfare was most successful in the UK when the institutions to reinforce pre-distribution were at their strongest, in the 1950s and 1960s (Coats et al., 2012, chapters 2 & 3; Pearce, 2012). Hacker (2011) points out that the massive increase in inequality in some of the most developed countries is linked to erosion of the protective institutional framework. As Heyes and Lewis demonstrate (Chapter 9 in this volume), there is substantial cross-national evidence that better working conditions are, in fact, associated with greater economic resilience.

Pre-distribution might include: institutional changes, such as a strengthening of the bargaining position and influence of workers through stronger trade union rights and representation on works councils; legislative interventions, such as enforcement of higher minimum wages or a living wage; better working conditions or shorter working hours; measures to curb wages at the top end through reforms to remuneration systems and possibly maximum wage legislation; and interventions to control the prices of items of common consumption such as utilities, transport or food (see also Pyke, Chapter 13 in this volume). Recent policy commitments from a future Labour government, such as the energy price freeze, fit into this category.

This approach is attractive for three reasons: it addresses the issue of redistributing power towards groups that have grown relatively weaker in the market; it increases the influence of institutions that might reinforce solidarity and promote greater reciprocity across groups that may then perceive a stronger common interest; and implementation costs are low.

The problems are to do with the impact on the structure of social relationships and on market interactions. Some of the proposals are directed at strengthening the bargaining power of organised labour, while some are directed to those at the margin of or outside work. At various times these groups have failed to recognise common interests and much of the tradition of a deserving/undeserving distinction derives from this division. One contribution is to direct interventions to investments that increase the supply of jobs while strengthening the protection of wages and standards in those jobs, the reverse of the current spending cut plus work programme strategy. At minimum, pre-distribution needs to engage with redistribution to protect those outside the labour market.

Pre-distribution confronts the operation of the capitalist market system directly and may affect international competitiveness. This leads to concerns about how well an approach which developed during the heyday of nation state capitalism is fitted to advance collective interests in a more globalised world (Glynn, 2006). This takes the argument in the direction of the greater cross-national regulation of inequalities stressed by Plan B in order to ensure that competitive pressures do not damage a high-wage economy.

This brief overview of progressive strategies indicates areas of consensus and of conflict. Consensus is found at the macro-level in relation to a stronger role for the state in moderating the economic cycle and in economic investment to secure growth. Damage to Labour's reputation for economic prudence may constrain willingness to spend. At the micro-level, disagreements are more marked and focus on issues of balance between different policies. This is particularly evident in two areas: first, between policies that direct their efforts to working with the deserving/ undeserving distinction (expanded notions of contribution, social insurance-based logics) as against those that seek to sidestep it (pre-distribution, social investment); and second, between those that stress the engagement of ordinary people (co-production, mutuals and co-operatives) as against those that rest on top-down initiatives (childcare spending, progressive tax, better social housing). Social investment and pre-distribution are strongly supported.

## Assessment

The above discussion identified three main criteria for progressive policies. They must enable government to address immediate and future budgetary challenges, they must be consonant with public opinion and be electable and they must lead public discourse in a progressive direction. In addition, they must acknowledge the issue of continuing economic pressures, the productivity constraints public services face and the degree of social inequality that exists. We move on to consider how well various proposals meet these conditions at macro- and micro-levels.

## Macro-level

There is a considerable measure of agreement at the macro-level on the themes of infrastructural spending to encourage growth and of more progressive taxation. The Coalition introduced a modest £6.3bn infrastructure package in the 2011 Autumn Statement, with the expectation of some £5bn in the longer-term and a possible £20bn leveraged from private sector pension funds. IFS calls for a further £10bn (2012) and NIESR suggests £15bn (2012). Compass proposes a much larger programme, with an initial £100bn fund (2011: 26) for the Investment Bank. Tax reforms are also not described in detail but include new taxes directed at the reduction of income and wealth inequalities. Similar ideas are included in most programmes.

It is unclear how far these policies would be more successful than current government initiatives in addressing the immediate problems of sluggish growth, mainly because developments in the UK are intertwined with those elsewhere. Apart from the arguments of *In the Black Labour*, there is little work examining in detail how spending plans would relate to budgetary constraints. If we assume that these constraints are, at least in the short-term, severe, it is necessary to identify areas for cutback.

Non-welfare state areas, especially defence, face sharp cuts, which could continue. A generous and inclusive policy would seek to spread the savings burden more evenly. IFS analysis (O'Dea, 2010; Browne, 2010; Crawford, 2010) bears out the arguments of Tepe-Belfrage (Chapter 12 in this volume) and shows that the cuts and tax changes bear most on those at the bottom, especially on women, and on a small group at the top, facing higher tax rates, and on families and children rather than benefits for older people. Further taxes on the distant wealthy (a capital value or land tax, perhaps or higher inheritance taxes) would fit with public discourse. One problem is how far it is possible to bring higher taxes down the income distribution, given public resistance to taxing the middle class. A further issue concerns the desire to mitigate benefit cuts. Some resources could be saved in the short-term by terminating the restructuring of benefits and public services. It is difficult to see how far further savings could be made without addressing state pensions. This would affect a large group in the electorate typically seen as deserving.

These considerations imply that new policies at the micro-level are essential if the macro-level problems are to be addressed. These policies must at least constrain spending. They must also fit with public opinion and build the public trust necessary to support future progressive reforms.

## Micro-level

*Social investment* is attractive because it offers a return, so that net spending commitments are contained; areas like child-care fit the public opinion constraint because they focus on an obviously deserving need group (young children) and are directed at supporting paid work. They also help support an inclusive solidarism since they can be universal across the group. For these reasons they have been vigorously promoted by progressives in Europe (Vanderbroucke et al., 2011). However, the case for investment is only persuasive in a limited range of areas, mainly around education and public health.

*Solidarity policies* based on principles such as contribution can operate across a wider range of areas, provided that the public will accept a relatively broad range of activities and not simply a social insurance payment or paid work as a relevant contribution. Spending commitments may generate problems, since inclusion is likely to involve extra spending on higher benefits for those who are unable to make equivalent cash contributions. The deservingness barrier creates difficulties in including people, typically from the most deprived groups, who are unable to make any contribution. Horton and Godfrey (2009: 168) address this by postulating activities which might enhance future contributions, such as attendance on training and work-readiness programmes for unemployed people. Benefit entitlement for those unwilling to accept these requirements would be reduced. The policies offer a progressive contribution because they build reciprocity and help channel debates towards the idea that citizens contribute and derive benefit from participating in society.

Policies which operate within the constraints of the *deserving/undeserving distinction*, such as National Salary Insurance, are likely to be financially viable, since their range is relatively small. They are electorally feasible and attractive to public opinion, but do not build inclusiveness.

*User engagement* programmes can use a wide range of techniques, involve little extra spending, are often attractive to a public feeling ignored by remote decision-makers, and may help build trust in public policies to facilitate difficult spending decisions in the future. There are real limits to how far a sense of inclusion and participation can be promoted, for example across a national education system or health service. Identification with, for example, a particular school in a more participative or co-operative system may strengthen social divisions. These considerations may limit participation to the more restricted forms, such as personal budgeting.

*Pre-distribution* is also highly attractive in terms of low direct public spending. It does not obviously involve extra spending and may well have longer-term benefits in reducing inequalities. The approach may encounter electoral and public opinion obstacles if it is seen to strengthen sectional interests. Again, it may fail to strengthen inclusivity and solidarity between those in secure work and those in less stable jobs. The energy price freeze combines policies which help the poor with solidarity policies directed at the general squeeze as pay falls behind price rises.

## Conclusion

This brief overview suggests that none of the proposed policies offers a complete solution to the problems outlined earlier. Any progressive future is likely to rely on a combination, so that issues arise in reconciling conflicts between groups addressed by different approaches. The budgetary pressures require policies that constrain current spending. By the criterion of economic sustainability, social investment, desert-centred, user engagement and pre-distribution policies seem attractive, because cheaper. Conversely, the social contribution approach seeks to offer a way of presenting substantial generous and inclusive welfare so that it is electorally feasible. The Left Trilemma results from the imperative to demonstrate economic competence, the need to gain public support and the Left's core commitment to progressive policies. It is particularly intransigent when resources are limited and public opinion is set against the poor. Policies that lead to savings are hard to reconcile with generosity and inclusiveness, which are hard to promote when public discourse is suspicious of the undeserving and lukewarm about taxing the better-off.

Under these circumstances, the Left must develop a policy programme which shifts public discourse. The five themes identified earlier have remained powerful over time but do fluctuate. In general, attitudes have moved against generosity and inclusiveness. The lack of sympathy for unemployed people and the harsh stigmatisation of the poor at the present time are striking. These shifts indicate that the Right is currently more successful in leading public debate. The theme of social solidarity through a broad-based contribution system, reinforced with pre-distribution and social investment policies may contribute to an attractive electoral platform. If contributory welfare involves increased spending this may limit its feasibility, so that it is only practicable through gradual introduction over time. Provided that the systems are designed to foster inclusiveness and to minimise barriers between groups, the potential for leading public debate in a progressive direction is strong.

These policies must be embedded within an overall approach that fosters a return to growth through investment in infrastructure, production and social provision, and seeks higher taxation of the better-off. The resources available will be limited in the medium-term, so that some cuts will be necessary to enable support for the most vulnerable. It is hard to see how generosity to pensioners can escape such constraints, because of the size of the programme.

This chapter has set out the difficulties any progressive social programme faces as a trilemma between economic viability, public acceptability and inclusiveness and generosity. This trilemma does not confront the Right, who promote an economic programme of cutbacks directed particularly at the poor, in tune with public attitudes and concerned with work incentives and poverty-level incomes rather than inclusiveness and generosity. No suggested programme is wholly satisfactory on all counts and there is a conflict, at least in the short-term, between policies that seem most likely to satisfy harsh spending pressures and an ungenerous public discourse, and those with the strongest potential to generate adequate and solidaristic welfare. This points to a broad and conjoint policy platform, and one which pays attention to ensuring that policies do not reinforce divisions and put obstacles in the path of any move towards greater inclusiveness.

## Note

1. The following builds on Baumberg's analysis (Baumberg, 2012).

## References

Atkinson, A. (2007) 'The Distribution of Earnings in OECD Countries', *International Labour Review*, 146, 2, 41–60.

Atkinson, A., Piketty, T. and Saez T. (2011) 'Top Incomes in the Long Run', *Journal of Economic Literature*, 49, 1, 3–71

Ayoubkhani, D., Baird, A., Munro, F. and Wild, R. (2010), 'Education Productivity', *Economic and Labour Market Review*, 4, 55–60.

Bailey, J. (2011) *Painful Separation*, Resolution Foundation, http://www.resolutionfoundation.org/publications/?page=2

Bamfield, J. and Horton, T. (2009) *Understanding Attitudes to Inequality*, JRF, http://www.jrf.org.uk/publications/attitudes-economic-inequality

Baumberg, B. (2012) 'Three Ways to Defend Welfare in Britain', *Journal of Poverty and Social Justice*, 20, 149–161.

Ben-Galim, D. (2011) *Making the Case for Universal Childcare*. IPPR London.

Blanden, J. and Machin, S. (2007) *Recent Changes in Intergenerational Mobility in Britain*. Sutton Trust report.

BMA (2012) 'BMA Welcomes Criticism of Healthcare Reforms', http://web2.bma.org.uk/nrezine.nsf/wd/CPAN-8QTGPD?OpenDocument&C=28+January+2012

Boyle, D. and Harris, M. (2009) *The Challenge of Co-production*, NEF/NESTA, http://www.nesta.org.uk/library/documents/Co-production-report.pdf (accessed 20 December 2011).

Brewer, M., Browne, J, and Joyce, R. (2011) *Child and Working Age Poverty and Inequality in UK: 2010*, IFS Commentary C121, http://www.ifs.org.uk/comms/comm121.pdf

Browne, J. (2010) *Distributional Analysis of Tax and Benefit Changes*. London: IFS, http://www.ifs.org.uk/publications/5313

Clarke, E. and Gardner, O. (2011) *The Red Book*. http://www.scribd.com/doc/73605264/Labour-Left-The-Red-Book-23-November-2011

Clegg (2012) *DPM's Mansion House Speech*, Cabinet Office, http://www.dpm.cabinetoffice.gov.uk/news/deputy-prime-minister-s-speech-mansion-house

Coats, D. (2012) *From the Poor Law to Welfare to Work*. Smith Institute, London.

Compass (2011) *Plan B*, http://www.compassonline.org.uk/news/item.asp?n=13946

Cooke, G. (2011b) *In the Black Labour*, Policy Network, http://www.policy-network.net/publications/4101/-In-the-black-Labour

Cooke, G. (2011a) *National Salary Insurance: Briefing Paper*. IPPR London.

Cooper, Y. (2010), *Women Bear Brunt of Budget Cuts*, http://www.yvettecooper.com/

Crawford, R. (2010), *Where Did the Axe Fall?* London: Institute for Fiscal Studies, http://www.ifs.org.uk/publications/5311 (accessed 28 May 2011).

Curtice, J. (2010) 'Public Reactions to Spending under New Labour', in A. Park et al. (eds), *British Social Attitudes, 2010–11*. London: Sage.

Dickson, M. and Smith, S. (2011) *What Determines the Return to Education?* CMP paper 11/256 http://www.bris.ac.uk/cmpo/publications/papers/2011/wp256.pdf (accessed 20 December 2011).

Dolphin, T. (2011) *10 Ways to Promote Growth*. IPPR, London.

Field, F. (2001) *Making Welfare Work*. Transaction Publishers, New Brunswick.

Fitzpatrick, S., Johnsen, S. and White, M. (2011) 'Multiple Exclusion Homelessness in the UK: Key Patterns and Intersections', *Social Policy and Society*.

Gamble, A. (2011) *Economic Futures*. A report for the British Academy project *New Paradigms in Public Policy*. London, British Academy Policy Centre.

Gann, T. (2011) 'Labour Winning in the South', 144–55, *The Red Book*, E Clarke and O. Gardner eds, Labour Left, http://www.scribd.com/doc/16016440/The-Red-Book

Gintis, H., Bowles, S., Boyd, R. and Fehr, E. (2005) *Moral Sentiments and Material Interests*. Cambridge, Mass: MIT Press.

Glasby, J., Le Grand J. and Duffy, S. (2010) 'A Healthy Choice? Direct Payments and Healthcare in the English NHS', *Policy and Politics*, 37, 4, 481–497.

Glasman, M. et al (2011) *The Labour Tradition and the Politics of Paradox,* http://www.soundings.org.uk/

Glennerster, H. (2010) *Financing the United Kingdom's Welfare States.* London: 2020 Public Services Trust.

Glynn, A. (2006) *Capitalism Unleashed.* Oxford University Press.

Gough, I. (2011b) *Climate Change and Public Policy.* BA and OUP.

Gough, I. (2011a) 'Welfare Cuts', in K. Farnsworth and Z. Irving (eds), *Social Policy in Challenging Times.* Bristol: Policy Press.

Hacker, Jacob (2011) *The Institutional Foundations of Middle Class Democracy,* Policy Network.

Hardie, M., Cheers, J. Pinder, C. and Qaeser, U. (2011) *Public Sector Outputs, Inputs and Productivity: Healthcare No 5,* London: ONS.

Hay, C. (2007) *Why We Hate Politics.* Cambridge: Polity.

Hills, J (2001) 'Poverty and Social Security', in A. Park et al. (eds) *British Social Attitudes,* 2001/2 edition, London: Sage.

Hills, J. (2012) 'The Changing Architecture of the Welfare State', *Oxford Review of Public Economics,* 27, 4.

Hills, J., Sefton, T. and Stewart, K. (2009) *Towards a More Equal Society?* Policy Press.

HM Treasury (2010) *Budget 2010,* HC 451, http://webarchive.nationalarchives.gov.uk/20100407010852/http://www.hm-treasury.gov.uk/d/budget2010_complete.pdf

HM Treasury (2011) *Autumn Statement,* cm 8231http://cdn.hm-treasury.gov.uk/autumn_statement.pdf

HoC Heath Committee (2012) *Public Expenditure on the Health Service,* http://www.publications.parliament.uk/pa/cm201012/cmselect/cmhealth/1499/149906.htm

HoC Public Accounts Committee (2011) *Management of NHS Hospital Productivity, 26th Report,* House of Commons, 9 March.

Horton, T. and Gregory, J. (2009) *The Solidarity Society,* Fabian Society, http://www.webbmemorialtrust.org.uk/download/publications_&_reports/Solidarity_Society.pdf

IFS (2012) *Green Budget.* http://www.ifs.org.uk/budgets/gb2012/12chap3.pdf

Johnston, R. and Pattie, C. (2011) 'Where Did Labour's Votes Go?' *British Journal of Politics and IR,* 13, 3, 283–303.

Judd, A. (2011) *Public Service Labour Productivity.* London: ONS.

Local Government Association (LGA) (2011) *Funding Settlement Disappointing,* http://www.lga.gov.uk/lga/core/page.do?pageId=16647103 (accessed 28 May 2011).

Mau, S. (2004) 'Welfare Regimes and the Norms of Social Exchange', *Current Sociology,* 52, 1, 53–74.

Mau, S. and Veghte, B. (2007) *Social Justice, Legitimacy and the Welfare State.* Aldershot: Ashgate.

Mauss, M. (1990 [1922]) *The Gift: Forms and Functions of Exchange in Archaic Societies.* London: Routledge.

Miliband, E. (2011) *Labour Party Annual Conference Speech,* http://www.labour.org.uk/ed-milibands-speech-to-labour-party-conference

Miliband, E. (2010) In Fabian Society, *The Labour Leadership.* [ebook] Available at http://www.fabians.org.uk/publications/extracts/labour-leadership-ed-miliband Accessed 27 October 2011.

Mulheirn, I. (2012) *Osborne's Choice*, Social Market Foundation, http://www.smf.co.uk/research/economic-policy/osborne-s-choice-combining-fiscal-credibility-and-growth/

NEF (2008) *Co-production*, http://neweconomics.org/sites/neweconomics.org/files/Co-production_1.pdf

NEP (2010) *An Anatomy of Economic Inequality in the UK*, Case Report 60, LSE, http://sticerd.lse.ac.uk/dps/case/cr/CASEreport60_summary.pdf

NIESR (2012) *World and UK Economy Forecasts*, NIESR, http://www.niesr.ac.uk/pdf/020212_170728.pdf

O'Dea, C. (2010) *Who Loses Most from Public Spending Cuts?* London: Institute for Fiscal Studies, http://www.ifs.org.uk/publications/5313 (accessed 28 May 2011).

OBR (2010) *Economic and Fiscal Outlook, November 2010*, Cmnd 7979. London: Her Majesty's Stationery Office.

OBR (2011a) *Economic and Fiscal Outlook, November 2011*, Cmnd 8218. London: Her Majesty's Stationery Office.

OBR (2011b) *Fiscal Sustainability Report July 2011 – Charts and Tables*, http://budgetresponsibility.independent.gov.uk/fiscal-sustainability-report-july-2011/

OECD (2010) *Economic Outlook*, no 88, November, Paris: OECD.

Orton, M. and Rowlingson, K. (2007) *Public Attitudes to Economic Inequality*, JRF, York, http://www.jrf.org.uk/publications/public-attitudes-economic-inequality

Ostrom, E. and Walker, J. (1997) 'Neither Markets Nor States', in D. Mueller (ed.) *Perspectives on Public Choice*. Cambridge: Cambridge University Press, 35–72.

Parkin, Frank (1979a). *Marxism and Class Theory: A Bourgeois Critique*, Columbia University Press.

Pearce, N. (2012) 'New Times New thinking', *New Statesman*, 23 March, http://www.ippr.org/articles/56/8905/new-times-new-thinking

Philpott, R. (ed.) (2011) *The Purple Book*. London: Biteback.

Radice, G. and Diamond, P. (2010) *Southern Discomfort Again*. London: Policy Network.

Richards, P. (2011) 'Back to the Future', in R. Philpott (ed.), *The Purple Book*. London: Biteback.

Rothstein, B. (2005) *Social Traps and the Problem of Trust*. Cambridge: Cambridge University Press.

Scholes, T. et al. (eds) (2011) *What Next for Labour?* London: Queensferry.

Sefton, T. (2005) 'Give and Take', in A. Park et al. (eds) *British Social Attitudes, 22nd Report*, London: Natcen.

Sterne, N. (2006) *The Economics of Climate Change*, HM Treasury, http://www.webcitation.org/5nCeyEYJr

Stoker, G. (2006) *Why Politics Matters*. Basingstoke: Macmillan.

Tajfel, H. (1978) *Differentiation between Groups*. London: Academic Press.

Uslaner, E. (2008) *Corruption, Inequality and the Rule of Law*. Cambridge: Cambridge University Press.

Taylor-Gooby, P. (2009) *Reframing Social Citizenship*. Oxford: Oxford University Press.

Taylor-Gooby, P. (2012) 'Root and Branch Restructuring to Achieve Major Cuts: The Social Ambitions of the Coalition', *Social Policy and Administration*, available via Early View.

Taylor-Gooby, P. and Hastie, C. (2002) 'Support for State Spending', in A. Park et al. (eds) *British Social Attitudes: the 19th Report*. London: National Centre for Social Research.

Titmuss, R. (1970) *The Gift Relationship*. Harmondsworth: Penguin Books.
van Oorschott, W. (2000) 'Who Should Get What, and Why? On Deservingness Criteria and the Conditionality of Solidarity among the Public', *Policy & Politics*, 28, 1, 33–48.
van Oorschott, W. (2006) 'Making the Difference in Social Europe: Deservingness Perceptions among Citizens of European Welfare States', *Journal of European Social Policy*, 16, 1, 23–42.
Vanderbrouke, F., Hemerijk, A. and Palier, B. (2011) *Why the EU Needs a Social Investment Pact*, OSE, http://www.ose.be/files/OpinionPaper5_Vandenbroucke-Hemerijk-Palier_2011.pdf (accessed 20 December 2011).
Walshe, K. (2010) *Reorganisation of the NHS in England*, BMJ 16 July, http://www.bmj.com/content/341/bmj.c3843.extract
Whittaker, M. (2012) *Squeezed Britain?*, Resolution Foundation, http://www.resolutionfoundation.org/publications/essential-guide-squeezed-britain/
Women's Budget Group (WBG, 2011) *The Impact on Women of the Coalition Spending*. women-bear-brunt-of-budget-cuts (accessed 28 May 2011).
Yeates, N. et al. (2011) *In Defence of Welfare*, Lincoln: Social Policy Association, http://www.social-policy.org.uk/downloads/idow.pdf (accessed 28 May 2011).010; Feinstein 1972; IFS 2011: 153.

# 6
# The UK Macroeconomic Policy Debate and the British Growth Crisis: Debt and Deficit Discourse in the Great Recession

*Ben Clift*

## Introduction

The central political battle in Britain's response to the global financial crisis (GFC) has been over the meanings of fiscal rectitude and economic credibility. This chapter analyses that battle by charting some of the key decisions taken by the UK Government, situating these in the context of ideas about management of public finances and Keynesianism. It explores what has happened to debt and deficit discourse, and its political salience in the UK after the GFC. One aim of this chapter is to demonstrate the historically contingent nature of fiscal policy and sustainability assessment by comparing their shifting, conjunctural constructions, rooted in underlying political economic assumptions, and how these different underlying assumptions have become the stuff of a contested politics within the UK and in wider economic policy debates. Assessment of fiscal policy and fiscal sustainability must be placed in the context not only of material conditions in the national and global economy, but also of ideational factors – conventional wisdoms and climates of opinion (and their normative underpinnings) about fiscal policy, fiscal positions, and sovereign debt.

The impact of these ideational factors is significant. Here we highlight the significance of the changing interpretive frameworks within which fiscal policy assessment is situated, charting the evolution of crisis narratives within the UK policy debate, and significant shifts in the presentation of Britain's debt and deficit position, and its sustainability. Crucially, the scale and speed of fiscal retrenchment presented as imperative (and without which a damaging loss of confidence and credibility becomes likely) differed appreciably between the different post-crisis narratives. The other aim of this chapter is to begin to explore the implications of these processes of fiscal rectitude construction for economic strategies to address Britain's paucity of economic growth and, more broadly, implications for the development of a revived British growth model. We consider the impact of the Coalition's construction of fiscal rectitude on the prospects for steering the UK economy on a path to growth, and potentially discovering a new British growth model.

## The elusive imperatives of post-GFC fiscal rectitude

Assessments of a country's fiscal position, and the appropriateness (or otherwise) of fiscal policy settings are not objective in the sense that what makes them 'true' or 'false' is 'independent of anybody's attitudes or feelings about them' (Searle, 1995: 8). Ideational factors, notably conventional wisdoms and climates of opinion (and their normative underpinnings) about fiscal policy and sovereign debt, play a constitutive role. As has been argued elsewhere in relation to the balance of payments, in areas with significant uncertainty over assessment mechanisms and where prior assumptions play an important role, the scope for construction and re-construction of economic rectitude assessment is particularly great (Clift and Tomlinson, 2008).

In relation to fiscal credibility, much hinges on inter-subjective beliefs, such as those about appropriate levels of debt and deficit, and the fiscal policies to help achieve them. Understandings of the relationship between fiscal policy and economic growth are also crucial, since the presence or absence of economic growth has implications for debt sustainability. Notions of fiscal credibility and fiscal rectitude are thus, in an important sense, social constructions; 'credibility is a social relationship as much as (or rather more than) an economic relationship' (Hall, 2008: 2). When particular shared understandings of appropriate debt, deficits and fiscal policy in a globalising economy become sufficiently embedded they develop the quality of 'social facts' (Searle, 1995: 24–25; Ruggie, 1998: 13, 20–21; Sinclair, 2005: 53–54; Hall, 2008: 9, 45–54).

Assessing appropriate macroeconomic policy requires an assessment of where we are in the cycle. This is central to any evaluation of the structural, or cyclically adjusted, fiscal balance (or deficit), which is the preferred international yardstick for a country's fiscal stance and position. Structural deficit assessment is considered preferable to headline nominal deficit targets, for the good reason that it avoids the pro-cyclicality (for example, inducing public expenditure cuts whilst the economy is already contracting, or failing to induce moderation during upswings) of nominal targets. This assessment in turn hinges on assumptions about the output gap and the potential rate of growth. This poses particular problems in the post-GFC world. In short, what proportion of the pre-2008 economic growth potential is now permanently lost capacity and how large, therefore, is the output gap? What proportion of unemployment is structural, what proportion cyclical?

The UK Government, IMF, OECD and EC each has its own preferred methodology for assessing the output gap, and the potential growth rate, plugging in its own assumptions. They all differ somewhat. Which is best? The answer is that nobody knows, and the picture will only become fully clear ten years from now. Nevertheless, economic forecasters and policy economists have to make assessments of these issues and make policy on the back of such assessments. Economic policy assessment of this kind is highly sensitive to a number of somewhat arbitrary assumptions. However, the methodology for such an assessment is a contested issue, with no accepted right way. Both the potential growth rate and the output gap assessment are highly sensitive to assumptions, which are also necessarily somewhat arbitrary. Yet the policy implications of these somewhat artificial constructs can be very great – over-estimating the structural deficit can lead to too much fiscal consolidation, whilst under-estimating it could lead to not enough.

These are pressing issues in relation to evaluating 'where we are at' in the economic cycle. Similar difficulties manifest themselves in assessing the relative health of the public finances. Again, somewhat arbitrary assumptions have a major impact on the interpretation and assessment of advanced economy debt dynamics. To the extent that this *is* a UK crisis of debt (something which remains contested) – its policy implications are rendered harder to read by the very nature of debt and deficit dynamics and their evaluation. This is inherently difficult because of the many imponderables in terms of changes in economic fundamentals, and because of the unpredictability of financial market assessments of particular country's fiscal, debt or deficit positions and prospects. A good deal hinges, therefore, on the prior assumptions (for example, about the relationships between debt and growth, debt and interest rates, or fiscal policy and growth) made by bond market participants, national governments and international economic institutions designed to counter these imponderable and unpredictable aspects of fiscal policy and debt dynamics. This unpredictability is all the more pronounced for fiscal consolidation and debt reduction strategies projected many years into the future.

This all means that for different countries, in different situations, different levels of debt are sustainable. In the UK case, the Coalition seems to assume the country is relatively close to the limits of sustainable debt, whilst other influential bodies such as the IMF – with their nationally differentiated assessment of debt conditions and dynamics – would see the particularities of UK debt structure and its track record as offering greater leeway, a point we return to later in the chapter. More hawkish international commentators, appalled at the vertiginous rises in advanced economy debt levels following the crisis, argued that all economies should target a return to 60 per cent debt by 2020 or 2030. The view that higher government debt gets progressively much worse for economic performance gained ground from 2010 onwards as attention shifted from staving off the next Great Depression to dealing with the public finances consequences of fiscal stimulus, bank bailouts, and lost post-GFC revenues. International economic policy debates evolved from a brief flourishing of Keynesian thinking in 2008–2009, when Strauss-Kahn (then Managing Director of the IMF) called for a co-ordinated global fiscal stimulus amounting to 2 per cent of global GDP in October 2008. This was superseded by a shift towards prioritising restoring the public finances, and addressing increased public debt through cuts in public expenditure and austerity policies, captured in the oxymoron 'growth friendly fiscal consolidation' at the June 2010 Toronto G20 (Blyth, 2013).

Shifts in the narration of policy priorities was bolstered by influential works from top economists Reinhardt and Rogoff, which asserted that, above 90 per cent of GDP, debt necessarily undermined growth. This seemed to posit a more powerful, immediate and direct negative correlation between very high debt and long-term growth. Its implications for the balance of prioritisation on policy debates appeared clear. It also appeared both pressing and prescient as average debt levels had either already been reached, or were set to exceed the 90 per cent threshold in many advanced economies.

As the post-GFC recession continued, the balance of prioritisation in economic policy commentary shifted once more. IMF Chief Economist Blanchard's analysis in late 2011 (Blanchard, 2011) suggested that too rapid a fiscal consolidation might be perverse, even on its own terms, as financial markets might see the adverse effects on growth of such *excessive* pace as reducing the credibility of such policies. This was a view also taken by some leading academic economists (Delong and Summers,

2012). A lack of growth affects the denominator of debt/GDP ratios, meaning government debt levels get apparently higher, whilst tax revenues continue to fall or flatline. Moreover, bondholders get ever more concerned about the repayment prospects of governments in growthless economies. At this time, claims from the influential Reinhardt and Rogoff about the 90 per cent debt threshold came under high-profile scrutiny as no one could reproduce their results. This fed a climate of intellectual and policy elite opinion that increasingly accepted that balancing the appropriate prioritisation between debt and growth might be more complicated than the single-minded austerity-focused advocates had hitherto presumed.

## The politics of economic ideas and the construction of fiscal rectitude since the crisis

Here we focus on two economic ideas which are revealing of assumptions about appropriate public debt and government spending. They entail different understandings of the rationale behind, and efficacy of, fiscal policy – especially in a recession. Differing assumptions about each has major implications for appropriate macroeconomic policy responses, both to the initial crisis and to the prolonged downturn which followed.

Firstly, the notion of multipliers associated with public spending is derived from Richard Kahn (1931) and closely associated with the classical Keynesian position as set out in the *General Theory* (Keynes, 1964: 113–131). The efficacy of fiscal policy as a tool in economic stabilisation hinges on assumptions made about the size of fiscal multipliers. These are the assumptions plugged into economic models about how much effect increasing (or reducing) government spending has on economic activity. As Backhouse puts it, following the Keynesian assumption that 'the expenditure multiplier [is] greater than one ... a rise in investment or government spending would produce a rise in income that was larger than the initial increase in spending' (2006: 32; see also Blaug, 1990).

This apparently arcane, technical topic is in fact revealing of crucially important underlying ideas about which economic policy levers governments can pull, and to what effect, when faced with a prolonged downturn. This recognition of the potentially beneficial effects of increased public spending and positive spillover effects of the aggregate demand boost on consumption, economic activity and confidence is important for the politics of fiscal policy. It strengthens the case for a focus on demand and the need to sustain it, and for increased public spending and activist, expansionary fiscal policy, in a recession and when monetary policy is already accommodating. Put crudely, a higher estimate of fiscal multipliers reveals a more Keynesian understanding of the economy, whereas low fiscal multiplier assessments reflect neoliberal economic assumptions.

This may be helpfully contrasted with the crowding out thesis associated with neo-classical and, subsequently, neo-liberal political economy. This mainstay of neo-liberal analysis of public finances and state/market relations, assumes increases in public spending will not enhance economic growth or economic activity, but simply crowd out (inherently more efficient) private spending and investment. This was the cornerstone of the UK's Treasury View of the 1930s (see Tomlinson, 1990: 60–61, 85–90) which Keynes was arguing against. R G Hawtrey's submission to the Macmillan Committee of 1930 captures the 100 per cent crowding out position; 'whether the spending came out of taxes or loans from savings, the increased government expenditure would merely replace private expenditure' (quoted in Klein, 1968: 45–46). Corollaries of this view include Say's Law, that supply will call forth demand and that the free market has an inherent tendency towards full employment of resources which does not require government stimulus. The crowding out effect argument links to a stance on debt, since rising government bond yields that reflect rising market fears of default, or at least eroding fiscal credibility, will adversely affect private investment. In short, 'with governments issuing so much debt, the private sector cannot compete for funds, and as such investment and output must fall' (Blyth, 2010: 37).

A related concept is Ricardian equivalence, which assumes that tax cuts or debt-financed increased government spending will not stimulate spending because they will be fully offset by the anticipation of higher taxes in the future to pay off the debt. These economic assumptions are intimately linked to an approach to debt and fiscal policy which prioritises fiscal consolidation. Such a stance is predicated upon 'dubious "Ricardian effects," which assume offsetting private expenditures for public cutbacks' (Blyth, 2010: 38). As Holland and Portes summarise the position, 'in the extreme example of Ricardian equivalence, the fiscal multiplier is effectively zero, as fiscal policy is simply offset by private sector adjustments to savings behaviour' (2012: 7). These two positions distil the essence of fundamentally different views of fiscal policy, of public debt, and of government spending.

In the current crisis, a modern take, which adheres to some of the same principles as the Treasury View, has been articulated by an influential economist, Alesina, into the expansionary austerity' thesis (see

Alesina and Perotti, 1995; Alesina and Ardegna, 2009; for a critique see Holland and Portes, 2012: 4–5; IMF, 2010a: 93–113). This is built on ideas about Ricardian equivalence and the confidence effects of fiscal consolidation efforts. This argues that the strenuous exertions to restore public finances will so reassure economic actors (that they won't have to foot a larger tax bill down the line) and financial market participants, that interest rates will come down. Buoyed by the prospect of improved national economic health, investment will then pick up, as will economic activity. Advocates claim to draw on empirical examples, notably Denmark and Ireland in the 1980s. This thesis has had adherents in high places, notably Rodrigo de Rato, Managing Director of the IMF between 2004 and 2007. As we shall see below, allusions to the expansionary austerity thesis were used by Osborne and others as part of the justification for the Coalition's economic policy settings from May 2010 onwards.

There are methodological question marks suggesting proponents of this thesis both mis-specify the timing of contractions, and over state their positive growth effects (IMF, 2010a: 93–113). The prevailing IMF view, shared by many leading economists, is that it is an empirical question whether or not such effects manifest themselves, but that they would likely do so only under very exacting conditions. Furthermore, in a context of low interest rates for the majority of advanced economies, as has been the case in countries like Britain since the GFC, it is difficult to see by what mechanism or channels these confidence effects could make themselves felt. Under current conditions of very low interest rates for most advanced economies, ideas about expansionary austerity, like those about crowding out effects, are not seen as germane to the post-GFC political economic conjuncture.

The 2007–2008 crisis and its aftermath also revitalised research on fiscal policy and fiscal multipliers – widely deemed more pertinent to the current conjuncture. Debates and disagreements over appropriate fiscal policy, and over debt and deficit discourse, also became increasingly part and parcel of the party political debate in Britain to a degree not seen for many years. As part of the IMF's extensive rethink about fiscal policy efficacy since 2008 under the very specific conditions of the GFC (see Spilimbergo et al., 2008), a string of IMF research papers have set out good reasons why we should expect expansionary fiscal policy, targeted towards lower earners, to be more effective in supporting demand and growth during a downturn. Theoretical arguments and operational advice advanced by the IMF chief economist and others have put the case that fiscal multipliers are asymmetric rather than constant, varying to significant degrees across the economic cycle, being higher in a downturn or prolonged period of slow or no growth (Auerbach and Gorodnichenko, 2012; Delong and Summers, 2012). Fiscal multipliers, recent scholarship and IMF research has argued, are likely to be particularly high in post-financial crisis conditions. This is because recessions mean more unused capacity in the economy and broken transmission mechanisms in the financial system following financial crises (credit crunch), which normally mean more liquidity constrained (or cash-strapped) households. Fiscal policy is more likely to be effective when monetary policy was doing all it could, with interest rates at or around zero (the, so-called, zero lower bound) (IMF, 2012a; Blanchard and Leigh, 2013).

Fiscal multipliers also vary according to national conditions (depending, for example, on the size and efficacy of the automatic stabilisers built in to the economic policy regime). They also vary according to which policy mechanisms are being used (public investment, for example has a high multiplier, targeted social transfers a little lower, generalised tax cuts lower still). The Fund's somewhat Keynesian rethinking of fiscal policy effectiveness has been backed by empirical assessments and sharp upwards re-evaluations of post-crisis fiscal multipliers (IMF, 2010a, c, 2012a; Blanchard and Leigh, 2013). In October 2012, the IMF's flagship *World Economic Outlook* publication explored the 'systematic relationship between fiscal consolidation and growth', finding that 'the multipliers used in generating growth forecasts have been systematically too low since the start of the Great Recession', and arguing that, whereas default assumptions have tended to use 0.5 as a reference value, 'actual multipliers may be higher, in the range of 0.9 to 1.7' (IMF, 2012c: 41). As Blanchard (2012c: xv) put it in the foreword, 'while this consolidation is needed, there is no question that it is weighing on demand, and the evidence increasingly suggests that, in the current environment, the fiscal multipliers are large'. The implications of this were to challenge the case for the kind of front-loading of fiscal consolidation undertaken in Britain from May 2010 onwards.

This second wave of fiscal multipliers research accompanied and pushed a rebalancing of emphasis from an exclusive focus on austerity policies, tempering these concerns with the need to support growth (Holland and Portes, 2012). Yet assessments of fiscal multipliers continue to vary widely, with different international institutions and different governments using a variety of assumptions. Interestingly, Office of Budget Responsibility (OBR) assessments, for example, do not align directly with IMF views (Chote, 2013). This difference is significant because the size of the fiscal multiplier assumption plugged into economic models used to assess the impact of fiscal consolidation has a very major impact on what the expected outcome of those economic policies will be, an issue we return to below. This provides sufficient backdrop to the debate about economic ideas so we turn now to the UK macroeconomic policy debate.

## UK macroeconomic policy after May 2010: tackling the 'crisis of debt'

After the formation of the Conservative/Liberal Democrat coalition in May 2010, a new budget was introduced in June. Consistent with the underlying assumptions and understandings of the relationship between debt, public spending and growth of the likes of Osborne and Cameron, this announced much larger spending cuts and a much faster fiscal tightening than Labour had planned. Underpinning the changes in fiscal policy settings was a different conception of the central problems facing the British economy and standing in the way of economic recovery. Broadly speaking, under the previous Labour Government, British economic problems had been understood in terms of a crisis of growth, focusing attention on what needed to be done to restore a UK growth model. Under the Coalition, the central problem was understood as a crisis of debt. Addressing the deficit and debt bias of the UK economy would, the Coalition assumed, in and of itself go a long way to resolving the UK growth crisis.

Consistent with this crisis of debt discourse, the UK Coalition government in 2010 conceived of the credibility and debt sustainability constraints its fiscal policy was operating under as very tight. Osborne and Cameron's understanding of the UK economic position saw very little potential for activist fiscal policy in support of growth, and paid little attention to aggregate demand in the economy or the distributive impact of fiscal policy. This aligned both chronologically and intellectually with the shifting prioritisation in the international economic policy debate discussed above. This was the phase where more hawkish voices advocated withdrawing from fiscal stimulus and focusing on austerity and fiscal consolidation, presented somewhat disingenuously at the Toronto G20 in 2010 as 'growth friendly' (G20, 2010).

The central claim of the Coalition government's first budget was that continuing Labour's prior fiscal trajectory would 'put the recovery at risk' and undermine the possibility of sustained economic growth (Treasury, 2010b: 1). The Coalition's economic analysis made bold assumptions about the adverse effects of debt on future growth, accordingly its priority was fiscal retrenchment, with fewer concerns about balancing this with securing growth. Hence the need for a much more rapid fiscal tightening than Labour had put in place, composed of approximately 80 per cent spending cuts and 20 per cent tax increases. The central fiscal aim of the new strategy was to achieve a cyclically adjusted current balance by 2015/2016.

Whilst not saying in so many words that fiscal consolidation was needed to stave off a Greek style crisis, Osborne, Cameron and Clegg subsequently presented and justified UK macroeconomic policy strategy in these terms during interviews and speeches. The June 2010 budget document itself did not make such a claim, recognising that 'the financing environment has remained supportive'. Nevertheless, it committed the Coalition government to accelerated fiscal consolidation to 'keep market interest rates lower for longer, supporting economic recovery' and also claimed that the government's 'credible deficit reduction plan' should 'provide businesses with the confidence they need to plan and invest, supporting the necessary recovery in business investment' (Treasury, 2010b: 9).

What was more explicit within the 2010 emergency budget was the expansionary austerity thesis as part of the rationale behind fiscal consolidation. The impression was consistently given in speeches that fiscal consolidation would be helpful for economic recovery. The logic of the expansionary austerity is evoked directly by the Coalition government and the Treasury. In discussing the 'wider economic effects' of fiscal consolidation, the budget document claimed these 'will tend to boost demand growth, could improve the underlying performance of the economy and could even be sufficiently strong to outweigh the negative effects' and 'the effect on private sector confidence and spending' of the governments 'concrete measures' to limit the rise of government debt 'could prompt households and companies to reduce precautionary saving, increasing consumption and investment' (Treasury, 2010b: 19; see Portes, 2012).

In sum, to achieve fiscal credibility the June 2010 budget, alongside the already noted cyclically adjusted fiscal balance by 2015/2016, set out the aim of a falling ratio of net debt to GDP by the same date. Both targets were to be monitored by the OBR in order to underpin the credibility of the government's stance (Treasury, 2010b: 12). The central assumption of the construction of fiscal rectitude and debt and deficit under the Coalition was that Britain faced a 'crisis of debt' (Hay, 2013). Fiscal consolidation on the scale proposed was deemed an immediate imperative for UK macroeconomic policy to avoid increased borrowing costs since Britain did not enjoy the fiscal space to do otherwise. Such appeals to adverse effects in bond markets are a consistent theme of the construction of crisis narratives, particularly those asserting the necessity of tighter and faster fiscal retrenchment. *Sotto voce,* another element was that the expansionary austerity thesis indicated that these economic policies might not adversely affect UK economic growth.

This construction of Britain's economic policy constraints arguably neglected or deliberately ignored any impact of the Bank of England's Asset Purchase Facility (QE) and, notably, Bank of England purchases of gilts through the secondary market. This contributed significantly to the low yields on Treasury bonds and this ability to use independent monetary policy making powers of the Bank of England, and new appetites for 'unconventional' monetary policy interventions which all central banks have discovered since the GFC, could in fact facilitate a much more expansionary fiscal policy. The Bank of England's expansion of its balance sheet through very substantial interventions in the bond market is one cause of ongoing, very low, UK Government borrowing costs. This willingness to buy up bonds sets the Bank of England apart from the ECB, which has shown a hesitancy to buy bonds, notwithstanding Draghi's crucial 'whatever is necessary' announcement, which stabilised the Eurozone debt crisis by implying the ECB would do so.

The Government's construction of UK economic problems as primarily a crisis of debt was at odds with IMF views of the debt issues facing an advanced economy like the UK after the GFC. A consistent feature of Fund discussion of fiscal sustainability is the recognition of 'heightening market sensitivity to variations in fiscal performance across countries', and 'increased attention being paid by markets to differences in underlying fiscal conditions across countries' (IMF, 2010c: 5; IMF, 2009: 18–19). This underscores the importance of specific national trajectories, involving distinctive debt structures, dynamics, conditions, varying revenue raising capacities and different track records increasing or reducing leeway. This in turn affects 'the degree to which each country has fiscal space' (Spilimbergo et al., 2008: 11).

The nationally differentiated assessments of fiscal sustainability favoured by the IMF put the UK in a very different category to the troubled Eurozone economies. For the IMF, that financial markets would see UK debt as lacking credibility, leading to rising borrowing costs *à la* Greece, Italy, or Spain was deemed a very low probability. The contingent, differentiated assessment of national debt conditions and dynamics bound up in the IMF notion of fiscal space brings to light a number of salient facts. The UK Government has strong revenue raising capacities and powers and a good track record on macroeconomic policy. UK debt structure is the longest in the world at an average maturity of 13–14 years (IMF, 2010d: 6–7). This all expands UK fiscal space and, sure enough, the actual evolution of bond market attitudes towards the UK remained extremely positive and benign overall, and rates very low, throughout this period (IMF, 2010d: 11). There was no direct evidence from the market of loss of confidence in the UK, either under Labour or the Coalition, as the IMF subsequently pointed out (IMF, 2012b: 39). Placed in an historical context and given low interest rates, UK debt servicing costs were far from unprecedented, *lower* than during the late-1980s and mid-1990s (IMF, 2009: 18).

The UK budget deficit was running at very high levels in the immediate post-GFC period. This was due partly to the fiscal stimulus, but it also resulted from reduced tax revenues as asset prices fell, notably in the financial and housing sectors, and overall economic activity reduced substantially. The UK debt rose substantially, principally as bank bailouts brought substantial additional liabilities from the UK's troubled financial sector onto the public debt book. Yet even in these trying circumstances, the IMF did not view fiscal sustainability as a major problem for the UK Government. Difficulties financing UK debts due to sharply rising borrowing costs – whilst obviously a very high cost policy problem were they to arise – were deemed a low probability.

A much more pressing concern were the adverse effects of macroeconomic policy on growth. As the IMF Mission in the UK conducting Article IV consultations in September 2010 noted, 'the precise headwinds from fiscal consolidation are difficult to predict – they could turn out more powerful than expected' (IMF, 2010b: 20). The uncertainty is partly because evaluating the 'precise magnitude' of medium-term fiscal adjustment required, and the impact of consolidation 'is sensitive to assumptions' (IMF, 2009: 24). The analogy used by the IMF was that the Coalition government had made a judgement call in buying an 'insurance policy' through strenuous fiscal consolidation from 2010, the premium being paid as lower growth (Chopra, 2010). Contained within Chopra's metaphor is a rejection of Osborne's assertion that fiscal consolidation on the scale he set out in June 2010 was a non-negotiable imperative of sustaining fiscal credibility.

The IMF's view that UK loss of market credibility was a low probability (albeit a potentially high cost) event affected their view of the lower growth 'insurance premium' paid. Endorsement offered by the IMF of the Coalition's fiscal consolidation strategy was built on the assumption that growth was returning to the UK economy, as the forecasts in 2010/2011 indicated was likely. It is interesting to note that the grounds for endorsing the Coalition's fiscal tightening discussed in the Article VI report (IMF, 2010b: 28) link strongly to the 'fact' of recovery of growth even as fiscal consolidation had begun. However, UK growth forecasts were downgraded subsequently, for example in June 2011 (IMF, 2011), suggesting that the balance of priorities might pan out differently.

The November 2010 Article IV report on the UK included debates for and against fiscal tightening, noting merit on both sides of the argument. One important criticism of fiscal tightening undermining fragile growth hinged on scepticism about the private sector 'picking up the slack' as the public sector retrenches. Secondly, 'a bleak assessment of the UK's structural deficit could be self-fulfilling: because policymakers assume a large permanent drop in potential output, they tighten policies too early; this causes capital scrapping and human capital losses that a faster recovery would help prevent', and finally, the need to placate bond markets is overstated, they argued, given the evolution of long-term UK interest rates (IMF, 2010b: 28).

Demonstrating the new concern with distributional impacts of the post-crisis IMF, and following a Keynesian logic of targeting those with a higher marginal propensity to spend, Chopra noted the need to be 'fair' and 'protect the poor and the vulnerable'. He also underlined: 'If there's a sharp and prolonged downturn in the economy, the pace of fiscal consolidation may need to be adapted.' (IMF, 2010e) The potential for 'resource slack', hysteresis effects leading to 'further scrapping of idle capital and persistent unemployment, reducing both actual and potential output' (IMF, 2010b: 25) was keenly appreciated. In this and later assessments, the Fund underline the need for flexible policy responses and contingency plans should the fiscal retrenchment choke off the economic recovery.

The IMF's assessment, expressed ever more confidently as growth continued to disappoint between 2010 and 2013, was that the 'cost' of the UK's fiscal consolidation 'insurance policy' was too high in terms of lost growth. Olivier Blanchard even said at the 2013 IMF spring meetings that Osborne was 'playing with fire' in pursuing his austerity policies. The IMF became increasingly pointed in its advice that more could/should be done through fiscal policy, and more activism on unconventional monetary policy, such as quantitative easing and other forms of credit easing, to address the UK economy's persistent deficient demand. The downside risk of the austerity focus was permanent lost output as it became harder to close the output gap (how far below potential growth rate the UK economy was operating). Hysteresis effects[1] were theorised and modelled and, by the 2012 consultations, formed an increasing part of the IMF's central scenario for the UK economy (IMF, 2010b: 25, 2012b: 24–25, 38, 70–76).

Crucially, the IMF's Article IV reports in 2010, 2011, 2012 and 2013 consistently and repeatedly warn about powerful 'headwinds' from fiscal consolidation, and underline the importance of 'nimble' fiscal and monetary policy responses (to lower than hoped for growth). The IMF recommended planning additional 'credibly temporary' tax cuts targeted at 'low income households employment creation or investment to increase their multipliers' alongside 'further support' from (unconventional) monetary policy (IMF, 2010b: 30). As stronger adverse effects of fiscal retrenchment on aggregate demand and on growth materialised after 2010, calls for contingency plans and a change of fiscal policy peppered surveillance (IMF, 2010b: 42–43; IMF, 2010c, e; IMF, 2011, 39, 46; IMF, 2012b, 2012d: 1–4).

## The fiscal consolidation debate: How far, how fast? how much will it hurt?

In June 2010, Olivier Blanchard, head of the research department at the IMF, and Carlo Cottarelli, Director of the IMF's fiscal affairs department, published the culmination of their reflections to that date on fiscal policy, fiscal consolidation, and fiscal sustainability. They offered their 'ten commandments for fiscal adjustment in advanced economies' on the IMF blog.[2] Where they sounded warnings against 'front-loading' of fiscal tightening, which they deemed in general to be 'inappropriate' given the need to preserve short- and long-term growth; 'too much adjustment could also hamper growth, and this is not a trivial risk' (Blanchard and Cottarelli, 2010).

Whilst the UK Chancellor has sought to present those arguing for a slower pace of fiscal consolidation as on the radical fringes of international debate, in fact this was the central position of the IMF and others from 2011 onwards. Their position (on fiscal consolidation) was not the mainstream view, but an outlier. The notion of expansionary austerity – which the Government clung to and used to justify its fiscal policy approach in official documents, including the June 2010 emergency budget (Treasury, 2010: 19) – has been widely discredited in some very respectable places, notable the IMF's *World Economic Outlook* in 2010 (IMF, 2010a: chapter 3).

These issues became increasingly prominent within the UK economic policy debate after 2010 as the downturn dragged on through 2011 and into 2012. As their concerns about hysteresis grew, the IMF central scenario for the UK economy began to reflect larger estimates of lost output (IMF, 2012b: table 3). The work on fiscal multipliers discussed above had convinced many in the IMF that these were asymmetric across the cycle, and this view informed IMF surveillance of the UK (2012b: 24–25, 38, 70–76). This begged tricky questions about whether it would be more costly to do the fiscal adjustment immediately or later. These estimates and policy modelling exercises are highly sensitive to assumptions, as noted above, and it is a mistake to over-estimate the possible level of precision these economic estimates can achieve. However, the IMF mission took the view that multipliers for the UK were considerably higher in 2011–2012 than they would be in the near future. This, compounded by their growing concerns about hysteresis effects and permanent lost capacity, led them to advocate an alternative course of action.

The IMF was more ready to reason with higher possible fiscal multipliers than the UK authorities assumed. In OBR chief Robert Chote's March 2013 letter to the Prime Minister, he noted OBR assessments of fiscal multipliers were within the range reported by the IMF, but not at the upper level. The OBR had not engaged in an upwards re-evaluation of fiscal multipliers of the kind advocated by the IMF chief economist in October 2012 (IMF, 2012c; Blanchard and Leigh, 2013). On balance the OBR assumed fiscal multipliers to be somewhat lower than some of the higher IMF assessments of post-GFC levels. Perhaps reflecting these different assumptions, the UK IMF mission noted that the OBR assumed higher medium-term growth for the UK, and 'a more rapid return to historical potential growth rates and less lingering effects from hysteresis and the crisis' (IMF, 2012b: 25).

## The 'plan B' that dare not speak its name

George Osborne staked the economic credibility of the Coalition government in 2010 on its commitment to stay the course of the harsh fiscal consolidation he presented as immediately necessary for the UK to avoid deeper economic and financial crisis. As growth disappointed between 2010 and 2012, the IMF were not alone in recommending a change of course. This was part and parcel of the party political debate, with Shadow Chancellor Ed Balls leading the charge, with more considered interventions from respected economic policy commentators who offered similar views (Wren-Lewis, 2011, 2014; Holland and Portes, 2012; Portes, 2012, 2013). The Chancellor countered these calls by claiming that no diversion was possible. Osborne rejected what he later termed the 'fiscalist' position of Coalition critics (Osborne, 2013), claiming they misread the relation between fiscal policy and growth. This was all part of the construction of fiscal rectitude in Britain around inexorable fiscal policy imperatives of the post-crisis condition.

However, as assiduous observers have picked up, the rhetorical adherence to 'no plan B' belied the reality of UK economic policy (IMF, 2013: 37). Despite claims that no change of course was possible because 'Britain must pay its way in the world' the UK Government *did* slow the pace of fiscal consolidation from late summer 2012 onwards. Indeed Robert Chote, Director of OBR, noted that their evidence indicated that deficit reduction had 'stalled' (quoted in Portes, 2013). OBR forecasts indicated a public sector net borrowing requirement broadly plateauing between 2011 and 2014 (7.7 per cent in 2011–2012, 7.3 per cent in 2012–2013, and 6.8 per cent in to 2013–2014), before beginning to come down again after that (OBR, 2013: chart 1.1). This was all a far cry from the trajectory announced in June 2010. The Coalition construction of fiscal rectitude was, in effect, being honoured in the breach. It turned out there was a plan B, and it had informed deficit reduction efforts since summer 2012. This all demonstrates the contingency and malleability of fiscal rectitude and the presentation of economic policy.

Yet Osborne continues to present the pace of fiscal consolidation as unchanged. In so doing he seeks to claim, whilst pointing to the return of growth to the UK economy during 2013, that those arguing that fiscal consolidation would hurt economic growth were wrong or misguided. This 'fiscalist position', which Osborne rejects (Osborne, 2013), is held not only by critical economists in the UK, such as Jonathon Portes and Simon Wren-Lewis, but also to a significant degree by the IMF. Osborne has sustained his prior assumptions about the relationship between fiscal policy and growth in a bid to challenge what he calls this 'fiscalist position'. This is expansionary austerity thinking rearing its head again, or what Simon Wren-Lewis refers to as an ideological attachment to 'demand denial' (2011). Further evidence of Cameron and Osborne's ideological refusal to admit the connection between fiscal policy and growth came when the Coalition government sought to claim in early 2013 that disappointing growth between 2010 and 2012 was unrelated to the fiscal consolidation effort. They even claimed that the OBR endorsed this view. The OBR Director promptly wrote to David Cameron in March 2013 to point out that this was *not* their view. Whilst the Eurozone crisis and other factors contributed to disappointing growth, fiscal consolidation in OBR estimates accounted for roughly 1.4 per cent of GDP in lower UK growth between 2011 and 2012 (Chote, 2013).

However, many commentators argue that the Coalition government did not slow the pace of adjustment *enough*, with the result that growth has come much later than it could have (Portes, 2013; Wren-Lewis, 2014). The output gap (how far below potential growth the UK economy is) is that much greater than it could have been. Furthermore, the modest pace of growth means that the recovery is relatively weak. It will in all likelihood take a long time to close the yawning output gap which characterises the evolution of the UK economy since 2007–2008, if indeed it can be closed.

## Conclusion: debt and deficit discourse and the British growth model

This chapter has argued that the singular construction of Britain's economic policy problems under the Coalition government since 2010, as a crisis of debt rather than as a crisis of growth, has serious implications for the British growth model and for the balance of emphasis and prioritisation in UK economic policy making. The analysis above demonstrates how fiscal rectitude construction is a transient historical phenomenon, and how the re-construction of economic and fiscal rectitude under the Coalition government since May 2010 is, to some degree, autonomous from actual fiscal policy practice, or its assessment by independent observers. Nevertheless, the consequences of this construction for UK economic performance, and for the nature of the British State, are important. Despite authoritative statements to the contrary from the likes of the IMF, from 2010 onwards Osborne presented his commitment to harsh fiscal consolidation as necessary to stave off a crisis of debt. Osborne justified his decision to 'accelerate the pace of fiscal consolidation' bluntly (and erroneously) in the emergency budget speech of June 2010 'the crisis in the Eurozone shows that unless we deal with our debts there will be no growth' (2010). This interpretive line continued even when the pace of deficit reduction was slowed in 2012. Osborne and Cameron then sought to claim that the fiscal consolidation had not adversely affected growth, despite an overwhelming consensus amongst the OBR, IMF and academic economists that it had.

An underlying ideological opposition to counter-cyclical fiscal policy, or 'demand denial' (see Wren-Lewis, 2011) is at the root of the contorted rhetorical manoeuvring through which Osborne sought to conceal the slowing pace of fiscal consolidation, and through which Cameron sought to claim that the OBR agreed with his erroneous assertion that slower growth in the UK economy in 2011 and 2012 owed nothing to spending retrenchment. More fundamentally, the Coalition government, and in particular the Conservative Chancellor and Prime Minister, demonstrated a desire to change the size of the British state. As Osborne put it in his budget speech of June 2010, 'the state today accounts for almost half of all national income. That is completely unsustainable ... we have made a start. But we need to go much further if we are to meet our fiscal mandate and see debt falling by the end of this Parliament.' (Osborne, 2010) This is tantamount to a different vision for the British state and the UK's public sector. The Coalition's particular construction of fiscal rectitude since May 2010 has implications for Britain's potential growth strategies and for the evolving nature of the British state.

The aim is to reduce public expenditure as a proportion of GDP from circa 50 per cent in the wake of the GFC to 40 per cent. The Coalition settlement, and the planned scaling up of deficit reduction between 2015 and 2018, contains indications as to the evolving character of the British state. According to the OBR, 80 per cent of the very sizeable reduction of the deficit between 2009 and 2018 is accounted for by lower public spending. Government consumption of goods and services will move 'to its smallest share of national income at least since 1948' (OBR, 2013: 7). Gamble notes how the Coalition government 'announced a major rethinking of the role of the state, spurred on by its decision to make a more rapid reduction in the budget deficit its priority', and this augured 'the most dramatic reshaping of the state that has taken place since 1945 ... a complete reevaluation of the Government's role in providing public services' (2010: 10; see also Wren-Lewis, 2013).

The presentation by the Coalition government of its austerity measures as non-negotiable necessary conditions of economic credibility and fiscal sustainability is not at one with assessments by IMF or other respected economic commentators. Nevertheless, the public spending cuts to bring down the deficit on the scale undertaken aggressively between May 2010 and summer 2012, a trajectory set to return between 2015 and 2018, is programmed to alter the future size and scope of the British state. The promised reductions in public investment have implications for the British model of capitalism, limiting the role for public power or the public sector in boosting investment in the economy to increase productive capacity and human capital, or stimulating the manufacturing sector to counter low growth (see Craig Berry, Chapter 7 in this volume). Here a key building block of the Coalition view – the crowding out argument – plays an important role. The crowding out arguments, which underpin the Government's fiscal consolidation strategy, entail focusing on the supply side of the economy and expecting the private sector to pick up the slack. This thinking pursues further the retreat from Keynesian approaches to managing the UK economy since the 1970s (see Coutts and Gudgin, Chapter 1 in this volume).

The Coalition government has adopted a very different vision for British state capacity than, for example, the idea of a British developmental state (see e.g. Shonfield, 1969; Marquand, 1988; Hutton, 1995). There could be scope for such themes to re-emerge, given widespread calls for a rebalancing of the British economy. Yet ironically, in contrast to the 1970s, the IMF currently advocates *more* UK public expenditure on growth-enhancing measures and public investment than the Coalition government has been willing to countenance. Significantly, even though the pace of fiscal consolidation was attenuated in the summer of 2012, there are ongoing concerns that too much of the fiscal consolidation is coming from cutting public investment. Critics highlight how early deficit reduction came from 'cutting public sector net investment (spending on schools, roads, hospitals, etc.) roughly in half' (Portes, 2013). A recent *Financial Times* in-depth report revealed a lack of delivery on infrastructure spending, with 'slow, if not minimal, progress on many schemes' (Plimmer and Pickard, 2013).

The key dissonance between the IMF mission and the UK government during 2013 Article IV consultations, over a number of billion pounds of intrastructure spending, reveals deeper differences about the public power's ability to positively affect economic outcomes. The IMF's UK mission noted 'to spur private demand, the drag from planned near-term fiscal tightening could be offset – notably by bringing forward capital investment' (IMF, 2013: 38). The significance of the difference between the UK government and IMF is not just the volume but the type of spending. The IMF's advocacy of more infrastructure spending indicates that its view of fiscal policy goes beyond improved capacity utilisation, to plans to increase capacity (i.e. a more fully fledged growth policy); the Mission calls for 'measures aimed at improving the economy's skills base and competitiveness' to 'help boost the productive potential' as well as 'support demand in the near-term by boosting expectations about long-term prospects and incomes' (IMF, 2013: 38). The IMF is not normally seen as an advocate of the developmental state model, yet they do not neglect the role of capacity building public investment in infrastructure, recognising its high fiscal multipliers and beneficial effects. Moreover, even in the UK's less than optimal public finances position, the IMF advocates *increasing* such infrastructure spending. However, the Coalition strategy sees little merit in this kind of expansion of state intervention. Indeed, the size of the state – and the scope of the state – entailed within the austerity and medium-term fiscal consolidation programme leaves limited space for facilitating growth oriented investment, or broader infrastructural development. The Coalition's levels and targets for public spending, and the parameters of its debt and deficit discourse, which it has reinforced consistently since 2010, rule out the kinds of institutional innovations that would be consistent with a British developmental state model.

## Notes

Ben Clift gratefully acknowledges the support of the Leverhulme Trust for the research fellowship funding (RF-2012-340) entitled 'Its Mostly Fiscal – The IMF, Evolving Fiscal Policy Doctrine and The Crisis', which enabled the research for this chapter to be undertaken. The author is grateful to the editors of this volume for helpful comments on an earlier draft of this chapter.

1. Hysteresis is a process whereby substantial persistence of higher unemployment leads, through loss of skills, human capital degradation, and insider/outsider effects within the labour market, to a permanent ratcheting up of the unemployment rate and reduction in the growth potential of the economy. See Blanchard and Summers (1986).
2. Olivier Blanchard and Carlo Cottarelli 'Ten Commandments for Fiscal Adjustment in Advanced Economies'. Posted on 24 June 2010 by iMFdirect. http://blog-imfdirect.imf.org/2010/06/24/ten-commandments-for-fiscal-adjustment-in-advanced-economies/

## References

Alesina, A. and Perotti, R. (1995) 'Fiscal Expansions and Fiscal Adjustments in OECD Countries', NBER Working Papers 5214.

Alesina, A. F. and Ardagna, S. (2009) 'Large Changes in Fiscal Policy: Taxes Versus Spending', NBER Working Paper No. 15438, October.

Auerbach, A. J. and Gorodnichenko, Y. (2012) 'Fiscal Multipliers in Recession and Expansion', *American Economic Journal: Economic Policy*, 4, 2, 1–27

Bagaria, N., Holland, D. and Van Reenen, J. (2012) 'Fiscal Consolidation during a Depression', *National Institute Economic Review*, 221, F42–F54.

Barrell, R., Fic, T. and Liadze, I. (2009) 'Fiscal Policy Effectiveness in the Banking Crisis', *National Institute Economic Review*, 207.

Barrell, R., Holland, D. and Hurst, A. I. (2012) 'Fiscal Consolidation Part 2: Fiscal Multipliers and Fiscal Consolidations', OECD Economics Department Working Paper No. 933.

Blaug, M. (1990) 'Second Thoughts on the Keynesian Revolution' In *Economic Theories: True or False,* edited by Mark Blaug.

Backhouse, R. (2006) 'The Keynesian Revolution', in *The Cambridge Companion to Keynes*, edited by Roger Backhouse and Bradley Bateman. Cambridge: Cambridge University Press, pp. 19–38.

Blanchard, O. (2010) 'IMF Explores Contours of Future Macroeconomic Policy' Interview with Olivier Blanchard IMF Survey online 12 February 2010. http://www.imf.org/external/pubs/ft/survey/so/2010/int021210a.htm

Blanchard, O. (2011) 2011 in Review: Four Hard Truths 21/12/2011. http://blog-imfdirect.imf.org/2011/12/21/2011-in-review-four-hard-truths/

Blanchard, Olivier. and Cottarelli, Carlo (2010) 'Ten Commandments for Fiscal Adjustment in Advanced Economies' Posted on 24 June 2010 by IMFdirect. http://blog-imfdirect.imf.org/2010/06/24/ten-commandments-for-fiscal-adjustment-in-advanced-economies/

Blanchard, O. and Leigh, D. (2013) *Growth Forecast Errors and Fiscal Multipliers.* IMF Working Paper WP/13/1, Washington, IMF.

Blanchard, O. and Summers, L. (1986) 'Hysteresis And The European Unemployment Problem', *NBER Macroeconomics Annual 1986*, 1, 15–90. http://www.nber.org/chapters/c4245

Blyth, M. (2010) 'This Time It Really Is Different: Europe, the Financial Crisis, and "Staying on Top" in the 21st Century', Paper Prepared for Breznitz and Zysman (eds), *The Third Globalisation: Can Wealthy Nations Stay Rich in the Twenty-First Century?* Oxford: Oxford University Press.

Blyth, M. (2013) *Austerity: The History of a Dangerous Idea.* Oxford: Oxford University Press.

Chopra, A. (2010) 'Transcript of a Conference Call on the 2010 Article IV Consultations with the United Kingdom', Tuesday, 9 November 2010 http://www.imf.org/external/np/tr/2010/tr110910.htm

Chote, R. (2013) Letter to the Prime Minister, March 2013. Office for Budget Responsibility.

Clift, B. and Tomlinson, J. (2008) 'Whatever Happened to the UK Balance of Payments "Problem"? The Contingent (Re)Construction of British Economic Performance Assessment', *British Journal of Politics and International Relations*, 10, 4, 607–629.

DeLong, J. B. and Summers, L. H. (2012) 'Fiscal Policy in a Depressed Economy', Brookings Papers on Economic Activity 2012.

G20 (2010) Communique´ from the Toronto summit, 26–27 June.

Gamble, A. (2010) 'The Politics of the Deficit: British Politics and the Financial Crisis', paper prepared for APSA Conference, Boston Ma. September 2010.

Hall, R. (2008) *Central Banking as Global Governance.* Oxford: Oxford University Press.

Hay, C. (2013) 'Treating the Symptom Not the Condition: Crisis Definition, Deficit Reduction and the Search for a New British Growth Model', *British Journal of Politics and International Relations*, 15, 1, 23–37.

Holland, D. and Portes, J. (2012) 'Self-Defeating Austerity?' *National Institute Economic Review*, 222, 1–8.

Hutton, W. (1995) *The State We're In.* London: Jonathon Cape.

IMF (2009) 'The State of Public Finances Cross-Country Fiscal Monitor: November 2009', SPN/09/25 IMF, Washington.

IMF (2010a) *World Economic Outlook: Recovery, Risk and Rebalancing,* October 2010, Washington: IMF.

IMF (2010b) IMF Country Report No. 10/338 United Kingdom: 2010 Article IV Consultation – Staff Report; Staff Supplement; Public Information Notice on the Executive Board Discussion; and Statement by the Executive Director for the United Kingdom. Washington: IMF.

IMF (2010c) 'Navigating the Fiscal Challenges Ahead: *Fiscal Monitor* May 2010'. Washington: IMF.

IMF (2010d) IMF Staff position note 'Default in Today's Advanced Economies: Unnecessary, Undesirable, and Unlikely' SPN/10/12, 1 September. IMF, Washington

IMF (2010e) IMF Executive Board Concludes 2010 Article IV Consultation with the United Kingdom http://www.imf.org/external/np/sec/pn/2010/pn10147. htm. Public Information Notice (PIN) No. 10/147 9 November 2010

IMF (2011) 'United Kingdom: 2011 Article IV Consultation – Staff Report' IMF Country Report No. 11/220. Washington: IMF.

IMF (2012a) *Fiscal Monitor: Balancing Fiscal Policy Risks.* April 2012, Washington: IMF.

IMF (2012b) 'United Kingdom: 2011 Article IV Consultation – Staff Report', Report No. 12/90. Washington: IMF.

IMF (2012c) *World Economic Outlook: Growth Resuming, Dangers Remain,* October, Washington: IMF.

IMF (2012d) 'United Kingdom – 2012 Article IV Consultation Concluding Statement of the Mission' http://www.imf.org/external/np/ms/2012/052212. htm

IMF (2013) 'United Kingdom: 2013 Article IV Consultation – Staff Report', Report No. 13/210. Washington: IMF.

Kahn, R. (1931) 'The Relation of Home Investment to Unemployment', *Economic Journal,* 41, 173–198

Keynes, J. M. (1964[1936]) *The General Theory of Employment, Interest and Money.* London: Macmillan.

Klein, L. (1968) *The Keynesian Revolution.* London: Macmillan.

Office for Budget Responsibility (2013) *Economic and Fiscal Outlook December 2013.* http://cdn.budgetresponsibility.independent.gov.uk/Economic-and-fiscal-outlook-December-2013.pdf

Marquand, D. (1988) *The Unprincipled Society.* London: Fontana Press.

Plimmer, G. and Pickard, J. (2013) 'Osborne under Pressure to Deliver Coalition Infrastructure Pledges', *Financial Times,* 2 December.

Osborne, G. (2010) 'Budget Statement by the Chancellor of the Exchequer', the Rt Hon George Osborne MP, 22 June 2010 http://webarchive.nationalarchives. gov.uk/20130129110402/http://www.hm-treasury.gov.uk/junebudget_speech. htm

Osborne, G. (2013) 'Chancellor Speech on the Economy: HM Treasury', 9 September 2013, https://www.gov.uk/government/speeches/chancellor-speech-on-the-economy

Portes, J. (2012) 'More on Multipliers: Why Does It Matter?' NIESR Blog, http:// niesr.ac.uk/blog/more-multipliers-why-does-it-matter#.UvkM2c4SPz9

Portes, J. (2013) 'What Osborne Won't Admit: Growth has Increased Because of Slower Cuts', *New Statesman,* 10 September.

Ruggie, J. (1998) *Constructing the World Polity: Essays in International Institutionalization.* London: Routledge.

Searle, J. (1995) *The Construction Of Social Reality.* London: Penguin.

Shonfield, A. (1969) *Modern Capitalism: The Changing Balance of Public and Private Power.* Oxford: Oxford University Press.

Sinclair, Tim (2005) *The New Masters of Capital: American Bond Rating Agencies and the Politics of Creditworthiness.* Ithaca: Cornell University Press.

Spilimbergo, A., Blanchard, O. Symansky, S. and Cottarelli, C. (2008) *Fiscal Policy for the Crisis,* IMF Staff Position Note, SPN/08/01, 29 December.

Spilimbergo, A., Symansky, S. and Schindler, M. (2009) 'Fiscal Multipliers', IMF Staff Position Note, SPN/09/11.

Tomlinson, Jim (1990) *Public Policy and the Economy.* Oxford: Clarendon.

Treasury (2010a) *Budget 2010 Securing the Recovery,* HC 451. London: HMSO.

Treasury (2010b) *Budget 2010,* HC 61. London: HMSO.

Wren-Lewis, Simon (2011) 'Lessons from Failure: Fiscal Policy, Indulgence and Ideology', *National Institute Economic Review,* 217, 1–15.

Wren-Lewis, S. (2013) 'The UKs Macroeconomic Battleground to Come', 11 December.    http://mainlymacro.blogspot.co.uk/2013/12/the-uks-macroeconomic-battleground-to.html

Wren-Lewis, S. (2014) 'Economic Standards', 4 January, http://mainlymacro.blogspot.co.uk/search?updated-max=2014-01-22T14:41:00-08:00&max-results=7

# 7
# The Final Nail in the Coffin? Crisis, Manufacturing Decline, and Why It Matters

*Craig Berry*

Recessions inevitably, and understandably, herald anxiety and much discussion about the headline performance of the economy, chiefly employment, income and GDP growth. Various indicators, such as exports, investment or consumer spending are closely monitored for evidence of economic recovery. The performance of individual sectors is important to this discourse, but sectors are largely treated as component parts – a way of disaggregating overall economic performance – rather than examined in terms of the intrinsic role they may play in the overall economic system. It is rare for mainstream economic commentators to dig very deeply into 'what' questions: exports *of what*, investment *in what*, or spending *on what*. Critical scholarship is not faultless in this regard. Colin Hay's (2013) depiction of failure of the Anglo-liberal growth model represents a persuasive account of the British growth crisis and the conditions that triggered the deep recession of 2009. Again, however, we are invited to worry about an economy that pays too little to most of its employees, fails to facilitate long-term investment, and relies too heavily on consumer spending fuelled by debt and the housing market – concerns that manifest at the macro level of analysis, not the meso. The prominent role played by the financial sector in this critical account is the exception that proves the rule, as the 'cuckoo in the nest' it is (rightly) condemned as a key progenitor of the macroeconomy's pathologies.

This chapter does not depart from Hay's account of the British growth crisis, instead it seeks to augment it by directing attention to an essential segment of the UK economy – indeed every capitalist economy, and of course the global capitalist economy – that is, manufacturing. The crisis has severely affected manufacturing, at the same time a crisis in UK manufacturing is constitutive of, and inseparable from, the wider crisis of growth; the nature and performance of the manufacturing sector is central to why the crisis emerged, why it was so profound, and why the UK economy has yet to meaningfully recover. The chapter's diagnosis of manufacturing in the UK is not entirely new, it draws upon and updates insights from scholarship on manufacturing generated through the long-running debate about the UK's economic decline, arguing that while declinism is an over-simplified narrative, the stories it tells about manufacturing help us to account for the UK's present predicament.

Interestingly, the most consistent attempt to direct attention to manufacturing has emanated from the political establishment, through the coalition government's rebalancing narrative. The economic imbalance imbibed with greatest significance by the coalition partners has of course been that between the public and private sectors, but correcting apparent imbalances between exports and imports, saving and spending, and manufacturing and finance has also been identified as a policy priority (HM Government, 2010; HMT and BIS, 2011; Osborne, 2010). Of course, the rebalancing narrative is in large part an attempt to downplay the significance of the economic crisis (Froud et al., 2011), and indeed the objective has largely been abandoned by government in favour of restoring the pre-crisis growth model (Berry, 2013). For our purposes here, the main problem with rebalancing is that, while it signifies anxiety about the state of particular sectors, it over-simplifies (perhaps intentionally) the relationships between sectors. As such, while the finance sector has endogenous defects, these defects take on greatest significance with respect to how they affect the performance of the rest of the economy. The chapter concludes, accordingly, that it is the UK political elite's persistent reluctance to address the impact of finance on other sectors, despite the unique opportunity created in this regard by the financial crisis, that determines manufacturing's fate.

The chapter is divided into three main sections. The first details manufacturing decline in the context of the UK's more general economic decline, and offers an overview of the condition of UK manufacturing amid recession and apparent recovery. Most importantly, it accounts for the difficulties experienced by manufacturing by locating it within the UK's national business model. The second section contemplates the significance of the manufacturing sector to both sustainable growth and social equality (and where they overlap), arguing that it is paramount on both counts. Finally, the third section looks briefly at efforts to improve the UK's manufacturing performance, arguing that an exclusive focus on advanced manufacturing is wrong-headed, and that any change depends on a wider economic transformation.

## Why are the British *even worse* at manufacturing?

In 1983, Karel Williams, John Williams and Dennis Thomas published the seminal *Why Are the British Bad at Manufacturing?* The study sought to explain the failure of Keynesian macroeconomic policies to arrest the UK's relative economic decline in the post-war era, it also served as a warning about the emergent monetarist framework of the Thatcher government. For Williams *et al.*, neither approach addressed either inter-sectoral relationships or the international economic context, which together shape everyday decisions by economic actors, including the state. These factors handicapped manufacturing in the UK, which in turn dimmed the propulsive force of manufacturing in delivering sustainable growth. Strong overall growth in most of the 1990s and 2000s appeared to have proved Williams *et al.* wrong about the latter, irrespective of their insights on the former issue. But the depth of the economic downturn since 2008 warrants revisiting both elements of their argument. First, however, this section looks briefly at the history of manufacturing decline.

### Manufacturing decline

There have been three main periods of manufacturing decline. The UK's share of manufacturing output fell steadily from the height of the Industrial Revolution in the early nineteenth century, but fell more rapidly following Germany and Japan's rapid industrialisation around the turn of the twentieth century. The UK's share of world manufacturing output fell from 23 per cent in 1880 to 14 per cent at the outbreak of the First World War (English and Kenny, 2000: 280). The period following the Second World War also saw significant decline, but should probably be divided into an immediate post-war period up to the 1970s, and a later period following the election of Margaret Thatcher. In the 1950s, what began as a natural post-war catch-up by West Germany and Japan developed into a significant undoing of the UK's industrial strength. Between 1950 and 1979, annual growth in manufacturing output averaged 2 per cent – significantly lower than all other leading OECD countries. Over the same period, only the United States saw lower growth in labour productivity in manufacturing, although the UK fared worse in terms of total factor productivity, and significantly worse than all leading competitors in terms of profitability (Matthews, 2007: 766–771).

If the immediate post-war period exhibited a relatively poor performance, it was the period from the late 1970s onwards that saw manufacturing in the UK significantly decline in terms of relative size. Manufacturing's share of overall economic output in the UK fell from around 30 per cent in 1980 to 15 per cent in the mid-2000s (PricewaterhouseCoopers, 2009: 7). More than two million jobs were lost in the manufacturing sector during the 1980s, with almost one million more in the early and mid-1990s, and around 1.5 million during New Labour's time in government (Froud et al., 2011: 18). The Thatcher government's pursuit of a strong pound during the 1980s had a deleterious impact on the international competitiveness of UK manufacturing, but it did boost the attractiveness of the City of London to international capital markets. The enormous expansion of North Sea oil production in the 1980s supported the high pound and at the same time diluted the imperative to support manufacturing by way of protecting the UK's export base. Much is often made of the fact that manufacturing productivity actually improved throughout the 1980s, after falling significantly in the 1970s, with this trend credited to the Thatcher government's offensive against the trade unions, and the impact of the early-1980s recession in 'killing off' the least productive manufacturing workers and firms. However, productivity in the 1980s did not grow as quickly as it had even in the 1960s, and slowed again in the 1990s (Cameron, 2003). Globalisation is often offered as an explanation for job losses in this period, and it is undoubtedly true that, from the 1970s onwards, global manufacturing became more international in character, with trade a higher proportion of world manufacturing output, and intra-industry trade a higher proportion of overall trade. However, over this period non-OECD countries have not, as a whole, seen increases in either the number of people employed in manufacturing, or the proportion of the world's manufacturing workforce located within their borders. The UK did lose many low-skilled manufacturing jobs to developing countries, but also many high-skilled jobs to OECD rivals as many countries were able to reinvest productivity gains in higher-value production (Pilat et al., 2006).

Unsurprisingly, the fate of manufacturing featured heavily in debates about the UK's general decline, as a reduction of *absolute* influence in world politics was related to poor *relative* economic performance (Gamble, 2000). For early decline theorists, the UK's 'gentlemanly' capitalism recast the Industrial Revolution as a historical anomaly, as British national culture was said to eschew the entrepreneurial approach required of industrialism. For others, it was precisely the UK's early success in industrialism that precipitated relative decline, as it lessened incentives to innovate (Kenny and English, 2000). Perhaps the most promising declinist approach for our purposes is that which emphasises the relationship between finance and industry, exemplified by Geoffrey Ingham's *Capitalism Divided* (1984). Ingham emphasised the importance of manufacturing to national prosperity, but outlined the deleterious impact of the UK's excessively large financial sector on attracting labour market talent, investment and macroeconomic policy support away from sectors such as manufacturing, while at the same time being incapable of delivering real economic value itself. Later decline theorists have, however, celebrated the end of decline for precisely the same reasons, as the UK political elite appeared to achieve sustained economic growth in the 1990s and 2000s by supporting financial sector growth and marginalising manufacturing, therefore marshalling the UK's historic and distinctive economic strengths (Brivati, 2007; Rubinstein, 1993, 2000).

### The national 'business model'

The financial crisis and subsequent recession casts considerable doubt on the notion that the UK's decline has been arrested or reversed and raises questions about the extent to which the UK's economic problems are synonymous with its performance in manufacturing. Karel Williams *et al.* steered clear of the decline debate, but offer an account of UK manufacturing similar to Geoffrey Ingham's. They posited four 'conditions of enterprise' which characterise the British national 'business model' and help to explain the decline of manufacturing in the UK. They were, of course, writing before the manufacturing sector shrunk so significantly in the 1980s, when the UK remained one of the world's leading manufacturers in terms of output. To argue that the UK was 'bad' at manufacturing at this time may have been excessive, although it did seem the country was increasingly 'less good' at it, compared to its main rivals.

The first condition is the control of enterprise over the labour process (Williams et al., 1983: 34–47). Williams *et al.* acknowledge the view, widely held at the time, that industrial relations in the UK led to 'bad work practices' encompassing over-staffed and poorly-maintained machinery and acting as a drain on management effort. However, they dispute the notion that trade union strength was the root cause of this condition, suggesting instead that it was trade union marginalisation in corporate decision-making that led to poor industrial relations. Moreover, insofar as bad work practices lead to lower productivity, generally speaking firms are compensated for this through lower wage costs. The continuing relevance of this condition has been underlined by Guy Vernon and Mark Rogers' (2013) comparison across fourteen OECD countries of the relationship between forms of trade union organisation and manufacturing productivity. Trade unions which take the form of enterprise unions, organising within a single firm or workplace, have little or no impact on productivity, irrespective of their size or strength (as in the United States). In countries where trade unions organise across multiple firms and occupations within a single industry (such as Germany), union strength is associated with higher productivity. In manufacturing sectors dominated by craft and general unionism (traditional organisation within particular occupations, increasingly characterised by large-scale, catch-all unions), union strength has a deleterious impact on productivity. The UK typifies this third formation. The limited and short-lived nature of productivity improvements in the 1980s vindicates the Williams *et al.* argument to some extent, and encourages us to consider not simply the size and strength of trade unions, but also the extent of their involvement in strategic decisions within the sector.

The second condition is market structure and the nature of demand (Williams et al., 1983: 47–58). Williams *et al.* argued that the Europeanisation of the manufacturing customer base made it difficult for the UK to compete on quality against its more nimble European rivals, situated closer to their final customers, and sterling's lofty value (discussed further below) similarly meant it could not compete on cost. Problems of market structure are related to two other conditions of enterprise, discussed further below, the failure of the banking sector to provide funding for transforming production processes and the government's *laissez-faire* approach to industrial policy. Williams *et al.* also made the specific point, offering the example of shipbuilding, that in UK manufacturing there existed a bifurcation between buyers and producers which was not evident in other European countries to the same extent. Ship owners in many countries had a financial stake in the shipbuilding yards, and therefore invested in production in order to meet their own demand. In the UK, ship owners simply looked elsewhere. It is interesting to note that, after decades of decline, the UK retains a strong, global position in only two industries, aerospace and pharmaceuticals – where the UK government has itself been the most important customer. However, even these industries have suffered in recent years, under both New Labour and the coalition government, as a result of the state's reluctance to take a strategic role in supporting them, whether in terms of incentivising domestic production (in the case of pharmaceuticals) or offering strong political backing for international activities (in the case of aerospace and related defence activities) (Comfort, 2013; Sissons, 2012).

The third condition, clearly the most important for Williams et al. (1982: 58–76), is the relationship of manufacturing to financial institutions. Compared to other European countries, British manufacturers rely far more on retained profits and equity finance than on bank loans for investment. This is problematic for two main reasons: firstly, British manufacturers are relatively unprofitable; and secondly, the new-issue equity market in the UK is relatively underdeveloped compared with the secondary issue market. Manufacturing sectors in most leading OECD nations use retained profits and equities to fund investment to a greater extent than the UK, even though overall they rely far more on bank lending. Williams *et al.* point to the 'liquidation' approach to determining loan viability in the UK, where the value of the borrowers' assets are the main consideration, rather than the 'going concern' approach more prevalent in Germany and the United States, which favours future revenue streams. They also identify the highly 'financialised' environment within which institutional investors operate – incentivising 'safe haven' investments such as the secondary equities market, gilts and property – as culpable for under-investment in manufacturing.

It hardly needs reporting that British financial institutions continue to fail the manufacturing sector. Since the publication of *Why Are the British Bad at Manufacturing?*, what Stewart Lansley (2011) calls the 'two-track economy' has become even more pronounced. Deregulation and technological innovation within the so-called 'money economy' centred in the City of London enables economic actors to derive strong returns simply from manipulating the financial structures of existing firms, rather than investing in 'productive economy'. The growth of hedge funds has exacerbated short-termism throughout the economy, and enabled the financial sector to profit from industrial failure as well as industrial success. Banks have grown in size and reoriented towards investment as well as lending, yet both activities are heavily skewed towards residential and commercial property. Institutional investors continue to turn over their portfolios at a rapid pace, disabling the prospect of long-term investment in manufacturing capacity (Woolley, 2011). Figure 7.1 offers an industrial breakdown of lending by banks resident in the UK, detailing how the 2000s largely exacerbated existing biases towards property (including mortgage lending to individuals). Accordingly, while research and development (R&D) spending rose from the early 1990s up until the financial crisis in Germany, France and the United States, in the UK it fell from 1 to 0.8 per cent of GDP (Lansley, 2013).

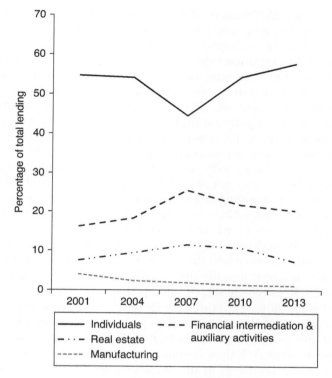

*Figure 7.1* Industrial breakdown of UK resident bank lending

Source: Bank of England. Figures from Bank of England data, available at http://www.bankofengland.co.uk/statistics/Pages/bankstats/2014/mar.aspx (accessed 15 May 2014).

It would be misleading to claim, however, that there exists a major *cultural* cleavage between finance and major manufacturing firms – this assumption is one of the weaknesses of the decline literature on this issue. Williams *et al.* remark that 'big business seems to have learnt to love its financial chains' (although this does not apply to smaller firms to the same extent) (1983: 75–76). This is because of the tendency – partly in response to the paucity of external finance – of manufacturing firms in the UK to increase in size through merger and acquisition (M&A) activity. Takeovers, which were rarely hostile, were a way to grow without strong profits or innovation. Given the unwillingness of UK banks to lend to the manufacturing sector, investment in the form of takeovers by foreign companies has proved to be an important source of capital for UK manufacturers, albeit at the same time it has led to a loss of control over where production is located (see Jeremy Green's contribution to this volume in Chapter 3 for a longer discussion of foreign direct investment and multi-national companies in the UK). This logic has therefore acted to *reverse* the trend towards ever-larger manufacturing firms; in a recent report for the Centre for Research on Socio-Cultural Change (CRESC), however, Karel Williams (with several co-authors), acknowledged the rapidly declining size of British manufacturers since the 1980s, with the sector now populated by small workshops without the capacity to move up the value chain (Froud et al., 2011: 29). Of course, the period since *Why Are the British Bad at Manufacturing?* has seen the global coalescence of supply chains and the growth of intra-industry trade, and the growing importance of manufacturing firms able to operate and form relationships across borders. M&A among British firms in the mid/late twentieth century represented a defensive strategy against steady decline which ultimately proved unsustainable. The smaller firms that remain, in the early twenty-first century, are the ones least able to integrate into the global production system. Foreign investment into UK manufacturing was, and perhaps still is, an endorsement of the strength of the sector in some fields – yet it has also exacerbated the destruction of the sector as these globally mobile investors have little incentive to protect the UK's manufacturing base for its own sake. As suggested above, it is these circumstances, far more than the apparent rise of low-cost producers in the developing world, that explains the 'offshoring' of UK manufacturing.

The fourth condition is, simply, government. Williams et al. (1983: 92–110) share with Robert Skidelsky (2013) the view that the state in the UK has never taken a strategic approach to manufacturing. A recent comparative study of industrial policy across Europe, Japan and the United States found that the UK lacks any tradition of active industrial policy (although persistent efforts to attract inward investment, at least in part through foreign takeovers, could be seen as an *implicit*, albeit deeply flawed, industrial strategy). Indeed, there have been few initiatives targeted directly at manufacturing, with industrial policy largely represented by support for regional development and small- to medium-sized enterprises (SMEs) that did not discriminate between sectors. Policy interventions are generally aimed at the micro level, and take the form of 'soft' support, such as advice services, gateway services and the dissemination of best practice. The UK prefers tax credits and weighted public sector procurement practices to direct subsidies and, insofar as subsidies are offered, they are generally targeted, understandably, at the most needy regions, rather than strategically important industries (Buigues and Sekkat, 2009). Reports from policy insiders confirm this picture. Sir Ian Gilmour, a 'wet' (that is, moderate) minister in the first Thatcher administration, accused his Thatcherite colleagues of 'a systematic belittling of manufacturing industry's importance' (cited in Lansley, 2011). Dan Corry, head of the 10 Downing Street policy unit and a special adviser at the Department of Trade and Industry under New Labour, admits that despite being concerned about the future of manufacturing, indicated by the launch of the Manufacturing Advisory Service in 2002, 'the Labour government was not quite sure what to do' (Corry, 2011: s128).

### The recession and its aftermath

It would be wrong to presume that 2008 represented a significant rupture within the manufacturing sector in the UK, as it did for the rest of the economy, because manufacturing had not shared in the pre-crisis boom. There had been no upturn in manufacturing output between 2002 and 2007 (Froud et al., 2011: 26–28). At the beginning of 2014 the notion that manufacturing was undergoing a resurgence became commonplace in media reports, based largely on the stabilisation of output growth witnessed in 2013 and a growing confidence among manufacturers (see Allen, 2014). Markit's monthly Purchasing Managers' Index (PMI) received regular coverage in *The Financial Times*, with Emily Cadman and Tanya Powley reporting in March 2014 that the index had shown activity increases for eleven months in a row – a period of consistency unlike that experienced since the 2009 recession, but rather mundane when considered over a longer timeframe.

Clearly, there is a danger of confusing levels and rates; consistent growth from a very low base is not a sign of success. The most remarkable aspect of manufacturing's recovery is that it is occurring so late after the official end of the recession. Furthermore, even the limited recovery evident in manufacturing had been fuelled by a single industry, that is, car manufacturing, largely consisting of Japanese-owned firms increasing production in the UK (ONS, 2013a). Clearly, these firms have been attracted by falling real wages and sterling's significant depreciation; that so few other industries have benefited from the same dynamic is therefore also quite remarkable, and demonstrates the UK's crippled manufacturing capacity in most industries. A weak pound should, in theory, offer an important fillip to manufacturers, yet it seems clear that the damage inflicted on UK manufacturing during the 1980s, when a strong pound was pursued to the benefit of the banking sector, has dismantled the logic of this equation (SPERI, 2014b). Interestingly, strong domestic demand is also part of the explanation for car manufacturing's relative success, with *The Guardian* reporting in January 2014 on the apparent (and hugely ironic) role that Payment Protection Insurance compensation has played in supporting this demand (Monaghan, 2014). Output in the transport equipment industry (principally cars) grew by more than 50 per cent between 2009 and 2013, whereas all other manufacturing industries saw either a fall in output or only a small increase over this period. In fact, in every non-transport industry that has seen rising output, the growth recorded between 2009 and 2010 was greater than that recorded from 2010 onwards (ONS, 2013b).

Overall, manufacturing output remains significantly below its 2007 level, and lower even than the level of output attained in 2010. In contrast, output in the services sector recently exceeded its pre-crisis peak (ONS, 2014b). More than 300,000 jobs have been lost in manufacturing since 2007, more than any other sector. Health and social work have seen the highest increase in jobs over this period (more than 400,000), but the largest percentage increase has been in real estate activities, that is, services related to property and the housing market (an increase in jobs of more than 20 per cent between the end of 2007 and end of 2013) (ONS, 2014a). Manufacturing has been hit particularly hard by the staggering sluggishness in business investment, which has fallen in two out of every three quarters since the coalition government took office, and remains significantly below its pre-recession peak and the G7 average (Berry, 2013: 21). Capital, however, is available. British businesses were estimated to be retaining around £500 billion in cash at the end of 2013 (Parker and Groom, 2013). Figure 7.1, in the previous section, details how steeply lending to manufacturers by UK financial institutions, relative to individuals and other sectors, has fallen since the financial crisis – even as total lending overall has risen significantly.

It is worth noting that, predictably, manufacturing output has recovered strongly in Germany, with car manufacturing also making a significant contribution to growth. The key difference between the UK and Germany in this regard is that Germany houses a greater proportion of its car manufacturing supply chain: 60 per cent of the content of cars assembled in Germany is manufactured in Germany, compared to 36 per cent in the UK (Stewart, 2013). Crucially, employment in the UK's, so-called, foundation industries – industries which predominantly supply the manufacturing and construction sectors – has fallen proportionately more than manufacturing in general (PricewaterhouseCoopers, 2014). Furthermore, Julie Froud *et al.* report that the three industries which account for almost four-fifths of the UK's manufacturing exports (machine tools and equipment, car manufacturing and chemicals) also account for almost half of the manufacturing trade deficit, because such a high proportion of their components are imported (2011: 28).

## Why manufacturing matters

This section makes the case that manufacturing is special. The decline of the manufacturing sector in the UK has, firstly, socially deleterious consequences, which have intensified since the recession, and secondly, exemplifies the flawed growth model which prevails in the UK.

### Manufacturing and social equality

The decline of manufacturing has negatively affected the ability of the UK labour market to produce high-quality and well-paid jobs. Manufacturing productivity has failed to keep pace with the UK's main competitors, yet manufacturing jobs tend to exhibit greater productivity than the service sector jobs that now dominate the UK labour market, because the latter are labour- rather than capital-intensive. This equates, primarily, to higher wages for manufacturing workers, but also higher quality jobs with a stronger utilisation of skills (Berry, 2014). The decline of manufacturing is also a constitutive part of the acute labour market problems faced by young people in particular, as the higher skills profile of employment in manufacturing is associated with good vocational pathways, such as apprenticeships. The services sector has been unable to replicate this (Heyes, 2012; Jones, 2013). The number of young people not in employment, education or training (NEET) is therefore alarmingly high (Cooke, 2013).

The recognition that the events of 2008 and the subsequent deep recession were preceded by an extraordinary squeeze on low and median incomes and living standards is one of the main reasons that the UK is experiencing an ongoing crisis of and for growth, not simply the aftermath of a financial crisis. Even during a period of relatively strong and consistent growth, from the early 1990s onwards, it became clear that not only were different segments of society benefiting disproportionately from growth, but that the majority were hardly benefiting at all. While earnings across the labour market as a whole grew strongly in the decade up to 2008, earnings in the bottom half of the earnings distribution 'flat-lined' from 2003 onwards. James Plunkett (2011) points out that the median earner in the UK did not earn noticeably more in 2008 than they had in 2003, and that had earnings growth in the middle continued on its 1977–2003 path during this period, the median earner would have entered 2008 being paid over £2,000 more a year. This pattern has continued and intensified since the recession. Overall earnings growth has largely halted, yet this is because incomes at the bottom and middle of the earnings distribution have consistently fallen in real terms, while incomes at the top have continued to rise (Berry, 2014; Plunkett et al., 2014).

What is sometimes missed in this line of argument, however, is that the earnings squeeze is not simply a product of the same jobs paying less, or not paying more. Rather, it is a product of the transformation of the sectoral balance of the British economy, that is, the reduction in employment within middle-paying sectors such as manufacturing. Before the return of the housing boom in 2013, the fastest growing sector was the economy's lowest paid sector, which saw a 17 per cent growth in employment between 2008 and 2012. The Resolution Foundation reports that, overall, 190,000 jobs were created in low-paying sectors over this period (defined as sectors where median pay is lower than two-thirds of the national median), while 169,000 jobs were lost in middle-paying sectors. All of the middle-paying sectors concentrated in the private sector (that is, manufacturing, construction, and transport, storage and communications) saw employment fall, apart from real estate. High-paying sectors saw employment grow by 139,000, although this is due almost exclusively to growth in a single sector, that is, business services (Plunkett et al., 2014: 31–34).

The Trades Union Congress (TUC, 2013) has taken this analysis further by detailing employment growth within individual industries, showing, for instance, that higher-paying manufacturing industries have lost more jobs than lower-paying manufacturing industries. This is the reason we have seen pay in manufacturing decline in relation to other sectors. In 2000, manufacturing workers were paid around 20 per cent more than the national average; by the end of 2013, this had fallen to around 15 per cent (SPERI, 2014a). We can conclude that the higher-paying manufacturing industries encompass more capital-intensive jobs, and are therefore disproportionately affected by the UK's stagnant investment rate. The loss of jobs in manufacturing is not only closing off routes into high-quality employment for many people, but the jobs that remain are increasingly lower-quality, further undermining the ability of the manufacturing sector to deliver equitable growth (see the discussion of decent work in Frank Pyke's Chapter 13 in this volume; from the current chapter's perspective, manufacturing's resurgence may be an essential ingredient for addressing poor quality and precarious employment).

Manufacturing decline also exacerbates regional inequality in the UK. Contrary to popular understanding, manufacturing output is fairly evenly spread throughout the UK, with the proportion of output created in both the South-East and South-West having grown in the 1990s and 2000s (although London's share declined) (Froud et al., 2011: 16). However, this overlooks the fact that regional economies within the UK are not equal in size. Figure 7.2 shows that manufacturing makes up a more significant portion of regional output in the Northern England's three regions, the East Midlands, and Wales, especially in comparison with London and the South-East. Manufacturing decline therefore exacerbates the so-called 'North-South divide'; it should come as no surprise that the regions exhibiting a greater dependence on the manufacturing sector also tend to have lower average pay (Berry, 2014), not only because manufacturing no longer pays as well as it once did, but also because manufacturing jobs have been replaced by low-skilled service sector jobs, or the dole queue.

## Manufacturing and sustainable growth

The chapter so far has made the case that the UK is bad at manufacturing, even worse following the recession, and that this has deleterious social consequences. It is necessary now, however, to bring a further argument more firmly to the surface, that is, that being bad at manufacturing

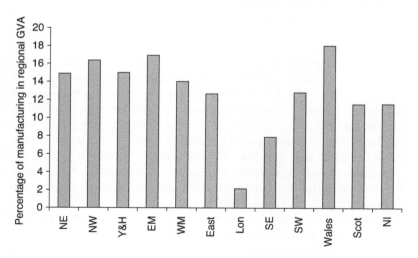

*Figure 7.2*   Share of manufacturing in regional output, 2011
*Source*: ONS (2013c).

threatens the sustainable growth of the UK economy (although the discussion of the role of manufacturing in the UK's post-war relative decline, and in the earnings squeeze evident in the 2000s, has hinted at this perspective). The crisis in UK manufacturing is constitutive of, and inseparable from, the wider crisis of growth.

Neoclassical economic theory – and its attendant ideological formation, neoliberalism – has seduced policy-makers and business leaders in the UK over several decades into marginalising concerns about productivity, employment and economic resilience. Guided by the metaphor of the marketplace, the core objective is removing perceived impediments to the efficient function of the pricing mechanism. It gives rise to the prescription that economies should focus on whichever products can be sold at a price which maximises the profit margin, and the notion that any form of embeddedness in social structures for economic practices is a barrier to the price mechanism – and, as such, is ironically labelled 'uneconomic' by Matthew Watson (2014). Growth is almost an afterthought, presumed to be merely a by-product of the market economy.

This perspective clearly helps to explain the UK's acquiescence to the increasing dominance of the services sector in its economy. Yet most services are, by definition, labour-intensive, which inevitably constrains the extent to which the economy can deliver productivity improvements (as it is far more possible to improve the technologies applied to production by human beings, than the functions of the human body itself). In contrast, manufacturing is, by definition, the application of technology to natural resources. As such, in a capitalist economy it is the economic fulcrum of technological development, and therefore of productivity improvements. Moreover, the material technologies that other sectors rely upon must also be 'manufactured', one way or another (Matthews, 2007: 772–775; Skidelsky, 2013). None of this is to suggest that the UK economy must manufacture *every* good it seeks to consume, because national economies have never been hermetically sealed. Yet a misplaced belief that the market economy had become an unfettered global economy and that the UK could prosper simply by pursuing a 'comparative advantage' in services sustained, up to 2008, the destructive myth that the UK hardly needed to concern itself with manufacturing anything at all (Berry, 2011).

It would be wrong, however, to see sectors themselves as distinct. Most sectors depend upon manufacturing to produce the equipment that can deliver productivity gains. This equipment, alongside consumable goods, could be, and is, imported into the UK economy. Yet this would leave, and has left, the economy reliant on exporting services, which are notoriously difficult to trade across borders. That financial services became increasingly tradable in the pre-crisis years was not a bad thing; rather, the problem was that the tradability of manufacturing output was consistently neglected. Individuals' increased capacity to consume, whether generated by personal debt, housing equity gains, public spending or, in theory, earned income, serves to suck in imports and further undermine the economy's resilience should domestic or international demand in key markets recede. Furthermore, while manufacturing output is utilised by other sectors, equally, other sectors also rely upon producing goods and services for manufacturers. Derek Matthews' review of evidence on the UK manufacturing sector's post-war decline finds therefore that output in the services sector in the UK grew far more slowly than France, Germany and Japan, where manufacturing output also grew much more strongly (Matthews, 2007: 773).

The growth of the financial sector in the UK, alongside the increasing tradability of its output and partial decoupling from the rest of the economy, has since weakened this relationship to some extent – and for a remarkably sustained period was able to generate strong growth in the UK without a significant contribution from manufacturing. This, however, has created new problems. As noted above, an over-sized financial sector infects the economy as a whole with short-termism, as investors and lenders have fewer incentives to support the long-term development of firms – despite the fact that most advancements in technology and productivity occur by stealth. It also attracts the most able graduates away from productive sectors such as manufacturing. This is not to suggest that the average City trader might have opted instead for a career in welding; the financial sector has also recruited an army of mathematicians and scientists to develop the increasingly complex systems through which trading occurs (Lansley, 2013). The financial sector is also inherently more volatile than sectors such as manufacturing. This means that even where the sector is able to generate wealth at a much faster rate than other sectors, these gains can just as quickly evaporate. This is also a problem for the sustainability of public finances; the budget deficit in the UK was created not by a bloated welfare state, but the sudden disappearance of tax revenue from the financial sector (Hay, 2013).

Before discussing how manufacturing decline might be addressed, it is worth reflecting on where the arguments about social equality and sustainable growth overlap. This sub-section has argued that manufacturing is an essential ingredient of a growing and resilient economy given the scope for improved productivity and tradability. However, the progressive social outcomes produced by a strong manufacturing sector, indicated in the previous sub-section, would also improve the sustainability of the British growth model. Insofar as progressive outcomes are delivered via higher incomes at the bottom and middle of the earning distribution, manufacturing helps to reduce the economy's dependence on debt-fuelled consumption and the housing market, both of which are significant sources of instability.

## A march of the makers?

This section briefly considers what might be done to revive British manufacturing. As noted in the chapter's introduction, the rebalancing narrative, to some extent, signifies renewed interest in manufacturing among UK policy-makers, after the negligence of the New Labour years. George Osborne famously promised a 'march of the makers' in his 2011 budget speech. Difficult to pin down, the rationale for the rebalancing agenda has probably been most effectively articulated by BBC radio and television presenter Evan Davis, in his book *Made in Britain*. In his mission to demonstrate 'why our economy is more successful than you think', Davis states boldly that manufacturing decline 'is a sign of success, not failure' (2012: 84). However, he concedes that 'the manufacturing enthusiasts'' instincts that our economy is not perfect are 'not entirely off the mark' (2012: 123). Therefore, we need to rebalance the economy:

> More than most other advanced economies, Britain has found ways of earning a living that are beyond manufacturing. We have probably taken this too far for our own good and have too small a manufacturing base, but if that is the case the argument is that we just need to make some adjustments to our course rather than reverse the direction we have taken. (Davis, 2012: 7)

The adjustment required is that individuals should save more; Davis assumes this will automatically translate into greater productive investment. Accordingly, he exonerates both the corporate sector and government from blame for manufacturing's afflictions:

> [T]he companies themselves are not to blame. Nor are the Bank of England or the Treasury or the department responsible for business. The problem is down to us...the decisions taken by each of us in terms of how much to spend determines the structure of our economy. (Davis, 2012: 125)

The logic of rebalancing lends itself to the notion that the UK, as an advanced economy, should be pursuing advanced manufacturing, that is, production involving a high degree of technological innovation. The coalition government's plan for growth, published alongside the 2011 budget, therefore identifies supporting advanced manufacturing as a key priority. It offered only moderate policy changes, however, including extending tax allowances, establishing more extensive forms of advice and dissemination networks, and some additional support for relevant university-based research centres (HMT and BIS, 2011). The clamour for manuservices – services connected to manufacturing processes, such as design, engineering, maintenance – occupies a similar intellectual territory to advanced manufacturing, contending as it does that the UK can make money from exporting its manufacturing expertise without having to get its hands dirty.

The advanced manufacturing agenda overlooks the fact that UK manufacturing is, on some measures, already more attuned to innovation than its closest competitors. High-tech products have a larger share of manufacturing exports in the UK than most other OECD countries (Brinkley, 2009: 14; Pilat et al., 2006: 21) (Germany exports a greater *volume* of high-tech goods, but also a greater *proportion* of lower-tech goods). Furthermore, while the government's plan for growth notes that only 40 per cent of British manufacturers are involved in technological innovation, compared to 70 per cent in Germany (HMT and BIS, 2011: 21), this statistic fails to take into account the smaller size of manufacturing firms in the UK. The larger firms, which account for the bulk of manufacturing output, are far more likely to be involved in technological innovation. Similarly, a focus on manuservices, while ostensibly promising insofar as it would increase the tradability of the UK services sector, seems to overlook the risk that the newly industrialising countries will, at some point, develop comparable expertise in designing, engineering and maintaining manufactured goods – leaving the UK with, relatively speaking, neither manufacturing goods nor manuservices to export.

Stronger industrial policy in the form of subsidies and picking winners has never been fashionable in the UK, but even industrial policy sceptic Andrew Sissons (2012) acknowledges it may be necessary in the 'special case' of advanced manufacturing, and both the Confederation of British Industry (CBI) and the TUC have called for this kind of reform. However, it is clear that a more general transformation of the UK manufacturing sector will require a radical realignment of the relationship between finance and the 'real economy' (and a related realignment of the trade union/employer relationship, and of unions themselves). Neoclassical theorists or neoliberal ideologues tend to eschew industrial subsidies insofar as they distort the market; on the contrary, its limitations lie in its failure to disrupt market-led capital allocation mechanisms, instead simply supplementing them through government-backed loans in some industries (see Bentham et al., 2013). No such realignment appears imminent, with the government indeed downplaying concerns about financial sector practices from manufacturers. The plan for growth reported the fact that – when asked as part of the 2009 Innovation Survey (HMT and BIS, 2011: 85) – 15–20 per cent of manufacturers considered a lack of information about technology and market structure as a barrier to innovation, yet the report omitted the fact that a far greater proportion reported that inaccessible or expensive finance was a barrier (BIS, 2010). Indeed, Evan Davis' account of the UK's failure to capitalise on its natural advantage in the offshore wind energy industry – clearly a key growth area for advanced manufacturing – is a compelling tale of lack of capacity, not lack of know-how (2012: 121–122).

Even if advanced manufacturing and manuservices could be expanded in the UK, it must also be acknowledged that there is less scope for these activities to deliver, directly, sustainable employment for large numbers of people, particularly in the Northern regions. It may be, however, that advanced manufacturing can deliver an *indirect* boost to jobs lower down the supply chain, but the hollow success of UK car manufacturing in recent years, noted above, should be a note of caution in this regard. CRESC advocate an alternative focus on the 'mundane' economy, arguing (based on studies into the railways and meat supply industries) that, contra to the conventional wisdom, lower-value manufacturing has declined in the UK not due to competition from developing countries, but to dysfunctional supply chains and predatory firm behaviour (Bentham et al., 2013; Bowman et al., 2012, 2013). The UK now imports more than 50 per cent of its bacon, for instance, from Denmark and the Netherlands, countries in which wages in the meat processing industry are double those in the UK (Bowman et al., 2012: 6). Of course, by the same token, mundane manufacturing probably offers less scope for productivity improvements. The coalition government's recent enthusiasm for reshoring – they have, predictably, established a reshoring advisory service for UK firms moving production back to the UK from overseas – suggests they are amenable to increasing mundane manufacturing. Yet it surely also betrays a quintessential acceptance of lower pay in the manufacturing sector, as it is currently this (rather than lower energy costs, as in the United States) that is driving reshoring (Groom and Powley, 2014).

## Conclusion

It is impossible to adjudicate on the possibility that the financial crisis has pushed manufacturing UK, once and for all, into terminal decline. Certainly, there is evidence of both wishful thinking and unclear objectives among policy-makers, and a lack of appetite to engender the more profound transformation – in the relationship between finance and the rest of the economy – required to meaningfully reverse the downward course British manufacturing has taken in recent decades. Yet it is important not to exaggerate the traditional strength of manufacturing in the UK; decline has been an enduring feature of manufacturing in the UK because the British economy has persistently failed to maintain or replicate the industrial strength developed in the eighteenth century.

The UK has long struggled to excel at manufacturing because the financial sector has long been empowered to pursue its own interests at the expense of the rest of the economy. These circumstances intensified from the 1980s onwards, meaning manufacturing waned further. Of course, the events of 2008 exposed this strategy as folly. It is not unreasonable, therefore, to expect a rebalancing toward manufacturing in its wake, especially if manufacturers are able to capitalise on ongoing wage stagnation, or a new enthusiasm for advanced manufacturing produces new forms of investment in manufacturing, if and when political conditions become more amenable. But even these prospects – which are barely visible at the moment – would not be sufficient to enable manufacturing to play a key role in resolving the British growth crisis, given that the sector would remain subservient to the whims of finance (in terms of both the power of the banking sector and the logic of financialised corporate governance) and, like the economy in general, destructively vulnerable.

## Acknowledgements

The author is very grateful for comments and suggestions from Jeremy Green, Colin Hay, and Mike Kenny on a first draft of this chapter.

## References

Allen, K. (2014) 'UK Manufacturing Tipped for Strongest Growth in Europe', *The Guardian*, 6 January 2014, available at http://www.theguardian.com/business/2014/jan/06/uk-manufacturing-forecast (accessed 28 February 2014).

Bentham, C., Bowman, A., Froud, J., Johal, S., Leaver, A. and Williams, K. (2013) 'Against New Industrial Strategy: Framing, Motifs and Absences', CRESC

Working Paper No. 126, available at http://www.cresc.ac.uk/sites/default/files/ WP126%20Against%20New%20Industrial%20Policy.pdf (accessed 28 February 2014).

Berry, C. (2011) *Globalisation and Ideology in Britain: Neoliberalism, Free Trade and the Global Economy.* Manchester: Manchester University Press.

Berry, C. (2013) 'Are We There Yet? Growth, Rebalancing and the Pseudo-recovery', SPERI Paper No. 7, available at http://speri.dept.shef.ac.uk/wp-content/uploads/2013/01/SPERI-Paper-No.7-Are-We-There-Yet-PDF-747KB.pdf (accessed 28 February 2014).

Berry, C. (2014) 'The Hyper-Anglicisation of Active Labour Market Policy: Facilitating and Exemplifying a Flawed Growth Model', SPERI Working Paper No. 14, forthcoming.

Bowman, A., Froud, J., Johal, S., Law, J., Leaver, A. and Williams, K. (2012) *Bringing Home the Bacon: From Trader Mentalities to Industrial Policy.* CRESC Public Interest Report, available at http://www.cresc.ac.uk/sites/default/files/Bringing%20 home%20the%20bacon.pdf (accessed 5 March 2014).

Bowman, A., Folkman, P., Froud, J., Johal, S., Law, J., Leaver, A., Moran, M., Williams, K. (2013) *The Great Train Robbery: Rail Privatisation and After.* CRESC Public Interest Report, available at http://www.cresc.ac.uk/sites/default/files/ GTR%20Report%20final%205%20June%202013.pdf (accessed 5 March 2014).

Brinkley, I. (2009) *Manufacturing and the Knowledge Economy.* The Work Foundation, available at http://www.theworkfoundation.com/downloadpublication/report/212_212_manufacturing%20and%20the%20knowledge%20 economy.pdf (accessed 28 February 2014).

Brivati, B. (2007) *The End of Decline: Blair and Brown in Power.* London: Politico's.

Buigues, P.-A. and Sekkat, K. (2009) *Industrial Policy in Europe, Japan and the United States: Amounts, Mechanisms and Effectiveness.* Basingstoke: Palgrave Macmillan.

Cadman, E. and Powley, T. (2014) 'UK Manufacturing Activity Increases for 11th Month in a Row', *The Financial Times,* 4 March 2014, available at http://www. ft.com/cms/s/0/ea806a50-a2d9-11e3-ba21-00144feab7de.html (accessed 28 February 2014).

Cameron, G. (2003) 'Why Did UK Manufacturing Productivity Growth Slow Down in the 1970s and Speed Up in the 1980s?' *Economica,* 70, 121–141.

Comfort, N. (2013) *The Slow Death of British Industry: A Sixty-Year Suicide 1952–2012.* London: Biteback.

Cooke, G. (2013) *No More NEETs: A Plan for All Young People to be Learning or Earning.* Institute of Public Policy Research, available at http://www.ippr.org/ publication/55/11516/no-more-neets-a-plan-for-all-young-people-to-be-learning-or-earning (accessed 4 March 2014).

Corry, D. (2011) 'Labour and the Economy 1997–2010: More than a Faustian Pact', *The Political Quarterly,* 88, s1, s128–s139.

Department for Business, Innovation and Skills (2010) *Innovation Survey 2009: Statisitical Annex,* available at https://www.gov.uk/government/publications/ innovation-survey-2009-statistical-annex (accessed 6 March 2014).

English, R. and Kenny, M. (2000) 'Decline or Declinism?' in R. English and M. Kenny (eds), *Rethinking British Decline.* Basingstoke: Macmillan, pp. 279–299.

Froud, J., Johal, S., Law, J., Leaver, A. and Williams, K. (2011) 'Rebalancing the Economy (or buyer's remorse)', CRESC Working Paper No. 87, available at http://www.cresc.ac.uk/publications/rebalancing-the-economy-or-buyers-remorse (accessed 28 February 2014).

Gamble, A. (2000) 'Theories and Explanations of British Decline', in R. English and M. Kenny (eds), *Rethinking British Decline*. Basingstoke: Macmillan, pp. 1–22.

Groom, B. and Powley, T. (2014) 'UK Reshoring Faces Battle, Industrialists Warn', *The Financial Times*, 24 January 2014, available at http://www.ft.com/cms/s/0/e4667f82-8511-11e3-8968-00144feab7de.html (accessed 28 February 2014).

Hay, C. (2013) *The Failure of Anglo-Liberal Capitalism*. Basingstoke: Palgrave.

Heyes, J. (2012) 'Vocational Training, Employability and the Post-2008 Jobs Crisis: Responses in the European Union', *Economics and Industrial Democracy*, 34,2, 291–311.

HM Government (2010) *The Coalition: Our Programme for Government*. London: The Stationery Office.

HM Treasury and Department for Business, Innovation and Skills (2011) *The Plan for Growth*. London: The Stationery Office.

Ingham, G. (1984) *Capitalism Divided? The City and Industry in British Social Development*. London: Macmillan.

Jones, K. (2013) *The Road Less Travelled? Improving the Apprenticeship Pathway for Young People*. The Work Foundation, available at http://www.theworkfoundation.com/DownloadPublication/Report/344_Apprenticeship%20policy%20paper%20FINAL.pdf (accessed 4 March 2014).

Lansley, S. (2011) *The Cost of Inequality: Three Decades of the Super-Rich and the Economy*. London: Gibson Square.

Lansley, S. (2013) 'Britain's Livelihoods Crisis', TUC Touchstone Pamphlet No.10, available at https://www.tuc.org.uk/sites/default/files/tuc-19639-f0.pdf (accessed 28 February 2014).

Matthews, D. (2007) 'The Performance of British Manufacturing in the Post-war Long Boom', *Business History*, 49, 6, 763–779.

Monaghan, A. (2014) 'UK Car Sales at Highest since Onset of the Crisis', *The Guardian*, 7 January 2014, available at http://www.theguardian.com/business/2014/jan/07/uk-car-sales-five-year-high-smmt (accessed 28 February 2014).

Office for National Statistics (2013a) *Economic Review: October 2013*, available at http://www.ons.gov.uk/ons/rel/elmr/economic-review/october-2013/art-october.html (accessed 28 February 2014).

Office for National Statistics (2013b) *Index of Production: December 2013*, available at http://www.ons.gov.uk/ons/dcp171778_351570.pdf (accessed 28 February 2014).

Office for National Statistics (2013c) *Regional Gross Value Added (Production Approach): December 2013*, available at http://www.ons.gov.uk/ons/rel/regional-accounts/regional-gross-value-added--production-approach-/december-2013/index.html (accessed 5 March 2014).

Office for National Statistics (2014a) *Labour Market Statistics: February 2014*, available at http://www.ons.gov.uk/ons/rel/lms/labour-market-statistics/february-2014/index.html (accessed 4 March 2014).

Office for National Statistics (2014b) *Second Estimate of GDP: Q4 2013*, available at http://www.ons.gov.uk/ons/rel/naa2/second-estimate-of-gdp/q4-2013/stb-second-estimate-of-gdp--q4-2013.html (accessed 4 March 2014).

Osborne, G. (2010) 'Mais Lecture: A New Economic Model', speech delivered on 24 February 2010, available at http://www.totalpolitics.com/print/speeches/35193/george-osborne-mais-lecture-a-new-economic-model.thtml (accessed 28 February 2014).

Osborne, G. (2011) 'Budget Speech', speech delivered in the House of Commons, 23 March 2011, available at http://www.publications.parliament.uk/pa/cm201011/cmhansrd/cm110323/debtext/110323-0001.htm#11032368000001 (acceded 6 March 2014).

Parker, G. and Groom, B. (2013) 'Danny Alexander Urges Business to Invest its £500 Billion Cash Pile', *The Financial Times*, 23 October 2013, available at http://www.ft.com/cms/s/0/23c886fe-3b32-11e3-a7ec-00144feab7de.html (accessed 28 February 2014).

Pilat, D., Cimper, A., Olsen, K. and Webb, C. (2006) 'The Changing Nature of Manufacturing in OECD Countries', Organisation for Economic Co-operation and Development STI Working Paper 2006/9, available at http://www.oecd.org/science/inno/37607831.pdf (accessed 28 February 2014).

Plunkett, J. (2011) *Growth Without Gain? The Faltering Living Standards of People on Low-to-Middle Incomes*. Resolution Foundation, available at http://www.resolutionfoundation.org/media/media/downloads/Growth_without_gain_-_Web.pdf (accessed 4 March 2014).

Plunkett, J., Hurrell, A. and Whittaker, M. (2014) *The State of Living Standards*. Resolution Foundation, available at http://www.resolutionfoundation.org/publications/state-living-standards/ (accessed 4 March 2014).

PricewaterhouseCoopers (2009) *The Future of UK Manufacturing: Reports of Its Death Are Greatly Exaggerated*, available at https://www.pwc.co.uk/assets/pdf/ukmanufacturing-300309.pdf (accessed 28 February 2014).

PricewaterhouseCoopers (2014) *Understanding the Economic Contribution of Foundation Industries*, available at http://www.tatasteeleurope.com/file_source/StaticFiles/Functions/Media/Foundation_Industries_Report.pdf (accessed 28 February 2014).

Rubinstein, W. D. (1993) *Capitalism, Culture and Decline in Britain, 1750–1990*. London: Routledge.

Rubinstein, W. D. (2000) 'Interview', in R. English and M. Kenny (eds), *Rethinking British Decline*. Basingstoke: Macmillan, pp. 64–75.

Sheffield Political Economy Research Institute (2014a) *Pay in Manufacturing and Finance*, available at http://speri.dept.shef.ac.uk/wp-content/uploads/2014/01/SPERI-British-Political-Economy-Brief-No.1-%E2%80%93-Pay-in-Manufacturing-Finance-FINAL.pdf (accessed 28 February 2014).

Sheffield Political Economy Research Institute (2014b) *Sterling Depreciation and the UK Trade Balance*, available at http://speri.dept.shef.ac.uk/wp-content/uploads/2014/01/SPERI-British-Political-Economy-Brief-No.2-%E2%80%93-Sterling-depreciation-the-UK-trade-balance.pdf (accessed 28 February 2014).

Sissons, A (2012) 'UK Manufacturing Needs More Than a Wing and a Prayer', *EGov Monitor*, 6 February 2012, available at http://www.egovmonitor.com/node/46310 (accessed 28 February 2014).

Skidelsy, R. (2013) 'Meeting our Makers: Britain's Long Industrial Decline', *New Statesman*, 24 January 2013, available at http://www.newstatesman.com/culture/culture/2013/01/meeting-our-makers-britain%E2%80%99s-long-industrial-decline (accessed 28 February 2014).

Trades Union Congress (2013) *The UK's Low Pay Recovery*, available at https://www.tuc.org.uk/sites/default/files/Lowpayreport.pdf (accessed 28 February 2014).

Vernon, G. and Rogers, M. (2013) 'Where Do Unions Add Value? Predominant Organizing Principle, Union Strength and Manufacturing Productivity Growth in the OECD', *British Journal of Industrial Relations*, 51, 1, 1–27.

Watson, M. (2014) *Uneconomic Economics and the Crisis of the Model World*. Basingstoke: Palgrave.

Williams, K., Williams, J. and Thomas, D. (1983) *Why Are the British Bad at Manufacturing?* London: Routledge & Kegan Paul.

Woolley, P. (2011) 'Why are Financial Markets So Inefficient and Exploitative – and a Suggested Remedy', in A. Turner et al. (2011) *The Future of Finance – And the Theory that Underpins It*. London: London School of Economics, available at http://harr123et.files.wordpress.com/2010/07/futureoffinance-chapter31.pdf (accessed 28 February 2014).

# Part III
# Global, Local and Sectoral Dimensions

# 8
# Local and Regional Economic Development in Britain

*Danny MacKinnon, Andrew Cumbers and David Featherstone*

## Introduction

Over the past couple of decades, the local and regional scales of political-economic organisation have gained a renewed prominence set against a backdrop of economic globalisation and state restructuring (Storper, 1997). Variously characterised as a 'new regionalism' or 'new localism' (Lovering, 1999), prevailing approaches to sub-national economic development regard the institutional capacity to foster bottom-up forms of growth based upon the harnessing of local skills and resources as a crucial source of competitiveness in an increasingly globalised economy (Bristow, 2010). Devolution has been identified as a key 'global trend', as a range of governments across the world have transferred power to regional institutions as a means of promoting political decentralisation and recognising distinct territorial identities, in addition to the promotion of economic development (Rodriguez-Pose and Sandall, 2008).

These broader trends have been played out in a distinctive fashion in Britain. While successive governments have promoted bottom-up forms of local and regional growth since the late 1980s (see Department of Employment, 1988; Department of Environment, Transport and the Regions, 1998; HM Government, 2010a), this has been accompanied by periodic institutional 'churn' and restructuring as incoming administrations have sought to stamp their own imprint on the landscape of sub-national economic governance. Thus, the Conservative government's espousal of local, business-led agencies in the late 1980s and 1990s gave way to Labour's model of asymmetrical regional devolution in the late 1990s and 2000s which has, in turn, been succeeded by a renewed localism under the Coalition government since 2010 (Clarke and Cochrane, 2013). This preoccupation with institutional reform has been described by one commentator as amounting to 'a pathology of compulsive re-organisation, involving the wholesale sweeping away and re-creation of organisations and an endless tinkering and meddling with what currently exists' (Jones, 2010: 374). Despite the recurrent rhetoric of localism and regionalism this reflects the underlying centralism of the UK state, which enables national government effectively to dictate the structure and practice of sub-national service design and delivery (Jones, 2013). While devolution to Scotland, Wales and Northern Ireland can be seen as somewhat exceptional in this respect, involving what is in practice a politically irreversible, and indeed ongoing, process of decentralisation (Jeffery, 2011), the devolved governments may act as centralising forces within their respective jurisdictions, engaging in their own forms of reorganisation and 'tinkering' (MacKinnon and Shaw, 2010).

This chapter examines the political economy of localism and regionalism in Britain over the past couple of decades, based upon the belief that the capacity to foster local and regional development is a necessary, though not sufficient, component of any national growth model. It discusses successive institutional reforms, assessing how the tensions between the process of decentralisation that they were purported to be unleashing and the opposing tendency towards centralised direction have been played out (see MacKinnon, 2000). It argues that the limits of decentralisation and the reproduction of centralised rule represent critical weaknesses of the British growth model relative to other developed countries. These limitations are compounded by an entrenched pattern of spatial inequality, symbolised by the North–South divide, which is being exacerbated by the spatially uneven effects of the prolonged economic downturn of 2008–2012 and the incipient economic recovery (Centre for Cities, 2014a). Indeed, the UK has both one of the highest levels of spatial disparities among developed countries and one of the most centralised systems of sub-national government finance, whereby local authorities are heavily dependent on transfers from central government (OECD, 2013), suggesting that greater decentralisation is required to promote the development of less-favoured localities and regions outside the South East of England (Centre for Cities, 2014).

The remainder of the chapter is structured in four main sections. First, we develop a conceptual framework for understanding the evolution of sub-national economic governance in Britain. This is followed by an account of local and regional economic governance and development under the Labour government of 1997–2010. We then turn to the politics of localism under the Coalition, viewing this as an 'austerity localism' whereby the local is reasserted as part of a project to restructure the public sector (Featherstone et al., 2012). Finally, a concluding section synthesises the main arguments of the chapter and begins to sketch the contours of an alternative progressive localist approach.

## State restructuring, neo-liberalism and political decentralisation

This chapter is closely informed by recent conceptual debates on the nature of the local in geography and the social sciences (Massey, 1994, 2005). A key theme of these debates has been the adoption of relational approaches which seek to overturn conventional conceptions of space as fixed, static and bounded, emphasising instead openness, connectivity and the social and political construction of space. Thus, localities and regions are actively constructed by particular social interests at specific points in time (Allen et al., 1998). Rather than existing as natural geographical entities with a singular and unproblematic identity, they incorporate a range of different social actors and interests, who may assert competing claims to place (Massey, 1994). Contrary to political discourses of decentralisation, which invariably portray localism and regionalism as inherently positive and necessary antidotes to an overweening centralism, they are neither progressive nor regressive in an *a priori* sense (Pratchett, 2004), but can be either in practice, depending upon how the terms are politically constructed and mobilised (Massey, 2005). The linkages between overlapping geographical scales, such as the local, regional and national, should also be seen in relational terms. Sub-national spaces of governance are in part constructed out of their relations with the national, focusing attention on the actors and networks which mediate these relationships (Allen and Cochrane, 2010).

Turning to more concrete issues, the reorganisation of states since the late 1970s has been shaped by several causal factors, including globalisation and the development of supra-national institutions like the European Union (EU), the prominence of neo-liberal notions of limited government (Peck and Tickell, 2002), and the rise of regionalist and nationalist movements (Keating, 1998). In a highly influential account of state restructuring, Jessop (1997) identified three main processes of reorganisation. First, the denationalisation of the state involving the transfer of some responsibilities and functions 'upwards' to supra-national institutions, such as the European Union (EU), and 'downwards' to local and regional agencies. Second, the 'destatisation' of the political system referring to an 'outwards' movement of responsibilities from the state to various arm's-length agencies, private interests and voluntary bodies. Third, the internationalisation of policy regimes as a complex phenomenon encompassing a growing volume of linkages between national, regional and local institutions and personnel in different countries. This enables policy transfer as initiatives introduced in one country are taken up and adapted by officials in another (Peck, 2011).

One of the key factors identified above is the political and ideological influence of neo-liberalism, defined by Peck (2010: xii) as 'an open-ended and contradictory process of politically-assisted market rule'. In essence, neo-liberalism involves the promotion of market forces, individual choice and a limited state as key principles of economic and social organisation (Jessop, 2002). Key political and economic reforms include the privatisation of state-owned enterprises, the deregulation of financial markets, the promotion of free trade, efforts to reduce welfare expenditure, and the introduction of market proxies to reform the public sector (ibid). The object of these reforms is not, as Peck (2001: 447) argues, the state *per se*, but a 'historically and geographically specific institutionalisation of the state' inherited from the Keynesian-welfarist model of the post-war decades. This state formation is being replaced 'not by fresh air and free markets', as some of the more simplistic accounts of globalisation imply, 'but by a reorganised state apparatus' (ibid).

Localism and regionalism often gain political and ideological traction within neo-liberalism as part of what Peck and Tickell (2002) term roll-back neo-liberalism, involving the dismantling of 'alien institutions' and attacks on public bureaucracies and collective entitlements through the 'now familiar repertoire of funding cuts, organisational downsizing, market testing and privatisation' (Peck, 2010: 22). In this context, the local in particular has been ideologically constructed as the spatial 'other' of centralised bureaucracy, being elided with notions of enterprise, self-reliance and civic responsibility. Accordingly, neo-liberal reforms, such as the establishment of unelected local agencies which bypass local government, have fostered a certain revival of the local as a strategically important site for the promotion of market-based reforms and initiatives over the past couple of decades (Brenner and Theodore, 2002). At the same time, such reforms typically embody a fundamental tension between a rhetorical emphasis on local initiative and continued central oversight and direction through a raft of managerialist technologies such as targets, audits, inspection and performance management (MacKinnon, 2000). In this context, particular variants of localism can be seen as highly functional for central government as both rhetorical devices and means of selectively delegating and 'down-loading' politically difficult decisions (for example, over cuts to services) to local actors under the guise of decentralisation and empowerment.

Processes of denationalisation, destatisation and internationalisation came together to shape a new system of local and regional governance in the 1990s. New organisations and agencies created by top-down reforms do not, however, operate in an institutional vacuum, but must operate within a pre-structured and already occupied organisational landscape. These relationships can be understood in terms of processes of institutional 'layering' as existing organisations are subject to waves of restructuring (Jones et al., 2004), producing distinctive 'geographies of governance':

> The process by which new geographies of governance are formed is not a pseudo-geological one in which a new layer (or round of regulation) supersedes the old, to form a new institutional surface. Rather, it is a dynamic process in which (national) regulatory tendencies and local institutional outcomes mould one another in a dialectical fashion. Geographies of governance are made at the point of interaction between the unfolding layer of regulatory processes/apparatuses and the inherited institutional landscape. (Peck, 1998: 29)

As such, successive 'layers' of centrally orchestrated reform interact with pre-existing institutional structures and practices at the regional and local scales to create new geographies of governance. These 'national regulatory tendencies' and 'local institutional outcomes' are not of course authorless or devoid of agency, but are actively shaped by politicians, local and regional state officials, business leaders, consultants and others, reflecting the nature of the state as a 'peopled organisation' (Jones et al., 2004).

As part of the new structures of governance created in the 1980s and 1990s, local and regional organisations have become increasingly active in supporting economic development within their regions and localities (Storper, 1997). In contrast to traditional regional policy, which aimed to direct investment into depressed regions through a range of 'top down' incentives and controls, this 'new regionalism' focuses largely on internal factors and conditions within regions, viewing these as the key to generating investment and growth. In this sense, 'locally-orchestrated regional development has replaced nationally-orchestrated regional policy' (Amin et al., 2003: 22). Key strands of policy include supply-side initiatives to stimulate innovation and learning within firms, measures to try and increase entrepreneurship and efforts to develop and upgrade the skills of the workforce through a range of training and education programmes. The aim of such policies is to try to 'hold down' or 'embed' global processes of economic development (Goodwin et al., 2005). In this context, decentralisation is important in granting regions and sub-state nations the political and institutional capacity to promote growth and tailor their policies to the needs of their economies.

In addition, political decentralisation is often advanced through a 'good governance' discourse of bringing decision-making closer to citizens (Hildreth, 2011; Rodriguez-Pose and Sandall, 2008). There is an important distinction to be made here between the decentralisation of power within the state, from central to local government, and the transfer of powers from the state to communities and the users or consumers of services. While the former tends to be the focus of many democratic reformers on the centre left, the latter is often emphasised by conservative and neo-liberal thinkers and politicians. Hildreth (2011) usefully elaborates upon this distinction to identify three models of localism which can be extended to regionalism. First, 'conditional localism' involves the central state decentralising power to local authorities on the understanding that these powers are used to meet national policy priorities and service standards. Second, 'representative localism' refers to the decentralisation of powers to independent, locally elected authorities whose powers are rooted in legally agreed principles. This corresponds to the model found in many Western European countries, emphasising accountability to local residents and representative leadership through elected mayors. Finally, 'community localism' is based upon the decentralisation of powers from the state to individuals and local communities, emphasising the direct involvement of citizens and the bypassing of local government.

## Local and regional governance in the UK under Labour, 1997–2010

Localism has operated in a largely top-down and centralised fashion in the UK since the 1980s, representing a recurring thread within the British variant of neo-liberalism. In the late 1980s and again since 2010, the local has been constructed as the locus of social responsibility and economic self-reliance and counter-posed with the unresponsive bureaucracies of the state as part of a process of roll-back neo-liberalism (Peck, 2010: 22). A more state-led and conditional form of localism and regionalism was apparent under New Labour, emphasising the delivery of national objectives and coordination between public sector agencies

(Lodge and Muir, 2010). This can be seen as reflecting a process of roll-out neo-liberalism through the establishment and consolidation of new institutional arrangements to further entrench marketisation and the associated regime of performance management (Davies, 2008; Peck, 2010).

As part of their effort to dismantle the 'alien' collectivist institutions of the 1960s and 1970s and extend the operation of market forces, the Conservative governments of the 1980s and 1990s sought to curtail and control the activities of elected local government, imposing rigid financial constraints and bypassing local authorities through the creation of special-purpose organisations (Urban Development Corporations, Training and Enterprise Councils, NHS Trusts, etc.) (see Jessop et al., 1988). In other areas, such as social work and housing, the state sought to devolve responsibility by involving voluntary and private agencies in service delivery. At the same time, compulsory competitive tendering imposed a market logic on many local services, drawing private interests into networks of providers. Rather than signalling the retreat of the state and the inexorable advance of the private sector, these reforms were part of a political project designed to 'reinvent' government through the wholesale introduction of business practices and norms into the public sector, often referred to as the 'new public management' (Dunleavy and Hood, 1994). The creation of local business-led agencies by the then Conservative government was accompanied by a rhetoric of local initiative and responsibility through the recruitment of local business leaders (Peck, 1995). This was located within a broader discourse of 'active citizenship' and community, viewed as an essential antidote to both the 'dependency culture' fostered by the welfare state and accusations that Conservative policy was over-reliant upon an amoral market individualism (Kearns, 1995).

After coming to power in 1997, New Labour retained much of the neo-liberal agenda developed by the Conservatives, particularly in terms of its adherence to market-orientated economic policies, while introducing more ameliorative and mildly redistributionist social policies, alongside an emphasis on the need for the renewal of the state (Hall, 2003; Peck, 2004). The major institutional reform was devolution, which involved the creation of an elected parliament in Scotland, elected assemblies in Wales and Northern Ireland, an elected mayor and assembly in London and the establishment of Regional Development Agencies (RDAs) in the English regions (Goodwin et al., 2005). Described as the most significant change to the institutional fabric of the British state for 300 years (Gamble, 2006), devolution involved a substantial, though highly asymmetrical, decentralisation of power. It has created new power centres in the form of elected parliaments and assemblies within the devolved territories and there is evidence that this has fostered some recentralisation of governance through the rationalisation and refocusing of organisational structures in the interests of 'national integration' (Danson and Lloyd, 2012; Jones et al., 2005). In Wales, for example, the Welsh Development Agency was abolished and its functions absorbed into the Welsh government in the so-called 'bonfire of the quangos' in 2006 (Morgan, 2006).

RDAs were established in an effort to address the 'economic deficit' of the English regions by granting them the institutional capacity to enhance regional competitiveness and growth (DETR, 1997; Jones, 2001). A key task of the English RDAs was the formulation and implementation of regional economic strategies, although their powers were insufficient to coordinate the activities of other agencies and central departments active in their regions (Jones, 2001; Pike and Tomaney, 2009). While introducing an overdue regional development component into the post-Thatcher 'British growth model', RDAs embodied something of a contradiction as effectively top-down agencies – funded, appointed and overseen by central government – charged with orchestrating bottom-up regional development (Jones, 2001). The regionalisation agenda in England was effectively stymied by the rejection of proposals for a North East Assembly in the referendum of November 2004, leaving in its wake a weak and fragmented pattern of sub-national economic governance (Pike and Tomaney, 2009). The supply-side approach embodied by the RDAs made little impression on entrenched regional disparities, which continued to widen in a period of sustained national economic growth from the mid-1990s to the financial crash of 2007–2008 (Pike et al., 2012).

Local government in England also provided an important institutional focus for New Labour modernisation through a succession of initiatives. Key initial reforms included a requirement for councils to replace their traditional committee structures with an executive in the form of a leader and cabinet or an elected mayor, based on a distinction between executive and legislative functions (Laffin, 2008: 110). In addition, new performance regimes were established, with Best Value succeeded by Comprehensive Performance Assessments and Local Public Service Agreements between local authorities and central government (ibid). As this suggests, the initial rhetoric of partnership soon gave way to an 'intense and over-prescriptive regime of targets and performance management' (Lodge and Muir, 2010: 99). Despite commissioning the

Lyons Review of 2007, Labour also failed to offer any additional financial powers to local government, with the Council Tax only raising about 25 per cent of local government funding (ibid). Periodically, however, the government sought to invoke the prospect of a renewed localism, providing an indication of the tendency of such neo-liberal informed initiatives to 'fail forward' (Peck, 2010) in terms of how the emergent limitations of earlier initiatives often generated pressure for more radical reform. This was particularly apparent in Labour's 2006 White Paper, which introduced a rhetoric of 'double devolution' in terms of decentralisation to both local government and local communities, although the powers offered to enact this proved to be rather modest (Davies, 2008).

In overall terms, then, there is a clear sense in which a recurring rhetoric of localism and community involvement was undermined by the realities of centralised performance management and policy direction under Labour (Davies, 2008; Lodge and Muir, 2010). This can be seen as a highly conditional and centrally orchestrated form of localism (Harrison, 2008; Hildreth, 2011), with local authorities emerging 'as largely passive recipients of central policy initiatives' (Laffin, 2008: 112).

## Austerity localism: local and regional governance under the Coalition government, 2010–

Localism has been embraced by the Conservative–Liberal Democrat Coalition government through a range of initiatives involving the abolition of certain existing state institutions and the transference of certain powers to local communities (Lowndes and Pratchett, 2012). While the highly conditional form of localism that operated under Labour can be seen as state-led, the approach of the Coalition government is avowedly anti-statist, with its construction of the local as the other of state direction and control evoking the notion of community localism (HM Government, 2010b; Hildreth, 2011). In the context of the Coalition's programme to dramatically curtail government spending, however, this can be seen as a kind of austerity localism, whereby the local is reasserted as part of a new round of roll-back neo-liberalism (Peck and Tickell, 2002) designed to restructure the public sector dramatically (Featherstone et al., 2012). Local government has faced a disproportionate share of public spending cuts in contrast to other sectors, such as health and foreign aid, which have been protected (Lowndes and Pratchett, 2012). While the scale and duration of public expenditure cuts is virtually unprecedented in the context of the UK in recent decades, the accompanying rhetoric of localism and decentralisation carries distinct echoes of the late 1980s and early 1990s (Jones, 2013).

Within its first few weeks of office, the Coalition announced the abolition of a number of 'alien' institutions and functions inherited from Labour, including: Regional Development Agencies; Government Offices for the Regions; the Audit Commission; Local Area Agreements; and the Standards Boards regime (Cochrane and Clarke, 2013). The abolition of RDAs was described by the Secretary of State for Business, Innovation and Skills as the Coalition's 'Maoist moment' (Scratton, 2010), reflecting the Conservative Party's long-standing opposition to RDAs as 'arbitrary', 'bureaucratic' and 'bloated' (Pugalis and Bentley, 2013; Tomaney et al., 2012). Associated regional functions, such as integrated Regional Strategies, Regional Observatories, Regional Leaders' Boards, Regional Select Committees and Regional Business Links were also curtailed in line with the government's 'distaste for almost all things "regional"' (Pugalis and Bentley, 2013: 666). Crucially, however, many of the functions previously exercised by regional bodies such as RDAs, including innovation, inward investment and trade promotion, adult skills provision and the management of European funds, have actually been renationalised in Whitehall rather than localised (Tomaney et al., 2012). The other key target for the Coalition government was the regulatory arrangements designed to monitor and direct the performance of local government and regarded as symptomatic of Labour's excessively centralised and bureaucratic approach (Lowndes and Pratchett, 2012).

The renewed prominence of localism was signalled by the Conservative Party's pre-election Green Paper *Control Shift: Returning Power to Local Communities*, which claimed to set out an agenda for a 'truly radical localisation' (Conservative Party, 2009: 14), with decentralisation 'described as the biggest thing that government can do to build the Big Society' (HM Government, 2010b: 2). While the Big Society project has faded somewhat as the government has struggled to articulate its meaning and significance, this commitment to decentralisation acquired rapid legislative expression in the shape of the Localism Bill, which became law in November 2011 (Clarke and Cochrane, 2013). Key measures for the transfer of power to local areas include: proposals to enhance the use of local referendums, particularly in relation to the vetoing of 'excessive' Council Tax rises; referendums for the election of local mayors in 12 cites; measures for the election of Police and Crime Commissioners; the creation of a general power of competence for local government; and the empowerment of community groups to take over state-run assets and services, especially when these are threatened with closure (HM

Government, 2010b). In addition, the Coalition government propose to grant local authorities limited powers to retain a proportion of (nationally-set) business rates and to partially localise Council Tax Benefit and social housing, while developing a structure of neighbourhood planning. Interestingly, Labour's targets seem to have been replaced by a set of economic incentives to encourage local compliance with central targets, including: the New Homes Bonus for authorities that allow development; the provision of additional funding in exchange for the freezing of Council Tax; plans to allow local authorities to keep more of their business rates in return for the introduction of pro-business policies; and the provision of additional funds for councils that have restored weekly bin collections (Clarke and Cochrane, 2013: 14). This illustrates how localism can actually serve to reinforce centralism in the context of austerity through the fiscal dependence of local authorities on central transfers.

At the same time, local authorities have borne a disproportionate share of spending cuts, with the local government budget of the Department of Communities and Local Government projected to undergo a cumulative real terms cut of 29.5 per cent between 2010/2011 and 2015/2016 (Emmerson et al., 2013: 161). In Scotland, a concordat has been in place between local authorities and the Scottish Government since 2007 (Waite et al., 2013), with councils given additional financial flexibility in return for freezing the level of council tax, contributing to a financial squeeze in combination with more limited budget cuts administered by the Scottish Government (Centre for Public Policy for the Regions undated). The Communities Secretary, Eric Pickles, sought to further tighten the squeeze on local authorities in the winter of 2013/2014 by reducing the cap by which local authorities can increase council tax from 1.5 to 2 per cent, without seeking approval from local residents through a referendum (Wintour, 2014). In overall terms, the rhetoric of 'localism, localism, and localism' (Pickles in Wilson and Game, 2011: 394) is being undercut by a combination of severe austerity and the offering of fiscal incentives that tie additional funding to the adoption of centrally approved policies. This equates to a form of compulsory localism, redolent of the rate capping and austerity of the 1980s, in which central control has actually been strengthened compared to the conditional localism that operated under Labour (Harrison, 2012), as indicated by Pickles' notion of guided localism (Communities and Local Government Committee, 2011: 27).

Proposals for the establishment of Local Enterprise Partnerships (LEPs) were invited by Pickles and Business Secretary Vince Cable in June

2010, culminating in the formation of 39 LEPs by local authorities and local business interests across England by the end of 2011 (Figure 8.1) (Shutt et al., 2012). This process reignited several turf wars between competing local interests (Haughton et al., 1997), with two rival bids being submitted for the Humberside area, for example, while the formation of the North East LEP triggered a, so-called, civil war between Newcastle and Sunderland (see Bentley and Pugalis, 2013; Harrison, 2012). The result of this interaction between the LEP initiative and the 'inherited institutional landscape' (Peck, 1998) is a highly differentiated, fragmented and localised geography, largely confounding government claims about LEPs mapping onto functional economic areas compared to the 'arbitrary' boundaries of RDAs (Tomaney et al., 2012). LEPs lack any statutory authority and the first LEP national survey revealed that around 50 per cent have adopted a form of legal incorporation, while the remainder operate as voluntary partnerships or as part of wider local authority-based structures (Marlow et al., 2013).

While provided with start-up funds by government, LEPs have been widely characterised as under-resourced and under-powered (Bentley et al., 2013; Heseltine, 2012; Jones, 2013; Marlow et al., 2013). This concern has been partly addressed by the provision of some core funding and the establishment of the Growing Places Fund by the Government, alongside an LEP's ability to bid for other nationally administered schemes, such as the Regional Growth Fund (Heseltine, 2012; Shutt et al., 2012). Moreover, in response to the Heseltine Review, the government announced the establishment of a new Single Local Growth Fund from 2015 to be allocated on the basis of Local Growth Deals supported by LEPs' Strategic Economic Plans (HM Treasury, 2013). As this indicates, beyond the rhetoric of decentralisation and a local empowerment (HM Government, 2010b), LEPs seem to represent a new form of centrally orchestrated localism (Harrison, 2008), echoing many of the limitations of the network of Training and Enterprise Councils and Local Enterprise Companies (LECs) established in England and Scotland in the early 1990s (Jones, 2013). In Scotland, by contrast, localism is now less apparent, with the functions of LECs having been either integrated into their 'parent' regional agencies, Scottish Enterprise and Highlands and Islands Enterprise, or transferred to local authorities (Danson, 2012).

The Coalition government also introduced City Deals in two distinct waves, the first in 2012, confined to the eight 'core cities' outside London and the second in 2013, extending to 20 second-tier cities (Marlow, 2013; Waite et al., 2013). According to the government, these bespoke deals are designed to give cities 'the powers and tools they

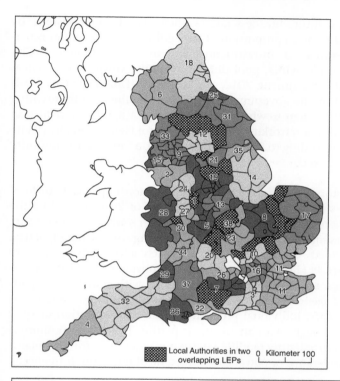

**List of local enterprise partnerships:**

1. Birmingham and Solihull with East Staffordshire, Lichfield and Tamworth
2. Cheshire and Warrington
3. Coast to Capital
4. Cornwall and the Isles of Scilly
5. Coventry and Warwickshire
6. Cumbria
7. Enterprise M3
8. Greater Cambridge and Greater Peterborough
9. Greater Manchester
10. Hertfordshire
11. Kent, Greater Essex and East Sussex
12. Leeds City Region
13. Leicester and Leicestershire
14. Lincolnshire
15. Liverpool City Region
16. pan London
17. New Anglia
18. North Eastern Partnership
19. Derby, Derbyshire, Nottingham and Nottinghamshire
20. Oxfordshire City Region
21. Sheffield City Region
22. Solent
23. South East Midlands
24. Stoke-on-Trent and Staffordshire
25. Tees Valley
26. Thames Valley Berkshire
27. The Black Country
28. The Marches Enterprise Partnership
29. West of England
30. Worcestershire
31. York and North Yorkshire
32. Heart of the South West
33. Lancashire
34. Gloucestershire
35. Humber
36. Dorset
37. Swindon and Wiltshire
38. Northamptonshire

*Figure 8.1*  LEPs in England, end of 2011

*Source*: Shutt et al. (2012: 14).

need to drive local economic growth' and to enable them to 'unlock projects and initiatives', while strengthening governance arrangements (HM Government, 2012: 1). Key measures include: innovative funding provisions, such as Tax Increment Financing, which allow authorities to borrow against future business rate revenues; Earnback provisions, by which cities get back a proportion of the additional tax revenues generated by investment in infrastructure; and the establishment of City Investment Funds, which pool different funding streams and sources together (HM Government, 2012; Waite et al., 2013). While City Deals are promoted by the government as offering genuine and far-reaching devolution, the extent to which they amount to a significant reduction in, as opposed to a reworking of, central control is questionable (Waite et al., 2013). According to David Marlow (2013), a former local authority and RDA chief executive:

> When history comes to evaluate the coalition's approach to local growth, I suspect the fundamental critique of 2010–15 will be the subsuming of political values and conviction – whether to localism, city leadership, rebalancing, really to anything – in a series of tactical and one-sided 'deals'. The 'deal' approach allows government to deconstruct 39 LEPs, 28 cities, and any number of other places' ambitions into a series of bilateral negotiations with individual departments and agencies. The 'deal' model requires local leadership teams to 'prove' each individual proposition in a demonstration of their abilities to 'haggle' with an oligarchic patron. The default position is agreement to a slightly modified status quo where government retains the preponderance of powers, resources, flexibilities and influence.

As such, the capacity of local leaders to negotiate with government is key, suggesting that this highly conditional and asymmetrical form of localism serves to incentivise entrepreneurial governance rather than growth investment (Waite et al., 2013), distributing resources on the basis of negotiating skill and institutional capacity rather than local need. As city leaders and think tanks become increasingly vocal in demanding further powers (Core Cities, 2013; Centre for Cities, 2014a), this may evolve into a more locally orchestrated form of localism, but one that continues to be defined by central control and direction.

Efforts to promote local growth have been confronted by a context of national economic recession and austerity since 2008, giving way to an uneven recovery in recent months. The effects have been to widen existing spatial disparities in Britain, with research showing that 'the places and people most severely impacted by the last five years of recession and hesitant recovery are those that were already the worst-off' (Townsend and Champion, 2014: 3). Analysis of nine large provincial city-regions (the eight English core cities plus Glasgow) shows that they have closely followed national macroeconomic trends of recession and recovery, but generally perform worse in contrast to London (ibid). Thus, the post-2008 decline in employment was steeper and more persistent in the provincial city-regions compared to Great Britain as a whole, while London diverged strongly by experiencing a marked recovery from 2010 (ibid: 7). Indeed, 79 per cent of private sector jobs created in the UK between 2010 and 2012 were created in London, compared to only 10 per cent in the next nine largest cities (Centre for Cities, 2014a: 7), while one public sector job has been created in London for every two lost in other cities in the same period (Centre for Cities, 2014b). Such trends starkly expose the economic and political limitations of the Government's discourse of sectoral and spatial 'rebalancing' (Shutt et al., 2012), making it hard to see how this piecemeal and fragmented form of centrally orchestrated localism outlined above can be expected to address widening spatial disparities in a climate of prolonged austerity (Tomaney et al., 2012).

## Conclusions

As we have emphasised, localism is an important recurring strand of UK neo-liberalism, articulated through periodic strategies of political and economic restructuring which have sought to foster global competitiveness, reduce welfare dependency and dismantle collectivist institutions. In this context, localism and sense of notion of community seem to provide a 'flanking compensatory mechanism for the inadequacies of the market mechanism' (Jessop, 2002: 455), particularly in terms of securing the legitimation of the state. Over time, market rationalities have become more deeply entrenched and institutionalised, although their recurring limitations in terms of the needs of social reproduction and, periodically, economic growth, require the development of 'flanking' and supplementary tactics to counteract, pre-empt and co-opt sources of resistance and blockage. Since 2010, conditional localism and centrally orchestrated regionalism under Labour have given way to the austerity localism of the Coalition government as part of a renewed round of roll-back neo-liberalism involving the dismantling of some of the inherited structures of regionalism and central scrutiny, alongside a strong ideological emphasis on (local) community as part of a renewed assault on collectivism and the public sector (Featherstone et al., 2012). The collision between the national state project of austerity localism and the 'inherited institutional landscape' (Peck, 1998) has produced a differentiated and fragmented geography, most evident in relation to LEPs and City Deals (Tomaney et al., 2012; Marlow, 2013). Beneath the rhetoric of radical localisation, central control has actually been extended in some respects through a combination of the renationalisation of certain regional functions, austerity and a mode of compulsory localism in which additional funds are only offered on the basis of compliance with central government priorities (Harrison, 2012). As such, centralism remains a pathological weakness of the British growth model, paralleling and reinforcing the economic dominance of London and the South East in an increasingly spatially unbalanced and uneven pattern of economic development.

This raises the critical questions of how a more far-reaching model of 'real localism' (Cox, 2010) might be enacted to address entrenched regional disparities. In response, we end by outlining what we term a progressive localist approach (Featherstone et al., 2012). By the term progressive localism, we are referring to political strategies that aim to strengthen local institutions and communities as part of a wider political project grounded in principles such as social and spatial justice, equity, democracy and solidarity (Pike et al., 2007). The introduction of a progressive localist approach would require the development of a new institutional framework for local government which constructs local–central relations in a more balanced and supportive manner, rather than the reductive, zero-sum conceptions that have dominated recent British political practice. Rather than focusing solely on the local level, this entails the adoption of a multi-scalar approach. Here, we highlight four key principles. The first is based on genuine autonomy, requiring constitutionally guaranteed powers for local government, bringing the UK much closer to the systems of representative localism found in Western European countries (Hildreth, 2011). Second, local institutions require greater financial powers to provide for genuine autonomy and local accountability, involving the removal of central constraints and the introduction of greater financial flexibility beyond the rather piecemeal and one-sided terms of City Deals (Cox, 2010). The third key feature is policy innovation and learning between authorities as key elements of a cooperative localism. There is scope for this to be to be encouraged by central government through the establishment of policy networks and fora. Finally, our approach also has implications for the role of central government, which would retain an important role in terms of the determination of overall (minimum) service standards, the redistribution of revenues and the facilitation and coordination of local policy development. This requires national policy-makers to adopt the enabling state model that they have often prescribed for local government. A genuine commitment to decentralisation in a context of entrenched regional inequalities would also require the dispersal of national institutions and facilities (Amin et al., 2003), ultimately aiming at the creation of multiple centres of decision-making.

# References

Allen, J. and Cochrane, A. (2010) 'Assemblages of State Power: Topological Shifts in the Organisation of Government and Politics', *Antipode*, 42, 1071–1089.

Allen, J., Massey, D. and Cochrane, A. (1998) *Rethinking the Region*. London: Routledge.

Amin, A., Massey, D. and Thrift, N. (2003) *Decentring the Nation. A Radical Approach to Regional Inequality*. London: The Catalyst Forum.

Brenner, N. and Theodore, N. (2002) 'Cities and the Geographies of 'Actually Existing Neoliberalism', *Antipode*, 34, 349–379.

Bristow, G. (2010) *Critical Reflections on Regional Competitiveness*. London: Routledge.

Centre for Cities (2014a) *Cities Outlook 2014*. London: Centre for Cities.

Centre for Cities (2014b) 'Annual Health Check of UK Cities Shows that the Capital is Booming While Other Cities Fall Further Behind', Press Release, 27 January. London: Centre for Cities.

Centre for Public Policy for Regions (CPPR) (undated) *Scottish Government's Draft Budget 2013–14*, Briefing No. 1. Glasgow, CPPR

Clarke, N. and Cochrane, A. (2013) 'Geographies and Politics of Localism: The Localism of the United Kingdom's Coalition Government', *Political Geography*, 34, 10–23.

Communities and Local Government Committee (2011) *Localism*. Third Report of Session 2010–2012. HC 447. London: The Stationery Office.

The Conservative Party (2009) *Control Shift: Returning Power to Local Communities*. London: The Conservative Party.

Core Cities (2013) *Competitive Cities, Prosperous People: A Core Cities Prospectus for Growth*. Manchester: Core Cities.

Cox, E. (2010) *Five Foundations of Real Localism*. Newcastle upon Tyne, IPPR North.

Danson, M. (2012) 'Localism and Regionalism in Scotland – Growth and Development in Another Country', in M. Ward and S. Hardy (eds), *Changing Gear: Is Localism the New Regionalism?* London: The Smith Institute, pp. 117–125.

Danson, M. and Lloyd, G. (2012) 'Devolution, Institutions and Organisations: Changing Models of Regional Development Organisation. *Environment and Planning C: Government and Policy*, 30, 78–94.

Davies, J. S. (2008) 'Double-devolution or Double-dealing? The Local Government White Paper and The Lyons Review', *Local Government Studies*, 34, 3–22.

Dunleavy, P. and Hood, C. (1994) 'From Old Public Administration to New Public Management', *Public Money and Management*, 14, 9–16.

Department of Employment (1988) *Employment for the 1990s*. Cm 540. London: HMSO.

Department of the Environment, Transport and the Regions (1997) *Building Partnerships for Prosperity: Sustainable Growth, Competitiveness and Employment in the English Regions*. Cm 3814. London: HMSO.

Emmerson, C., Johnson, P. and Miller, H. (eds) (2013) *IFS Green Budget 2013*. London: Institute for Fiscal Studies.

Featherstone, D., Ince, A., MacKinnon, D., Cumbers, A. and Strauss, K. (2012) 'Progressive Localism and the Construction of Political Alternatives. *Transactions of the Institute of British Geographers*, NS 37, pp. 177–182.

Gamble, A. (2006) 'The Constitutional Revolution in the United Kingdom', *Publius: The Journal of Federalism*, 36, 19–35.

Goodwin, M., Jones, M. and Jones, R. (2005) 'Devolution, Constitutional Change and Economic Development: Explaining and understanding the NEW Institutional Geographies of the British State', *Regional Studies*, 39, 421–436.

Harrison, J. (2008) 'Stating the Production of Scales: Centrally Orchestrated Regionalism, Regionally Orchestrated Centralism', *International Journal of Urban and Regional Research*, 32, 922–941.

Harrison, J. (2012) 'Competition between Places', in M. Ward and S. Hardy (eds) *Changing Gear: Is Localism the New Regionalism?* London: The Smith Institute, pp. 85–95.

Haughton, G., Peck, J. and Strange, I. (1997) 'Turf Wars: The Battle for Control of English Local Economic Development', *Local Government Studies*, 23, 88–106.

HM Government (2010a) *Local Growth: Realising Every Place's Potential*. Cm 7691. London: HM Government.

HM Government (2010b) *Decentralisation and the Localism Bill: An Essential Guide*. London: HM Government.

HM Government (2012) *Unlocking Growth in Cities: City Deals Wave 1*. London: HM Government.

HM Treasury (2013) *Government's Response to the Heseltine Review*. Cm 8587. London: HM Treasury.

Heseltine, M. (2012) *No Stone Unturned in the Pursuit of Growth*. London: Department of Business, Innovation and Skills.

Hildreth, P. (2011) 'What is Localism, and What Implications do Different Models have for Managing the Local Economy?' *Local Economy*, 26, 702–714.

Jeffery, C. (2011) *Wales, the Referendum and the Multi-level State*. St David's Day Lecture 2011. Cardiff: The Wales Governance Centre.

Jessop, B. (1997) 'Capitalism and Its Future: Remarks on Regulation, Government and Governance', *Review of International Political Economy*, 4, 561–581.

Jessop, B. (2002) *The Future of the Capitalist State*. Polity: Cambridge.

Jessop, B., Bonnett, K., Bromley, S. and Ling, T. (1988) *Thatcherism: A Tale of Two Nations*. Polity, Cambridge.

Jones, A. (2010) 'Here We Go Again: The Pathology of Compulsive Re-organisation', *Local Economy*, 25, 373–378.

Jones, M. (2001) 'The Rise of the Regional State in Economic Governance: "Partnerships for Prosperity" or New Scales of State Power?' *Environment and Planning A*, 33, 1185–1211.

Jones, M. (2013) 'It's like déjà vu, all over again', in M. Ward and S. Hardy (eds), *Where Next for Local Enterprise Partnerships?* London: The Smith Institute, pp. 85–94.

Jones, R., Goodwin, M., Jones, M. and Simpson, G. (2004) 'Devolution, State Personnel and the Production of New Territories of Governance in the United Kingdom', *Environment and Planning A*, 36, 89–109.

Jones, R., Goodwin, M., Jones, M. and Pet, K. (2005) '"Filling in" the State: Economic Governance and the Evolution of Devolution in Wales', *Environment and Planning C, Government and Policy*, 23, 337–360.

Kearns, A. (1995) 'Active Citizenship and Local Governance: Political and Geographical Dimensions'. *Political Geography*, 14, 2, 155–177.

Keating, M. (1998) *The New Regionalism in Western Europe*. Cheltenham: Edward Elgar.

Laffin, M. (2008) 'Local Government Modernisation in England; A Critical Review of the LGMA Evaluation Studies', *Local Government Studies*, 34, 109–125.

Lodge, G. and Muir, R. (2010) 'Localism under New Labour', *The Political Quarterly*, 81, S96–S107.

Lovering, J. (1999) 'Theory Led by Policy: The Inadequacies of the "New Regionalism" (illustrated from the case of Wales), *International Journal of Urban and Regional Research*, 23, 379–395.

Lowndes, V. and Pratchett, L. (2012) 'Local Governance under the Coalition Government: Austerity, Localism and the "Big Society"', *Local Government Studies*, 38, 21–40.

MacKinnon, D. (2000) 'Managerialism, Governmentality and the State: A Neo-Foucauldian Approach to Local Economic Governance', *Political Geography*, 19, 293–314.

MacKinnon, D. and Shaw, J. (2010) 'New State Spaces, Agency and Scale: Devolution and the Regionalisation of Transport Governance in Scotland', *Antipode*, 42, 1226–1252.

MacKinnon, D., Shaw, J. and Docherty, I. (2008) *Diverging Mobilities? Devolution, Transport and Policy Innovation*. Oxford, Elsevier Science.

Marlow, D. (2013) 'What Do Wave Two City Deals Tell Us About Potential Offers and Asks for Local Growth Deals?' Blog on Regeneration and Renewal website, 5 December 2013. Available at http://davidmarlow.regen.net/2013/12/05/what-do-wave-two-city-deals-tell-us-about-potential-offers-and-asks-for-local-growth-deals/ (accessed 21 January 2014).

Marlow, D., McCarthy, A., O'Brien, P., Pike, A. and Tomaney, J. (2013) 'The State of the LEPs – A National Survey', in M. Ward and S. Hardy (eds), *Where next for Local Enterprise Partnerships?* London: The Smith Institute, pp. 65–74.

Massey, D. (1994) *Space, Place and Gender*. Minneapolis: University of Minnesota Press.

Massey, D. (2005) *For Space*. Sage: London

Morgan, K. (2006) 'Devolution and Development: Territorial Justice and the North-South Divide', *Publius: The Journal of Federalism*, 36, 189–206.

Peck, J. (1995) 'Moving and Shaking: Business Elites, State Localism and Urban Privatism', *Progress in Human Geography*, 19, 16–46.

Peck, J. (1998) 'Geographies of Governance: TECs and the Neo-liberalisation of Local Interests', *Space and Polity*, 2, 5–31.

Peck, J. (2001) 'Neoliberalising States: Thin Policies/Hard Outcomes', *Progress in Human Geography*, 25, 445–455.

Peck, J. (2010) *Constructions of Neoliberal Reason*. Oxford: Oxford University Press.

Peck, J. (2011) 'Geographies of Policy: From Transfer-diffusion to Mobility-mutation', *Progress in Human Geography*, 35, 773–797.

Peck, J. and Tickell, A. (2002) 'Neoliberalising Space', *Antipode*, 34, 380–404.

Pike, A., Rodriguez-Pose, A. and Tomaney, J. (2007) 'What Kind of Local and Regional Development and For Whom?' *Regional Studies*, 41, 1253–1269.

Pike, A., Rodriguez-Pose, A., Tomaney, J., Torrisi, G. and Tselios, V. (2012) 'In Search of the "Economic Dividend" of Devolution: Spatial Disparities, Spatial Economic Policy and Decentralisation in the UK', *Environment and Planning C: Government and Policy*, 20, 10–28.

Pike, A. and Tomaney, J. (2009) 'The State and Uneven Development: The Governance of Economic Development in England in the Post-devolution UK', *Cambridge Journal of Regions, Economies and Societies*, 2, 13–34.

Pratchett, L. (2004) 'Local Autonomy, Local Democracy and the "new localism"', *Political Studies*, 52, 358–375.

Pugalis, L. and Bentley, G. (2013) 'Economic Development under the Coalition Government', *Local Economy*, 28, 665–678.

Organisation for Economic Cooperation and Development (OECD) (2013) *Regions at a Glance*. Paris: OECD.

Rodriguez-Pose, A. and Sandall, R. (2008) 'From Identity to the Economy: Analysing the Evolution of Decentralisation Discourse', *Environment and Planning C, Government and Policy*, 21, 54–72.

Scratton, A. (2012) 'Vince Cable: Abolition of Development Agencies was "Maoist and chaotic"', *The Guardian*, 12 November.

Shutt, J., Pugalis, L. and Bentley, G. (2012) 'LEPs – Living Up to the Hype? The Changing Framework for Regional Economic Development and Localism in the UK', in M. Ward and S. Hardy (eds), *Changing Gear: Is Localism the New Regionalism?* London: The Smith Institute, pp. 11–23.

Storper, M. (1997) *The Regional World: Territorial Development in a Global Economy*. London: Guildford Press.

Tomaney, J., Pike, A. and McCarthy, A. (2012) 'The Governance of Economic Development in England', in M. Ward and S. Hardy (eds), *Changing Gear: Is Localism the New Regionalism?* London: The Smith Institute, pp. 65–74.

Townsend, A. and Champion, T. (2014) 'The Impact of Recession on City Regions: The British Experience, 2008–2013', *Local Economy*, Online First, pp. 1–14. DOI: 10.1177/0296094213518885

Waite, D., MacLennan, D. and O'Sullivan, T. (2013) 'Emerging City Policies: Devolution, Deals and Disorder', *Local Economy*, 28, 770–785.

Wilson, D. and Game, C. (2011) *Local Government in the United Kingdom*. 5th Edition. Basingstoke: Palgrave.

Wintour, P. (2014) 'Eric Pickles Plans Tax Squeeze on "Democracy Dodger" Councils', *The Guardian*, 10 January.

# 9
# Employment Protection Legislation and the Growth Crisis

*Jason Heyes and Paul Lewis*

## Introduction

In his recent book *Zombie Economics*, John Quiggin (2010) reviewed a number of economic theories and assumptions that have refused to die despite strong evidence that they are highly flawed. These include the claim that spending by the state crowds out private investment, the belief that efficient (i.e. weakly regulated) financial markets provide an accurate guide to the value of economic assets, and that policies that favour the well-off will, in the long-run, produce trickle down effects that benefit everyone. The belief that employment protection legislation (EPL) necessarily causes unemployment and is bad for competitiveness might be added to this list, and it is a belief that is at the heart of the Conservative–Liberal Democrat coalition government's strategy for jobs growth and enhancing the competitiveness of the UK economy. Since coming to power in May 2010, the government has unleashed a series of reforms that have eroded constraints on employers' ability to dismiss their employees and made it harder for dismissed workers to pursue compensation. The government has claimed that its reform programme will lighten the regulatory burden for employers and thereby encourage them to hire a greater number of employees. The main aim of this chapter is to subject this claim to critical scrutiny.

The chapter begins by discussing the belief that EPL is harmful to employment and tracing its influence over time on social policies relating to employment and the labour market. The chapter goes on to describe the reform agenda in the UK and the ways in which the government has loosened restrictions on dismissals and created new obstacles to block workers' access to justice. We then assess the extent to which reforms of employment protections are being pursued elsewhere in the EU. This is followed by a consideration of the potential consequences of the UK government's reforms for jobs, innovation and productivity. Drawing on published studies and our own research, we argue that the reforms are unlikely to stimulate a growth in good quality jobs and may have deleterious consequences for economic performance. In the conclusion we argue that the government has failed to develop a strategy for dealing with key work and employment related challenges and difficulties that have emerged or escalated since the start of the recent economic crisis.

## The shifting policy terrain

EPL regulates individual and collective dismissals and the use of temporary contracts by employers. It sets limits on an employer's ability to dismiss their employees and provides workers with rights in respect of consultation and severance payments. The consequences of EPL for the labour market have long been debated by economists and policy makers. The relationship between employment protection and unemployment has been of particular concern. Orthodox economists (e.g. St Paul, 2004; Siebert, 1997) tend to claim that restrictions on dismissal and requirements relating to severance payments contribute to unemployment by presenting firms with a disincentive to hire labour. Employers supposedly take into consideration potential future costs of dismissal, which leads them to recruit fewer workers than they would otherwise. A further twist on the argument is that employment protections reduce both inflows and outflows from unemployment, enabling insiders (i.e. employees) to extract higher wage increases from employers while exacerbating long-term unemployment to the detriment of outsiders (unemployed workers and, in particular, disadvantaged groups such as young workers) (Lindbeck and Snower, 1990; Blanchard and Portugal, 2001). The policy prescriptions that flow from this analysis include a weakening of employment protections and a reduction (or elimination) of minimum wages, which are deemed harmful to the employment prospects of low-skilled workers.

The claim that EPL is damaging to the labour market became a dominant theme in policy debates in the 1980s, as the Keynesian preoccupation with the relationship between aggregate demand and unemployment came to be replaced with an emphasis on the importance of supply-side phenomena. Drawing unfavourable comparisons between the supposedly over-regulated and sclerotic labour markets of continental Europe and the flexible labour markets of the US and the UK, the OECD and IMF argued that European governments would need to reduce the strictness of EPL if they were to cut unemployment (e.g. OECD, 1994). This message found favour with an increasing number of national policy makers. During the 1980s and 1990s employment protections were weakened in some EU countries, although this is not to say that there was an untrammelled race to the bottom: employment rights were strengthened for some groups within some countries, for example Italy (Michelotti and Nyland, 2008), while in the UK, a country with one of the most weakly regulated labour markets in the EU, there was an improvement in the late-1990s as a result of the Labour government's decision to implement European social policies following the 1997 general election. In many European countries, labour market reforms were largely associated with measures to facilitate an extension of fixed-term employment (OECD, 2004). In Germany, for example, the Employment Promotion Act (Beschäftigungförderungsgestz) of 1985 reduced restrictions on the use of fixed-term contracts, a process that was furthered in the early-2000s by the implementation of the recommendations of the Hartz Committee (Eichorst and Marx, 2011). Restrictions on employers' freedom to make use of non-standard contracts were similarly loosened in Spain in 1984, in Belgium in 1991 and in France in 1993.

Within the EU the prospect of a general levelling down of EPL to levels associated with the UK and Ireland appeared to be rejected in the 2000s as the European Commission began instead to encourage EU member states to pursue 'flexicurity', defined as an 'integrated strategy to enhance, at the same time, flexibility and security in the labour market' (European Commission, 2007: 10). According to the Commission, the introduction of greater contractual flexibility, along with active labour market measures and increases in lifelong learning would promote employment, reduce the duration of unemployment and improve the prospects of labour market outsiders. The Commission adopted an ambiguous, but on balance sceptical, position in relation to the benefits of EPL, arguing that achieving flexicurity would require policies that promoted 'employment security' rather than 'job security' (European Commission, 2007: 7). It also claimed that strict protections against economic dismissal further disadvantaged vulnerable workers, including the long-term unemployed, and encouraged 'recourse to a range of temporary contracts with low protection – often held by women and young people – with limited progress into open-ended jobs' (European Commission, 2007: 12).

Efforts by European policy makers to secure support for a common set of flexicurity principles in 2007 resulted in a de-emphasising of implied threats to employment protections and job security so as to appease flexicurity sceptics, including trade unions and some (particularly southern) EU member states (Mailand, 2010). Since the onset of the current economic crisis, however, the Commission has come to adopt a less ambiguous position in relation to EPL. Supply-side reforms of the labour market are central to the European Commission's proposals for generating economic growth in the aftermath of the crisis. The Franco-German initiated 'Euro plus pact', adopted in March 2011, called upon Eurozone countries to pursue flexicurity, although governments were expressly directed to consider the sustainability of the security aspects (e.g. unemployment benefits, pensions) (European Council, 2011). The Commission's 2011 Joint Employment Report similarly emphasised that unemployment benefit schemes should 'provide the right incentives to work' and called for greater sanctions for non-compliance. A renewed scepticism about the consequences of strong EPL can also be detected in the report, which recommends 'removing institutional obstacles that prevent proper functioning of Members States' labour markets' (EPSCO, 2011: 9).

## The context and content of UK reforms

EU member states have a considerable amount of discretion in respect of the content and strength of national EPL. While European Directives have established minimum standards in areas such as working time, holidays and equality of treatment, matters relating to probation periods for new employees, redundancy procedures, compensation, severance payments and the enforcement of employment rights are largely left to national governments to determine. These key employment relations issues have been targets for reforms introduced by the UK's Conservative–Liberal Democrat coalition government.

The government's employment law reforms have formed part of a wider set of measures aimed at removing regulations that are deemed to be detrimental to business. The Cabinet Office has spearheaded a red tape challenge, aimed at axing domestic regulations. Across government since January 2013 there has been a shift towards a one-in-two-out approach to regulation, whereby any new regulatory measure that imposes a cost on firms has to be offset by a reduction in other regulations sufficient to save double the costs imposed by the new measure (this scheme replaced a one-in-one-out approach that had operated since 2010). The regulatory reform agenda in respect of employment rights has had two principal components: firstly, a weakening of constraints

on an employer's ability to dismiss employees; and secondly, the introduction of new restrictions on a worker's ability to access justice. Work
on the first component commenced when the government asked the
venture capitalist Adrian Beecroft to undertake a review of UK employment law. The starting assumptions that informed Beecroft's review are
clear from the introductory section of his subsequent report, published
in October 2011:

> Britain has a deficit crisis, from which the only escape route is
> economic growth ... Yet much of employment law and regulation
> impedes the search for efficiency and competitiveness. It deters small
> businesses in particular from wanting to take on more employees:
> as a result they grow more slowly than they otherwise might. Many
> regulations, conceived in an era of full employment, are designed to
> make employment more attractive to potential employees. That was
> addressing yesterday's problem. In today's era of a lack of jobs those
> regulations simply exacerbate the national problem of high unem-
> ployment. (Beecroft, 2011: 2)

Beecroft's far-reaching recommendations included the abolition of the
Gangmaster's Licencing Authority (a body that regulates labour suppliers
in the agricultural and food sectors), dropping plans to introduce new
rights for agency workers (as required by the EU's Agency Workers
Directive), the closure of the Employment Agencies Inspectorate, a
substantial cut to the consultation period required for collective redundancies, enabling small businesses to opt out of laws relating to unfair
dismissal and the right to request flexible working patterns, and the
introduction of compensated no-fault dismissal.

Beecroft's recommendations were broadly supported by the CBI, the
British Chambers of Commerce and the Institute of Directors. Business
Secretary Vince Cable sounded a more sceptical note,[1] yet the government has since acted in the spirit of Beecroft's recommendations, even
if it has not followed them to the letter. The attack on employment
protections commenced in April 2012 when the minimum period of
employment service for unfair dismissal claims was increased from one
to two years (it is worth noting that prior to the 1979 general election
the minimum period of employment service required for unfair dismissal
claims was just six months). In April 2013 the government reduced the
minimum consultation period required in respect of large-scale collective redundancies involving more than 100 workers from 90 to 45
days. The following month, measures were introduced that permitted

private sector employers to offer prospective employees a financial stake in their business, on the condition that key employment rights were foregone. The, so-called, employee ownership scheme, first proposed during the 2012 Conservative Party Conference by George Osborne, the Chancellor of the Exchequer, enables employers to provide a new recruit with between £2,000 and £50,000 worth of tax-exempt shares, in return for which the new employee will have to agree to waive their rights in respect of unfair dismissal, redundancy and the right to request flexible working.[2] The measure was introduced despite scepticism on the part of key employer organisations. John Cridland, Director General of the CBI, described the scheme as a 'niche idea'. John Longworth, Director General of the British Chambers of Commerce (BCC), argued that the idea deserved to be 'tried out', but was 'unlikely to be a game-changer'. The Chartered Institute for Personnel and Development (CIPD), the leading professional body for people managers, has voiced unambiguous opposition to the measure. The organisation's employment relations advisor, Mike Emmott, argued that 'employees have little to gain by substituting their fundamental rights for uncertain financial gain and employers have little to gain by creating a two tier labour market'.[3] Opposition to the scheme was also strong in the House of Lords, which twice voted against the proposal. The government chose to plough on regardless, while making minor concessions, including the addition of requirements that workers be provided with free independent legal advice before accepting a rights for shares job offer and be given up to seven days to make up their mind. The government has emphasised that the scheme will be voluntary, although it is conceivable that many unemployed workers will find the offer preferable to continued joblessness. They will then have no legal protection against unfair dismissal and no right to redundancy compensation. Furthermore, redundancy implies a struggling (or insolvent) business, in which case the value of their shares is likely to be negatively affected.

The government has also made it easier for employers to dismiss staff who are deemed to be under-performing by introducing measures to facilitate consensual termination of the employment relationship through Acas conciliation, settlement agreements and protected conversations between employees and employers. Where an employer offers to end an employment relationship on agreed terms (i.e. for financial compensation), the details of the conversation cannot be used as evidence in an Employment Tribunal, should the employee subsequently wish to claim that they were unfairly dismissed. The Employment Tribunal service has itself been subject to reforms that have served to erode workers' access to justice. The key changes relate to the costs of bringing a case and the potential compensation if a case is upheld. Claimants are now required to pay a fee in order to bring a case (£400 for a wages claim; £1,200 for an unfair dismissal claim; £1,600 for discrimination claims) and must pay part of the fee up front in order to register the claim for a preliminary hearing (the remainder is paid if the claim goes to a full hearing). The maximum unfair dismissal compensation award has been cut from £72,300 to the worker's annual salary (or the UK average salary, currently £26,000), depending on which is lower. Furthermore, the principle of tripartism, which has been central to the Employment Tribunal system, has been challenged. Since the creation of the (then) Industrial Tribunals in the mid-1960s, lay-persons nominated by employer and trade union organisations have sat alongside judges at hearings and been able to provide advice based on their experience. The government has removed the requirement of tripartism in respect of unfair dismissal cases, which judges are now permitted to hear alone.

The government justified its reforms on the grounds that the Employment Tribunal system had become too costly and over-burdened as a consequence of caseload increases beginning in the 1990s. The government also claimed that the reform would ease the burden on businesses by discouraging workers from bringing weak or baseless cases which employers then need to spend time and money defending. However, the number of claims began to fall in 2009, prior to the implementation of the reforms. More importantly, the claim that there are too many cases is highly questionable. Most claims never reach a full hearing (because they are withdrawn, dismissed at a preliminary hearing stage or are settled, perhaps with the help of Acas). Moreover, the number of claims is not a reflection of the extent of unfairness or bad practices. The 2008 Fair Treatment at Work Survey found that only 3 per cent of employees who experience a problem at work register an Employment Tribunal claim. Even if a worker is successful, compensation tends to be relatively low[4] and is frequently not paid in full (Adams et al., 2009).

## How does the UK compare to other EU member states?

In order to assess whether the reforms implemented by the coalition government are likely to benefit the UK economy, it is first necessary to place them in a comparative context. International comparisons of EPL tend to be based on the synthetic EPL indicators developed by the OECD (Venn, 2009). These indicators, which are constructed on the basis of national employment laws relating to dismissals, facilitate cross-country benchmarking. Since the mid-1980s, the earliest period for which OECD data are available, the UK has had among the lowest overall EPL score of any OECD member state (the US being the only country that has consistently been awarded a lower score) and has had the lowest scores of any OECD member country within the European Union. Over the past three decades, however, the EPL scores associated with EU member states have tended to converge as governments have sought to deregulate labour markets, particularly in relation to constraints on temporary employment (Heyes, 2011).

The economic crisis has given further impetus to EPL reforms. Table 9.1 compares EU member states according to various synthetic EPL measures developed by the OECD. Comparing 2008 and 2013, it is clear that efforts to erode employment protections have not been confined to the UK. Typical measures have included longer probationary periods for new recruits, cuts in severance pay and weaker negotiating and consultation rights for employee representatives. However, the EPL scores suggest that steps to weaken employment rights have mainly been confined to the most financially distressed economies and the Central and Eastern European economies that have joined the EU since 2004. The former have been obliged by the, so-called, Troika of the European Commission, European Central Bank and IMF to implement reforms in return for financial assistance intended to ameliorate their sovereign debt crises and stabilise the Eurozone. Spain, Italy and Portugal have increased employers' freedom to make use of fixed-term contracts and made it easier for employers to dismiss workers. Italy has weakened workers' rights to reinstatement in cases of wrongful dismissal. Spain has ended administrative authorisation for large-scale redundancies and cut the basis for calculating compensation for unfair dismissals. While Portugal has cut overtime payments, reduced the number of bank holidays, increased employers' freedom to select workers for dismissal and cut severance payments. Greece has cut starting salaries for young people, increased employers' freedom to extend working time, established a 12-month probation period for new employees, and made it possible for company-level collective agreements to take precedence over sectoral-level agreements. By comparison, Ireland's reforms have been more limited and the country is something of an exception among the financially distressed EU member states in that its EPL scores for regular and temporary contracts have increased since 2008, albeit from a very low base. The main improvements have been: the transposition of the European directive on temporary agency work into Ireland's

*Table 9.1*  OECD measures of EPL for EU member states, 2008–2013 compared

| | Regular contracts | | | | | | Fixed-term and temporary agency contracts | |
|---|---|---|---|---|---|---|---|---|
| | EPR_V3 | | EPC | | EPRC_V3 | | EPT_V3 | |
| | 2008 | 2013 | 2008 | 2013 | 2008 | 2013 | 2008 | 2013 |
| Austria | 2.119 | 2.119 | 3.25 | 3.25 | 2.442 | 2.442 | 2.167 | 2.167 |
| Belgium | 2.076 | 2.076 | 5.125 | 5.125 | 2.947 | 2.947 | 2.417 | 2.417 |
| France | 2.668 | 2.602 | 3.375 | 3.375 | 2.87 | 2.823 | 3.75 | 3.75 |
| Germany | 2.719 | 2.719 | 3.625 | 3.625 | 2.978 | 2.978 | 1.542 | 1.75 |
| Netherlands | 2.902 | 2.838 | 3.0 | 3.188 | 2.93 | 2.938 | 1.167 | 1.167 |
| Luxembourg | 2.279 | 2.279 | 3.875 | 3.875 | 2.725 | 2.735 | 3.833 | 3.833 |
| Czech Republic | 3.002 | 2.875 | 2.125 | 2.125 | 2.751 | 2.66 | 1.875 | 2.125 |
| Estonia | 2.559 | 1.743 | 1.75 | 2.875 | 2.328 | 2.066 | 2.292 | 3.042 |
| Hungary | 1.821 | 1.454 | 3.375 | 3.625 | 2.265 | 2.074 | 1.917 | 2 |
| Poland | 2.197 | 2.197 | 2.875 | 2.875 | 2.391 | 2.391 | 2.333 | 2.333 |
| Slovakia | 2.189 | 1.808 | 3.75 | 3.375 | 2.635 | 2.256 | 2.167 | 2.417 |
| Slovenia | 2.434 | 1.992 | 3.375 | 3.375 | 2.703 | 2.387 | 2.5 | 2.125 |
| Denmark | 2.035 | 2.098 | 2.875 | 2.875 | 2.275 | 2.32 | 1.792 | 1.792 |
| Finland | 2.383 | 2.383 | 1.625 | 1.625 | 2.167 | 2.167 | 1.875 | 1.875 |
| Sweden | 2.524 | 2.524 | 2.5 | 2.5 | 2.517 | 2.517 | 0.792 | 1.167 |
| Greece | 2.69 | 2.075 | 3.25 | 3.25 | 2.85 | 2.41 | 3.167 | 2.917 |
| Italy | 2.595 | 2.412 | 4.125 | 3.75 | 3.032 | 2.794 | 2.708 | 2.708 |
| Portugal | 4.167 | 3.01 | 1.875 | 1.875 | 3.512 | 2.685 | 2.292 | 2.333 |
| Spain | 2.224 | 1.948 | 3.75 | 3.125 | 2.66 | 2.284 | 3.5 | 3.167 |
| Ireland | 1.37 | 1.497 | 3.5 | 3.5 | 1.978 | 2.069 | 0.708 | 1.208 |
| UK | 1.248 | 1.115 | 2.875 | 2.625 | 1.713 | 1.546 | 0.417 | 0.542 |

*Note:* The EPL index varies between 0 (least restrictions) and 6 (most restrictions). EPR_V3 measures the strictness of regulations of individual dismissal of employees on regular/indefinite contracts and incorporates nine data items. EPC measures additional costs and procedures involved in dismissing more than one worker at a time and incorporates four data items. EPRC_V3 is the weighted sum of sub-indicators concerning the regulations for individual dismissals and additional provisions for collective dismissals. It incorporates 13 data items. The measure reported for the strictness of regulation on the use of fixed-term and temporary work agency contracts is EPT_V3, which incorporates eight data items.

national legislation, which has strengthened rights for this group of workers; greater protection for whistleblowers; and efforts to improve compliance. However, social protections, including unemployment benefits, have been cut since the start of the crisis.

Reforms have also been widespread among the CEE economies. Some improvements in rights have taken place, mostly as a consequence of the transposition of EU Directives into national legislation (e.g. in 2009 Slovakia implemented the EU Directives on part-time and fixed-term workers). Other measures, however, have been directed at weakening protections. Slovakia has made notice and probation periods more flexible, Slovenia has cut severance payments and increased employers' freedom to dismiss workers, while Lithuania has extended working time and also relaxed constraints on lay-offs. Several countries, including Lithuania, the Czech Republic and Romania, have weakened restrictions on the use of fixed-term contracts (Clauwaert and Schömann, 2012: 11). The CEE economies in the OECD have not been subject to direct pressure from the Troika. However, as can be seen from Table 9.2, most experienced a surge in unemployment following the start of the crisis or, as in the case of Slovakia, were suffering from comparatively high rates of unemployment even before the crisis began. The countries that have been least interested in diluting EPL are those that avoided sovereign debt crises and substantial increases in unemployment after 2008. In countries such as Germany, Austria and the Netherlands, job saving measures such as work-sharing played an important role in cushioning the impact of the crisis on the labour market (Bosch, 2010). It is likely that relatively robust apprenticeship training systems also helped to protect young people.

## Will weaker EPL help to restore jobs growth and competitiveness?

The reductions in EPL strictness that have been implemented in the UK and elsewhere in the EU have been intended to reduce unemployment and enhance competitiveness. There are, however, reasons for doubting that substantial improvements will result, particularly in countries such as the UK, where EPL was already weak prior to the crisis. The first reason for scepticism is the lack of a linear relationship between EPL and employment or unemployment, which means that lower levels of EPL are not necessarily associated with superior employment outcomes. Figures 9.1 and 9.2 plot the average employment and unemployment rates for EU member states in 2007 against the OECD's composite

*Table 9.2*   Unemployment rates in the EU, 2006–2012

| GEO/TIME | 2006 | 2007 | 2008 | 2009 | 2010 | 2011 | 2012 |
|---|---|---|---|---|---|---|---|
| EU28 | 8.3 | 7.2 | 7.1 | 9.0 | 9.7 | 9.7 | 10.5 |
| Austria | 4.8 | 4.4 | 3.8 | 4.8 | 4.4 | 4.2 | 4.3 |
| Belgium | 8.3 | 7.5 | 7.0 | 7.9 | 8.3 | 7.2 | 7.6 |
| France | 9.2 | 8.4 | 7.8 | 9.5 | 9.7 | 9.6 | 10.2 |
| Germany | 10.3 | 8.7 | 7.5 | 7.8 | 7.1 | 5.9 | 5.5 |
| Netherlands | 4.4 | 3.6 | 3.1 | 3.7 | 4.5 | 4.4 | 5.3 |
| Luxembourg | 4.6 | 4.2 | 4.9 | 5.1 | 4.6 | 4.8 | 5.1 |
| Bulgaria | 9.0 | 6.9 | 5.6 | 6.8 | 10.3 | 11.3 | 12.3 |
| Croatia | 11.4 | 9.6 | 8.4 | 9.1 | 11.8 | 13.5 | 15.9 |
| Czech Rep. | 7.1 | 5.3 | 4.4 | 6.7 | 7.3 | 6.7 | 7.0 |
| Estonia | 5.9 | 4.6 | 5.5 | 13.8 | 16.9 | 12.5 | 10.2 |
| Hungary | 7.5 | 7.4 | 7.8 | 10.0 | 11.2 | 10.9 | 10.9 |
| Latvia | 7.0 | 6.1 | 7.7 | 17.5 | 19.5 | 16.2 | 15.0 |
| Lithuania | 5.8 | 4.3 | 5.8 | 13.8 | 17.8 | 15.4 | 13.4 |
| Poland | 13.9 | 9.6 | 7.1 | 8.1 | 9.7 | 9.7 | 10.1 |
| Romania | 7.3 | 6.4 | 5.8 | 6.9 | 7.3 | 7.4 | 7.0 |
| Slovenia | 6.0 | 4.9 | 4.4 | 5.9 | 7.3 | 8.2 | 8.9 |
| Slovakia | 13.5 | 11.2 | 9.6 | 12.1 | 14.5 | 13.7 | 14.0 |
| Denmark | 3.9 | 3.8 | 3.5 | 6.0 | 7.5 | 7.6 | 7.5 |
| Finland | 7.7 | 6.9 | 6.4 | 8.2 | 8.4 | 7.8 | 7.7 |
| Sweden | 7.1 | 6.1 | 6.2 | 8.3 | 8.6 | 7.8 | 8.0 |
| Cyprus | 4.6 | 3.9 | 3.7 | 5.4 | 6.3 | 7.9 | 11.9 |
| Greece | 8.9 | 8.3 | 7.7 | 9.5 | 12.6 | 17.7 | 24.3 |
| Italy | 6.8 | 6.1 | 6.7 | 7.8 | 8.4 | 8.4 | 10.7 |
| Malta | 6.9 | 6.5 | 6.0 | 6.9 | 6.9 | 6.5 | 6.4 |
| Portugal | 8.6 | 8.9 | 8.5 | 10.6 | 12.0 | 12.9 | 15.9 |
| Spain | 8.5 | 8.3 | 11.3 | 18.0 | 20.1 | 21.7 | 25.0 |
| Ireland | 4.5 | 4.7 | 6.4 | 12.0 | 13.9 | 14.7 | 14.7 |
| UK | 5.4 | 5.3 | 5.6 | 7.6 | 7.8 | 8.0 | 7.9 |

*Source*: Eurostat [une_rt_a]. Data are not seasonally adjusted.

measure of regulations for individual dismissals and additional provisions for collective dismissals.[5] The scatterplot suggests that there was no clear relationship between EPL and national employment and unemployment rates in the year preceding the crisis. While the correlation between EPL and employment rates is negative ($r = -.22$, $p = .34$) and the correlation between EPL and unemployment positive ($r = .29$, $p = .20$), neither correlation is statistically significant. Although the UK and Portugal respectively had the lowest and highest EPL scores of all EU member states, their employment rates did not differ greatly in 2007.

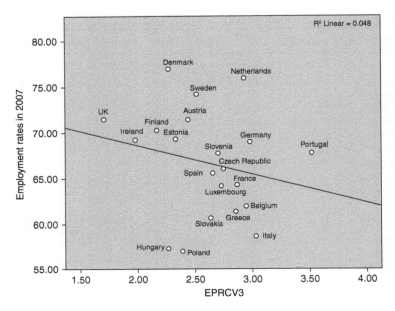

*Figure 9.1* 2007 employment rates in EU member states plotted against OECD EPL scores

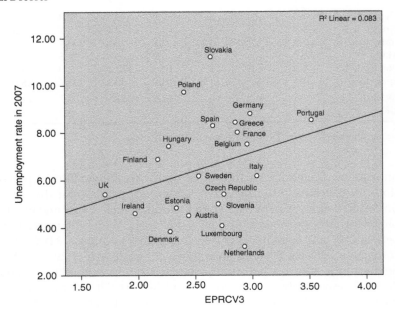

*Figure 9.2* 2007 unemployment rates in EU member states plotted against OECD EPL scores

The scatterplots provide only a static snapshot. A sizeable number of studies have, however, examined the relationship between unemployment and labour market institutions, including EPL, over time. Some have suggested that unemployment (particularly long-term unemployment) is positively related and employment negatively related to increases in the strictness of EPL (see, for example, Elmeskov et al., 1998; Bertola et al., 2001; Botero et al., 2004). However, Baker et al. (2005) have highlighted that the estimates contained in these studies vary considerably, are in some cases implausible and are highly sensitive to the measures, time periods and estimation methods on which they are based. Their own analysis, based on data from the 1960s to the 2000s, provided no support for the view that EPL is positively associated with unemployment. Other recent studies have produced similar results. Oesch (2010), for example, found that the employment prospects of low-skilled workers in OECD countries were unaffected by employment protections during the period 1991–2006, while Avdagic and Salardi's (2013: 750) analysis of 32 EU and OECD countries over a 30-year time period found that '[e]mployment protection legislation does not have any discernible impact on unemployment, regardless of the choice of estimators and specifications'. Furthermore, a recent analysis by Cazes et al. (2012) has suggested that negative impacts of EPL on employment are observable only among countries with very high EPL index scores and that 'at very low levels of employment protection, increases in EPL stringency are associated with a *higher* employment rate', (Cazes et al., 2012: 14, emphasis added).

Even if the impact of EPL is broadly neutral with respect to aggregate unemployment, it is possible that it might have a disproportionate impact on certain disadvantaged groups, such as the disabled and young people. Given the threat of a lost generation, perhaps the most important question is whether a reduction in the stringency of EPL might improve the job prospects of young people. Once again, however, the evidence relating to the consequences of EPL for employment is mixed. Some studies have found that stringent EPL has adverse effects on young people (e.g. Allard and Lindert, 2007; Bertola et al., 2007) while others, such as Noelke (2011) have found that the strictness of EPL has no implications for youth unemployment. Cazes et al. (2012) found that, once GDP changes are controlled for, national experiences of youth unemployment since the start of the Great Recession were unrelated to differences in EPL strictness. Furthermore, an examination of long-term unemployment for young people in those countries that have reduced the strictness of EPL for regular contracts suggests little sign of an improvement: indeed, as shown in Figure 9.3, rates have continued to increase in most of these countries.

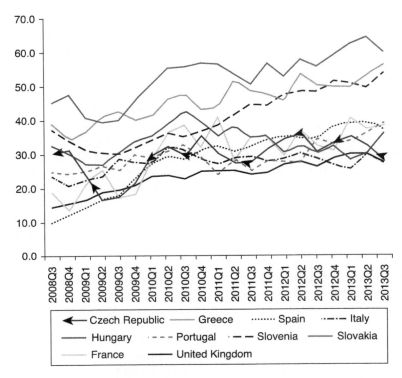

*Figure 9.3*  Quarterly changes in long-term youth (15–24 yrs) unemployment, 2008–2013

*Source*: Eurostat [lfsq_upgal].

There is also a risk of overlooking the potential value of robust employment protections in preserving jobs during economic downturns. Figure 9.4 suggests that EU countries with relatively strong employment protections tended to experience less severe job losses than those with weaker protections during the early stages of the crisis (for a fuller discussion see Heyes and Lewis, 2013). While EPL did not prevent subsequent employment rate reductions, particularly in countries experiencing financial distress and pursuing austerity, it is likely that it served to stem job losses in the initial period and encouraged employers to look for internal means of reducing labour costs. This was particularly the case in countries such as Germany, where short-time working was used extensively (Bosch, 2010; Heyes, 2013).

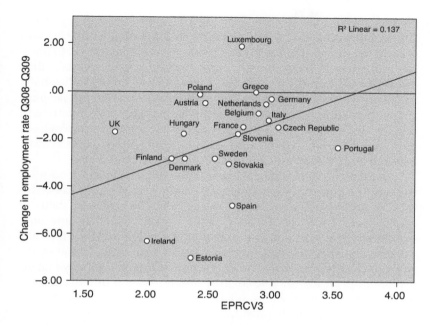

*Figure 9.4*  EPL and employment rate changes, Q3 2008–Q3 2009
*Note:* r = .37, p < 0.1.

Although the academic literature relating to EPL has tended to focus on its consequences for employment, the implications of weaker EPL for management–worker relations, innovation and productivity also need to be considered. Every employment relationship involves a power imbalance, but workers who have been stripped of their statutory rights are less likely to feel able to challenge unreasonable demands or voice honest opinions. Moreover, weaker employment protections may undermine the trust, cooperation and worker participation required for the successful introduction of new processes and products (Buchele and Christiansen, 1999). To that extent, the erosion of employment protections will serve to impede rather than stimulate innovation and investment. It is therefore possible that by weakening EPL, the UK government will impede productivity growth (Buchele and Christiansen, 1995, 1999; Storm and Naastepad, 2009). The UK has long suffered from a vicious cycle of low wages, low investment and low productivity (Nolan, 1991). Although the economy appears to be recovering from the economic crisis and unemployment is (at the time of writing) beginning to fall, productivity has yet to pick up (Financial Times, 23 January 2013). Furthermore, average real wages have fallen substantially since the start of the crisis (Gregg et al., 2013) and economic recovery has yet to translate into renewed wages growth. Firms that are able to maintain their competitiveness on the basis of low wages and the numerical flexibility and intensive working practices that weaker employment rights facilitate are perhaps unlikely to perceive benefits in making costly investments in skills and technology. To that extent, the government's employment protection reforms may be further entrenching the structural weaknesses of the UK economy.

By weakening EPL and making it easier for employers to dismiss workers, the government is supposedly addressing the risks associated with an information asymmetry – specifically, the general inability of employers to know the qualities of the workers that they hire until the worker is in post and the possibility that they will therefore hire workers who they subsequently deem to be unsuitable. However, the government has exacerbated other types of information gaps by making it more difficult for firms to identify and access authoritative sources of employment information, advice and support. The Business Link Advisory Service, which provided advice, support and mentoring to small businesses, was closed in 2011. Although Acas' telephone-based advice service has been retained, the government has imposed a moratorium on advertising activities across government services, which means that Acas does not currently have a budget to enable it to reach out to employers and prospective employers. The question of how an employment relationship, having been created, can be most effectively managed and sustained appears not to have been considered. The analysis of the formation of the employment relationship has simply been reduced to a cost (notional) benefit analysis of more flexible termination rights in employment law. The government has legislated to cut potential employer costs for worst case situations in which employment relationships cease to be viable in the, largely evidence-free, hope that this will stimulate jobs growth. It has not legislated to build the foundations for high-trust employment relations that are more likely to contribute to long-term sustainable growth and make the UK more competitive in global markets.

## Conclusion

The turn to austerity has breathed new life into the idea that cutting employment rights will lead to reduced unemployment and improved competitiveness. The reforms enacted by the current Conservative–Liberal Democratic coalition government have effectively turned back the clock in key areas of employment law. The increase in the period of service required in unfair dismissal claims has undone a reform implemented by the Labour Party in the late-1990s and re-established the rule that had existed under the Thatcher and Major governments. The changes to the Employment Tribunal system have gone even further by imposing restrictions on access to justice and attacking principles of tripartism in an area that even the Thatcher governments had not challenged. While the current government's ability to weaken employment rights in certain areas, such as equality of treatment and working time, is restricted by European law, Prime Minister David Cameron has made it clear that he would like control over social policies relating to work and employment to be repatriated to the UK and that this would be an objective of any future renegotiation of the UK's ties to the EU. If this were to happen, it would be highly likely that further employment rights would be stripped away.

The economic crisis has left a substantial impression on work and employment in the UK. The government has focused on reducing the level of unemployment and increasing job quantity while neglecting crucial issues relating to the distribution of work and the quality of jobs. Many of those workers who are in employment have less paid work than they require, as reflected in the substantial increase in the proportions of workers who are involuntarily employed in temporary or part-time jobs (Heyes and Lewis, 2013). There has also been an increase in highly precarious forms of employment, such as zero-hours contracts that provide no guarantee of work or payment, yet typically require workers to submit to a contractual obligation of exclusivity. The CIPD (2013) has estimated that approximately one million UK workers are employed on such contracts. Furthermore, it is widely recognised that many of the new jobs that have been created since the start of the crisis are low-waged (Mayhew, 2012). The expansion of low-paid work has fuelled in-work poverty and helped to push the issue of the living wage up the policy agenda. Each of these problems is likely to be exacerbated by the weakening of employment protections, given that workers will be more vulnerable to implicit or explicit threats of dismissal. Increasing employers' freedom to dismiss workers falls far short of a viable strategy for creating sustainable quality jobs. It also threatens to further erode the necessary conditions for the development of trust and cooperation that might in turn support innovation, internal flexibility and improved performance.

The attack on EPL has been one important element in a drive by the government to cheapen the cost of employing British workers. Following the start of the crisis, the Labour government attempted to incentivise employers to take on employees by offering them employment subsidies. This scheme was abandoned following the 2010 general election. Instead, the coalition government has adopted a wider strategy that has included public sector pay freezes and cuts, a reduction in the real value of the national minimum wage and the stripping away of labour market regulations and enforcement mechanisms that supposedly impose unnecessary and harmful costs on businesses and stifle entrepreneurial behaviour. These policy measures are the labour market face of austerity, introduced in the belief that renewed economic growth will ensue as businesses are freed from shackles that stymie their efforts to improve efficiency and expand the scale of production. As this chapter has demonstrated, this belief is not well supported by the evidence. It is far more likely that the coalition government's recalibration of employment rights will produce a shift in the balance of power at the workplace in favour of employers, emboldening the worst employers and increasing the vulnerability and insecurity of those they employ. This will do nothing to shift the UK onto a high skill, high investment growth path.

The stated aim of the coalition government has been to achieve sustainable growth and a balanced budget through rebalancing the economy towards the increased export of high value-added goods and services. The influential Heseltine report on economic growth (2013), which was broadly accepted by the government, cast an envious glance at the performance of Germany. However, the report's proposed solutions to the weaknesses of the UK economy were based on an incomplete assessment of the institutional features of the UK's more competitive and economically balanced EU neighbours. The report emphasised the importance of infrastructure investment, active industrial policy and a greater role for the local and national associations of business. There was no consideration of the nature of the employment relationship or manager–worker relations. The benefits that strong institutions, including robust employment protections, provide in terms of skill development (Harcourt and Wood, 2007), internal investment, trust and cooperation were ignored, as were the 'beneficial constraints' (Streeck, 1997) that regulation and institutional systems place upon management in their choice of competition strategies and the macroeconomic demand benefits associated with relatively high wages and compressed wage structures (Stockhammer et al., 2009). Market flexibility, particularly in relation to the labour market, remains the leitmotif of the UK government's growth strategy, yet the consequence is that an increasing proportion of the UK economy is being locked into low-wage, low investment and low productivity forms of competition.

Renewed enthusiasm for weaker employment protections has not been confined to the UK. Since 2008 several other European governments have eroded constraints on dismissals and encouraged temporary employment in the hope of reducing unemployment and promoting competitiveness. Yet, given a lack of compelling evidence that cuts to EPL directly result in a lowering of aggregate unemployment, it would, as Countouris and Freedland (2013: 93) have recently argued, be best to focus on the role of employment law in 'protecting the dignity and working conditions of workers' rather than viewing it as a means by which to stimulate economic growth. The policy tendency within the EU at the present time threatens to ratchet down protections for both workers employed on non-standard contracts and those with regular contracts. The proliferation of temporary jobs and other precarious forms of work (such as internships) may further fuel arguments in favour of weakening the protections associated with standard employment as the number of labour market outsiders grows relative to the number of insiders. Some (for example, Kenner, 2009) have argued in favour of a harmonisation of worker status and a contractual unification in which employment rights would accrue over time, according to length of tenure. This might help to lessen inequalities in the labour market, although it is important that a move to unify contractual structures should not result in a general levelling down of protection. The aim, as Countouris and Freedland (2013) argue, should be to deliver dignity and decent conditions for all workers, as well as access to opportunities for skill development, capability building and employment stability. The implication is that employment law should be treated as a means of promoting social justice (Supiot, 2012) rather than an instrument for delivering labour market flexibility.

## Notes

1. https://www.gov.uk/government/news/beecroft-report-on-employment-law (accessed 4 March 2014).
2. In addition, employees taking maternity leave are required to provide 16 weeks' notice of their intention to return to work, as opposed to the standard 8 weeks.
3. http://www.cipd.co.uk/pressoffice/press-releases/share-ownership-no-substitute-employment-rights-good-people-management-081012.aspx (accessed 4 March 2014).

4. In the period April 2011–April 2012 the median awards for unfair dismissal and race discrimination were £4,560 and £5,256 respectively. Compensation was less than £2,000 in 30 per cent of awards.
5. The 2008 EPL values are used as the OECD did not provide information about combined individual and collective protections until that year and, moreover, earlier version of the separate indicators for individual and collective provisions are not available for Slovenia, Luxembourg and Estonia. They are available for all other countries and, with the exception of Finland, the values of the indicators for individual and collective protections did not change between 2007 and 2008. The value of the measure of additional provisions for collective redundancies fell from 1.876 to 1.675 between 2007 and 2008. The implications for the analysis are negligible.

# References

Avdagic, S. and Salardi, P. (2013) 'Tenuous Link: Labour Market Institutions and Unemployment in Advanced and New Market Economies', *Socio-Economic Review*, 11, 4, 739–770.

Beecroft, A. (2011) *Report on Employment Law*. Department for Business, Innovation and Skills. http://news.bis.gov.uk/imagelibrary/downloadmedia.ashx?MediaDetailsID=5551.

Bertola, G. M., Blau, F. D. and Kahn, L. M. (2001) 'Comparative Analysis of Labor Market Outcomes: Lessons for the United States from International Long-run Evidence', *National Bureau of Economic Research Working Paper*, No. W8526, October.

Blanchard, O. and Portugal, P. (2001) 'What Hides Behind an Unemployment Rate: Comparing Portuguese and US Labour Markets', *American Economic Review*, 91, 1, 187–207.

Bosch, G. (2010) 'Dismissing Hours Not Workers: Work-sharing in the Economic Crisis', *Principios: Estudios De Economía Política*, 17, 29–51.

Botero, J. C., Djankov, S., La Porta, R., Lopez-de-Sinales, F. and Shleifer, A. (2004) 'The Regulation of Labor', *Quarterly Journal of Economics*, 119, 1339–1382.

Buchele, R. and Christiansen, J. (1995) 'Productivity, Real Wages and Worker Rights: A Cross-national Comparison', *Labour*, 9, 3, 405–422.

Buchele, R. and Christiansen, J. (1999) 'Employment and Productivity Growth in Europe and North America: The Impact of Labour Market Institutions', *International Review of Applied Economics*, 13, 3, 313–332.

Cazes, S. and Tonin, M. (2010) 'Employment Protection Legislation and Job Stability: A European cross-country Analysis', *International Labour Review*, 149, 3, 261–285.

Cazes, S., Khatiwada, S. and Malo, M. (2012) 'Employment Protection and Collective Bargaining: Beyond the Deregulation Agenda', *Employment Sector Employment Working Paper* No. 133, Geneva: ILO.

CIPD (2013) *Zero-Hours Contracts: Myth and Reality*. Research Report November 2013. London: CIPD.

Clauwaert, S. and Schömann, I. (2012) *The Crisis And National Labour Law Reforms: A Mapping Exercise*. European Trade Union Institute. Working Paper 2012.04. Brussels: ETUI.

Countouris, N. and Freedland, M. (2013) 'Labour Regulation and the Economic Crisis in Europe: Challenges, Responses and Prospects', in J. Heyes and L. Rychly (eds), *Labour Administration in Uncertain Times: Policy, Practice and Institutions.* Cheltenham: Edward Elgar/ILO.

Elmeskov, M. J. and Scarpetta, S. (1998) 'Key Lessons for Labor Market Reforms: Evidence from OECD Countries Experience', *Swedish Economic Policy Review,* 5, 2, 205–252.

Gregg, P., Machin, S. and Fernández-Salgado, M. (2013) *Real Wages and Unemployment in the Big Squeeze.* Mimeo. LSE.

Harcourt, M. and Wood, G. (2007) 'The Importance of Employment Protection for Skill Development in Coordinated Market Economies', *European Journal of Industrial Relations,* 13, 2, 141–159.

Heyes, J. (2011) 'Flexicurity, Employment Protection and the Jobs Crisis', *Work, Employment & Society,* 25, 4, 642–657.

Heyes, J. (2013) 'Flexicurity in Crisis: European Labour Market Policies in a Time of Austerity', *European Journal of Industrial Relations,* 19, 3, 71–86.

Heyes, J. and Lewis, P. (2013) 'Employment Protection Under Fire: Labour Market Deregulation and Employment in the European Union', *Economic & Industrial Democracy.* Online version available at http://eid.sagepub.com/content/early/2 013/07/25/0143831X13491842

Kenner, J. (2009) 'New Frontiers in EU Labour Law: From Flexicurity to Flex-security', in M. Dougan and S. Currie (eds), *50 Years of the European Treaties: Looking Back and Thinking Forward.* Oxford: Hart.

Lindbeck, A. and Snower, D. J. (1990) 'Demand and Supply-side Policies and Unemployment: Policy Implications of the Insider-outsider Approach', *Scandinavian Journal of Economics,* 92, 2, 279–305.

Noelke, C. (2011) *The Consequences of Employment Protection Legislation for the Youth Labour Market.* Working Paper 144, Mannheimer Zentrum für Europäische Sozialforschung, University of Mannheim.

OECD (1994) *Job Study: Facts, Analysis, Strategies.* Paris: OECD

Oesch, D. (2010) 'What Explains High Unemployment among Low-skilled Workers? Evidence from 21 OECD Countries', *European Journal of Industrial Relations,* 16, 1, 39–55.

Quiggin, J. (2010) *Zombie Economics: How Dead Ideas Still Walk Among Us.* Princeton: Princeton University Press.

St Paul, G. (2004) 'Why are European Countries Diverging in their Unemployment Experience?' *Journal of Economic Perspectives,* 18, 4, 49–68.

Siebert, H. (1997) 'Labour Market Rigidities: At the Root of Unemployment in Europe', *Journal of Economic Perspectives,* 11, 3, 37–55.

Simonazzi, A. and Villa, P. (1999) 'Flexibility and Growth', *International Review of Applied Economics,* 13, 3, 281–311.

Stockhammer, E., Onaran, O. and Ederer, S. (2009) 'Functional Income Distribution and Aggregate Demand in the Euro Area', *Cambridge Journal of Economics,* 33, 1, 139–159.

Storm, S. and Naastepad, C. W. M. (2009) 'Labour Market Regulation and Productivity Growth: Evidence for Twenty OECD Countries (1984–2004)'. *Industrial Relations,* 48, 4, 629–654.

Supiot, A. (2012) *The Spirit of Philadelphia: Social Justice vs. the Total Market.* London: Verso.

Venn, D. (2009) *Legislation, Collective Bargaining and Enforcement : Updating the OECD Employment Protection Indicators.* www.oeced.org/els/workingpapers.

# 10
# Globalisation and the UK Economy since the 1990s

*Jonathan Perraton*

## Introduction

Both the current UK coalition government and its New Labour predecessors have emphasised the impact of globalisation in shaping economic performance and appropriate economic policy. David Cameron and George Osborne have talked of Britain needing to be a winner in the global race, whilst Tony Blair and Gordon Brown repeatedly stressed the challenges of the global economy. Whilst there have been differences of emphasis, there is a large degree of continuity in their approach to globalisation for national economic policy. Not only traditional areas of macroeconomic and industrial policy, but also other areas, such as welfare and education policy, have increasingly been framed in terms of the challenges of globalisation. Moreover, the UK economy was already highly integrated internationally, with relatively high trade integration and longstanding international financial and trading links, as well as multinationals going back to nineteenth century trading companies (Held et al., 1999; Hirst and Thompson, 2000).

This chapter provides a critical analysis of official approaches to economic globalisation by successive British governments. It argues that this has been driven by a hyper-globalisation view that distorts understanding of impact and thereby provides a misleading analysis of the remaining policy space and the possibilities for shaping global integration and institutions open to a leading economy. Further, the sanguine view that globalisation will provide general gains ignores the interaction between globalisation and longstanding structural weaknesses of the UK economy. The crisis since 2008 has highlighted not just the vulnerability of the UK economy, but also the problems with achieving rebalancing in a sustained recovery. The chapter is organised as follows:

the next section outlines recent official conceptions of the trends and implications of economic globalisation processes. In light of this, the third section examines the UK's trade and current account position, the fourth its foreign direct investment position and the fifth section examines the impact of globalisation on UK macroeconomic policy. The final section concludes.

## Globalisation and UK economic policy

The prevailing New Labour policy view that globalisation had fundamentally altered the parameters of economic policy – both in terms of macroeconomic management and the longer-term framework of economic policy – was clearly set out in a series of policy documents.[1] A broadly similar approach has been advanced by the coalition government,[2] asserting that, rhetoric aside, in practice the New Labour administrations pursued policies that actively undermined the UK economy's ability to realise potential gains from globalisation and left it less well equipped to do so than its major competitors:

> Britain has lost ground in the world's economy, and needs to catch up. If we do not act now, jobs will be lost, our country will become poorer and we will find it difficult to afford the public services we all want. If we do not wake up to the world around us, our standard of living will fall, not rise ... We literally cannot afford to go on like this. (HM Treasury, 2011)

Beyond political accusations, there are strong common themes in policy documents and approaches.[3] Others in Conservative policy circles advocate an even more thoroughgoing deregulation agenda to boost UK competitiveness (cf. Redwood and Wolfson, 2007; Kwateng et al., 2012).

In summary, the official view is roughly as follows: global integration of product and capital markets and the growth of multinational production have led to a major shift in global patterns of production with the continuing rise of China, India and other emerging economies. These countries' exports are rapidly rising up the quality ladder by acquiring technology through inward investment, developing their own innovation capacity and investing heavily in human capital development. The result is increased competitive pressure on developed economies like the UK, leading not only to greater specialisation in production but also stronger rewards (or potential rewards) for higher end production and to highly skilled labour and greater returns on innovation. Whereas in the post-war period multinational production was concentrated amongst developed economies, there is now increased competition for Foreign Direct Investment (FDI) inflows from emerging market economies and a growing spread of multinational production. Swathes of services once considered intrinsically non-tradable are increasingly subject to international competition through trade and/or international production as new communications technologies make them more tradable. Unambiguous policy conclusions are drawn from this. The standard gains from trade specialisation still apply, reinforced by dynamic gains from trade through pro-competitive effects of exporting and importing. The appropriate policy response is not intervention, but to promote deregulation, a competitive tax regime and flexible labour, product and capital markets (cf. esp. HM Treasury, 2004a, 2011; HM Treasury and DTI, 2004). The key prerequisite to realising gains and limiting costs from adjustment is market flexibility to transfer resources from declining to expanding firms and industries; indeed, one official study estimated that in the 1990s almost all productivity growth in UK manufacturing was accounted for by the entry and exit of firms (DTI, 2006: 18n36).[4]

On this analysis, the UK economy is well placed to benefit from these trends provided that appropriate policies are pursued. The UK has a longstanding comparative advantage in several high-tech and/or skilled labour-intensive manufactures as well as in services exports; its sectors of comparative advantage tend to be significantly different from that of the BRICs and other emerging market economies, so the UK largely does not face head-to-head competition with them in export markets (BIS, 2010; OECD, 2007). The benefits from inward FDI in terms of boosting the capital stock and transferring technology are widely claimed; outward FDI benefits the UK economy not simply in terms of receipts, but also through strengthening company performance domestically. Thus, outward investment may boost output and employment in the UK rather than leading to a net transfer of activity overseas. Similarly, out-sourcing may also boost core business in the UK. Parts of this account acknowledge historic problems with physical and human capital accumulation in the UK economy. Although there are clear differences in macroeconomic policy between the current government and its predecessors. Both regarded a stable macroeconomic environment as a prerequisite for high domestic investment and both also see the UK as increasingly part of an integrated global capital market, with a policy regime likely to attract inward investment. Human capital formation, particularly for the least skilled, has been highlighted as a key area for government intervention and there is some recognition of the low skill equilibrium trap problems of the UK economy (HM Treasury, 2004c).

Some qualifications to this analysis are offered. DTI (2004a) acknowledges that there are limits to these globalisation processes in practice. Patterns of international economic activity fall short of fully integrated global markets with activity in many sectors still largely determined by domestic factors. Even amongst manufacturing industries there is little relationship between performance and overseas sales but a strong relationship with domestic sales (DTI, 2004a: 14–15). Although much is made of the increased tradability of services, the DTI (2004a: 52) cites estimates that only around 12–16 per cent of service sector jobs could be potentially outsourced overseas and only around 5 per cent are contestable by low wage economies. Overall, the UK economy is predicted to continue to be a net gainer from services trade liberalisation, in particular if a major General Agreement on Trade in Services can be negotiated through the World Trade Organisation (WTO) (HM Treasury, 2005). The potential gains from services liberalisation at both the EU and global level have been repeatedly emphasised by both the coalition government and its New Labour predecessors.

There are two notable features of this assessment. First, the conception of globalisation as both an opportunity and a challenge comes close to a knife-edge assessment: pursue inappropriate policies and the UK economy faces the prospect of major welfare losses and unemployment; but the UK is also well-placed to gain significantly from these trends if the right policies are pursued. The global economy may be reaching a 'tipping point' for services trade and outsourcing (HM Treasury, 2004B: 29), although, as noted above, studies indicate that elsewhere the potential tradability of many services remains limited. This is related to the second feature: although the gains are largely presumed to be very widespread, there is minimal discussion of the possibility of significant groups of losers within Britain in the context of overall welfare improvements. Although there is a strong emphasis on structural adjustment induced by foreign competition as a source of productivity growth and gains from trade (e.g. DTI, 2004A; HM Treasury and DTI, 2004), provided markets are sufficiently flexible, displaced factors of production can move quickly and easily from declining to expanding firms and sectors whilst cheaper products provide a key source of general gains. The analysis claims both that structural adjustment is a major potential source of gains from trade, and that displacement costs and unemployment problems are likely to be low and short-term in nature relative to these gains (e.g. BIS, 2011a). Although trade and FDI may have significant effects on employment patterns they should not, in this analysis, affect employment levels; beyond frictional unemployment, continued integration would only raise unemployment if market restrictions inhibited the transfer of labour from declining to expanding sectors. Whereas standard trade analysis indicates that a corollary of significant gains from trade is that they would also be likely to give rise to significant income distribution effects for plausible elasticity values, this is largely not considered in this chapter.

The potential for successful policy intervention is largely dismissed here, on the basis of standard arguments that market failures are best addressed at source, and that international and regional agreements restrict the potential for industrial policy. Apart from education and training, the key exceptions here to the general conclusions against intervention are measures to support exporters and to attract inward investment (DTI, 2006; BIS, 2011b). Arguments for industrial policy and measures to promote industrial clusters are explicitly rejected on the grounds that governments cannot pick winners. Even with human capital formation, the emphasis here is less on systemic private under-provision than on information problems that may limit provision: 'for instance there may be information asymmetries, whereby firms are unaware of how useful training is likely to be for their staff or how to obtain it' (DTI, 2004a: 45). In the context of a general emphasis that the simple existence of market failures does not necessarily justify intervention, this is an odd collection of other interventions. Although there is some attempt to justify them individually in terms of evidence of market failure (DTI, 2006; BIS, 2011b), there is no wider justification of why these particular interventions are chosen as exceptions to the general non-interventionist rule.

Thus the official view of both the current and previous UK administrations is that Britain is well-placed to reap the benefits from globalisation trends, both in terms of its patterns of comparative advantage and its flexibility in responding to structural change. More recent government assessments have argued the need for further reform to strengthen the flexibility of the UK economy, but both the current government and its predecessors have emphasised both market flexibility and human capital formation (somewhat undermining claims that these are alternative strategies for governments of the right and left). In the more optimistic versions of this assessment the UK's relative advantage lies in products and services that will allow it to reap the gains from increased trade with emerging market economies without a major negative impact on particular groups or significant adjustment costs. OECD analysis provides some support for the notion that the UK is relatively well placed to benefit from globalisation given its flexibility and that its patterns of specialisation differ significantly from the major emerging market economies, although they also identify problems in UK skills levels, productivity gaps and infrastructure provision (OECD, 2007).

At least before the 2008 crisis, the implications for macroeconomic policy were seen to follow from this. The New Labour administration effectively accepted the new consensus macroeconomics framework of inflation targeting by an independent central bank, with fiscal policy playing an essentially passive role. In this context the exchange rate was assumed to play a stabilising role as a macroeconomic shock absorber. Earlier certainties about macroeconomic policy may have been undermined by the 2008 crisis, but the emphasis on rebalancing the UK economy through fiscal austerity presumes a model of open economy adjustment that would lead to higher net exports and private investment.

There are a number of difficulties with the largely sanguine view of economic globalisation taken by successive governments, which are considered in turn below.

## Trade and current account developments

The UK economy has relatively high trade shares that grew throughout the post-war period. The UK current account was close to balance in 1997 for the first time since the early 1980s, but has been in continuous deficit since. This should be set in the context of a relatively high real sterling rate up until 2007, in large measure from capital account developments, discussed below. As noted above, the official view is a sanguine one, that disturbances to the exchange rate from its equilibrium level are largely self-correcting and that the process of adjustment to restore external balance is unlikely to pose serious problems for the maintenance of internal balance.

There is a strong sense of déjà-vu about any assessment of the UK balance of payments. When examining the 1980s experience, Muellbauer and Murphy (1990) found the deterioration of the balance of payments to be due to the effects of financial liberalisation and a house price boom, in the context of continued weakness on the trade account. There was extensive debate as to whether there had been a trend improvement in UK manufacturing export performance from the 1980s and/or whether external balance constraints would become binding in the absence of either an unprecedented improvement in manufacturing or an implausible growth in services exports. In practice neither happened: the manufacturing balance continued to deteriorate over this period; domestic manufacturing output stagnated so that with rising productivity manufacturing employment continued to fall. The current account position was partially cushioned by favourable terms of trade developments, returns on UK overseas investments and improvements on the part of the services account (Coutts et al., 2007; Coutts and Rowthorn, 2013).

Over the 1970–1995 period the UK saw the largest falls in indicators of relative advantage in technologically specialised products amongst major developed economies, although it retained a relative advantage in science-based industries, particularly reflecting its advantage in pharmaceutical products (Guerrieri, 1999). Since the 1990s the UK has continued to lose market share in manufacturing industries trade, with the key exceptions of pharmaceuticals, computers and communication equipment – all high technology sectors (BIS, 2010, 2011a; see further: Barrell et al., 2006; Buisan et al., 2006). The UK has continued to lose market share in high technology manufactures. These developments are not simply indicative of structural weaknesses. The evidence here points to UK exporters as price-takers in global markets and that the evolution of market shares largely reflects exchange rate movements, although there is also evidence of relatively low income elasticities of demand for UK exports. UK manufactures exports tend to be relatively high price, possibly due to lower end production being sited overseas by UK multinationals. The entry of China and other emerging economies into global markets was associated with lower export shares for most major developed economies. Nevertheless, there are other indicators of structural weaknesses. The relative technology intensity of exports is significantly associated with changes in export share. Britain's falling relative technology intensity since the mid-1990s partly explains the decline in Britain's export share over this period. Further, although completion of the Single European Market programme acted to raise trade levels within Europe, British exports rose less rapidly than those of its major competitors. The outcome has been a falling British export share. Successive UK governments have stressed measures to encourage UK firms to export, but UK SMEs are less likely to export than the EU average (BIS, 2010). Unfavourable developments are not just down to adverse exchange rate movements, UK exports continue to suffer from longstanding weaknesses in non-price competitiveness and larger exporters often respond to favourable exchange rate movements by raising margins rather than increasing supply (BIS, 2010, 2012).

Recently there has been a clear official acknowledgement of limited UK trade with emerging markets; India apart, the UK has disproportionately low exports to the BRICs and other major emerging economies (BIS, 2010, 2012). The UK has been in deficit in trade in goods with the Asian newly industrialised economies (NIEs) since the 1990s. To raise a more general point, although the UK has consistently run a surplus on services trade with these economies, this has fallen some way short of offsetting the deficits in goods trade with them. The position of China is particularly noteworthy here. China accounts for the majority of the goods trade deficit with these Asian NIEs. Indeed, by 2005 China accounted for around a fifth of the UK's deficit in goods trade and whereas the deficit in goods trade with China was less than half that with Japan a decade ago now it is over double the deficit with Japan. It was these countries that dominated the UK's trade with NIEs. Elsewhere its goods trade with India is roughly in balance (although a small deficit in services trade has opened up) and trade with industrialising economies in Latin America and with the CEE transition economies remains small.

The longstanding problems of UK manufactured export performance were due largely to deficits with countries at similar levels of development where intra-industry trade predominated. Manufactures trade with NIEs, as more clearly inter-industry trade, might be expected to be based on specialisation stemming from differences in relative factor supplies. Overall, the worsening goods trade position with Asian NIEs since the mid-1990s suggests that the problems with UK manufacturing external performance are now affecting its competitive position relative to emerging manufactures exporters. China's comparative advantage increasingly reflects its integration with international production networks and specialisation in stages of production process. Nevertheless, trade with Europe is more clearly characterised by the exchange of dissimilar final products with much more limited trade in components and semi-finished goods, compared to China's trade with North America or Asia (Lemoine and Unal-Kesenci, 2002). Instead, whereas Europe has a predictable deficit in trade of final consumption goods, it has a larger surplus with China on capital goods trade than other trading blocs. This is a sector in which the UK does not enjoy a clear comparative advantage.

The official view is that the UK can be expected to gain significantly from increased services trade with high income elasticity of demand for commercial (business and financial) services and on-going negotiations to reduce barriers to services trade both regionally and globally (HM Treasury, 2005D, esp. chapter 3). Trade restrictions are held to lead to services trade being significantly below potential levels, but with faster than average productivity growth in the UK amongst these services, the UK could experience significant growth in this trade. Nevertheless, since 1990 'other commercial services trade' – including business and financial services, but excluding the traditional trades service of transport and tourism – has only grown globally at or slightly above the growth of world merchandise trade. The UK succeeded in increasing its share of global services from the 1990s through the mid-2000s, but has fallen slightly since (BIS, 2010, 2012). The UK clearly does have a relative advantage in key service sectors. Nevertheless, the issue here is whether the combination of global growth and possible services trade liberalisation could generate the expansion in commercial services trade that could compensate for a deteriorating manufacturing goods balance. Thus far, there is limited evidence that services trade growth of such magnitude is likely.

Wells (1989) pointed out that earlier claims that the UK's deficit on goods trade was unimportant, insofar as it reflects increased specialisation in services, were not supported by the data during the Thatcher era. The position on net services trade has improved since the mid-1990s, although this is not out of line with the picture in the previous two decades. Since labour income flows are in approximate balance, this is overwhelmingly due to the investment account. More specifically, the tendency in the post-war period was for net surpluses on the direct investment income account to be partially offset by other flows, particularly net income payments by banks. The first half of the current decade has seen an improvement in income from direct investment, much of this accounted for by income accruing to firms in the financial sector. This appears to reflect not just changes in the net overseas asset position, but also improvements in the rates of return on outward FDI that had declined over the latter half of the 1990s.

Thus, overall, the services trade picture has changed relatively little from the earlier period analysed by Wells (1989). The UK has a clear relative advantage in some services, particularly financial and businesses services, but this has been partially offset by growth of services imports (particularly in tourism). In the mid-1990s surpluses on services trade and incomes approximately offset the trade deficit but thereafter the current account deficit has worsened, despite improvements on the 'invisibles' account.

One upshot of this is that a key feature of the downturn since 2008 is that the UK current account position has remained weak. Although a recession would normally be expected to improve the current account, this could be attributed to downturns in major export markets.

Nevertheless the evidence here points to a longer-term weakening that predates the 2008 crisis. Muellbauer and Murphy (1990) noted evidence of a worsening of trade-offs between unemployment and the current account position during the 1980s. Similarly, current account positions experienced during the post-2008 period were historically high relative to the low levels of economic activity; a major depreciation of sterling was insufficient to have a major impact on the deficit, indicative of the structural weaknesses already noted.[5]

Official studies cite earlier estimates that indicated a limited impact of trade on wage inequality in the UK in line with much of earlier work on initial expansion of manufactures trade with developing countries; the corollary, though, is that the gains from this would be relatively small. The expansion of manufactures trade with developing countries and its extension to economies with significantly lower wages might be expected to magnify income distribution effects. Large (potential) gains without significant income distribution effects are possible if trade between the UK and these countries has effectively reached complete specialisation and consists of the exchange of dissimilar products with global specialisation increasing demand for goods in which an economy like the UK would be expected to have a comparative advantage. In practice, this may not be straightforward. Beyond very simple models it is not clear-cut that increased specialisation will lead to rising demand for the relevant products.

The sanguine view that trade with developing countries has had a limited, and largely beneficial, impact on UK labour markets may be dated. Income distribution effects are expected to impact where there is overlap in patterns of specialisation; if imports from NIEs were largely confined to non-competing manufactures any impact on wages would be small. Not only have manufacturing (and services) imports from developing countries increased substantially since initial estimates indicated that their impact was limited, but this trade is also increasingly with countries with much greater wage differentials. It has already had a significant impact on wages and price-setting (e.g. Auer, 2013) and recent trends are likely to accentuate this. It is not simply that the 'great doubling' with the integration of China and India substantially increased trade with developing countries, and thus its income distribution effects, but that, as these economies move into increasingly sophisticated product ranges, this may imply labour market effects that go beyond specialisation adversely affecting the least skilled British workers and towards increasingly global labour markets for a much greater proportion of the workforce (cf. Brown et al., 2011).

Changes in global trade have increasingly led to task-based relative advantage, reinforced by similar trends in technological progress, for instance in relatively routine areas, if previously of medium skill, the activity can be outsourced. Recent labour market trends bear this out, with increased job polarisation in the UK and elsewhere (Goos and Manning, 2007), and these trends seem set to continue (Brown et al., 2011). A high skilled minority of the workforce will continue to be employed in tradable industries reflecting Britain's comparative advantage. However, the notion that most of the UK workforce can be educated and up-skilled to compete directly in the world economy misses the impact of contemporary globalisation and technical change.

By definition the current account deficit must have its counterpart in a capital account surplus. This, however, is not the counterpart to the position on FDI, both inward and outward, which boomed at the end of the 1990s in the context of a global mergers and acquisitions (M&A) boom. However, outward FDI consistently exceeded inward FDI, although this was only marked during the late 1990s boom. Portfolio investment has fluctuated over the period, while tending to show a net inflow initially reflecting demand for UK equities. Since 2010, demand has shifted towards bonds, reflecting relatively high UK rates of return. Since 2010, there has been a sharp rise in gross other financial flows, chiefly international deposits and loans by UK banks, but in net terms this only shows a small surplus.

A noteworthy feature here is that the UK economy, like that of the US, appears to be able to earn net investment income despite the fact that its net foreign liabilities exceed its foreign assets, with a net foreign liability position of around 14 per cent of GDP in 2005 (Whitaker, 2006). This may be a statistical artefact since there are global discrepancies between recorded foreign assets and liabilities and, in particular, problems with the valuation of outward FDI stocks. Nevertheless, there is *prima facie* evidence that the UK economy is able to earn net investment income as a net investor from higher relative rates. This yield differential emerged in the mid-1980s but has largely persisted since. In part this reflects the clear trend of the UK economy towards a net asset position in FDI, which would be expected to have relatively high returns, and in part it reflects differences in the nature of the banking system's foreign asset and liability profiles.

## Foreign direct investment and multinational operations

Over the past decade the UK has maintained its position as both one of the world's leading holders of FDI and one of the leading host nations;

its share of world outward FDI stocks rose from 10.6 per cent in 1995 to 11.6 per cent a decade later and its share of global inward FDI stocks rose from 6.8 to 8.1 per cent over the same period. In the context of a persistent current account deficit UK outward net flows consistently exceeded inward net FDI flows over this period. The UK has particularly high stocks of both inward and outward FDI, but the net asset position of the UK is also strong. Nevertheless, this masks the role of inward FDI in UK industry. The overseas share of manufacturing output has risen from around a quarter to a third, and around a fifth of total business activity. Foreign multinational companies (MNCs) are now undertaking a significant minority of private R&D activity in the manufacturing and services sectors, with their share of R&D having risen from 30.8 per cent to 39.4 per cent since 1995 and their share of total business R&D having risen from 32.8 per cent to 38.6 per cent over the same period.[6] Foreign affiliates in manufacturing have a relatively high export propensity and contribute disproportionately to UK manufacturing exports.

Eschewing any sector-specific policy, the policy objective has been to establish a tax, regulatory and industrial relations system that would attract inward investment for its presumed benefits in terms of employment and technology spillovers. Much of the inward investment, particularly in the late 1990s, was in the form of M&A, with research indicating that the positive impact of such acquisitions on performance is questionable. Strategic asset-seeking investment has been significant and the long-term welfare implications for the UK of this are unclear as MNCs tap into existing clusters of relative technological advantage. Although there is evidence of technology spillovers from inward investment in manufacturing, the gains from this do not appear to be sufficiently large to justify the inducements offered (cf. Haskell et al., 2007). In the services sector the productivity differentials between foreign affiliates and domestic MNCs appear to be less pronounced (Griffith et al., 2004). Over 70 per cent of UK outward investment FDI stocks are in other developed countries.[7] There has been a longstanding predominance of intra-industry FDI in the UK's position (Driffield and Love, 2005), which tends to be associated with FDI in other developed economies. There has been little shift of UK MNCs investing in China or other emerging low wage manufactures producers. The impact on domestic capital accumulation and wages thus largely depends upon conditions in the UK relative to other developed countries. There is some evidence on outsourcing that does appear to support expectations that it tends to raise domestic economic activity by improving the competitiveness of UK companies (Amiti and Wei, 2005), but overall amongst OECD countries there is no clear evidence that lower tax rates have a significant effect on FDI flows (Gorg et al., 2009).

## Policy impact

The period of non-inflationary continuous expansion before the 2008 crisis was widely attributed to globalisation, a claim supported in part by Bank of England officials (Bean, 2006). On one level falling prices of imports from developing economies represent a relative price shift rather than a change in price level; deflation in the price of goods has been more pronounced in the UK than in the US or the Eurozone (reflecting its higher trade shares with low wage producers and real exchange rate appreciation), but services price inflation has been higher in the UK leading to a roughly similar inflation performance overall. Nevertheless, the positive terms of trade effect would be expected to ease the achievement of low inflation; although developing country industrialisation may indirectly offset this positive terms of trade effect through the impact on commodity prices, overall the net effect appears to be positive. Globalisation is also held to have affected inflation dynamics leading to a pronounced flattening of the Phillips curve (the trade-off between unemployment and inflation) over this period. The assumption that globalisation reduces the capacity of traders to increase prices and reduces wage pressures as workers effectively face greater competition, together with a reduced responsiveness of the output gap to domestic conditions and an increased responsiveness to overseas ones, leads to the opposite predictions about UK economic performance. Problems arise in disentangling the effects of globalisation relative to the increased effectiveness of monetary policy, analysing how inflationary expectations are anchored or accounting for the impact of luck in the absence of adverse shocks (cf. Benati, 2007). Bank of England modelling of UK inflationary processes is consistent with the claims about changes in the mark-up process and the increased impact of import prices so that even in phases where the labour share rose the inflationary impact was counteracted by import price effects (Batini et al., 2005). IMF estimates indicate that globalisation processes account for somewhere between a quarter and a half of the flattening of the UK Phillips curve from the 1990s (Iakova, 2007). Higher employment appears to have less effect on inflation.

Global financial flows nevertheless posed problems for monetary policy through their effects on the exchange rate, although the official view has been that destabilising movements in exchange rates are very much the exception, whilst acknowledging that some academic opinion viewed the appreciation of sterling from 1996 as exceeding levels that could be justified by developments in the real economy (HM Treasury, 2003: 61). The appreciation of sterling relative to the German mark in the latter half of the 1990s was all the more puzzling since for much of the period it went contrary to interest rate differentials. Subsequently sterling appreciated against the euro in the first years of the latter's existence and also saw a phase over 2001–2004 of change against the dollar that largely went in the opposite direction from interest rate differentials. Of course *ex post* it is always possible to rationalise these movements in terms of wider variables, but it is not clear if such relations are maintained over time, are exploitable by policy makers and whether or not they compromise the assumed automatic adjustment of the exchange rate. Although such exchange rate moves are cases where foreign exchange market intervention is most likely to be successful, intervention was discussed within the Bank of England but ultimately dismissed as likely to be ineffective. The evidence on automatic adjustment of the exchange rate is questionable and is more consistent over this period with the view that exchange rate movements continue to be a source of disturbance to the macroeconomy (cf. Cobham, 2002). There are specific British aspects to this, but it should also be seen in the context of more general global trends towards destabilising exchange rate movements (cf. UNCTAD, 2007: chapter 1).

The impact of trade and FDI on wage inequality within the UK has been widely debated, but there is evidence that both have a significant impact. Whilst initially it might be thought that such effects from North-South interactions would be limited as effectively complete specialisation set in, as NIEs up-grade their exports this can no longer be presumed. Far less attention though has been paid to the wider point of Rodrik (1997) that trade and FDI in general may be expected to increase the elasticity of demand for labour and thus reduce its power to extract rents. Recent evidence points to the expected increase in the elasticity of demand for labour (OECD, 2007) and a decline in the labour share of national income. Moreover, Guscina (2006) found that shifts in the labour share of national income were significantly and negatively related to openness to trade and FDI flows, with the actual evolution of labour's share in the UK closely following the fitted relationship from a regression on these globalisation variables. This moderation of real product wage growth has affected the Phillips curve relations discussed above.

Developments since the financial crisis raise questions over the established framework for UK macroeconomic policy and suggest a space for new policy developments. The Bank of England, along with other central banks, slashed interest rates to historic lows and kept them there; with quantitative easing, the Bank of England now holds around 30 per cent of UK government debt. These developments are some way from a politically independent central bank pursuing a low inflation target, the core macroeconomic policy framework in the UK (and elsewhere) since 1997. That framework itself was predicated upon inflationary processes that look increasingly dated in the context of large global capacity. More generally, decisive state action in response to the financial crisis is widely seen as having prevented it from worsening. Whereas once such state intervention, accompanied by strongly expansionary monetary and fiscal deficits, would have been expected to trigger an adverse response in the financial markets, since 2008 the markets have taken a generally benign view of such measures. The UK government has not so far shown any explicit appetite for more thoroughgoing state intervention, although its Foresight Future of Manufacturing Project does show an interest in various options. As noted, UK governments assumed that globalisation imposed strong limits on economic policy during the 1990s and 2000s. This stance may be shifting since the crisis.

## Conclusions

Before the crisis, the OECD (2007) supported the official assessment that the 'United Kingdom's good macroeconomic performance over the past decade has been underpinned by a willingness to embrace the opportunities offered by globalisation.' For analysts such as Turner (2008) globalisation was central to the developments underlying the current financial crisis. Globalisation pressures on inequality and real incomes led to households taking on increasing levels of debt. The muting of inflationary pressures from increased trade with low wage countries masked underlying developments so that the Bank of England pursued monetary policy that fuelled the house price bubble and rising debt. A full assessment of this awaits, but the period has seen continuing trade deficits with the opening up of significant deficits with the NIEs; ambiguous developments in respect of the development of indigenous technological capacity in an economy highly integrated through FDI but, partly through a strengthened net external direct investment position, improvements in overseas investment earnings.

Rebalancing the UK economy was central to the post-crisis economic strategy, both as a general aim and specifically through the coalition government's emphasis on expansionary fiscal consolidation. The policy was predicated upon projections that reducing the fiscal deficit would crowd in private investment and higher net exports. The lack of response of net exports has already been noted.

The broader approach of both the Coalition government and previous governments to globalisation remains problematic. It is unhelpful to conceive of it as a global race or as presaging either success or failure (even sympathetic critics have noted this is perilously close to a zero sum view of the world). Policies centred on deregulation, flexible markets and low corporation taxes have been deemed necessary and sufficient to prosper in the global economy, despite evidence of structural weaknesses in tradable industries. Recent analysis acknowledges the UK's limited presence in emerging markets, but emphasises barriers in those markets – which are likely to be faced by other countries, too – over weaknesses in the UK economy (BIS, 2010, 2012). Projections that expanded services trade could compensate for declining manufactures exports appear over-optimistic.

Whatever the broader merits of human capital policies, it is not realistic to expect that raising education and skills will lead to a substantial expansion in employment amongst high end, globally competitive industries. The cases of intervention to support exporting or to attract inward FDI are less obvious, indeed somewhat anomalous with the general presumption against industrial policy intervention. Support for exporters, including export credit insurance, is justified in terms of the positive productivity gains from exporting in the context of barriers to trading in the form of non-policy barriers from information failures and network effects and the absence of an effective private insurance market for certain groups of exporters. Even here though, it is noted that the direction of causality between productivity gains and exporting is unclear and there is no systematic cost-benefit analysis of the measures (DTI, 2004b: chapter 6, 2006). Specifically on export credit guarantees, the government increased funds for the subsidy element of this programme, although an independent report disputed the evidence that market failures justified subsidies (instead of simply public provision of the service on a cost recovery basis) and estimated that phasing out of the subsidy element would have trivial effects on UK export levels. Similarly, although inward FDI may generate positive externalities the evidence that incentives to attract it are cost-effective is ambiguous at best. Successive governments have eschewed systematic industrial policy, despite evidence of structural weaknesses, and maintained faith that deregulated markets and low taxes are sufficient responses to globalisation.

# Notes

1. See Balls (1998) and, particularly, DTI (2004a, 2004b), HM Treasury (2004a, 2004b), HM Treasury and DTI (2004).
2. This precludes analysis of immigration, where there is a clearer policy divide between the coalition government and its New Labour predecessors.
3. See, e.g., BIS (2011a), HM Treasury (2011)
4. Arguably this undermines the official emphasis on other pro-competitive effects of trade.
5. See further, *Sterling depreciation and the UK trade balance*. SPERI British Political Economy Brief No. 2.
6. Data from OECD, Measuring Globalisation database.
7. Defined as the other EU15, EFTA countries, Canada, USA, Japan, Australia and New Zealand.

# References

Amiti, M. and Wei, S.-J. (2005) 'Fear of Service Outsourcing: Is It Justified?' *Economic Policy*, 42, 308–347.

Auer, R., Degen, K. and Fischer, A. (2013) 'Low-Wage Import Competition, Inflationary Pressure, and Industry Dynamics in Europe', *European Economic Review*, 59, 141–166.

Balls, E. (1998) 'Open Macroeconomics in an Open Economy', *Scottish Journal of Political Economy*, 45, 2, 113–132.

Barrell, R., Choy, A. and Kirby, S. (2006) 'Globalisation and UK Trade', *National Institute Economic Review*, No. 195, 63–67.

Batini, B., Jackson, B. and Nickell, S. (2005) 'An Open-economy New Keynesian Phillips Curve for the UK', *Journal of Monetary Economics*, 52, 6, 1061–1071.

Bean, C. (2006) 'Globalisation and Inflation', *Bank of England Quarterly Bulletin*, 46, 4, 468–475.

Benati, L. (2007) 'The "Great Moderation" in the United Kingdom', ECB Working Paper No. 769.

BERR (2008) *Globalisation and the Changing UK Economy*. London: HMSO.

BIS (2010) *UK Trade Performance: Patterns in UK and Global Trade Growth*. BIS Economics Paper No. 8.

BIS (2011a) *Trade and Investment for Growth*. White Paper Cm 8015. London: HMSO.

BIS (2011b) *International Trade and Investment: The Economic Rationale for Government Support*. BIS Economics Paper No. 13.

BIS (2012) *UK Trade Performance Across Markets and Sectors*. BIS Economics Paper No. 17.

Brown, P., Lauder, H. and Ashton. D. (2011) *The Global Auction: The Broken Promises of Education, Jobs, and Incomes*. Oxford: Oxford University Press.

Buisan, A., Learmouth, D. and Sebastia-Barriel, M. (2006) 'UK Export Performance by Industry', *Bank of England Quarterly Bulletin*, 46, 3, 308–316.

Coutts, K., Glyn, A. and Rowthorn, R. (2007) 'Structural Change under New Labour', *Cambridge Journal of Economics*, 31, 845–861.

Coutts, K. and Rowthorn, R. (2013) 'The UK Balance of Payments: Structure and Prospects', *Oxford Review of Economic Policy*, 29, 2, 307–325.

Driffield, N. and Love, J. (2005) 'Intra-industry Foreign Direct Investment, Uneven Development and Globalisation', *Contributions to Political Economy*, 24, 55–78.

DTI (2004a) *Liberalisation and Globalisation: Maximising the Benefits of International Trade and Investment*. DTI Economics Papers No. 10.

DTI (2004b) *Trade and Investment White Paper 2004: Making Globalisation a Force For Good*. Cm 6278. London: HMSO.

DTI (2006) *International Trade and Investment – The Economic Rationale for Government Support*. DTI Economics Papers No. 18.

Goos, M. and Manning, A. (2007) 'Lousy and Lovely Jobs: The Rising Polarization of Work in Britain', *Review of Economics and Statistics*, 89, 1, 118–133.

Görg, H., Molana, H. and Montagna, C. (2009) 'Foreign Direct Investment, Tax Competition and Social Expenditure', *International Review of Economics and Finance*, 18, 1, 31–37.

Griffith, R., Redding, S. and Simpson, H. (2004) 'Foreign Ownership and Productivity: New Evidence from the Service Sector and the R&D Lab', *Oxford Review of Economic Policy*, 20, 3, 440–456.

Guerrieri, P. (1999) 'Patterns of National Specialisation in the Global Competitive Environment', in D. Archibugi et al. (eds), *Innovation Policy in a Global Economy*. Cambridge: Cambridge University Press.

Guscina, A. (2006) *Effects of Globalization on Labor's Share in National Income*. IMF Working Paper No. 06/294.

Haskel, J., Pereira, S. and Slaughter, M. (2007) 'Does Inward Foreign Direct Investment Boost the Productivity of Domestic Firms?' *Review of Economics and Statistics*, 89, 3, 482–496.

Hatzius, J. (2000) 'Foreign Direct Investment and Factor Demand Elasticities', *European Economic Review*, 44, 1, 117–143.

Held, D., McGrew, A., Goldblatt, D. and Perraton, J. (1999) *Global Transformations: Politics, Economics and Culture*. Cambridge: Polity Press.

Hirst, P. and Thompson, G. (2000) 'Globalization in One Country? The Peculiarities of the British', *Economy and Society*, 29, 3, 335–356.

HM Treasury (2003) *The Exchange Rate and Macroeconomic Adjustment*. EMU Study. London: HMSO.

HM Treasury (2004a) *Globalisation and the UK: Strength and Opportunity to Meet the Economic Challenge*. London: HMSO.

HM Treasury (2004b) *Long-term Global Economic Challenges and Opportunities for the UK*. Pre-Budget Report. London: HMSO.

HM Treasury (2004c) *Skills in the Global Economy*. Pre-Budget Report. London: HMSO.

HM Treasury (2005) *Financial Services in the Global Economy*. London: HMSO.

HM Treasury (2011) *The Plan for Growth*. London: HMSO.

HM Treasury and DTI (2004) *Trade and the Global Economy: The Role of International Trade in Productivity, Economic Reform and Growth*. London: HMSO.

Iakova, D. (2007) *Flattening of the Phillips Curve: Implications for Monetary Policy*. Working Paper No. 07/76. Washington DC: IMF.

Kwarteng, K., Patel, P. Raab, D. Skidmore, C. and Truss, E. (2012) *Britannia Unchained: Global Lessons for Growth and Prosperity*. Basingstoke: Palgrave Macmillan.

Lemoine, F. and Unal-Kesenci, D. (2002) *China in the International Segmentation of the Production Process*. CEPII Working Paper No. 2002–02.

Muellbauer, J. and Murphy, A. (1990) 'Is the UK Balance of Payments Sustainable?' *Economic Policy*, No. 11, pp. 347–395.

OECD (2007) *OECD Economic Surveys: United Kingdom*. Paris: Organisation for Economic Co-operation and Development.

Redwood, J. and Wolfson, S. (2007) 'Freeing Britain to Compete: Equipping the UK for Globalisation'. Economic Competitiveness Policy Group Report.

Rodrik, D. (1997) *Has Globalization Gone Too Far?* Washington DC: Institute for International Economics.

Turner, G. (2008) *The Credit Crunch: Housing Bubbles, Globalisation and the Worldwide Economic Crisis*. London: Pluto Press.

UNCTAD. (2007) *Trade and Development Report 2007*. New York: United Nations.

Wells, J. (1989) 'Uneven Development and De-industrialisation in the UK since 1979', in F. Green (ed.), *The Restructuring of the UK Economy*. Hemel Hempstead: Harvester Wheatsheaf.

Whitaker, S. (2006) 'The UK International Investment Position', *Bank of England Quarterly Bulletin*, No. 3, pp. 290–296.

# 11
# The Need for an Engaged, Expert and Inclusive British Capitalism

*Andrew Tylecote and Paulina Ramirez*

## Introduction

It is a familiar proposition that economies such as Britain and the United States have an advantage in radical innovation and therefore in sectors in which this is relatively important, in general, high-technology ones. Hall and Soskice (2001) call such economies liberal market economies (LMEs), a term which is now too familiar to need definition here; we shall call them *shareholder capitalist*, following Tylecote and Visintin (2008). Hall and Soskice (H&S) also argue that economies such as Germany and Japan have an advantage in incremental innovation and therefore in sectors in which this is more important (in general, medium or medium-to high-tech). H&S call these, business co-ordinated market economies, CMEs, in which there is 'considerable non-market co-ordination directly and indirectly between companies' (Soskice, 1999: 103); again, we follow Tylecote and Visintin and call Germany and Japan *stakeholder capitalist*. This is a rather narrower grouping because it is defined by business co-ordination *à la* H&S *and* employee inclusion, which we shall define below.

We certainly agree with the general drift of H&S, though we would prefer to contrast *disruptive* with *cumulative* innovation. We focus our international comparisons on corporate governance (broadly defined) and finance (CG&F), and we argue in Ramirez and Tylecote (2006) and Tylecote and Visintin (2008) that cumulative innovation is best supported by CG&F systems with high *engagement* by shareholders and financiers, which allows them to appreciate and support *low-visibility* innovative activity. These systems should also show a high *inclusion* of stakeholders (notably employees and supplier/customer firms); that is, a relationship with the firm which leads them to go *beyond contract* in their support of its innovations, and which leads it to go somewhat beyond its formal obligations. Disruptive, competence-destroying innovation on the other hand demands high *industrial expertise* by shareholders and financiers – which is the basis of a strong venture capital industry.

In general it is true that medium- to high-tech sectors (motor vehicles, machinery, chemicals) put more emphasis on cumulative innovation, and less emphasis on disruptive, than do high-tech sectors (aerospace, pharma, IT hardware and software, medical and scientific instruments) (Tylecote and Visintin, 2008 – T&V). And in general it is true that the relative advantage of Britain and the United States is in high-tech sectors and that of Germany in medium- to high-tech sectors, but Japan does not quite fit; it is strong in many areas of IT hardware, and rather weak in chemicals. As T&V argue, this reflects the fact that there are many high-tech areas which do not, in fact, demand disruptive innovation. Other stakeholder capitalist countries – notably Denmark, Sweden and Finland – have been establishing strong positions in biotechnology, software and telecommunications (T&V on Sweden; Ornston, 2012 on Denmark and Finland).

The Hall and Soskice (H&S) approach rather implies that economies which are badly adapted for success (say) in medium- to high-tech, because they are LMEs/shareholder capitalist, are therefore well adapted for success in high-tech. Unfortunately, we find that this is not the case in practice for the UK and in the next section we trace its decline in R&D intensity since 1979, to a level well below any of its main rivals except Italy. This is in spite of the fact that, other things being equal, an economy specialised in high-tech sectors (so defined because they have high R&D intensity) should have high R&D intensity overall. At the same time the UK's growth rate of GDP per capita fell substantially below that of the pre-Thatcher period, 1948–1979, and it developed a large and persisting deficit on the current account of the balance of payments. This pattern is scarcely consistent with success in high-technology. We note two contrasts: first, with the other main shareholder capitalist economy, the United States, which roughly held its position in R&D intensity, and continued to lead in most high-tech sectors; second, with most of the stakeholder economies, led by Finland and Sweden, which steadily increased their R&D intensity to a level well above the UK's, as they strengthened their position in high-tech sectors.

In the third section we explain these contrasts and how the United States, though the evolution of its corporate governance is widely criticised, has advantages over Britain in engagement, inclusion and expertise. The stakeholder capitalist economies have long had major advantages in engagement and inclusion, and some of them – roughly, the Nordic countries – have developed strength in expertise too, which takes them in the direction of shareholder capitalism. In conclusion we discuss what is to be done about the failings of the British system.

## The long decline of the UK industrial research system

Over the thirty years prior to 2014 the UK experienced a fundamental weakening of its innovation system in both absolute and relative terms. During this period, R&D spending as a percentage of GDP in the UK economy steadily declined, so that by 2013 the UK economy was substantially less research-intensive than in the late 1970s (Jones, 2013). This decline in UK R&D spending took place at the same time that a number of other countries (including stakeholder economies such as Germany, Japan, Finland and Sweden, as well as shareholder economies such as the US) either maintained or increased their research intensity (Hughes and Mina, 2012). Data from the OECD cited in BIS (2012) show that

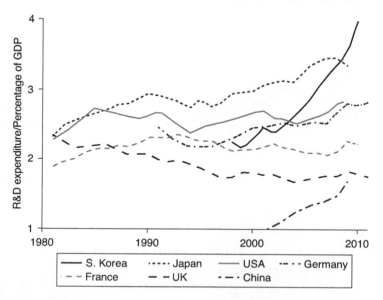

*Figure 11.1*   R&D expenditure as a percentage of GDP of selected economies over the period 1980–2011

Source: *Eurostat*, cited in Jones (2013).

throughout the 1990s and 2000s R&D as a percentage of GDP was lower in the UK than the US, France, Germany and Japan. Only Italy fared worse than the UK. Moreover, the gap between the UK and competitor countries worsened after the financial crisis with R&D spending falling only in Japan, Canada and the UK (BIS, 2012).The result has been that while the UK was one of the most research-intensive economies in the world in 1979 (Jones, 2013) by 2010 it had become one of the least research-intensive advanced economies (BIS, 2012; Hughes and Mina, 2012; Jones, 2013).

### What explains the decline of the UK's R&D performance?

Two factors explain the decline in the UK's R&D intensity. The first is a reduction in direct government spending on industrial R&D as a result of the privatisation of a number of industries (for example, energy). The second is a steady decline since the 1980s of UK-owned private sector business expenditure on R&D (BERD) (Figure 11.2) which, according to Jones (2013), appears to be unique among the main competitor nations.

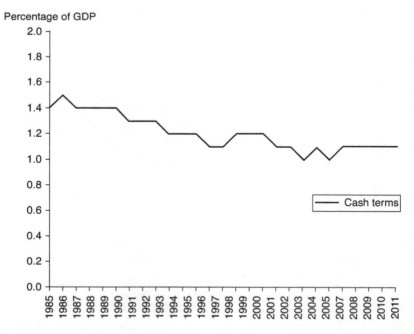

*Figure 11.2*   Expenditure on R&D by businesses in the UK as a percentage of GDP
*Source*: ONS (2012).

This is in contrast to publicly funded scientific research that takes place in universities, which has experienced a sustained, though modest, increase in funding thereby increasing as a proportion of GDP (Jones, 2013; Hughes and Mina, 2012). It is therefore the decline of the UK's industrial research system that explains the severe weakening of the UK's innovation system. As a result Germany, Denmark, Japan, South Korea, Sweden and Finland (all but South Korea are stakeholder countries) as well as the US (another shareholder capitalist economy) all have industrial sectors devoting substantially more to R&D than in the UK.

There is general agreement that, by international standards, business expenditure on R&D (BERD) in the UK is low (Hughes and Mina, 2012; Jones, 2013; Nesta, 2010; BIS, 2012). This tends to be predominantly concentrated in a few large firms in a small number of industrial sectors. Despite much discussion on the role of SMEs in innovation systems, in the UK only 3.5 per cent of independently-owned SMEs (i.e. SMEs that are not part of larger firms) undertook R&D activities in 2009 (Hughes and Mina, 2012). Moreover, while in most leading economies the majority of R&D is funded by national firms, in the UK nationally-owned businesses fund less than half of the country's R&D expenditure with the rest being funded by government and overseas firms (Hughes and Mina, 2012). The increasing role of overseas subsidiaries in the UK's industrial research system is clearly revealed by R&D data which show the very large increase in BERD by foreign-owned firms located in the UK since the 1980s. Figures from ONS (2011) show that from 2000 R&D expenditure by UK-owned businesses fell in real terms and that the very small increase in total BERD was driven entirely by the rise of R&D foreign inward investment (Jones, 2013). In 1993, 73 per cent of UK BERD was performed by UK-owned businesses. In 2011, for the first time, the money spent on R&D by foreign-owned businesses equalled that spent by UK-owned businesses (ONS, 2012; Jones, 2013). This is a much higher proportion than in similar countries.

It has been suggested that the low R&D intensity of the UK economy could be explained by the sectoral mix of the UK economic structure, which includes a relatively high proportion of service industries that are by nature of lower R&D intensity (BIS, 2012). If this was the case the UK economy would show high levels of investment in other intangible assets associated with innovation, such as training, software, design, copyrights and spending associated with organisational innovation. OECD data show, however, that investment in innovation in the UK remains low, even when investment in intangible assets is accounted for, although the gap narrows (Hughes and Minas, 2012). There is no

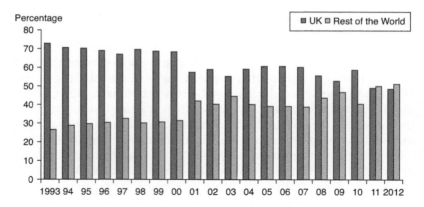

*Figure 11.3*    Ownership of businesses who perform R&D in UK

sign that the weakening R&D is being offset by more investment in intangibles. Moreover, even when focusing only on the manufacturing sector, the figures show low levels of BERD as a percentage of value added (Hughes and Mina, 2012). The evidence indicates that manufacturing has not only become smaller as a share of the UK economy but it is also less R&D intensive than that of other developed economies (Hughes and Mina, 2012; Jones, 2013). Therefore, even after adjusting for the structural differences between the UK and other economies, the UK industrial research system still underperforms.

### Venture capital

One of the areas in which LMEs/shareholder capitalist systems are generally regarded as superior, is in the quantity and quality of their venture capital. Table 11.1 gives recent data on venture capital investments/GDP. The data show that the UK is towards the top end of a group of European countries with similar venture capital markets but it is by no means the highest in Europe (Sweden, and Finland are higher) and it is considerably weaker than the US. The data make clear that a number of countries characterised as stakeholders have caught up and even surpassed the UK in an area considered central to the financing of high-technology, disruptive innovations. They suggest that the UK is not only weaker than stakeholder countries in cumulative innovation but that its finance system does not give much more than average support to industries associated with disruptive innovation. This weakness of the UK system of innovation – commonly referred to as 'the

*Table 11.1*   Venture capital investments as a percentage of GDP

|  | Seed/start-up/ early stage | Later stage | Total |
|---|---|---|---|
| United States | 0.055 | 0.116 | 0.171 |
| Sweden | 0.025 | 0.029 | 0.054 |
| Finland | 0.034 | 0.007 | 0.041 |
| United Kingdom | 0.025 | 0.013 | 0.038 |
| Switzerland | 0.017 | 0.016 | 0.033 |
| Denmark | 0.021 | 0.012 | 0.032 |
| Netherlands | 0.014 | 0.015 | 0.029 |
| Norway | 0.016 | 0.012 | 0.029 |
| Japan (2011) | 0.017 | 0.009 | 0.026 |
| Germany | 0.013 | 0.007 | 0.021 |
| Austria | 0.009 | 0.001 | 0.011 |

*Source*: OECD Venture Capital database (2012).

valley of death' – has increasingly been recognised by the UK parliament and government (e.g. House of Commons Science and Technology Committee, 2013), resulting in a number of initiatives aimed at directing public sector funds to support SMEs in new technology sectors.

UK venture capital has (by comparison with the US) an aversion to high-technology and early stage financing – which together might be thought of as its key contribution. While 75 per cent of venture capital investment in the US goes into the high-technology sectors of information technology, communication and health/biotechnology, the equivalent figure for the UK is just over 52 per cent (Nesta, 2010), with the rest going to energy and consumer and business.

## Britain versus the US versus the stakeholder capitalist economies

### The nature of the British system of corporate governance and finance: Engagement and expertise

We have, in work done around 2000, assessed the engagement, inclusion and expertise of the British system. We were able to do this comparatively with the United States because although all our interviews were in London, many of our interviewees (particularly the top managers of British multinational firms) were thoroughly familiar with the US system. Our findings were extremely disturbing from a British point of view.

In order to understand why the UK CG&Fs represents an obstacle to innovation and industrial upgrading it is necessary to understand the workings of investors and the nature of the relationship they establish with firms. Since the 1980s the main characteristics of the UK system have been the prevalence of financial institutions in the ownership of UK companies, and a management system focused almost exclusively on the need to maximise shareholder value over short time-periods. In 1993 British financial institutions owned 69 per cent of listed UK stocks (against 37 per cent in the US), with 'foreign owners' holding 16 per cent, assumed also to be preponderantly financial institutions (Tylecote and Visintin, 2008: 97). Table 11.2 shows that by 2012 the share held by foreign owners (rest of the world) had risen to 53.2 per cent, a rise of 9.8 per cent in two years. British financial institutions owned a share of 28.8 per cent in total, so within the overall UK share they were still preponderant; and we assume again that within the foreign share the bulk would be held by the 'usual suspects' dominant in the UK: insurance companies, pension funds, unit trusts and investment trusts (mutual funds).

The management of these shares however is even more concentrated as a number of financial institutions, such as the smaller pension funds and charities, outsource the management of their assets to asset management houses, mostly part of investment banks, which also control most of the mutual funds.[1] This internationalisation of the ownership of UK

*Table 11.2*   Beneficial ownership of UK shares by value. At 31 December in 1998, 2010 and 2012.

|  | 1998 | 2010 | 2012 |
|---|---|---|---|
| Rest of the world | 30.7 | 43.4 | 53.2 |
| Insurance companies | 21.6 | 8.8 | 6.2 |
| Pension funds | 21.7 | 5.6 | 4.7 |
| Individuals | 16.7 | 10.2 | 10.7 |
| Unit trusts | 2.0 | 8.8 | 9.6 |
| Investment trusts | 1.3 | 2.1 | 1.7 |
| Other financial institutions | 2.7 | 12.3 | 6.6 |
| Charities, church etc. | 1.4 | 0.8 | 0.6 |
| Private non-financial Companies | 1.4 | 2.3 | 2.3 |
| Public sector | 0.1 | 3.1 | 2.5 |
| Banks | 0.6 | 2.5 | 1.9 |
| **Total** | **100** | **100** | **100** |

*Source*: Office of National Statistics. http://www.ons.gov.uk/ons/dcp171778_327674.pdf

shares is an increasing trend among UK CG&Fs. UK individuals held only 10.7 per cent of all UK shares listed in the London Stock Exchange – a figure which is exceptionally low by international standards.

Empirical studies of institutional investors carried out between 1999 and 2005 and reported in Tylecote and Ramirez (2006, 2008) and Ramirez and Tylecote (2004) showed that, in general, institutional investors and their fund managers saw themselves as *traders* of shares – buying cheap and selling dear – rather than *owners* of companies. From the point of view of fund managers (those who actually make the decisions of where to invest) their business is 'to defend the financial interests of our clients' whose assets they manage, that is the pension funds, mutual funds and so on, and they have preferred to do this as outsiders, operating on a portfolio investment basis with as little engagement with the firms they invest in as possible. Our interviews show that 'the clients' (e.g. the pension funds) monitor the performance of their funds on a quarterly basis focusing the attention of fund managers on the short-term performance of the portfolio of financial investments under their management rather than the longer-term needs of the companies whose shares they own. It is from here that the focus on the short-term performance of companies, which has characterised the UK CG&Fs, arises.

It is this preference for the trading of shares that has shaped the arms-length 'outsider' relationship between institutional investors and the firms they invest in, and has been central to the policy of non-engagement which has characterised UK institutional investors. A very important consequence of this policy, from the point of view of innovation, is that it places important limits on the amount and nature of information that firms can give and that fund managers can receive. The point to emphasise here is that the limitation to the development of a greater understanding by investors of the firms they invest in, that is of *firm-specific understanding* (as opposed to knowledge of its sector more generally), is a direct result of shareholder preference for 'outsider' involvement. This limits appreciation of low-visibility innovative activity which we have already put forward as key to cumulative innovation.

So, although fund managers have very good access to the firms they invest in, their questioning and probing of senior management is limited by their desire not to receive information considered market-sensitive[2] or 'insider information' (Tylecote and Ramirez, 2008). This constraint has meant that managers could not give investors information that they did not want to make generally available to the public (for instance, information that the firm does not want competitors to know) nor did these investors want to receive any information which would restrict their trading. It is clear therefore that intrinsic to the present UK CG&Fs is the failure of investors and shareholders to establish any long-term engagement with the firms they invest in and as a consequence to develop any meaningful firm-specific understanding.

Our research also shows that institutional investors in the UK develop only a very superficial understanding of the industrial sectors 'their' firms operate in (Tylecote and Ramirez, 2008). Most fund managers have little in-depth industry knowledge or understanding of the technologies in which the companies, whose shares they own, are investing. One of the reasons for this is the rapid turnover of sectors for which fund managers are responsible, which impedes the development of a long-term under-standing of an industry and its technological trajectory. Though institu-tional investors do buy information from industry analysts this data is usually gathered from publicly available information and therefore gives little insight into what is really going on inside firms. As a result very few actors in the system have both industrial expertise and engagement with, and therefore understanding of, individual firms.

There is much in this account which could have been said in much the same terms about Wall Street. Indeed it *has* been said about Wall Street, more or less, by William Lazonick (e.g. Lazonick and O'Sullivan, 2000; Lazonick, 2011). But it was clear that there were differences, gener-ally in the US's favour. The investment analysts who play a key role in reporting to fund managers were judged by top managers of British firms to be distinctly inferior in industrial expertise to their US coun-terparts. Likewise, US institutional investors, even operating away from home, engaged more with the firms in which they owned shares than did British ones.

*Britain since 2000*

In a very limited sense British institutional shareholders do now engage more with the firms in which they have invested than they generally did in the 1990s; they engage to control but not to understand. Thus, hedge funds may suddenly build up substantial shareholdings in a firm with a view to pressing it to sell off a division which is currently under-performing and thus depressing the share price. This sort of interven-tion is known as activist shareholding, and was learnt from the United States (Economist, 2014). More important is the continuing policy of major institutional investors to largely control key appointments – of the (non-executive) chairman, the chief executive, and the finance director (Young and Scott, 2004). The first and the third are regarded as having generic skills, so they can be brought in not just from other firms but from other sectors, on the grounds that they have performed satis-factorily from the City's point of view. The chief executive is (one might think) a different proposition. But the most trustworthy CEOs – from the point of view of British institutional investors – are now brought in from outside; and they are generally not encouraged to stay too long (they might 'go native'). Young and Scott found that just under two thirds of CFOs in FTSE100 firms had been appointed from outside, half of chairmen, and about a third of CEOs.

Again, this situation is very similar to that described by Lazonick and O'Sullivan (2000) for the United States (we shall enter a reservation about this for the US, below). It is hardly surprising that we find such a convergence, since we saw above that foreign owners now dominate the share registers of listed British firms – and that the largest asset manager in London as elsewhere is the US BlackRock (Economist, 2013).

### The US, UK and stakeholder capitalist economies: A broader comparison.

Earlier we compared Britain with the United States from the point of view of 'outsider' institutional investors and the firms which they control – and found a large degree of convergence. This is a rather lop-sided comparison since virtually all large British-based firms are controlled in this way, but in the United States there are two very important catego-ries of large firm which are controlled by fully engaged 'insider' capital:

1. Young firms in high-technology sectors.

These firms are generally still controlled by their founders: clearly the case for Google and Amazon; and, at least until recently, true of Microsoft and Apple.

2. Older firms in which the founding family has chosen to continue to exercise control (e.g. Ford, Dupont).

The 'insider capitalists' are aided by the more permissive legislation of the United States, as regards 'poison pills' and other 'shark defences' against hostile takeover. This is particularly true for the state of Delaware where many large firms (including Rupert Murdoch's News Corp) are incorporated. Such protective devices also help incumbent manage-ment in other large firms to maintain a greater degree of autonomy from outsider shareholders (Plender, 2006). By contrast, as Davis *et al.* point out, 'UK takeovers are more common, more likely to be hostile bids, and more likely to succeed than in any other major economy in the world. Evidence suggests that a significant proportion of takeover activity is neither beneficial to the creation of long-term shareholder value nor to the UK industrial base, economy and society as a whole.' (Davis et al., 2013). This is not surprising when we consider the attitude of City institutional shareholders as expressed in our interviews: 'The market includes takeovers. Exit includes takeovers and this is the way to change management, this is the market mechanism' (senior investor, Prudential).

What holds for the United States holds *a fortiori* for the main stakeholder capitalist economies: outsider control, although increasing, remains the exception. In Japan an elaborate system of cross-shareholding between firms in the same group continues to give management in most large firms almost complete protection from the intrusion of outsider shareholders. In Germany the big banks have, since the early 2000s, largely disentangled themselves from the web of industrial shareholdings they had built up over many decades and exercised in an 'insider' manner. However, founding families have generally held on to the controlling stakes they hold in many firms – particularly the middle-sized firms, which are of great importance in the German economy. Moreover, Germany is one of the EU countries that has refused to introduce legislation dismantling protective devices against hostile takeover (Andrew Johnson, personal communication). In any case it is said in Germany that the most effective 'poison pill' against takeover is their system of co-determination.

Co-determination in some form is a distinguishing feature of the European stakeholder economies (Japan has some similar arrangements but, unlike European co-determination, they are not imposed by law). The German form is the strongest and simplest: the non-executive directors of the supervisory board have ultimate control of the firm, and the employees elect 50 per cent of them.

Co-determination puts at issue rather starkly the assumption commonly made about corporate governance in mainstream economics: that it is or should be designed to get firms to maximise shareholder value. Agency theory in mainstream economics traditionally supposes that salaried managers will under-invest in R&D because it is risky and they are risk-averse – unlike outsider shareholders who have diversified portfolios which spread their risk. So their remuneration should reward management for taking risk, for example through stock options. More recent arguments, broadly consistent with agency theory, assert that outsider investors are in fact the main culprits, through short-termism.

As Haldane (2011) shows, the pressures they put on management, largely through the share price, are to reduce investment, particularly in R&D, below what would maximise long-term shareholder value (let us call this level the 'shareholder optimum').

Co-determination creates a corporate governance mechanism which, in principle, could induce firms not simply to go *up to* the shareholder optimum, but to go above it.[3] For employees have more to gain than to lose from most forms of innovation (disruptive innovation is the main exception). Product innovation, which we suppose is the main purpose of R&D, will maintain or improve the firm's position in the market and thus give them security of employment. *Process* innovation might reduce employment, by increasing labour productivity, but in the long-term this too is indispensable for holding down costs and thus maintaining the firm's position in the market (also for persuading it not to 'offshore' employment to countries with cheaper labour).

In practice, what co-determination is likely to produce is a creative compromise. The shareholders will strenuously resist innovation that is likely to be unprofitable. But marginally profitable product innovation will be conducted, on the understanding that employees will be co-operative with regard to process innovation, and moderate in demands for wage increases; as a package that may indeed maximise shareholder value.

Stakeholder capitalism has other ways of producing a shareholder optimum involving heavy spending on innovation. Whether a given quantum of spending on R&D will yield commensurate profit to the firm will depend on a number of circumstances. One of them is the extent of complementary spending by the public sector on basic research, and indeed applied R&D on strategic innovations like the internet. As Tassey (2007) and Mazzucato (2013) among others have pointed out, the innovations of firms like Apple were possible and profitable because of such *prior* complementary spending. Another form of complementary spending by the public sector is *simultaneous*: co-funding of R&D via such institutions as the Fraunhofer Gesellschaft in Germany, which is important in stakeholder capitalist economies. It is also important in the United States, in the form of the Small Business Innovation Research and Small Business Technology Transfer programmes.[4]

A distinguishing feature of European stakeholder capitalism is the extent of co-operation among firms – alliance co-ordination, as Whitley (2003) describes it. It is a truism in mainstream economics that competition among firms can be deleterious to innovation: to the extent that R&D and other innovation spending creates a public good, it will suit firms B, C and D to wait for firm A to lead, and then use the knowledge that A has created. Patents are intended to guard against this, but patents can be 'invented round': it is notorious in pharmaceuticals, for example, that 'me-too' drugs can be at least as profitable as the original radical innovation (Nuffield, 2012: chapter 9). Co-operation on R&D among the firms in one industry is relatively common in European stakeholder capitalism; it is encouraged by government through mechanisms like the Fraunhofer Gesellschaft. But there is a more general form of co-operation which must also support innovation: on training. Employers in Germany (and other stakeholder capitalist economies) co-operate to establish common standards of skill and to train adequate numbers of workers, through apprenticeships in particular. They co-operate with the unions in their sector to ensure that low pay for apprenticeships is compensated by real skill formation. Such investment is beneficial from any point of view – it obviates the destructive 'poaching' in the UK of skilled staff from companies that train adequately, by companies that do not. But it must be particularly beneficial in innovation to have adequately trained workers, capable not only of carrying out their current jobs competently but even of seeing how they might improve.

It is interesting to compare the US, stakeholder capitalism and the UK from the point of view of inclusion. As we defined it in the Introduction, it is 'a relationship with the firm which leads [employees and suppliers/ customers] to go *beyond contract* in their support of its innovations, and which leads it to go somewhat beyond its formal obligations'. As we have argued, co-determination must strongly support inclusion, but we must enter the reservation that employees will naturally be much more supportive of cumulative innovation than of disruptive innovation, since the latter threatens their jobs; and indeed much the same can be said of existing suppliers and customers. That may limit stakeholder capitalist success in those parts of high-tech which have experienced disruptive innovation. On the other hand there is no reason why *new* firms should not be set up successfully to exploit disruptive innovations, if there is adequate venture capital and if labour markets are reasonably flexible (so that able workers are willing to take a chance on new firms). This appears to be the case in the Nordic countries, as we saw above for VC, and as Ornston (2012) shows.

The nature of work organisation must both reflect the extent of employee inclusion and affect the success of innovation and of high-tech industry. Lorenz and Valeyre (2006) have found that the type

*Table 11.3*  Discretionary learning work organisations as a percentage of the total workforce, selected European countries

| | Discretionary learning | Lean production learning | Taylorist organization | Simple |
|---|---|---|---|---|
| Netherlands | 64.0 | 17.2 | 5.3 | 13.5 |
| Denmark | 60.0 | 21.9 | 6.8 | 11.3 |
| Sweden | 52.6 | 18.5 | 7.1 | 21.7 |
| Finland | 47.8 | 27.6 | 12.5 | 12.1 |
| Germany | 44.3 | 19.6 | 14.3 | 21.9 |
| France | 38.0 | 33.3 | 11.1 | 17.7 |
| UK | 34.8 | 40.6 | 10.9 | 13.7 |
| Italy | 30.0 | 23.6 | 20.9 | 25.4 |
| Spain | 20.1 | 28.1 | 18.5 | 22.5 |
| Greece | 18.7 | 25.6 | 28.0 | 27.7 |
| EU15 | 39.1 | 28.2 | 13.6 | 19.1 |

*Source*: Table 3 in Lundvall (2009).

of work organisation which they define as discretionary learning (self-explanatory) is very much more common in the Nordic countries (and the Netherlands) than elsewhere in Europe, including the UK.

The US does not have any form of co-determination, but it does have another institution which fosters inclusion of a kind. It is extremely common in the United States for employees to hold substantial shareholdings in their own firms. It is also common in US high-technology – in fact more or less mandatory in 'ventured' firms (firms in which venture capital has been invested) – for all employees (at least early on) to be paid partly in stock options. Employee shareholding gives employees little or no power; stock options certainly give none; so the conservative potential of inclusion based on co-determination is absent in the US. What US-style inclusion gives employees is a stake in the success of the firm, and thus it gives management a reason to trust them not to abuse high discretion. It is thus tilted very much in favour of disruptive innovation. Just as the UK is almost unique in Europe in the absence of employee power, so it has gone nowhere near as far as the United States in the development of employee shareholding. And, while stock options are normal in 'ventured' firms in the UK, as in the US, such firms do not dominate UK high-technology as they do in the US (Tylecote and Ramirez, 2006).

## Conclusion

We have set out some stark facts of industrial decline during the period of alleged Thatcherite renaissance of the British economy after 1979. While almost all other advanced economies were increasing their spending on R&D as a proportion of national income, the UK was going in the other direction. The decline was in business spending on R&D, and above all in spending on R&D by British-owned businesses. This was odd: as a stereotypical liberal market economy the UK should be successful in high-technology sectors and, by definition, such sectors require heavy R&D spending. The other stereotypical LME, the United States, is certainly successful in such sectors and has a much higher business R&D intensity than the UK – even if it has fallen behind stakeholder capitalist competitors over the last two decades. This was reflected in international comparisons of venture capital funding, in which the US is far ahead of the UK, which has now fallen behind some stakeholder capitalist economies.

So what is wrong with the UK? We argued that for an advanced economy to succeed, it must put adequate resources into innovation, and spend them well. For that, its corporate governance system must display *engagement*, *inclusion* and *expertise*. Of these ingredients for success, engagement was particularly important in medium- to high-tech, where stakeholder capitalist economies/CMEs traditionally excel, expertise is particularly important in high-tech, where the US excels. We found that the corporate governance of UK listed firms was weaker than the US in all three of these. This was largely because the managers of these firms were uniquely exposed to short-term pressures from disengaged 'outsider' shareholders. They were ruled by the market – including the market for corporate control, operating through hostile takeovers.

### What is to be done?

The globalisation of finance and capital greatly complicates the task of any policy-maker trying to address the faults of a corporate governance system. If a British government, *per impossibile*, were to opt for co-determination, the large majority of British listed firms would no doubt redefine themselves as Irish or Luxembourgish before the legislation had passed the House of Commons. If a tax on share transactions in the London markets were imposed, such transactions might well take place elsewhere.[5] Such obstacles to implementation may help to explain the extraordinary limpness of the recommendations of the Kay Review, a document which showed considerable understanding of the problem but seemed to rely largely on exhortation for the solution.

We do nonetheless believe that some moves towards co-determination are worth making: to have ONE non-executive director elected by the employees together, might not frighten too many firms. We would also advocate what could be called peripheral reforms:

1. The return of the Industrial Training Boards, set up by the Labour government of 1974 and abolished by Margaret Thatcher. These addressed the 'under-training' problem by imposing a 'training levy' on all firms not spending at least 2 per cent of turnover on training – and then spending the money for them.
2. A network of public sector-owned banks on the German model (the Sparkassen) with a duty to lend to small and medium-sized businesses.[6]
3. Extensive emulation of the various German, Nordic and US methods for public sector co-funding of R&D.

This still leaves the awkward fact that British business is dominated by large listed firms which, for the most part, have ample reserves of cash they prefer not to spend, whether on physical investment or R&D. Without major changes in the system of corporate governance we believe this situation will continue and that there are two crucial facts in this situation:

• British institutional investors of equity, together with the American asset managers who, with them, dominate the UK market, prefer to trade, not to hold.
• These investors do not put their own people as non-executive directors on boards.

In spite of the difficulties of imposing a transactions tax on share sales on the London market, it should be possible to construct tax arrangements – particularly on pension funds – which give them incentives to hold shares long-term. In such a situation the only way that asset managers could hope to out-perform the market – and certainly to justify the fees they charge for 'actively managed' funds, as opposed to cheap 'passive management' which simply follows the index – would be by engagement with management, such that they contribute to the future value of the shares that they would now be almost condemned to hold. The simple old-fashioned way of doing that, practised for a long time by the most successful investor in the world, Warren Buffett, is to take a seat on the board. This has been out of the question because it would make the investor an 'insider' and thus prevent them trading. But if the investor is going to hold, not trade…. Really effective involvement would require that they not only engage, but develop industrial expertise – as venture capitalists have, when they take seats on the board of firms in which they have invested.[7]

It would facilitate such a complete change in relationships between investors and managers if a rule were also introduced to deny new shareholders a vote until (let us say) two years had elapsed. Those investors who had switched to a hold-not-trade strategy would thus find their voting leverage increased. At the same time the trustees of pension funds, the largest single category of UK shareholdings, should be given a fiduciary duty to act as befits long-term owners of companies, as opposed to speculators in pieces of paper. It would be difficult to frame this duty in a way that *obliged* trustees to act in this way, just as the Companies Act of 2006 achieved nothing (so far as we are aware) by giving directors such duties.[8] But with the other pressures in this direction…

A further incentive for shareholders to engage would be provided by any move to make hostile takeover more difficult. As the Kay Review puts it in Section 8.16: 'There is considerable variation between jurisdictions in the legal powers a government has to block unwanted takeovers.' The British government should take more. 'There is also considerable variation between jurisdictions in the ability of private actors to block takeovers to which they are opposed. In continental Europe, there are many legal differences and more concentrated shareholding is common. In the United States, law and market practice have been more favourable to "poison pills" and other means of resistance by incumbent management to unwanted bids.' We should move in the direction of the US – more particularly, the state of Delaware.

To borrow a phrase from the apocryphal Irishman, if one wanted to go to an engaged, inclusive and expert corporate governance system in the UK, one wouldn't start from here. Not only has British capital abandoned the governance of large British firms, it has in large measure abandoned even the management of its own asset portfolios. At the same time those portfolios have been globalised and diversified to the point where the ownership of large British firms is mostly foreign. We have to provide incentives for whoever – British or foreign – has substantial shareholdings in British firms, to develop and deploy engagement and expertise. If it is perhaps too late to transform the governance arrangements of existing large firms, such changes may be timely to protect and nurture new firms which arise from the remaining strengths of the British innovation system – in its science base.

## Notes

1. The 'asset management houses' are often part of investment banks; some of the largest operating on the UK stock market are now US-owned, such as Merrill Lynch (now part of Bank of America Merrill Lynch). However, the biggest of them is now BlackRock, which is a pure asset manager. Economist (2013) 'BlackRock: The monolith and the markets', 7 December
2. Market-sensitive information is information that could influence the short-term share price if it became public. Thus receiving it before it becomes public gives the opportunity to make a profit by buying or selling shares: this is insider-trading, which is of course illegal.
3. When control is exercised by insider capitalists or autonomous managers who want growth or the satisfaction of innovation, this too may take innovation spend above the shareholder optimum.
4. 'The Small Business Innovation Research (SBIR) program is a highly competitive program that encourages domestic small businesses to engage in Federal Research/Research and Development (R/R&D) that has the potential for commercialization. Through a competitive awards-based program, SBIR enables small businesses to explore their technological potential and provides the incentive to profit from its commercialization ... Small Business Technology Transfer (STTR) is another program that expands funding opportunities in the federal innovation research and development (R&D) arena. Central to the program is expansion of the public/private sector partnership to include joint venture opportunities for small businesses and nonprofit research institutions. The unique feature of the STTR program is the requirement for the small business to formally collaborate with a research institution in Phase I and Phase II. STTR's most important role is to bridge the gap between performance of basic science and commercialization of resulting innovations.' www.sbir.gov/about.
5. Would the transactions have to be registered in Britain? Then perhaps the tax could not be evaded.
6. British commercial banks became, in the years before the financial crisis broke, steadily less interested in engaging with the firms they lent to. They replaced layers of middle managers who had been expected to talk to and try to understand borrowers, actual and prospective, with algorithms drawing on databases: a quick, cheap and (with suitable collateral) apparently safe approach to lending. The collateral is not now what it was (or seemed to be), and the algorithms are now pointing away from lending (*vide* V Cable's remarks on bank lending to NE firms, 8 July 2012).
7. At least one organisation submitting evidence to the Parliamentary Committee reviewing the Kay Review, agrees with us: '42. Albion Ventures took a different view. It told us that consultation of major shareholders was a start, but that Professor Kay had not gone far enough. It recommended that "long-term substantial shareholders should have representation on the boards of companies in which they invest". 77 It argued that this would "allow longstanding

investors to have personal, reciprocal and trust-based relationships with the company management".78'

8. (1) A director of a company must act in the way he considers, in good faith, would be most likely to promote the success of the company for the benefit of its members as a whole, and in doing so have regard (amongst other matters) to:

(a) the likely consequences of any decision in the long-term,
(b) the interests of the company's employees,
(c) the need to foster the company's business relationships with suppliers, customers and others,
(d) the impact of the company's operations on the community and the environment,
(e) the desirability of the company maintaining a reputation for high standards of business conduct, and
(f) the need to act fairly as between members of the company.

The Companies Act 2006 c. 46 Part 10 Chapter 2 The general duties section 172.

# References

Blasi, J., D. Kruse and A. Bernstein (2003a) *In the Company of Owners: The Truth About Stock Options*. New York: Basic Books.

Blasi, J., D. Kruse, J. Sesil and M. Kroumova (2003b) 'An Assessment of Employee Ownership in the United States with Implications for the EU', *International Journal of Human Resource Management*, 14, 66, 893–919.

Business, Innovation and Skills (2012) *Annual Innovation Report: Innovation, Research and Growth*. BIS, November 2012.

Davis, A., Offenbach, D., Stevens, R. and Grant, N. (2013) *Takeovers and the Public Interest*. Policy Network Paper, July.

Economist (2013) 'BlackRock: The Monolith and the Markets', 13 December.

Economist (2014) 'Corporate Governance – Anything You Can Do, Icahn Do Better', 14 February.

Haldane, A. G. (2011) *The Short Long*. Speech at 29th Societe Universitaire de Recherches Financieres Colloquium: New Paradigms in Money and Finance? Brussels, May.

House of Commons Science and Technology Committee (2013) 'Bridging the Valley of Death: Improving the Commercialisation of Research', http://www.publications.parliament.uk/pa/cm201213/cmselect/cmsctech/348/348.pdf

Hughes, A. and Mina, A. (2012) The UK R&D Landscape, UK-ICR, UK Innovation Research Centre, Judge Institute University of Cambridge.

Jones, R. (2013) *The UK's Innovation Deficit and How to Repair It*. Sheffield Political Economy Research Institute, SPERI paper No. 6.

Kay, J. (2012) The Kay Review of UK Equity Markets and Long Term Decision Making, July 2012, Dept of Business, Innovation and Skills. Available at http://bis.gov.uk/assets/biscore/businesslaw/docs/k/12-917-kay-review-of-equity-markets-final-report.pdf

Lazonick, W. (2011) 'From Innovation to Financialization: How Shareholder Value Ideology is Destroying the US Economy', chapter in Gerald Epstein and Martin H. Wolfson (eds), *The Political Economy of Financial Crises*. Oxford: Oxford University Press.

Lazonick, W. and O'Sullivan, M. (2000) 'Maximizing Shareholder Value: A New Ideology for Corporate Governance', *Economy and Society*, 29, 1, 13–35.

Lorenz, E. and Valeyre, A. (2006) 'Organizational Forms and Innovative Performance: A Comparison of the EU-15', in E. Lorenz and B-A. Lundvall (eds), *How Europe's Economies Learn: Coordinating Competing Models*. Oxford: Oxford University Press.

Lundvall, Bengt-Åke (2009) *The Danish Model and the Globalizing Learning Economy: Lessons for Developing Countries*. UNU-WIDER Research Paper No. 2009/18, March. http://www.wider.unu.edu/stc/repec/pdfs/rp2009/RP2009-18.pdf

Mazzucato, M. (2013) *The Entrepreneurial State: Debunking Public vs. Private Sector Myths*. Anthem: Other Canon Economics.

Nuffield Council on Bioethics (2012) 'Emerging Biotechnologies: Technology, Choice and the Public Good'. December.

OECD Venture Capital Database 2012.

ONS (2012) ONS Statistical Bulletin, Business Enterprise Research and Development (2011) Office for National Statistics. http://www.ons.gov.uk/ons/dcp171778_287868.pdf |

ONS (2013) ONS Statistical Bulletin, Ownership of UK Quoted Shares 2012. http://www.ons.gov.uk/ons/dcp171778_327674.pdf

Ornston, D. (2012) *When Small States Make Big Leaps*. Ithaca: Cornell University Press.

Plender, J. (2006) 'An Acceptable Poison Pill? It's Not an Oxymoron', *Financial Times*, 6 April, pp. 20.

Ramirez, P. and Tylecote, A. (2004) 'Hybrid Corporate Governance and Its Effects on Innovation: A Case Study of AstraZeneca', *Technological Analysis and Strategic Management*, 16, 1, 97–119.

Rébérioux, A. (2002) 'European Style of Corporate Governance at the Crossroads: The Role of Worker Involvement', *Journal of Common Market Studies*, 40, 1, 111–134.

Tassey, G. (2007) *The Technology Imperative*. Cheltenham and Northampton MA: Elgar.

Tylecote and Ramirez (2006) 'Corporate Governance and Innovation: The UK Compared with the US and "Insider" Systems', *Research Policy*, 35, 1, 160–180.

Tylecote and Ramirez (2008) 'Finance, Corporate Governance and the New Techno-Economic Paradigm', *Louvain Economic Review*, 4, 583–613.

Whitley, R. (2003) 'The Institutional Structuring of Organizational Capabilities: The Role of Authority Sharing and Organizational Careers', *Organization Studies*, 24, 5, 667–695.

Young, D. and Scott, P. (2004) *Having Their Cake: How the City and Big Bosses are Consuming UK Business*. London: Kogan Page.

# Part IV
# Alternatives Beyond Growth?

# 12
# A Feminist Critique of the 'Politics of Community'

*Daniela Tepe-Belfrage*

This chapter critically interrogates the Coalition government's Politics of Community (Robinson, 2008) agenda. Specifically, it looks at how the concept of The Broken Society is understood as the key hindrance to growth and prosperity and how the government proposes to solve this problem by empowering communities and local people via The Big Society. The chapter argues that this serves to legitimise both the politics of austerity and welfare retrenchment and a politics of discipline and criminalisation. By drawing on a theoretical framework inspired by the work of Loïc Waquant, this chapter highlights some of the devastating effects the Politics of Community agenda has had on the lives of women and in particular its effect on single mothers.

The Politics of Community are in part a continuation and intensi-fication of crucial aspects of the community agenda of the previous Labour government. Both agendas emphasise the individual's respon-sibility for their own fate through 'workfare' rather than 'welfare', de-emphasise material deprivation and socio-economic marginalisa-tion, and are accompanied by disciplinary and criminalising discourses and practices (Hancock et al., 2012). Thus, the Politics of Community sits firmly within the process of an ongoing neoliberalisation of the welfare state (Peck, 2002) where the market is presented as the best, if not the only, means of securing the wellbeing of the individual. At the same time, social assistance is understood as an obstruction to this aim. The Politics of Community under the Coalition government has therefore served to legitimise an extension of neoliberalism (Fraser and Murphy, 2013: 38) in the context of 'severe austerity' (Rubery and Rafferty, 2014: 123) as a response to the 'deepest and most protracted global economic crisis after 1929' (Karamessini, 2014: 7). A regime of market citizenship (Bakker, 2008) provides the ideological foundation for a sharp reduction in benefits and a rise in workfare practices. This serves to construct welfare recipients as undeserving (Peck, 2001) and their lifestyles as open to critique and legitimately subject to discipline.

Gendered analysis of the politics of austerity, which followed the 2008 financial crisis, demonstrates that 'the current crisis is far from simply a standard downside of a business cycle. Rather, it is likely to lead to far-reaching social and economic change' (Rubery, 2014: 25). Women have been disproportionately affected in terms of their relative position in the labour market compared to men (Bettio and Verashchagina, 2014) and the introduction of workfare schemes have had problematic consequences in terms of gender equality (Perrons and Plomien, 2014). Critical feminist political economy has shown how responses to the crisis accelerated the already existing crisis of social reproduction (Elson, 2009) and, more generally, how the 'neoliberal state's aggressive reordering of people's daily lives extends...into the household and spheres of reproduction' (LeBaron, 2010: 890).

This paper builds on these approaches. However, I argue that dimensions of criminalisation and disciplining and their consequences for the lives of women have been marginalised in the literature (for a notable exception, see LeBaron and Roberts (2010) on the carceral state) but should be brought to the forefront given their devastating effects on people's lives. The UK's Politics of Community serves as a case study to highlight these dimensions.

Drawing on the work of Waquant I argue for an understanding of neoliberalism which moves from a concern with 'economic policies promoting the virtues of lightly regulated markets over state activity, towards a more sociological conception' where we recognise that there is a 'functional need for interdependent linkages between strategies of "state-craft" – state orchestrated economic and social control' (Stenson, 2013: 42). Economic policies are thus accompanied by 'tough, punitive modes of policing, criminal justice and punishment, along with a shift away from state-funded welfare benefit safety-nets for the poor towards more conditional "workfare" policies' (Stenson, 2013: 42). While gender is unfortunately largely ignored in Wacquant's work itself (see Gelsthorpe, 2008), I argue that his theoretical insights help us to shed light on the destructive effects that these neoliberal developments have on the lives of women – in particular single mothers – beyond the effects on their (non)position in the marketplace.

## The politics of community: From Broken Britain to Big Society

Initially popularised by the former leader of the Conservative Party Iain Duncan Smith and the Centre for Social Justice, the terms Broken Society and Broken Britain have become catchphrases summarising the social, political and economic health of Britain today (Mooney, 2011). They have also been used to frame public debates on the future of social welfare in Britain. These terms have been especially prominent in right-leaning newspapers and tabloids, with *The Sun* even running a series on the theme focusing on crime and anti-social behaviour between 2008 and 2009. The concept formed an important part of the Conservative Party's message before the general election in 2010 and afterwards in the context of legitimating austerity politics (Clark and Newman, 2012).

Yet, despite the seeming importance of this policy – Cameron even described it as at the 'top of his political agenda' in 2011 – the concept of a Broken Society remains vague and largely undefined. David Cameron lists under it 'irresponsibility, selfishness, behaving as if your choices have no consequences, children without fathers, schools without discipline, reward without effort, crime without punishment, rights without responsibilities' (Cameron, 2011).

As such, Broken Britain seems to refer to the state of British society, in that it describes a perceived loss of moral integrity, norms, values and community spirit. The implication is that these *were* in place in another (unspecified) time and place. In addition, there is a focus on law and order within the theme and a strong call for more discipline. At the same time, this analysis of British society does not affect all parts of British society equally in the sense that not all sections of society are considered to be broken or to have lost their community spirit. Rather, the narrative focuses upon particular elements of a social underclass that are somehow perceived to impact upon the whole of society. For example, Iain Duncan Smith has argued that, 'Britain is witnessing a growth in an underclass whose lifestyles affect everyone' (Smith, 2008). A further aspect of the Broken Britain concept seems to be that these elements are individually made responsible for perceived failures to live up to a particular and unclear societal standard of norms. Wider societal responsibility for the breakdown of particular norms and values is largely denied.

Despite the term being employed to justify an economic policy of cutting the welfare which goes to the 'underserving poor', the meaning of

Broken Britain is largely detached from political processes and economic relations. This in turn reveals an ideological focus on family breakdown and economic dependence, crime control and criminalisation (Hancock and Mooney, 2012: 3, see also Finlayson, 2010: 2). Crucially, the demise of 'community' is presumed 'to be the key driver of this breakdown in society' (Flint and Robinson, 2008: 1).

Alan Finlayson points out that the Conservatives understand the current crisis as a consequence of social decay, detaching social from economic and political decisions (Finlayson, 2010: 2). He cites an interview with Oliver Letwin, the Chairman of the Conservative Party in 2008 (after the onset of the financial crisis!), who argues that while Britain is facing huge economic problems the main challenge is of a social nature: 'the biggest long-term challenge we face today is a social one... I think that the social revolution we need to achieve is as great as the economic revolution which was required in the 1980s and 1990s' (Letwin, in Finlayson, 2010: 3). As such, the economic problems Britain is facing are understood to be rooted in the social and moral crisis associated with the concept of Broken Britain (see also Mooney, 2011).

Yet, as has been argued, Broken Britain is linked by Conservative discourse to the politics of the welfare state and in particular to legitimate welfare cuts in the context of austerity (Clark and Newman, 2012). The Conservatives thus blame the existence of welfare on the lack of societal aspirations. This analysis is connected to the Conservative's general diagnosis of the key causes of poverty (Lister and Bennett, 2010). This diagnosis marks a U-turn from previous Conservative policy.[1] A recent Conservative policy report identifies five 'pathways to poverty': family breakdown, educational failure, economic dependence, indebtedness and addictions (Social Justice Policy Group, in: Lister and Bennett, 2010: 86), again with family breakdown and economic dependence being considered the main causes of poverty. An individual's actual income is deemed unimportant as a marker of poverty.

In common with the Politics of Community more generally, this is not a novel analysis of society but is in large part a continuation and intensification of New Labour perceptions of poverty and economic dependence. Welfare dependence is viewed as one of the main causes of poverty and the solution offered is a turn towards 'workfare' rather than 'welfare' in the context of intensified neoliberalisation of the welfare state (Jessop, 2002).

The Big Society is the government's principal response to the Broken Society. This discourse similarly de-emphasises material deprivation and socio-economic marginalisation (Lister and Bennett, 2010), by focusing on how to empower individuals through policies that support community initiatives and local people. This is therefore linked with the same Politics of Community (Robinson, 2008: 31).

The idea is to create policies that re-establish order in the short-term and create 'communities that nurture a sense of belonging and citizenship' in the long-term (Flint and Robinson, 2008: 2). The concrete political measures of the programme are in line with the ideological focus of the Broken Britain narrative – such as appointing Louise Carey to address Britain's 'problem' families through intensive parenting classes, or through restricting welfare benefits and severe criminal sentences for rioters and their families.

These discourses and policies are particularly disturbing as they put blame for societal failure on those in society who should be protected and on those who are not responsible for the economic misery we are facing. Indeed, this resonates nicely with the broader neoliberal idea of individual responsibility for one's own fate (Bakker, 2008) and helps to further legitimise welfare cuts and wider austerity measures, which have been accelerated after the financial crisis of 2008. Individuals are no longer perceived as deserving of support as their misery is their own fault and, crucially, this misery and accompanying life choices impact negatively upon those 'hard-working' people in society that are not reliant on welfare support. Furthermore, this discourse legitimises interventionist policies, disciplining and criminalising people's lives, as their lifestyles affect everyone.

Again, disciplining and criminalising social policy were a prominent feature of the Politics of Community under New Labour along with changing understandings of social solidarity and of what should be done about 'antisocial behaviour' (Rodger, 2008). Indeed, one of the key features of social policy under New Labour and under the Coalition government today are to link the 'reform of the welfare system and the development of a criminal justice agenda [to] dealing with dysfunctional families, anti-social behaviour in children and early intervention to rescue the ill-disciplined "feral children" in the peripheral housing estates and poor inner cities from entrapment in...inferior life trajectories' (Rodger, 2012: 415). According to Rodgers, The Crime and Disorder Act of 1998 and the Anti-Social Behaviour Act 2003 exemplify this point of continuity. 'The two key principles that underpinned criminal justice legislation were early intervention into families that were failing and reinforcing parental responsibility.' (Rodger, 2012: 415) Indeed, both acts were linked up with attempts to create community efficiency and crime prevention partnerships.

Yet, just as societal discourses are changing, the target of *what* or *who* is to be made cohesive, disciplined or integrated is changing as well.

Initially the Politics of Community, popularised through the idea of community cohesion, 'applied to the problems of urban society in the aftermath of the street disturbances in various Pennine mill towns in the summer of 2001'. This discourse identified particular ethnic and religious groups as living 'parallel lives' thereby 'undermining a common sense of belonging' (Flint and Robinson, 2008: 1). Prominent community cohesion initiatives were set up to address these problems (Cantle, 2008). This focus on ethnicity and religion was fuelled by the terrorist attacks in New York, London and elsewhere in the 2000s.

In the aftermath of the 2011 riots and against the background of accelerating austerity, the focus on who 'breaks Britain' has shifted almost entirely to an *underclass* that, through benefit fraud and lack of societal values, shows 'a shortage of respect and boundaries' (Cameron, 2011) , thereby contributing to social disintegration. I am not arguing that under New Labour this underclass was not addressed. New Labour legislation explicitly targeted the very poor in society. Yet, the discourses identifying 'problem' groups focused more clearly on ethnic minorities and Muslim communities in particular. As such, the focus of who most urgently needs to be made cohesive in order to 'mend' the Broken Society has changed.

As indicated above, this shift in 'cohesion focus' has not resulted in a shift of focus to address the increasing polarisation of society on the basis of income and class (Dorling and Thomas, 2004). The role of the wealthy and their part in generating the crisis is often ignored when it comes to legislation, in spite of rhetorical claims that 'we are all in this together'.

## Critical political economies of crime and discipline

The entanglement of welfare and crime control, disciplinary practices, criminality and criminalisation as evidenced in the Broken Britain, Big Society and the Politics of Community discourses has not been at the forefront of political economy approaches concerned with gender. Some work has been done on New Constitutionalism, but this has not been really integrated into the core of gendered research on the welfare state. Therefore, I propose to look seriously at insights from critical criminology/critical sociology (Wacquant, 2009; van Swaaningen, 1997; Pantazis, 2008; Rodger, 2008) to achieve a deeper understanding of current political and economic developments. This is particularly crucial at a time when 'the relationship between welfare and discipline, and between social policy and criminal justice, is changing from being an implicit feature of the welfare state development [to] becoming a more explicit and strategic characteristic' (Rodger, 2008: 4). This change in the nature of welfare is driven by 'a shift from a concern about structural causes of social problems to a preoccupation with "choices, lifestyle and the culture of the poor themselves"' (Rodger, 2008: 6) as evidenced in the Broken Britain and Big Society themes. Here, factors such as poverty, lack of income, poor housing, bad health and lack of access to health-care and educational possibilities are not considered the most important factors. Rather, the lifestyles of the poor are considered as the root cause of society's shortcomings.

Wacquant's work[2] on poverty, the criminalisation of poverty and the neoliberal governance of social insecurity is especially helpful here. His argument about the development of an advanced marginality resulting from uneven development in the capitalist core is important. He writes that, 'the novel regime of socio-spatial relegation and exclusionary closure ... has crystallised in the post-Fordist city as a result of the uneven development of the capitalist economies and the recoiling of welfare states' (Wacquant, 2008: 2–3). Hancock and Mooney (2012) argue that the particular strength of Wacquant's argument is that it shifts attention to the role of the state in (re)producing advanced marginality rather than playing to a pathological discourse of an underclass free of moral and ethical consciousness – again as evidenced in the Broken Britain narrative:

'Wacquant's arguments highlight the central role of the state in both producing and reproducing inequality in the context of neoliberalism while also managing the effects of rising inequality in terms of a growing punitiveness and steady drift to authoritarianism.' (Hancock and Mooney, 2012: 4)

Advanced marginality is characterised by six principal features:

1) Unstable work patterns accompanied by the reproduction of insecurity and social disintegration.
2) The exclusion of certain communities from economic growth, leaving the most marginalised members of society with reduced life chances.
3) 'Territorial fixation and stigmatisation' (2008: 237): advanced marginality is concentrated in particular locations in cities and both those who reside outside such locales and those within them regard such places as dangerous, degraded and degrading.

4) Territorial or spatial alienation and what Wacquant refers to as the 'dissolution of "place"' (2008: 241) as community bonds fragment and residents withdraw from public spaces characterised more and more by conflict and division.

5) 'Loss of hinterland' (2008: 243): the withering of social support for workers provided by families, neighbours and locally based institutions in earlier periods of cyclical downturn. Such support may have included informal working, but the path to regular employment would have been facilitated by these connections, which have now been shattered. Furthermore, collective means of representing and resisting are enfeebled by

6) 'Social fragmentation and symbolic splintering' (2008: 244) as working-class organisations, such as trades unions, find organising beyond the workplace difficult and pressure groups find little common ground and achieve still fewer real gains.

A focus on 'advanced marginality' provides a strong counter-narrative to the Politics of Community Agenda. Unfortunately, however, Wacquant's work pays little attention to gender (Gelsthorpe, 2010). At most, Waquant draws attention to the 'precariousness of poor women and the extent to which they are disciplined and controlled by the state through an emphasis on "workfare" rather than welfare' (Martin and Wilcox, 2013: 151). Wacquant, for example identifies a 'remasculisation' of the state where it is a high priority to tame men through penal policies (Waquant, 2009: 15).

Nevertheless, I argue that Wacquant's work can be usefully drawn upon in feminist research. In particular, his work helps us to focus on aspects of the welfare state that have received little attention to date, but which nevertheless can have crucial effects on women's lives. A good example of this is the changing discourse about family values and disciplinary–criminalisation practices that have formed part of the Politics of Community.

## The politics of community: Women's lives

Employing Wacquant's theoretical insights – especially his focus on the state's attempts to control moral deficiencies and to discipline perceived criminality – enables us to shed light on two particular moments of importance to women's lives in the Politics of Community, as evidenced in the idea of the Broken and Big Societies.

*(1) Particular femininities and masculinities are reproduced through discourse and practice, reproducing problematic understandings of socialisation and authority.*

In the case of the US welfare state, Waquant identifies a 'tenacious ideology of gender and the family that makes poor unwed mothers (and fatherless children) into abnormal, truncated, suspect beings who threaten the moral order and who the state must place under harsh tutelage' (2009: 81).

Applying his insights to the contemporary context in the UK, we can identify a similar shift in the perception of single motherhood and a shift in family values back to the family values of the 1950s. Here, women are taken as solely responsible for 'care' work and fathers are understood as crucial authority figures, the absence of which supposedly creates amoral individuals.

'Support for the marriage-based family has become the focal point of Conservative social policy under Cameron's leadership' (Kirby, 2009). There is an understanding that 'married' families are crucial for the Big Society envisaged and necessary to maintain and/or recreate a healthy, moral Britain. As Cameron puts it, 'the values of marriage are give and take, support and sacrifice – values that we need more of in this country' (Cameron, 2013). A transferable tax allowance of £1,000 for married couples from 2015 was announced in September 2013 to benefit – according to Cameron – mainly stay at home mothers and part-time workers. The effects on women's lives of similar measures in other welfare states, such as the *Ehegattensplitting* in Germany, have been well documented. Such measures tend to support traditional family structures, with women mainly responsible for social reproductive work and, at best, only in part-time work.

There is an underlying implication that marriage is somehow a morally superior form of life. Feminists have long pointed to problems associated with the institution of marriage (see de Beauvoir, 1997; Wollstonecraft, 1996; Moller Okin, 1989); arguing that historically it has been a crucial site of female oppression, associated with and tending to reinforce a female/male division of labour, with women taking on the burden of social reproductive responsibilities associated with the reproduction of particular femininities and masculinities. Also, the issue of violence in marriage and how marriage can serve to protect the violent behaviour of men has not changed significantly in spite of the criminalisation of marital rape and violence (Card, 1996, see also Chambers, 2012).

As such, it is at least questionable to support the institution of marriage as a protector of morality; in some cases it means supporting the institutionalised repression of women.

Yet the Conservatives do not stop here. In addition to supporting marriage as a superior way of life, they problematise single household families, in particular single mother households, as somehow incapable of socialising children into becoming moral human beings.

The first time Cameron spoke of Britain being 'broken' was in 2007, in the wake of the shooting of three London teenagers. In this case, he blamed absent fathers and, by extension, broken families: 'When you look at the people caught up in these events you see an absence, in many cases, of fathers.' He argues that this absence somehow corresponds to a lack of respect for authority.

He took up these themes again prominently in 2011 in an article published in the Sunday Telegraph to mark Father's Day. He stressed the crucial role of father figures in the upbringing of their children. While acknowledging that we live in an age where 'people don't like to see differences between the sexes', he argued that differences between the sexes mean that men and women bring different 'things to the table'. He went on to argue that society has a responsibility to shame 'runaway dads':

> they should be looked at like drunk drivers, people who are beyond the pale ... They need the message rammed home to them, from every part of our culture, that what they're doing is wrong; that leaving single mothers, who do a heroic job against all odds, to fend for themselves isn't acceptable. (Cameron, 2011a)

Ironically, Cameron's Father's Day speech was published only days after the passing of a welfare reform bill that made the Child Support Agency (CSA) charge mothers an upfront fee of £100 if they want to pursue outstanding payments from non-paying fathers, in addition to a permanent commission fee of between 7 per cent and 12 per cent of the pursued sum.

As Polly Toynbee in the Guardian pointed out, the intention was to deter single parents from chasing these fathers via the CSA and, in line with the Big Society agenda, make the families themselves responsible for coming to an agreement. She quoted Maria Miller, the Work and Pensions Minister, who was asked by a Tory MP why earning fathers would not be charged for the service. Her response, given at a DWP select committee, was to say: 'that wouldn't fit with our strategy of prioritising responsibility for themselves' (Miller, cited in Toynbee, 2011).

As such, single mothers are expected not just to provide singlehand-edly for their children, but also to personally communicate and nego-tiate with absent fathers who are unwilling to pay.

The theme of absent fathers causing more than financial hardship, but also being responsible for the lack of respect in their children, was brought up by Cameron once more in the wake of the riots in 2011.

> I don't doubt that many of the rioters out last week have no father at home. Perhaps they come from one of the neighbourhoods where it's standard for children to have a mum and not a dad ... where it's normal for young men to grow up without a male role model, looking to the streets for their father figures, filled up with rage and anger. (Cameron, 2011)

As Iain Duncan Smith argues:

> A further consequence of breakdown in the family is that boys have no male role models to display the traditional virtues of stability, fidelity and the work ethic. (Smith, 2014)

As mentioned earlier, there seems to be an assumption in the minds of Conservative politicians that these 'traditional virtues' are mainly and/or even necessarily socialised into children via male authority figures. The idea that a male role model is crucial to fostering societal values such as respect and fidelity stands in marked tension with years of feminist research and practice. The idea that a 'work ethic' is inherently 'male' is historically inaccurate and problematically devalues female work in and outside of the household. It reproduces the 'male provider myth', not recognising 'that women have always contributed significantly to the household economy, including through paid employment in and out of the home'. In addition, 'it brings men's work into view as part of a gendered structure of employment that has changed significantly over time' (Marx Feree, 1999: 871).

The complete absence of any mention of economic and social hard-ship, lack of welfare support and/or deprivation as contributing to the antisocial and/or rioting behaviour of young people is astonishing, but it sits nicely with the discourse of blaming the poor for their own and society's failures, while providing legitimacy for further welfare cuts and criminalising and disciplining policies.

*(2) Women, particularly single mothers, are the victims of disciplining and criminalising discourses and practices that accompany the Politics of Community.*

As Martin and Wilcox (2013) highlight, Waquant's work leads us to look at the 'precariousness of poor women and the extent to which they are disciplined and controlled by the state' (151).

> The activation of disciplinary programmes applied to the unemployed, the indigent, single mothers, and others 'on assistance' so as to push them onto the peripheral sectors of the employment market, on one side and the deployment of an extended police and penal net with a reinforced mesh, in the dispossessed districts of the metropolis, on the other side are the two components of a single apparatus for the management of poverty that aims at effecting the authoritarian rectification of the behaviours of populations recalcitrant to the emerging economic and symbolic order. (Waquant, in: Martin and Wilcox, 2013: 151)

As some of the quotes cited in the section above have highlighted, an explanation of the 2011 riots was very quickly found. The riots were due to 'broken families', in particular families without father figures. Indeed, a significant proportion of the rioters did come from single-parent households, although many came from diverse social backgrounds.

As a result, one of the discourses that developed very quickly as a response to the riots was to call for measures to withdraw benefits from convicted rioters and their families and to withdraw benefits from families that would not fulfill their 'societal obligations', such as failing to turn up at school or being outside on the streets after ten o'clock. This played nicely into the wider legitimation of the withdrawal of benefits in the context of austerity.

An e-petition on the government website (http://epetitions.direct.gov.uk/petitions/7337) that stated 'Convicted rioters should lose all benefits' drew more than 250,000 signatures. As stated on the website, the 'Department for Work and Pensions is also looking at whether further sanctions can be imposed on the benefit entitlements of individuals who receive non-custodial sentences. In addition the Department is considering increasing the level of fines which can be deducted from benefit entitlement.' Furthermore, ministers have encouraged social landlords to use their powers of eviction for anti-social behaviour and/or criminal activity.

The idea is to withdraw benefits so as to discipline those who do not live up to community standards. This can be understood as a further escalation of family intervention policies which started with the Respect Agenda under New Labour in 2005. The aim is to show families what is expected of them in terms of 'their responsibility to care for and monitor their children's behaviour' (Rodger, 2008: 117). As Rodger (2008) argues, 'family policy and the benefits agency [under New Labour] are geared to ensuring that mothers with children will work whenever possible – especially lone parents with children at primary school' (117), and to ensure that those unable to find work are exposed to supervision as a 'problem population'.

New Labour tended to deal with dysfunctional families with a range of policy initiatives beyond the disciplinary Anti-Social Behaviour Orders (ASBOs) and Parenting Orders, such as Sure Start and the Children's Fund. The Coalition government has downgraded the importance of such initiatives, which were designed to tackle child poverty and the disadvantaged, focusing instead on policies aimed at disciplining the poor.

One of the flagship programs of the Coalition government is the Troubled Families Programme, designed to turn around the lives of 120,000 families in England by 2015 in order to bring down public expenditure in this area. Troubled families are defined as families 'that have problems and cause problems to the community around them, putting high costs on the public sector'. More specifically, troubled families are those 'involved in youth crime or anti-social behavior, have children who are regularly truanting, have an adult on out-of-work benefits, cost the public sector large sums in responding to their problems, an estimated average of £75,000 per year' (https://www.gov.uk/government/news/14000-troubled-families-turned-around). Ruth Levitas highlights how this definition shifts the New Labour focus of families in 'trouble' to troublesome families causing 'trouble'. She cites David Cameron in a speech after the riots 2011:

That's why today, I want to talk about troubled families. Let me be clear what I mean by this phrase. Officialdom might call them 'families with multiple disadvantages'. Some in the press might call them 'neighbours from hell'. Whatever you call them, we've known for years that a relatively small number of families are a source of a large proportion of the problems in society. Drug addiction. Alcohol abuse. Crime. A culture of disruption and irresponsibility that cascades through generations. We've always known that these families cost an extraordinary amount of money.' (Cameron, in Levitas, 2013)

Local authorities are rewarded with £4,000 on a payment-by-results basis for 'turning around' the lives of families identified as troubled under the above criteria. The programme encourages councils to appoint dedicated case workers to individual 'failing' families to help them change their lives.

Ruth Levitas clearly exposes the ideological nature of the programme. She shows how an individual's behaviour is blamed for 'failure' rather than looking at more pressing structural factors that cause failure, such as 'ill-health, poverty and poor housing' (Levitas, 2012). Similarly, Danil points out how this ideology of individual failure is present in the 'Working with Troubled Families: A guide to the evidence and good practice', which takes on an agential approach that focuses entirely on the families themselves, treating their problems as endogenous and self-generated rather than examining the structural factors, and larger socio-economic context in which those families operate (Danil, 2013: 11).

As Parr and Nixon's (2008) work shows, the bulk of family intervention projects in the UK are aimed at female-only households. This is representative of a tendency 'to blame female tenants for the "inappropriate" behaviour of their male partners or teenage sons. A similar finding is also seen in the use of Parenting Orders, which have been predominantly given to lone mothers' (Martin and Wilcox, 2013: 157).

Since the accuracy of the statistics on 'troubled families' has been disputed (Leviatas, 2012), it is unclear how many of the troubled families are female-only households. Freedom of information requests which I have sent to central government and to the ten councils with the highest rates of 'troubled families' have shown that government and local councils (with the exception of Bradford) do not collate statistics on the composition of 'troubled families'. This is highly surprising given the strength of blame that is apportioned to absent fathers. There seems to be a tendency, however, exposed in the discourse on absent fathers, to assert that single mother households are over-represented among Britain's 'troubled families'. An indication that a high proportion of troubled families includes a large number of single mother households is that of six case studies of troubled families compiled by the government, five are headed by single mothers        (https://www.gov.uk/government/uploads/system/uploads/attachment_data/file/10961/Troubled_families_case_studies.pdf).

As Garrett (2007: 221–222) recognises, projects such as the Troubled Families Programme are 'schooling families to accept new temporal frameworks' by infantilising adults. Welfare cuts, restrictions on accessing welfare and intensive teaching and monitoring are combined to discipline the poor. Poor women, in particular single mothers, are particularly affected by these policies, which entirely neglect structural factors of poverty and violence.

To conclude this section with Rodger's observation: 'It is precisely the combination of family support and civil law that creates an uneasy relationship between social policy and criminal justice' (2008: 122).

## Conclusion

This paper has argued that under the Coalition government, neoliberal policies have intensified. This is particularly visible in the context of disciplining and criminalising policy and discourse that targets the very poor in society, and disproportionally affects poor women.

The financial crisis of 2008 can be seen as providing a 'state of urgency', where discourses blaming the most vulnerable in society for societal failure legitimises policies that target these very same people. The Broken Britain narrative, and its increased focus on an underclass that is damaging social norms and values, provides the background against which welfare cuts and disciplining and criminalising policies can be implemented.

While political economy approaches concerned with gender have paid attention to the ways in which austerity politics have disproportionally affected women, less attention has been paid to how criminalising and disciplining policies impact upon women's lives. This chapter has sought to correct this lack of attention by turning to the work of Waquant and by arguing for an integration of political economy approaches with insights from critical criminology. While this chapter has pointed towards some of the contributions critical criminology research can make to a political economy approach, further work is needed to develop a theoretical framework integrating these different approaches.

In this context, I would like to point to one particular issue that such a framework will need to address from a feminist perspective.[3] The role of the state in punishment and workfare is obvious, yet, somehow the state as a provider of welfare is implicitly and explicitly presented as the solution to this problem. This is as true for Wacquant's work as for sociological and social policy work inspired by him. From a feminist and critical perspective, such a 'solution' is highly problematic given the crucial role of the welfare state in securing and preserving problematic gender and class relations. The envisaged theoretical framework will have to be based on an understanding of the capitalist and gendered state that allows for a meaningful problematisation of both 'welfare' and 'workfare' functions of the state.

# Notes

1. In the late 1980s Conservatives conceived of relative poverty as simply inequality with former social security secretary John Moore announcing the 'end of the line for poverty' in 1989. According to him, relative poverty was, in reality, simply inequality, 'espoused as a concept by those on the left in order to condemn capitalism' (Lister and Bennett, 2010: 86).
2. It is worth pointing out that Wacquant's work should not be read without acknowledging the criticism he has faced, especially from feminist writers (for example, Gelsthorpe, 2010), in particular for his lack of attention to 'cultures of resistance'. For lack of space these criticisms are largely ignored in this chapter. Still, while acknowledging these shortcomings, for the purpose of this chapter it is worth recognising that Waquant's work directs our attention to moments in the neoliberalisation of the welfare state. This helps us to shed light on specific discourses and practices that impact on women in particular ways.
3. Thank you to Genevieve LeBaron for highlighting this aspect once again!

# References

Bettio, F. and Verashchagina, A. (2014) 'Women and men in the "Great European Recession"', in M. Karamessini and J. Rubery (eds), *Women and Austerity. The Economic Crisis and the Future of for Gender Equality*. London and New York: Routledge.

Brent, J. (2004) 'The Desire for Community: Illusion, Confusion and Paradox', *Community Development Journal*, 39, 3, 213–223.

Cameron, D. (2007) 'Speech in Constituency', http://www.telegraph.co.uk/news/uknews/1542914/Cameron-blames-absent-fathers.html (accessed 17 January 2014)

Cameron, D. (2011) 'Speech on the Fight-back After Riots, 15.8.2011', http://www.newstatesman.com/politics/2011/08/society-fight-work-rights (accessed 17 January 2014).

Cameron, D. (2011a) http://www.telegraph.co.uk/news/politics/david-cameron/8584238/David-Cameron-Dads-gift-to-me-was-his-optimism.html (accessed 15 January 2014).

Cameron, D. (2013) http://www.dailymail.co.uk/debate/article-2435723/DAVID-CAMERON-Marriage-good-Britain--thats-Im-backing-tax-break.html (accessed 15 January 2014).

Cantle, T. (2008) *Community Cohesion: A New Framework for Race and Diversity*. Basingstoke: Palgrave Macmillan.

Card, C. (1996) 'Against Marriage and Motherhood', *Hypatia*, 11, 3.

Chambers, C. (2012) *Feminism, Liberalism and Marriage*, http://ebookbrowsee.net/feminism-liberalism-and-marriage-doc-d16304541 (accessed 14 January 2014).

Clark, J. and Newman, J. (2012) 'The Alchemy of Austerity', *Critical Social Policy*, 32, 299–319.

Connor, S. (2010) 'The Myth of Community?' *Concept*, 1, 3, http://concept.lib.ed.ac.uk/index.php/Concept/article/viewFile/89/99 (accessed 22 August 2012).

Danil, L. R. (2013) 'Families First': A Study into the Coalition Government's 'Troubled Families Programme' in Leeds, West Yorkshire, UK, https://www.academia.edu/2762324/_Families_First_A_study_into_the_Coalition_

Governments_Troubled_Families_Programme_in_Leeds_West_Yorkshire_UK (accessed 20 January 2014).

De Beauvoir, S. (1997) *The Second Sex*. London: Vintage

Dorling, D. and Thomas, B. (2004) *People and Places: A 2001 Census Atlas of the UK*. Bristol: The Policy Press.

Elson, D. (2009) *Social Reproduction in the Global Crisis*. Paper presented at UNRISD Conference on Social and Political Dimensions of the Global Crisis, available at http://unrisd.org/80256B3C005BD6AB/(httpAuxPages)/934F4B5486C1FA40 C1257678002E09F3/$file/1-1Elson.pdf (accessed 19 May 2014).

Finlayson, A. (2010) 'The Broken Society Versus the Social Recession: How Should We Approach the Problems of a Post-crash Britain?' in R. Grayson and J. Rutherford (eds), *After the Crash: Reinventing the Left in Britain*. London, Lawrence and Wishart, 2009, pp. 27–37.

Flint, J. and Robinson, D. (2008) 'Introduction', in F. John and R. David (eds), *Community Cohesion in Crisis? New Dimensions of Diversity and Difference*. Bristol: The Policy Press.

Fraser, A. and Murphy, E. and Kelly, S. (2013) *Deepening Neoliberalism via Austerity and 'Reform': The Case of Ireland*. Human Geography, 6, 38–53.

Fraser, Nancy (2009) 'Feminism, Capitalism and the Cunning of History', *New Left Review*, 56, 97–117.

Garrett, P. M. (2007) '"Sinbin" Solutions: The Pioneer Projects for "Problem Families" and the Forgetfulness of Social Policy Research', *Critical Social Policy*, 27, 2, 203–230.

Gelsthorpe, L. (2010) 'Crime and Crime Control', *Criminology and Criminal Justice Studies*, 10, 4, 375–386.

Grimshaw, D. and Ruberty, J. (2012) 'The End of the UK's Liberal Collectivist Social Model? The Implications of the Coalition Government's Policy During the Austerity Crisis', *Cambridge Journal of Economics*, 39, 1, 105–126.

Hancock, L. and Mooney, G. (2012) '"Welfare Ghettos" and the "Broken Society": Territorial Stigmatization in the Contemporary UK', *Housing, Theory and Society*, 30, 1, 46–64.

Hancock, L., Mooney, G. and Neal, S. (2012) 'Crisis Social Policy and the Resilience of the Concept of Community', *Critical Social Policy*, 32, 3, 343–364.

Harrison, J. and Stephenson, M-A. (2011) 'Unravelling Equality? A Human Rights and Equality Impact Assessment of the Public Spending Cuts on Women in Coventry', http://www2.warwick.ac.uk/fac/soc/law/chrp/projectss/human-rightsimpactassessments/cwv/report/127948_cwv-chrp_report.pdf (accessed 15 August 2012).

Harvey, D. (2005) *A Brief History of Neoliberalism*. Oxford: Oxford University Press.

Husband, C. and Alam, Y. (2011) *Social Cohesion and Counter-Terrorism. A Policy Contradiction?* Bristol: The Policy Press.

Jenson, J. (1990) 'Representations in Crisis: The Roots of Canada's Permeable Fordism', *Canadian Journal of Political Science*, 23, 4, 653–683.

Jessop, B. (2002) *The Future of the Capitalist State*. Cambridge: The Policy Press.

Karamessini, M. (2014) 'Introduction – Women's Vulnerability to Recession and Austerity: A Different Crisis, a Different Context', in M. Karamessini and J. Rubery (eds), *Women and Austerity. The Economic Crisis and the Future of for Gender Equality*. London and New York: Routledge.

Kirby, J. (2009) 'From Broken Families to the Broken Society', *The Political Quarterly*, 80, 2, 243–247.

LeBaron, G. (2010) 'The Political Economy of the Household: Neoliberal Restructuring, Enclosures, and Daily Life', *Review of International Political Economy*, 17, 5, 889–912.

LeBaron, G. and Adrienne, R. (2010) 'Toward a Feminist Political Economy of Capitalism and Carcerality', *Signs: Journal of Women in Culture and Society*, 36, 1, 19–44.

Leviatas, R. (2012) 'There May Be "trouble" Ahead: What We Know about those 120,000 Troubled Families', *Policy Response Series*, No. 2, http://www.poverty. ac.uk/system/files/WP%20Policy%20Response%20No.3-%20%20'Trouble'%20 ahead%20(Levitas%20Final%2021April2012).pdf (accessed 15 January 2014).

Lister, R. and Bennett, F. (2010) 'The New "Champion of Progressive Ideals"? Cameron's Conservative Party: Poverty, Family Policy and Welfare Reform', *Renewal*, 18, 1/2, 84–109.

Martin, D. and Wilcox, P. (2013) 'Women, Welfare and the Carceral State', in P. Squires and J. Lea (eds), *Criminalisation and Advanced Marginality. Critically Exploring the Work of* Loïc *Wacquant*. Bristol: Policy Press, pp. 151–172.

Marx Feree, M. (1999) 'Beyond Separate Spheres: Feminism and Family Research', *Journal of Marriage and the Family*, 52, 866–884.

Moller Okin, S. (1989) *Justice, Gender and the Family*. New York: Basic Books.

Pantazis, C. (2008) 'The Problem with Criminalisation', *Criminal Justice Matters*, 74, 4, 10–12.

Parr, S. and Nixon, J. (2008) 'Rationalising Family Intervention Projects', in P. Squires (ed.), *ASBO Nation: The Criminalisation of Nuisance*. Bristol: Policy Press.

Peck, J. (2001) *Workfare States*. New York: Guilford Press.

Peck, J. (2002) 'Political Economies of Scale: Fast Policy, Interscalar Relations, and Neoliberal Workfare', *Economic Geography*, 78, 3, 331–360.

Perrons, D. and Plomien, A. (2014) 'Gender, Inequality and the Crisis: Toward More Equitable Development', in M. Karamessini and J. Rubery (eds), *Women and Austerity. The Economic Crisis and the Future of for Gender Equality*. London and New York: Routledge.

Ratcliffe, P. and Newman, I. (2011) *Promoting Social Cohesion. Implications for Policy and Evaluation*. Bristol: Policy Press.

Robinson, D. (2008) 'Community Cohesion and the Politics of Communitarianism', in J. Flint and D. Robinson (eds), *Community Cohesion in Crisis? New Dimensions of Diversity and Difference*. Policy Press: Bristol.

Rodger, John J. (2008) *Criminalising Social Policy: Anti-Social Behaviour and Welfare in a De-Civilised Society*. Willian Publishing: Portland.

Rodger, J. (2012) '"Regulation the Poor": Observations on the "Structural Coupling" of Welfare, Criminal Justice and the Voluntary Sector in a "Big Society"', *Social Policy & Administration*, 46, 4, 413–431.

Rubery, J. (2014) 'From "Women and Recession" to "Women and Austerity"', in M. Karamessini and J. Rubery (eds), *Women and Austerity. The Economic Crisis and the Future of for Gender Equality*. London and New York: Routledge.

Rubery, J. and Rafferty, A. (2014) 'Gender, Recession and Austerity in the UK', in M. Karamessini and J. Rubery (eds), *Women and Austerity. The Economic Crisis and the Future of for Gender Equality*. London and New York: Routledge.

Smith, I. D. (2008) http://www.telegraph.co.uk/comment/personal-view/3645075/ Shannon-Matthews-abuse-shows-we-will-all-pay-the-price-for-broken-Britain. html (accessed 14 January 2014).

Smith, I. D. (2014) http://www.dailymail.co.uk/news/article-477388/IAIN-DUNCAN-SMITH-Britain-gangs-family.html#ixzz2qO5GIjax (accessed 15 January 2014).

Squires, P. and Lea, J. (2013) 'Introduction: Reading Loïc Wacquant – Opening and Overview', in P. Squires and J. Lea (eds), *Criminalisation and Advanced Marginality. Critically Exploring the Work of Loïc Wacquant.* Bristol: Policy Press, pp. 1–18.

Steans, J. and Tepe, D. (2010) 'Introduction – Social Reproduction in International Political Economy: Theoretical Insights and International, Transnational and Local Sitings', *Review of International Political Economy,* 17, 5, 807–815.

Stenson, K. (2013) 'The State, Sovereignty and Advanced Marginality in the City', in P. Squires and J. Lea (eds), *Criminalisation and Advanced Marginality. Critically Exploring the Work of Loïc Wacquant.* Bristol: Policy Press, pp. 41–60.

Swaaningen van, R. (ed.) (1997) *Critical Criminology: Visions from Europe.* London: Sage Publications.

Tolly Toynbee (2011) 'Comment is Free', *The Guardian,* http://www.theguardian. com/commentisfree/2011/jun/20/doublethink-on-absent-fathers

Van Leeuwen, T. (2008) *Discourse and Practice: New Tools for Critical Analysis.* Oxford: Oxford University Press.

Wacquant, L. (2008) *Urban Outcasts: A Comparative Sociology of Advanced Marginality.* Cambridge: Polity Press.

Wacquant, L. (2009) *Punishing the Poor. The Neoliberal Government of Social Insecurity.* Durham, NC: Duke University Press.

Wollstonecraft, M. (1996) *A Vindication of the Rights of Women.* London: Constable and Company Ltd.

# 13
## Towards a New Growth Strategy: Promoting Decent Work in the United Kingdom

*Frank Pyke*

### Introduction

This chapter addresses the role of the social dimension in economic growth strategies, in particular in regard to the United Kingdom. In 2011, a meeting of international experts and senior technical officials from 16 different multilateral organisations concluded that the economic crisis had prompted a rethink of orthodox economic approaches to development and begun a search for alternative models (ILO, 2011a). Concurrently, there have been increased calls for a greater recognition of how social and economic dimensions intertwine for development (see, for example, Townsend, 2009), and demands for new models that better integrate economic and social policies. Such integration will, as pointed out by Jenkins (2010) and Ryder (2010), require new conceptual paradigms.

One institution that explicitly refers to social elements in its growth perspective is the International Labour Organization (ILO), which advocates the promotion of 'decent work'. Decent work includes both: in-work elements, such as working conditions (including, for example, health and safety, rest periods and holidays, and reasonable day lengths), fair pay, employment security, opportunities for training and learning, and possibilities for collective representation; and outside-of-work elements, such as unemployment insurance, retirement pensions, sickness benefits, and other aspects of a welfare system, as well as decent living conditions and environmental sustainability. This article utilises the decent work concept as a synonym for the social dimension in development.

Economic growth is widely seen as the route to lowering poverty rates and raising social and economic living standards. In recent years, however, the assumption of a one-way direction of causality, of growth leading to poverty reduction and an improvement in social conditions, has been increasingly challenged. A growing amount of international evidence indicates that although growth might indeed be a key factor, there is also a direct 'reverse' causal link from poverty and decent work deficits to rates of growth. The implication is that high poverty levels and decent work deficits could undermine efforts to grow an economy, potentially reducing growth rates, leading in turn to lower incomes and, potentially, lower welfare spending, and maybe ultimately to a vicious circle of stagnation or decline.

Such observations could have strong implications for the United Kingdom to the extent that aspirations for long-term productivity-based growth might be undermined by recent falls in standards of social protection, rising levels of poverty, greater casualisation and insecurity, and continuing inequality. This chapter reviews the international evidence that a range of social elements do, in fact, have potentially important inputs to sustainable growth, and it discuss the implications for the UK economy.

## The social and the economic in conceptual perspectives

Neo-liberal theories, typical business school perspectives, and the political influence of particular interest groups have tended to combine to produce a particular perspective on principles for promoting growth. It is referred to here as the business first perspective because it tends to exclude social concerns as key inputs.

### A business first perspective

In this perspective the social and economic dimensions are typically only weakly integrated, with the former mostly not considered for their impact on economic growth. In fact, frequently, social issues are thought of as essentially derivatives or outcomes of successful business or economic strategies involving non-social components (such as finance, marketing, infrastructures, business services, or supply chain organisation). Successful business policies and strategies create the surpluses required to fund social expenditures.

Often in such perspectives, social expenditures might be considered as luxuries to be afforded once growth has been achieved, or perhaps it might be thought that by achieving growth social benefits will naturally trickle down, or permeate, to all who need them. In short, policies for business development should come first and policies for social improvement later.

Indeed, the provision of decent conditions might be seen by some as impediments to competitiveness by, for example, raising production costs, stifling labour flexibility, encouraging people to choose unemployment rather than paid work, diverting public funds from infrastructure projects, imposing regulations and costs which inhibit new business start-ups, and interfering with the natural workings of markets. Some policymakers might even advocate reducing in-work and external welfare expenditures, and/or removing protective legislation, in order to reduce costs in the short run, maybe with the expectation of affording such expenditures later on. A simple diagram outlining the essentials of this perspective is presented in Figure 13.1.

From the perspective of Figure 13.1, the relationship between economic or business development, on the one hand, and social development, on the other, tends to be one of dependency with good social conditions essentially deriving from strong business growth. Strong growth, at the individual firm or broader level, provides the capacity for raising standards. Without first raising profits and growing existing and new enterprises, social expenditures cannot be afforded, and indeed risk undermining development. Consequently, business promotion and broader growth strategies, as taught in academic departments and promoted in policy circles and amongst providers of technical assistance, typically do not explicitly include as essential elements welfare systems, labour regulations, and other social or decent work aspects.

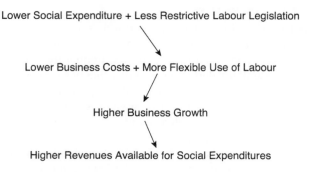

*Figure 13.1*   Growth through promoting business first

For example, Behrendt et al. (2009) point out that investments in social security have not been part of OECD donor governments' development strategies in low-income countries. In Zambia, Bell and Newitt (2010) suggested that central government commitment to large-scale social protection programmes was weak 'because they were not perceived to have a strong connection to economic growth'. In other cases, it seems that social expenditures, and/or the regulating of labour markets for employee protection, have been treated as luxuries, or even as drags on development by pushing up government borrowing, diverting public monies, and hindering labour market flexibility.

However, even if it is accepted that higher profits and stronger growth are prerequisites of increased social expenditure, there is no guarantee that a consequence would be the general provision of higher welfare benefits, or that all incomes would increase fairly and equally. Moreover, some would argue that should a government consider it necessary to pursue, perhaps in principle or temporarily, a strategy of minimising labour costs and social standards as a means of raising business competitiveness and growth, there is a risk of other economies then following suit, inducing in turn further labour and social cuts, and a generalised downward spiral or 'race to the bottom'.

### A decent work first perspective

An alternative view exhorts practitioners to recognise the role of decent work not just as an output or derivative but also as an important input to competitiveness, and, as the ILO has highlighted in its Global Agenda for Employment, 'a factor leading to increased productivity and economic growth (ILO, 2001: ix)'. Indeed, the view that decent work elements are simply derivatives of business growth, and that business promotion must come first and social expenditures later, is open to challenge on a number of key developmental dimensions, including in the areas of: workplace production; social protection and non-workplace living conditions; access to markets; and long-term economic, social and environmental sustainability.

These dimensions will be considered in turn:

*Workplace production*

Rather than decent work being considered simply a luxury, or a derivative of business development, there is a lot of evidence that aspects such as good working conditions, fair wages and job security can be important inputs to competitiveness and growth, by promoting flexibility and cooperation in work, innovation and productivity, which, if workers receive their fair share of revenue improvements, should in turn feed into higher demand in the economy.

A connection has been made between good working conditions, including a fair sharing of profits, and improved enterprise performance. For example, an international literature review carried out by Croucher et al. (2013) found links between Occupational Safety and Health and positive firm outcomes. Also, profit sharing has been associated with increases in firms' productivity (ILO, 2011b). In France, in 2009, 35 per cent of private sector companies with ten or more employees offered some kind of profit sharing scheme. In Peru and Ecuador profit sharing is compulsory (ILO, 2011b).

In the knowledge era, optimum workplace organisation and learning has risen to the forefront of competitive strategies. Ashton and Sung (2002) have highlighted the expansion of high performance work organisations utilising high performance work practices. In these kinds of organisations, a number of typical human resource practices have the potential to raise an enterprise's performance, while increasing worker satisfaction and earnings. Such practices include: job redesign, team working and self-managed workgroups, multi-skilling, performance related pay systems, much training and workplace learning, extensive internal communication, and greater employee autonomy and involvement in decision making.

Research has found that enterprises which have adopted such practices have raised their productivity and profits, while workers have benefited by receiving higher earnings, greater job satisfaction, higher skills, greater engagement in the decision making process, and greater security.

An important precondition for introducing high performance work practices is the need to generate an atmosphere of trust in the workplace. Good industrial relations are therefore important. Worker representation through trade unions can promote greater participation and trust and, through bargaining, help to ensure that workers receive a fair share of productivity improvements.

For high performance work practices, labour regulations matter. In fact, labour regulations are an integral part of all economies. In the case of China, a growth strategy based on leveraging cheap flexible labour and competing largely on price was accompanied, it seems, by labour laws which facilitated casualisation. More recent Chinese labour regulations that offer somewhat enhanced worker protection and security,[1] and efforts to expand industrial relations institutions (Lee, 2009), are arguably more appropriate to China's ambitions to promote productivity and innovation.

*Social protection and non-workplace living conditions*

Social protection in the form of insurance against unemployment, illness, disability, retirement or other life contingencies, and the guaranteeing of minimum wages or social floors for those in and out of work, is another 'social' aspect which might be considered a luxury, or a hindrance to competiveness, or maybe perceived as lying outside the normal business development sphere. However, views on this conceptual division between economic, business and social spheres are changing.

There are increasing views that cash transfers, public employment schemes, minimum wage guarantees, and social insurance schemes should be seen less as luxury expenses or social welfare initiatives to protect the poor and provide them with safety nets, and more as tools for addressing risk and economic vulnerability and as integral parts of a growth strategy (see, for example, Perry et al., 2006; Bonfiglioli, 2007; CPRC, 2008; also, see the deliberations of the meeting of multilateral experts, ILO, 2011a).

In fact, we know that the provision of social protection systems can: help micro-entrepreneurs and the self-employed preserve or invest in physical and financial capital necessary for small scale activities, and generally help people to manage economic and social risks; help to maintain demand in the local economy, including when acting as an automatic stabiliser during economic downturns; help industries retain their skilled labour forces at times of unemployment; allow people to spend money on education and training, both for themselves and for their children; help the maintenance of physical health levels; and facilitate social cohesion and reduce crime.

The downward spiral effect on local economies following reduced incomes, perhaps pursuant on unemployment without adequate social protection, is well known: businesses suffer from a lack of demand; local authorities reduce tax bases and might be forced to reduce public spending and/or increase public debt; families might spend less money on food, basic necessities and education – thereby harming future development; and crime and social disorder might increase. The detrimental effect of mass unemployment, following the closure of thousands of diamond processing enterprises, amongst workers who are weakly socially protected has been documented in Surat, India (See, for example, Hirway, 2009; Kapoor, 2009).

The self-employed and micro-entrepreneurs are aware of how the business and social aspects of their lives intertwine. For example, an unexpected expensive disaster, such as a family illness or even death, can soak money away from investment in equipment. Reflecting such precariousness, ILO research in the Philippines found that micro-entrepreneurs in the informal sector expressed a strong demand for social protection and a willingness to pay for social insurance. Social protection was necessary to remove risk, just as participation in micro-finance schemes allowed people access to funds that could bridge gaps in payment by debtors (Pascual, 2007). In fact, micro-business self-help associations can offer both business and social services. For example, in India the Self Employed Women's Association supports its members with a range of enabling services, including savings and credit, health care, child care, insurance, legal aid, housing improvement, capacity building and training.

Governments have increasingly recognised how economic and social spheres intertwine in real life and there have been numerous examples of social expenditures being integrated into macro-economic policies as part of growth strategies. In some countries, minimum wage or guaranteed social floor policies have been introduced, in part because of the economic role that demand plays in boosting growth. In Vietnam, in 2012, minimum wages were increased by 40 per cent not only for social reasons but also in order to stimulate growth through increased domestic demand. In Malaysia similar thinking was apparently behind the decision to introduce a national minimum wage for the first time (Grant and Bland, 2012). In China, there are indications that the economic development role of social factors, such as social protection, have been taken into account in the country's macro-economic management (Torres, 2011). In India, a government welfare scheme, the National Rural Employment Guarantee Act that guarantees 100 days of unskilled non-farming paid work to one member of every rural family, is reported to be one of the factors (along with higher food prices and easier credit) which have served to raise rural demand in the economy (Fontanella-Khan and Lamont, 2012).

Also, the International Institute for Labour Studies (IILS, 2013) cites an ECLAC (2012) report that in many Latin American countries actions to raise minimum wages resulted in support for consumption and the boosting of investment and growth. In Brazil, the government promoted social policies – such as social cash transfers, increased periods of entitlement to unemployment insurance, and minimum wage increases to prop up domestic demand – as part of its strategy to replace an over-dependency on exports by boosting domestic sources of economic growth (Berg and Tobin, 2011).

Not only are wage levels important for demand. Some would argue that a strong prevalence of low-wage labour in an economy can deter businesses from investing in productivity enhancing technologies and work practices. Conversely, wage hikes might have an opposite effect, as in encouraging productivity and higher value adding production. In Singapore, the government deliberately used wage hikes as a means of incentivising enterprises to move to higher value activities. In addition, the government promoted other means to stimulate labour productivity, including education and vocational training, and social welfare policy (Sengenberger, 2009). In China, the minimum wage tool was widely implemented at a time when concerns were raised by rising inequality, with an express desire to rely less on exports as a driver of growth and more on domestic demand, and when there are strong efforts to increase productivity and encourage enterprises to move up the value chain.

The demand for macro-economic policies to promote growth through cash transfers to the poor is also growing. Examples of the positive economic development role of social protection mechanisms have been documented, for example in Mozambique, Zambia, Lesotho and Ethiopia, where cash transfers are not only spent on just living but also on micro-economic activities, equipment, livestock, supporting education, or other development activities (CPRC, 2008; Sabates-Wheeler et al., 2008, citing Devereux et al., 2005; Bonfiglioli, 2007, citing Middlebrook, 2003).

In South Africa, social assistance transfers were found to play a key role in economic investments: seed money for informal economic activity; inputs for agriculture; for enlarging assets; for improving homes; for supporting education; and for facilitating migration in search of work (CPRC, 2008).

### Access to markets

A further argument for the importance of businesses adhering to good labour, social and environmental standards stands on the fact that there is clearly a market for such products, and that failure to comply with expectations risks market exclusion. The standard of the conditions under which products are produced are often factored into people's evaluations of whether or not to buy – just as people might also evaluate other aspects, such as the quality of the finish, the design and fashion elements, and colour. In other words, perceptions of social and environmental conditions can influence consumer choice.

Negative consumer perceptions of a company's ethical standards may goad major enterprises into using their influence to encourage suppliers to change their practices. For example, the electronics company Apple, which faced widespread negative online comments in response to allegedly poor working conditions in the large Chinese supplier Foxconn, has been reported as being particularly keen to remove underage labour from its supply chain. Apple's chief executive, Tim Cook, has been quoted as saying: 'Underage labour is a subject no company wants to be associated with', and, according to Garside (2013), he has vowed to eradicate the practice from the company's supply chain.

Many major retailers, brand holders and others at the head of global value chains, have designed codes of conduct that set out the acceptable working and environmental conditions expected from suppliers. Fear of bad publicity and a devalued brand image seems to be the main motivator. Often, individual companies establish their own codes, but there are also cases where enterprises and trade unions have negotiated international framework agreements. There are also cases where groups of businesses in the same industry, possibly together with trade unions, agree to adhere to a common group code or to address specific labour or environmental conditions of concern. For example, it was reported that following a major fire in 2013 at the Rana Plaza factory in Dhaka, resulting in many deaths, around 150 retailers and brand holders signed up with national and international trade unions to an international factory safety agreement, the Bangladesh Accord on Fire and Building Safety, which aims to survey and rectify conditions in Bangladeshi factories (Brignall and Butler, 2014). There are also multi-stakeholder agreements involving employers, trade unions, NGOs and/or others.[2]

It is not only major companies who are acting as gatekeepers to markets. National governments and international governmental institutions, such as the European Union (EU), have increasingly insisted on labour and environmental conditionality if their markets are to be accessed. Although attempts to insert a 'social (labour conditionality) clause' in the rules of the World Trade Organization failed, subsequently there has been a proliferation of bilateral and regional trade agreements, which include an expectation that exporters adhere to certain labour standards.

Between 1995 and 2009, the number of bilateral and regional trade agreements which included labour provisions rose from 4 in 1995, to 11 in 2000, to 21 in 2005, and to 37 in 2009. The percentage of all bilateral and regional trade agreements which included labour provisions rose from 4 per cent in the period 1995–1999, to 11 per cent over 2000–2004, to 31 per cent over 2005–2009 (IILS, 2009).

Adherence to such trade agreements can both provide access to markets and help to raise standards. In the case of Cambodia, for example, a bilateral textiles trade agreement with the USA included labour standards conditionality, which, combined with ILO monitoring mechanisms, is said to have resulted in increased textiles exports, a rise in standards compliance, and access to an ethically safe source for buyers wishing to protect their reputation (See, for example, Wells, 2006; Polaski, 2009).

Of course, not all consumers insist on compliance with labour and environmental standards, but a sufficient number do so to underline the fact that social considerations are an important input to the array of factors which make for market success. Products labelled Fair Trade are now a common sight.

*Long-term economic, social and environmental sustainability*

What can seem rational behaviour by a particular business to raise profits and growth can have unintended externality effects on another's development prospects. For example: a business or group of businesses might decide to reduce short-term costs by expelling untreated waste products into rivers or the atmosphere, with external costs for other businesses and society at large: or, there might be a decision to cut back on training, thereby reducing the pool of skills available to all; or, short-term savings on safety equipment might increase the long-term social costs of looking after injured workers. In brief, unregulated actions by individual enterprises can have harmful effects on the public good.

A recent ILO report (ILO, 2013) argued that environmental pollution and other externality deficiencies threaten aggregate productivity growth, but the 'grow now pay later' approach is increasingly being challenged. China is a country said to have pursued a 'growth at all costs' strategy but which now has to deal with serious environmental costs. International businesses may also be recognising that environmental calamities, perhaps caused by climate change, can push up supply costs. Scott (2013) reports that in Thailand, floods caused by a severe monsoon pushed up the price of hard drives for international computer manufacturers. In general, the effects of climate change could have serious consequences for agricultural and other enterprises, and the general population, worldwide.

The depression of wages is another area where savings could have (possibly short-term) benefits for some businesses but (possibly long-term) negative externality effects for others. Enterprises can be competitive while workers' wages remain low. Provided there are workers somewhere in the world who can afford the products of such enterprises then, in the short-term at least, for some businesses this model might work. A problem can arise, however, if rising inequality and low workers' income becomes a generalised phenomenon and there is an insufficient aggregate demand.

Research by the IILS, of the ILO, has tracked over recent decades a growing intra-country income inequality, a rising share of GDP going to profits, and a failure by workers to receive fair shares of productivity growth. For example, over the period 1990–2000, the Institute found that more than two-thirds of the 85 countries for which data was available experienced an increase in income inequality, as measured by changes in the Gini index (IILS, 2008).[3] Moreover, between 2000 and 2009, out of 56 countries with available information, more than 83 per cent were found to have experienced an increase in the share of profits in GDP (IILS, 2011); and for the period 1990–2006, in 24 out of 32 countries, productivity growth was found to have exceeded wage growth (IILS, 2008). By 2013, the IILS was reporting a continuance of inequality in developing and emerging countries, and a worsening situation in the majority of advanced countries for which data was available (IILS, 2013).

Inequality, and a failure by workers to receive fair shares of productivity gains, could have important implications for sustainable growth. It is reported that research by the International Monetary Fund found that inequality can make countries more prone to financial crises and that, indeed, sustainable growth over time is associated with a more equal income distribution (Strauss-Kahn, 2011). Also, Stiglitz (2009) has argued that inequality over the previous 30 years was one of the root causes of the 2008 global economic crisis.[4] Inequality is also reported to be associated with a range of social problems, including worse mental health, lower life expectancy, higher crime rates and greater social conflict (see, for example, Wilkinson and Pickett, 2009).

High levels of unemployment can be another unintended externality, especially where full employment and good quality jobs are not explicit policy objectives. Unemployment and underemployment are likely to exacerbate a loss of social cohesion, especially if adequate social protection mechanisms do not exist. Commentators have suggested that unemployment played a role in provoking the demonstrations and uprisings in North Africa in 2011 (for example, for Tunisia, see Saleh, 2014). Social conflict can have a huge economic (as well as social) cost, especially when it goes beyond social demonstration and/or increased crime to outright physical conflict, and maybe war. The war in 2003 in Iraq, for example, cost huge amounts of money.

Inter-generational social sustainability can be another victim of a failure to regulate the effects of negative externalities on social institutions, to invest in practices as 'public goods' for future development, and to mitigate the effects of poverty on inter-generational educational and skills renewal. The promotion of high levels of health, good education, strong social cohesion, and decent living and working conditions may have general beneficial effects on long-term business competitiveness and growth, while social expenditure cutbacks might provide immediate economic savings but have long-term inter-generational detrimental consequences.

In summary, it can be said that there is a wealth of international evidence that decent working and living conditions are as important to economic growth as other factors of development, such as finance, skills, and infrastructures. Consequently, we can suggest that an alternative way of thinking about growth to that outlined in Figure 13.1 could be as proposed in Figure 13.2, with a focus on social expenditures and decent work as growth facilitators and necessary investments for sustainable development.

For the United Kingdom, it begs the question as to whether current trends in standards of social conditions, or decent work, are conducive to the promotion of economic growth. In the United Kingdom it is generally accepted that competitiveness and growth must be based on productivity, innovation, and the provision of higher value products and services. But relatively low productivity has been a persistent problem (see, for example, Lansley, 2011), with a considerably worsening

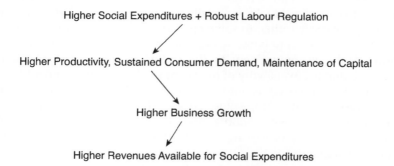

*Figure 13.2* Growth through decent work first: the United Kingdom

situation since 2008. In fact, by 2013, output per hour was 12.8 per cent below the pre-recession trend (Disney et al., 2013). In 2012, output per hour in Britain was reported to be 16 percentage points below the average of other G7 industrialised nations, 29 percentage points behind the USA alone, and 24 points behind both France and Germany (Chang, 2013, citing Office for National Statistics figures). Given past performance, what of the future? Is the United Kingdom laying the social foundations for future strong productivity growth? The evidence suggests not.

In fact, there is evidence that for a substantial part of the economy there has been a decline in decent work with increasing precariousness and a proliferation of casualised work patterns. Particularly emblematic of this process of casualisation has been the huge increase in the use of zero-hours contracts, which do not guarantee minimum hours or pay and which are often accompanied by weaker access to social benefits.[5] In addition, there have been record increases in the numbers working as self-employed, amounting to around 14 per cent of the labour force (Cohen, 2012). Part-time jobs, temporary jobs, internships, work placement schemes, and other measures largely for young people have all increased. Casualisation has been accompanied by a weakening of labour protection regulations (see, for example, Heyes and Lewis, Chapter 9 in this volume).[6]

Since 2008, the United Kingdom has experienced a widespread fall in real wages, induced in part by an oversupply of cheap labour and a shortage of well paid jobs (Disney et al., 2013). Cuts in social expenditure, the growth in casualisation, and the increase of part-time workers, many declaring themselves to be underemployed, have all played a part in a lowering of incomes.[7] Also, there has been a big increase in the number of self-employed, a proportion of whom appear to have been taking less productive lower paid jobs, especially in services (Cohen, 2012; Groom, 2012). As we saw earlier, in some countries minimum wage regulation has been used both to boost demand and to incentivise higher productivity forms of competition. In the United Kingdom, however, it is possible that the availability of much cheap, flexible labour might have encouraged employers to under-invest in productivity raising capital equipment (Elliott, 2013; Milne, 2014).[8] Thus, with the exception of specific sectors notwithstanding, there is some indication that the UK as a whole is at risk of moving towards a lower-wage/lower-productivity level of competitiveness.

Contributing to concerns about future threats to productivity-led growth are worries about a possible skills deficit. Aggregate improvements in education and skill levels are crucial for a United Kingdom growth strategy based on increasing productivity and innovation, but there are questions of whether many of the jobs being created are offering much in the way of learning on the job – a crucial aspect of skills acquisition; whether some people are, in effect, 'trading down', in other words deskilling as they take jobs below their abilities; and whether casual jobs in particular are offering much in the way of pathways for further learning and career enhancement. There are also the pernicious skill-inhibiting effects of rising poverty (see below). Yet, even while unemployment rates stay high, especially for young people, there have been reports of skill shortages in certain industries such as engineering, construction and ICT.

The decline of decent work and of non-work social protection is also a cause for concern for the United Kingdom's long-term growth prospects. Severe cuts in spending on social protection, such as housing benefit and council tax support, have made 1.75 million of the poorest British families even poorer (Aldridge and Macinnes, 2014), while there have been reports of a huge increase in those resorting to charity food banks (See Allen, 2014; Butler, 2014).[9] As a World Bank study (Perry et al., 2006) has pointed out, poverty can be an important drag on long-term growth, thanks to a number of feedback mechanisms, including the effects that coming from a poor household can have on nutrition, education, and the acquisition of skills, which in turn are crucial for raising productivity levels. Cuts to social protection also reduce the automatic stabiliser function of non-work payments, thereby reducing aggregate demand, and it could be argued that reductions to unemployment payments puts pressure on workers to accept jobs that are inappropriate or below their skill levels, implying a loss of productive contribution to the economy. Further, rising poverty and inequality has serious implications for social cohesion, maybe even resulting in serious disorder, as dramatically evidenced by the British youth riots of 2011.

As we saw earlier, inadequate levels of decent work can also negatively affect business growth prospects by inhibiting access to markets. Consumers are liable to punish companies that develop a reputation for acting in an ethically unacceptable way. In the United Kingdom, campaigns against poorly perceived, home based employers have hitherto not been as evident as those against overseas suppliers, typically from developing countries, but nevertheless there are signs that, in future, customers might vote with their wallets against British-based businesses seen as acting unethically. There have been protests against companies believed to have 'unfairly' avoided corporate tax payments, and there has been bad publicity for businesses allegedly exploiting young people on work schemes, and for others said to be making excessive use of zero hours contracts, or otherwise providing poor conditions. Moreover, there has been an increasing demand for public and private employers to sign up to a commitment to pay a living wage. Enterprises with decent work deficits might find market access more difficult in the future.

Of further concern for the United Kingdom is high and persistent inequality. For decent work-led growth to result in a dynamic development path it is important that the gains from growth are fairly distributed. Unfortunately, however, workers have not been receiving their fair share of productivity gains. According to Whittaker and Hurrell (2013), in the United Kingdom before the year 2000 wage gains were broadly in line with productivity, but from 2000 to 2013 growth of median wages and below increased much more slowly than overall productivity, and from 2008 to 2013 stagnant or even falling productivity has been accompanied by proportionately greater falls in wages. Inadequate sharing of the benefits of growth exacerbates inequality; reduces income growth and thereby domestic consumer demand; raises the risk of poverty, potentially contributing to the creation of a working poor; and undermines trust and motivation for cooperation, important for high performing enterprises. Further, in the worst scenario, excessive inequality might contribute to the creation of an economic crisis, as it is said to have done in 2008.

## Conclusions

In recent years the Business First perspective, and associated policies, have been prevalent, including in the United Kingdom. However, as we have seen, this approach has been challenged by mounting international evidence that a range of social or decent work expenditures have not only the character of safety nets or protection mechanisms but also play important roles in economic development. That is to say, adequate social conditions can be important inputs to business growth and broader economic development. Thus, they are not just derivatives. This was shown to be the case in the spheres of: workplace production environments; social protection and non-workplace living conditions; accessing markets; and long-term economic and social sustainability.

For the United Kingdom, it has been argued that a range of decent work deficits do not augur well for long-term productivity-led growth. Of particular concern is rising poverty, increased casualisation, and high levels of inequality, with likely implications for vital skills attainment, social cohesion, workplace cooperation for high performance, and the maintenance of sustainable demand. In brief, there is some indication that short-term cost cutting efforts might be laying the seeds for long-term decline, unless actions are taken to amend the situation.

Enterprises that seek to accrue competitive advantage by cutting social expenditures and reducing labour standards are often said to be engaging in a destructive 'race to the bottom' with like-minded competitors. Something similar could be said for national 'growth' strategies that engage in similar approaches, only in this case whole communities and societies are involved. To avert a threat of a spiralling decline the opposite thinking is needed, whereby the building up of social capacities is seen as a crucial input to a 'race to the top', as countries seek to compete by promoting higher productivity, higher incomes and higher standards.

Of course, decent work costs money. Indeed, that is one reason why some people argue that social expenditures are luxuries to be spent from the fruits of growth. On the other hand, if the view is taken that social expenditures are necessary to business growth then it could be argued that spending on decent work is a necessary investment – in the same sense that education and training cost money but are necessary investments in the global knowledge economy. Successful growth strategies look to a long-term building up of capabilities. Short-term cost cutting measures can undermine those capabilities.

## Notes

1. For example, in 2008, a new Labour Contract Law was enacted which specifies that workers should be given written contracts, which provides workers with more job security (Dueck, 2010).
2. There are many codes of conduct. For example, in the late 1990s, Urminsky (ILO, undated) reported on 258 codes of conduct addressing labour practices, created by enterprises, enterprise associations, trade unions, NGOs, universities, or combinations of those actors.
3. See also OECD (2011), where it was found that in the three decades prior to 2008, wage gaps widened and household income inequality increased in a large majority of OECD countries.
4. Stiglitz argued that inadequacy of aggregate demand caused by a transfer of money from the poor to the rich (who are less prone to spend) encouraged the loosening of monetary policy and easy credit in the USA, allowing workers to carry on spending and businesses to sell their products, but resulting eventually in an overextension of credit, the American sub-prime crisis, and the global crisis (Stiglitz, 2009). In other words, inequality on a grand scale contributed to an undermining of global economic sustainability.

5. By 2014, it was reported that more than one in ten employers are using such contracts (Inman and Monaghan, 2014, citing Office for National Statistics data).
6. It can be argued that such a deregulated regime might be appropriate for a low-wage/low-productivity, price driven growth model, but is inadequate for ambitions to grow through productivity enhancement, utilising high performance work practices that require trust and worker commitment.
7. Casual and part-time jobs tend to be lower paid. For example, in 2012, 33 per cent of UK temporary or casual workers and 43 per cent of part time workers, were found to be low paid (earning less than £7.44p per hour), compared with 20 per cent of permanent and 12 per cent of full time employees (Whittaker and Hurrell, 2013).
8. By 2013, business investment had fallen to a level 16 per cent below the pre-recession high (Disney et al., 2013).
9. Also, the BBC has reported that according to a poll of 2,444 adults carried out by the British Heart Foundation, over a third of UK adults are struggling to eat healthily. Two thirds of respondents say they want to eat more healthily but of these half are being hindered by the cost (BBC, 2014).

# References

Aldridge, H. and Macinnes, T. (2014) 'Multiple Cuts for the Poorest Families', Oxfam Research Reports, New Policy Institute and Oxfam, April 2014, UK.

Allen, K. (2014) 'Welfare Cuts Harm 1.75m of Poorest Families, Says Oxfam', *The Guardian*, 22 April 2014.

Ashton, D. and Sung, J. (2002) 'Supporting Workplace Learning for High Performance Working', International Labour Office (ILO), Geneva.

BBC (2014) 'A 'Third of UK Adults Struggle' to Afford Healthy Food', BBC Health, BBC website, 23 April 2014.

Behrendt, C., Cichon, M., Hagemejer, K., Kidd, S., Krech, R. and Townsend, P. (2009) 'Rethinking the Role of Social Security in Development', in P. Townsend (ed.), *Building Decent Societies: Rethinking the Role of Social Security in Development*. International Labour Office (ILO), Geneva.

Bell, S. and Newitt, K. (2010) 'Decent Work and Poverty Eradication: Literature Review and Two Country Study', a study for the Decent Work and Labour Standards Forum, London, UK.

Berg, J. and Tobin, S. (2011) 'Income-Led Growth as a Crisis Response: Lessons from Brazil', in ILO, 2011, 'The Global Crisis: Causes, Responses and Challenges', International Labour Office (ILO), Geneva.

Bonfiglioli, A. (2007) 'Food and the Poor', United Nations Capital Development Fund, New York.

Brignall, M. and Butler, S. (2014) 'No Improvement for Bangladesh Workers', *The Guardian*, 6 February 2014.

Butler, P. (2014) 'Hunger a 'National Crisis', Religious Leaders Tell Cameron', *The Guardian*, 16 April 2014.

Chang, S. P. (2013) 'Britain's Poverty Gap with G7 Largest Since 1994', The Telegraph (online), 18 September 2013. Web site: http://www.telegraph.co.uk

CPRC (Chronic Poverty Research Centre) (2008) 'The Chronic Poverty Report, 2008–2009: Escaping Poverty Traps', Brooks World Poverty Institute, Manchester, UK.

Cohen, N. (2012) 'Puzzling Picture on Jobs Foxes Experts', *Financial Times*, 16 August 2012.

Croucher, R., Stumbitz, B., Vickers, I., Quinlan, M., Banfield, W., Brookes, M., Lange, T., Lewis, S. McIlroy, J., Miles, L., Ozarow, D. and Rizov, M. (2013) *Can Better Working Conditions Improve the Performance of SMEs? An International Literature Review*. International Labour Office (ILO), Geneva.

Devereux, S., Marshall, J., MacAskill, J. and Pelham, L. (2005) 'Making Cash Count: Lessons from Cash Transfer Schemes in East and Southern Africa for Supporting the Most Vulnerable Children and Households', Save the Children, London, UK, and the Institute of Development Studies, Brighton, UK.

Disney, R., Jin, W. and Miller, H. (2013, chapter) 'The Productivity Puzzles', in C. Emmerson, P. Johnson and H. Miller (eds), *The IFS Green Budget*. Institute for Fiscal Studies, UK.

Dueck, C. (2010) 'Foreign Workers Replacing Chinese Migrants', *Financial Times*, 19 January 2010.

Economic Commission for Latin America and the Caribbean (ECLAC) (2012) 'Preliminary Overview of the Economies of Latin America and the Caribbean', ECLAC, United Nations, Santiago, Chile.

Elliott, L. (2013) 'Britain's Economy Sets Course for Fantasy Island', *The Guardian*, 28 October 2013.

Fontanella-Khan, J. and Lamont, J. (2012) 'Consumption Rises as Wealth Spreads to Countryside', *Financial Times*, 1 March 2012.

Garside, J. (2013) 'Investigators Uncover Child Labour at Apple's Suppliers', *The Guardian*, 26 January 2013.

Grant, J. and Bland, B. (2012) 'Strong Demand at Home Shelters South East Asia Economies', Financial Times, 24 May 2012.

Groom, B. (2012) 'Why do Job Figures Seem to Defy Gloom?', Financial Times, 13 September 2012.

Heyes, J. and Lewis, P. 'Employment Protection Legislation and the Growth Crisis', this volume.

Hirway, I. (2009) 'Losing the Sparkle: Impact of the Global Crisis on the Diamond Cutting and Polishing Industry in India', United Nations Development Programme (UNDP), India.

Jenkins, H. (2010) 'Decent Work and Fair Globalisation: A Guide to Policy Dialogue', *NGLS*, United Nations, New York.

IILS (International Institute for Labour Studies) (2008) 'World of Work Report 2008: Income Inequalities in the Age of Financial Globalisation', International Institute for Labour Studies, International Labour Office (ILO), Geneva.

IILS (International Institute for Labour Studies) (2009) World of Work Report 2009, IILS, International Labour Office (ILO), Geneva.

IILS (International Institute for Labour Studies) (2011) 'Brazil: An Innovative Income-led Strategy', IILS, International Labour Office (ILO), Geneva.

IILS (International Institute for Labour Studies) (2013) 'World of Work Report: Repairing the Economic and Social Fabric', IILS, International Labour Office (ILO), Geneva.

ILO (International Labour Office) (2001) 'A Global Agenda for Employment', a Discussion Paper, International Labour Office (ILO), Geneva.

ILO (International Labour Office) (2011a) 'Building Employment and Decent Work into Sustainable Recovery and Development: the UN Contribution', report of an inter-agency meeting, 29th November–1st December 2010, International Labour Office (ILO) Training Centre, Turin, Italy.

ILO (International Labour Office) (2011b) 'World of Work Report 2011: Making Markets Work for Jobs', International Labour Office, Geneva.

ILO (International Labour Office) (2013) 'Sustainable Development, Decent Work and Green Jobs', Report V to the International Labour Conference, 102nd Session, 2013, International Labour Office, Geneva.

Inman, P. and Monaghan, A. (2014) 'Huge Surge in Workers Tied to Zero-hour Deals', *The Guardian*, 1 May 2014.

Kapoor, A. (2009) 'Diamonds are for Never: The Impact of Economic Crisis and Coping Mechanisms in the Diamond Polishing Industry in India', Graduate School of Development Studies, International Institute of Social Studies, The Hague, Netherlands.

Lansley, S. (2011) 'Britain's Livelihood Crisis', Pamplet No. 10, Touchstone, UK.

Lee, C. (2009) 'Industrial Relations and Collective Bargaining in China', Working Paper No. 7, Industrial and Employment Relations Department, International Labour Office, Geneva.

Middlebrook, P. J. (2003) 'Fighting Hunger and Poverty in Ethiopia: Ethiopia's Experience in Implementing Employment Generation Schemes as part of the National Policy for Disaster Prevention and Management', Doctoral Thesis, University of Durham, UK.

Milne, S. (2014) 'Osborne's Record is a Dismal Failure Even in His Own Terms', *The Guardian*, 20 March 2014.

OECD (Organisation for Economic Cooperation and Development) (2011) 'Divided We Stand: Why Inequality Keeps Rising', Directorate for Employment, Labour and Social Affairs, Paris

Pascual, C. G. (2007) 'Impact Case Study of Sikap Buhay: Action Research on Promoting Decent Work for the Informal Economy in Quezon City', a study prepared for the International Labour Office (ILO) Philippines Office.

Perry, G. E., Orias, O. S., Lopez, J. H., Maloney, W. F. and Severn, L. (2006) *Poverty Reduction and Growth: Virtuous and Vicious Circles*. World Bank Latin American and American Studies, The World Bank, Washington D.C., USA.

Polaski, S. (2009) *Harnessing Global Forces to Create Decent Work in Cambodia*. International Institute for Labour Studies (IILS), International Labour Office (ILO), Geneva.

Ryder, G. (2010) 'Introductory Comments' to H. Jenkins (ed.), *Decent Work and Fair Globalisation: A Guide to Policy Dialogue*. NGLS, United Nations, New York.

Sabates-Wheeler, R., Devereux, S. and Guenther, B. (2008) 'Building Synergies Between Social Protection and Smallholder Policies', paper for the conference: 'Social Protection for the Poorest in Africa: Learning from Experience', 8–10 September, 2008, Kampala, Uganda.

Saleh, H. (2014) 'Post-revolution Tunisia Faces up to Challenge of High Jobless Rates', *Financial Times*, 6 February 2014.

Scott, C. (2013) 'Sustainability Means Business', The Guardian, 31 October 2013.

Sengenberger, W. (2009) 'Globalisation and Social Progress: The Role and Impact of International Labour Standards'. A report prepared for the Friedrich Ebert Foundation, May 2005, Bonn, Germany.

Stiglitz, J. (2009) 'The Global Crisis, Social Protection and Jobs', *International Labour Review*, 148, 1–2.

Strauss-Kahn, D. (2011) 'The Global Jobs Crisis – Sustaining the Recovery through Employment and Equitable Growth', *International Monetary Fund (IMF)*, 13 April 2011, Washington.

Torres, R. (2011) 'Responding to the Global Crisis: Achievements and Pending Issues', in ILO (ed.), *Essays from an ILO Perspective*. International Labour Office (ILO), Geneva.

Townsend, P. (ed.) (2009) *Building Decent Societies: Rethinking the Role of Social Security in Development*. International Labour Office (ILO), Geneva.

Urminski, M. (undated) 'Self-regulation in the Workplace: Codes of Conduct, Social labelling and Socially Responsible Investment', Working Paper No. 1, Series on management and Corporate Citizenship, Job Creation and Enterprise Development Department, International Labour Office (ILO), Geneva.

Wells, D. (2006) 'Best Practice in the Regulation of International Labor Standards: Lessons of the US-Cambodia Trade Agreements', *Comparative Labor Law and Policy Journal*, 27, 3, 357–376.

Whittaker, M. and Hurrell, A. (2013) 'Low Pay Britain, 2013', September 2013, Resolution Foundation.

Wilkinson, R. and Pickett, K. (2009) *The Spirit Level: Why More Equal Societies Almost Always Do Better*. Allen Lane, UK.

Printed and bound by CPI Group (UK) Ltd, Croydon, CR0 4YY

University Centre at
# Blackburn
College

**Telephone: 01254 292165**

Please return this book on or before the last date shown